THE IRISH SC[ ]
SOMERVILLE A[ ]

*Dedicated to my mother, Nuala,
and in memory of my father,
Christian D. Stevens.*

THE IRISH SCENE
IN
SOMERVILLE
AND
ROSS

JULIE ANNE STEVENS

IRISH ACADEMIC PRESS
DUBLIN • PORTLAND, OR

First published in 2007 by
IRISH ACADEMIC PRESS
44 Northumberland Road, Dublin 4, Ireland

and in the United States of America by
IRISH ACADEMIC PRESS
c/o ISBS, Suite 300, 920 NE 58th Avenue
Portland, Oregon 97213-3786

WEBSITE: www.iap.ie

British Library Cataloguing in Publication Data
An entry can be found on request

ISBN 0 7165 3366 9 (cloth)
978 0 7165 3366 5
ISBN 0 7165 3367 7 (paper)
978 0 7165 3367 2

Library of Congress Cataloging-in-Publication Data
An entry can be found on request

Printed by MPG Books Ltd., Bodmin, Cornwall

Contents

Martin Ross and the dog Sheila (1911)

Dr. Edith Œnone Somerville, Honorary D. Litt. Trinity College Dublin (29 June 1932)

Foreword

The intensity and richness of Julie Anne Stevens's encounter with Somerville and Ross is everywhere apparent in this meditation on two writers who wrote as one. Merging and yet retaining their individual sensibilities, the cousins became a kind of metaphor for their own work, clinically detached from their situations and characters, yet at the same time intimately aware of the hidden forces that shaped behaviour and events. Edith Œnone Somerville and 'Martin Ross' (Violet Martin) studied Irish life with the detachment of the Anglo-Irish landlord class, separated from most of their countrymen and women by economics, education, religion, and politics. But the mutual, if often mistrustful dependence between landlords and tenantry gave them what it had earlier given Maria Edgeworth, an intimate knowledge of how farmers, servants, and small town traders lived, thought, and spoke.

Yeats described Ireland as a theatre in which the Anglo-Irish gentry had once performed in 'a play that had for spectators men and women that loved the high wasteful virtues'.[1] In his own time their descendants had become 'querulous and selfish', and their audience had ceased to be impressed. Dr Stevens tacitly develops Yeats's theatrical metaphor, but she suggests that Somerville and Ross recognized that the unhyphenated Irish were performing their own counter-drama. It involved the manipulation of those very masks that Oscar Wilde considered essential in society, and Yeats literally re-introduced upon the stage. In their masterpiece, *The Real Charlotte* (1894) – a novel with two heroines as well as two authors – we watch Charlotte Mullen artfully conceal her real self behind an aggressive affability. She is a performer, always ready with an anecdote about some local encounter, some *drôlerie* based on the doings of the local people. At a picnic she tells 'stories about her cats . . . with admirable dramatic effect and a sense of humour that made her almost attractive', then moves on to her specialty, the comic language of the people:

> inspired by another half glass of champagne, Miss Mullen continued, "Donovan . . . said he wanted 'Little Johanna for the

garden'. 'Ye great lazy fool,' says I, 'aren't ye big enough and ugly enough to do that little pick of work by yerself without wanting a girl to help ye?' And after all," said Charlotte, dropping from the tones of fury in which she had rendered her own part in the interview, "all he wanted was some guano for my early potatoes!" [2]

Charlotte enjoys these encounters with servants and tradespeople. ' "Whoever says thim throuts isn't leppin' fresh out o' the lake he's a dom liar, and it's little I think of tellin' it t'ye up to yer nose!" ' shouts an angry fish-seller, when Charlotte has doubted the freshness of her wares;

> "There's not one in the country but knows yer thricks and yer chat, and ye may go home out o'that, with yer bag sthrapped round ye, and ye can take the tay-leaves and the dhrippin' from the servants, and huxther thim to feed yer cats, but thanks be to God ye'll take nothing out
> o' my basket this day!"
> There was a titter of horrified delight from the crowd.
> "Ye never spoke a truer word than that, Mary Norris," replied [Charlotte]; "when I come into Lismoyle, it's not to buy rotten fish from a drunken fish-fag, that'll be begging for crusts at my hall-door to-morrow. If I hear another word out of yer mouth, I'll give you and your fish to the police, and the streets'll be rid of you and yer infernal tongue for a week, at all events, and the prison'll have a treat that it's pretty well used to!"
> Another titter rewarded this sally, and Charlotte, well pleased, turned to walk away.[3]

Charlotte is probably right about the fish. But Mary Norris's knowledge of how Charlotte runs her household suggests a more intimate and less admiring scrutiny of the gentry and their affairs than Yeats's theatrical metaphor imagined.

Charlotte's stories, with which she maintains her right of entry to the at-homes and tea parties of local Protestant society, are in fact not unlike those that will later feature in the two cousins' most popular work. *Some Experiences of an Irish RM* (1899), and its two sequels, often rely on a broad 'Oirish' accent for comic effect. Somerville and Ross listened carefully to the language of the people, and noted colourful or absurd phrases for future use. But the detached narrator of *The Real Charlotte* also shows Charlotte without her masks of affability and boisterous good humour, and reveals her ruthless ambition and her manipulative skill. Dr. Stevens deploys Baudelairean ideas of masking and unmasking to show us how Somerville and Ross maintain Charlotte as at once affable and sinister, familiar and strange. At the end of the novel she has the house and land she has long coveted, and has destroyed those who were in her way.

As for the other heroine, Francie Fitzpatrick, she is Charlotte's cousin and victim. Francie is an outsider in Lismoyle, and violates the local *mores* with her flirting and her ignorance of convention. An unskilled rider, and unaware that etiquette required stopping her horse while a funeral passes, she dies when the flapping cloak of a keening peasant frightens the horse, the totemic animal of Anglo-Ireland.

In Yeats's valedictory list of suitable subjects for the Irish poets who will succeed him, he specifies the peasantry, 'Hard-riding country gentlemen', monks, and porter-drinkers. The Irish middle-class, Protestant and Catholic, are deliberately omitted. But they are central in *The Real Charlotte*, which is, as Dr Stevens points out, a Balzacian anatomy of the Protestant middle-class in a small town, aware that they are a diminishing species but clinging to the status their religion, and their occasional reception by the local aristocrats, the Dysarts of Bruff, confer. They are hardly the 'Hard-riding country gentlemen' of Yeats's imagination, though Roddy Lambert, agent for the Dysart estate, aspires to be considered one. He embezzles money from the estate to buy horses, and has set himself up at 'a new house at least a mile from the town, built . . . at his employer's expense'.[4] There Lambert has contrived a view, concentrating 'all his energies on hiding everything nearer than the semi-circle of lake and distant mountain held in an opening cut through the rhododendrons', deliberately screening out 'the petty humanities of Lismoyle'.[5] What Lambert tries to exclude is the subject of *The Real Charlotte*.

Dr Stevens's central theme is her authors' depictions of the Irish landscape, and their ability to use that landscape as a metaphor for the conditions that shape their characters. In *The Real Charlotte* we travel the roads to Bruff and to Gurthnamuckla, the property Charlotte successfully schemes to make her own. Near Gurthnamuckla the landscape changes from 'pasture and sleek cattle and neat stone walls' to 'shelves and flags of gray limestone [that] began to contest the right of the soil with the thin grass and wiry brushwood' until 'The rock was everywhere. Even the hazels were at last squeezed out of existence'. The stone slabs make up an 'iron belt' for a time, but then,

The grass began to show in larger and larger patches between the rocks, and the indomitable hazels crept again out of the crannies, and raised their low canopies over the heads of the browsing sheep and goats. A stream, brown with turf-mould, and fierce with battles with the boulders, made a boundary between the stony wilderness and the dark green pastures of Gurthnamuckla.[6]

This Darwinian landscape, with its battles between stone and plants for survival, becomes a metaphor for the contest between Charlotte and those who stand in her way, and more generally an implicit metaphor for the two rival nations who contest the ownership of Ireland, at the time embodied in the Land League and the landlords and authorities who fought against it.

Dr Stevens carries the theatrical metaphor into her discussion of the Irish RM stories, arguing that Somerville and Ross share Jack Yeats's 'conviction that Irish life manifested the spirit of performance usually found on stage' so that 'life in Ireland is also an act . . . [and] the characters' antics become a performance'.[7] An angry woman's gestures are 'worthy of the highest traditions of classic drama', a servant departs 'like an exit in a pastoral play', the narrator compares himself to 'the leading gentleman' in 'a drawing-room drama'.[8] Stevens convincingly argues that Flurry Knox is a Harlequin figure, a trickster like the fox he hunts, Lord of Misrule, a playboy in his rural world. Like Charlotte, Flurry is accepted among the local Protestant gentry, and like her he is entertaining and manipulative. A hard-riding country gentleman, always the leader of the hunt, he is also a shrewd horse-trader. But he understands the people and shares their appreciation for wit, style, and audacity. When the patriarch of an ancient family must give up his beloved white hounds 'of the old Irish breed, with their truly national qualities of talent, rebelliousness, and love of sport', he gives Flurry ' "his pick of my hounds . . . and that's what no other man in Ireland would get" '.[9] Major Yeates, the Resident Magistrate who narrates the RM stories, envies 'Flurry's incommunicable gift of being talked to',[10] which makes him privy to all the secrets of the district. Yeates, who represents the authority and majesty of British law locally, is often the victim of Flurry's pranks. Like Harlequin, Flurry can maintain dual realities.

Flurry's intermediate role between the local establishment and 'the people' allows Yeates access to the stories he tells. If the action of *The Real Charlotte* is performed before an audience of one, the omniscient narrator, the RM stories imagine Ireland as a theatre in which Flurry contrives the discomfiture of an authority figure, frequently an

English visitor, at the hands of the unhyphenated Irish. In 'The Last Day of Shraft', for example, Flurry entices Yeates to Hare Island to shoot ducks, bringing along an Englishman eager to hear the pure Irish spoken there. The only duck shot is a tame one; Yeates, muddy and drenched, has to shelter in the local *shebeen* and borrow trousers adapted for a one-legged man; the Englishman listens to an interminable and unintelligible recital of an Irish poem. Flurry sends the police to raid the *shebeen* while Yeates is there; they find the local RM with a glass of *poitín* in front of him and one leg to his trousers. The Englishman is knocked down as the *shebeen* patrons rush to escape.

In the RM stories landscape also works as metaphor. Many of them feature hunts, frantic dashes over hills and dales in pursuit of the wily fox, a pursuit Dr Stevens links to the beast fables about Reynard. The landscape is full of obstacles, stone walls and streams that must be jumped, bogs where horses can sink. It is a valid metaphor for the Irish political and social landscape when Somerville and Ross were writing, full of challenges to the accepted order. Their RM stories do not mock the unhyphenated Irish. They raise instead the question of who controls an Irish story: Major Yeates, who tells it, or the actors who orchestrate and perform it, improvising a script Yeates often fails to understand. At the end of his misadventures on Hare Island he realizes that 'to-morrow' his mishap will be an Irish story and the district 'would ring with Flurry's artistic version of the day's events'.[11]

Sensitively examining her writers' metaphors and narrative methods, Dr Stevens has found a way of defining the achievement of Somerville and Ross in portraying the Ireland of their time. She catches the restlessness that characterized the period between the fall of Parnell and 1916, a time of apparent stasis and half-felt stirrings. Her study makes it clear that Somerville and Ross are central figures in any discussion of Irish writing.

Robert Tracy
Berkeley, September 2006

List of Illustrations

PLATES

Acknowledgements

Many people have inspired and helped me in writing this book. I especially appreciate the encouragement and criticism of my early mentors, Antoinette Quinn, Nicholas Grene, Robert Tracy and my father, the late Chris Stevens. I am also most grateful for the advice of Eve Patten and Terence Brown, and I appreciate the help of Tadgh O'Sullivan and Elizabeth Fitzpatrick whose suggestions were most helpful. Special thanks are due to Anne Macdona who worked with me in setting up the Somerville and Ross exhibition in Trinity College Library in 2002. Lady Coghill also added to the success of this work, which has added so much to my research. I owe a large debt of gratitude to Gifford Lewis and Declan Kiberd whose work has added so much to the study of Somerville and Ross and who have been wonderfully encouraging to me over the past few years. Otto Rauchbauer's establishment of the Drishane Archive has great significance, and I thank him and Christopher Somerville for all their help. I am particularly grateful to have worked with Anne Crookshank and Síghle Bhreathnach-Lynch on Edith Somerville's artwork. Finally, I much appreciate the assistance of Jane Maxwell and Bernard Meehan of the Manuscripts Department and Charles Benson of Early Printed Books in Trinity College Library.

I very much appreciate the continual support of Jonathan Williams – many thanks. Lisa Hyde and Irish Academic Press have my great gratitude. In addition a number of readers have been generous with their time, and I wish to thank Fionnuala Dillane, Sharon Murphy, Birgit Lang and my brother Kevin Stevens for their assistance and advice. Colleagues and friends have been most encouraging and I appreciate the support of many people: Dorothy Keelan, Carol Stewart, Michelle Sweeney, Noreen Doody, Gillian O'Brien, Selina Guinness, Derek Hand, P.J. Mathews, Eleanor O'Neill, Brenna Clarke and friends in St Patrick's College in Drumcondra. Finally, this work would never have been finished without the support of my family, Hugh McCann, Steven and Christy – thanks to you all.

Some material in this book, particularly sections of chapters five and six, appeared as essays in the *Journal of the Cork Historical and Archaeological Society* edited by Neil Buttimer (2000), and *Out of Context*, edited by Heidi Hansson (2006).

The reproduction of Edith Somerville's pictures is with the kind permission of Curtis Brown Group Ltd, London on behalf of the Estate of Edith Somerville © Edith Somerville 1888, 1902,1903, 1905, 1912.

Julie Anne Stevens
September 2006

Introduction

EDITH SOMERVILLE AND MARTIN ROSS possessed an inveterate sense of the dramatic nature of reality. They exploited the scenic quality of Irish life in their comic writing, showing an acute awareness of the self-conscious and ironic sensibilities of their fellow countrymen. They also took advantage of the scenic possibilities of the Irish landscape, drawing attention to the deceptively charming nature of a picturesque Ireland. Their detachment from the exploits and arguments of their time, a distance caused more by their comic sensibilities than the garrison walls surrounding their caste, allowed them to position themselves as commentators on Irish affairs. Martin Ross's unionist politics assisted in the writers' rather aloof position in relation to the Irish Literary Revival. Today that commentary is invaluable because it embraces nineteenth-century popular culture, often dealing with people and ideas that have been submerged or neglected because of a dominating nationalist argument or a general wariness of shoneenism, the imitation of all things English. This book draws attention to the network of connections—both fictional and fact—that Somerville and Ross's satire and parody trace. The writers' strong sense of family and pedigree ensured the maintenance of a past from which we can now benefit. At the same time their relative freedom as roaming artists with feminist tendencies made them look forward to the future so that their comic writing gives witness to an Anglo-Irish tradition in the face of modern development.

Somerville and Ross wrote and published in the midst of the vibrant consumer culture of the *fin de siècle*. They were closely involved with the periodical press throughout their writing career, publishing in mainstream magazines like *Strand*, *Blackwood's*, and *The Graphic*. They worked in Germany, France, and England, and in 1897 took on as their literary agent the forward-thinking Scotsman James Pinker, who included the Irish pair within his stable of commercial and non-commercial writers: H. G. Wells, Joseph Conrad, Stephen Crane, Henry James. Pinker brought Somerville and Ross right into the middle of things, and they handled with finesse both the demands of the

different magazines and the tastes of an expanded middle-class readership by publishing their immensely popular Irish RM series. Somerville
and Ross worked successfully within a fast-moving British culture preoccupied with the issues of New Woman thought, Social Darwinism,
colonial expansion, and the revived romance. Thus, their awareness of
themselves as Anglo-Irish writers, as spokeswomen for particular traditions in a turbulent Irish world, is refracted and altered by a modern
self-consciousness and an ironic sensibility which just as frequently
subverts as it promotes certain ideologies.

When Martin Ross met W. B. Yeats in Coole Park in 1901, she
defended the comic Irish stories and pictures she and Edith Somerville
were producing with great success. Yeats and Lady Gregory believed
that Somerville and Ross should return to writing novels about the
Irish middle class, as demonstrated in their impressive 1894 novel,
The Real Charlotte. Yeats could not 'approve of humour for humour's
sake'. Martin Ross disagreed and defended humour as a 'high art'.[1] A
few years later when Edith Somerville, always alert to opportunities
to publish her illustrations within a popular form, wrote a series of
comic verses to accompany the pictures of *Slipper's ABC
of Foxhunting*, Martin Ross wrote to their agent and expressed her
anxiety regarding her writing partner's work. She feared that the
'doggerel' of Somerville's verse would mar their reputation as comic
writers.[2] Somerville needed money to subsidize her hunting costs,
however, and published her work.

Martin Ross took comedy seriously. When the talented artist Edith
Somerville met her second cousin, the writer Violet Martin, in 1886,
they discovered in their collaboration as Somerville and Ross a successful writing partnership that derived its mainspring from a comic
vision. Together they presented an Anglo-Irish front that spanned the
southern counties of the island: from Galway to West Cork. They
seemed to write as one, and yet collaboration – the fact of two voices
and two points of view – always disturbs the unity of purpose their
works are meant to convey. One author can hide behind the other so
that no absolute authority exists, no single ideological purpose stands.
From the very start, then, they determined to write in chorus, drawing
both strength and the possibility of evasion from a double authorship.

Both writers, especially Edith Somerville, who always maintained
that she was an artist by choice and a writer by chance, took particular
interest in uniting visual and literary representation of Ireland. Their
forays into travel writing, illustrated books and children's literature
served in part as means to include pictures with words. Their writing

often drew attention to visual perspective, subverting what one might describe as the 'picture' of Ireland (a picturesque version) and showing that what one sees is not always what one gets in the Irish country-side. Despite the humour of their fiction and Somerville's pictures, their work draws upon significant land issues of the nineteenth century: eviction, improvement, estate management, agrarian outrage, boycotting, the land war between casual labourers, peasant proprietors, and gombeen entrepreneurs. Novels, like *Naboth's Vineyard* (1891) and *The Real Charlotte* (1894), satirize the scramble for land, using caricature and the grotesque to mock land greed. Two realistic sporting novels, *The Silver Fox* (1898) and *Dan Russel The Fox* (1911), concentrate on the Irish hunt to show how different ranks and races come together in a series of mock skirmishes across the bogland of Connemara and the hillocks of West Cork. The final decade of their joint career saw them concentrating on the publication in English magazines of illustrated comic stories that relied on the folk humour of Irish country living, eventually collecting these story-cycles into three volumes known as the Irish RM series: *Some Experiences of an Irish RM* in 1899, *Further Experiences of an Irish RM* in 1908 and *In Mr Knox's Country* in 1915.

Somerville and Ross's dedication to the 'high art of comedy' throughout their career includes an appreciation of its saturnine aspect. The writers' interest in the land delves deeper than its surface. They are fascinated by Ireland's subterranean depths. As Martin Ross explains in an unpublished manuscript called 'An Irish Goldmine', going underground reveals as much as it conceals:

> The sun poured into the little creek, between the grey jaws of cliff, & we sat on the warm rocks, & realised for the first time that to appreci-ate to any fitting extent the careless miracles and cunning common-places of the outer earth it is well to go behind the scenes for a while.[3]

Martin Ross's fascination with Ireland's boggy depths, described again in 'A Subterranean Cave at Cloonabinnia [*sic*]', and an essential part of the landscapes of Somerville and Ross's fiction,[4] lies not only in the darkness which such journeys suggest but also in the possible treasure which the darkness conceals. The centre of the Irish universe resides not in the heavens but in the earth where the quarry of many Irish RM stories, sly Reynard the fox, hides his gold.

Somerville and Ross's landscapes are unsteady, full of dangerous holes, like the 'shifting bog' in Bram Stoker's and Emily Lawless's writings.[5] The literary terrain of Somerville and Ross's fiction also shifts as the authors stage a tradition and then subvert it. This process demands that we ask, what is the real Ireland? What hidden treasure lies concealed in an Irish goldmine or a subterranean cave in Cloonabinna? The landscape, in both a literal and a literary sense, possesses a 'shifting' or 'shaking' surface. In *The Silver Fox*, the treacherous bog conceals under its peaty crust vast waterways, so mysterious and unknown that the locals tell unbelievable stories about its magical dimensions:

> There's holes up in Cahirdreen that's sixty feet deep, and wather run-nin' in the bottom o' them. 'Tis out undher Tully that wather goes. Sure there was a man had a grand heifer – God knows ye'd sooner be lookin' at her that atin' yer dinner – she fell down in one o' them holes, and went away undher the ground with the wather. As sure as I'm alive, they heard her screeching up through the bog![6]

Appropriately, the inhabitants of this country, 'where all was loose, and limitless, and inexact',[7] display chameleon-like characteristics, what earlier nineteenth-century writers such as Lady Morgan and Sheridan Le Fanu described as 'shifting faces'.[8] The title of Somerville and Ross's best-known novel, *The Real Charlotte*, indicates how changeable Irish character might be.

   Landscape in this book, then, offers a range of meanings. It usually refers to the representation of the countryside, both the occupations and the pastimes of country living, as well as the topography with its natural and man-made artefacts. It also relates to the process of designing or landscaping the estate garden and its environs according to the owners' principles and ideologies. At the same time landscape possesses a more abstract meaning. Anyone who reads Somerville and Ross's works becomes aware of how the past has marked Irish topog-raphy with traces of different settlements and the impact of various traditions. Landscape can incorporate meanings larger than what may be immediately apparent to the eye. The countryside bears testament to the cultural and political struggles of the past and certain features (the bog, the lack of forests, the ruins) retain a range of meanings. This study's treatment of the Irish countryside thus draws upon the idea of landscape as a cultural construct, as a manifestation of certain ideologies and traditions, as well as a composition, an artful arrangement of the people and their surroundings in a natural setting. Landscape may thus refer not only to concrete reality but also to an imagined vision of place. Writers and artists deal with different land-scape myths and traditions to construct a place of the imagination.

Bog, trees and crumbling ruins can be interpreted to mean different things according to their treatment in art. In Ireland, then, the countryside is closely associated with Irish identity.

The 'quaking sod' of Irish national consciousness[9] inevitably forces one to question the nature of identity in a search for some essential quality which distinguishes a people. Somerville and Ross's fiction deals with the resulting self-consciousness of national awareness, the process of acting Irish and being aware of the fact that one is doing so. As Major Yeates concludes while relaxing outside a western hotel in one of the later stories of the Irish RM series, being Irish can be a highly self-conscious performance.[10] He and Dr Hickey drink their evening coffee in the summer house of the hotel. They sit under a battered Chinese lantern, which the latter points out to be a ludicrous rival to the ascending rosy moon (recalling Bottom's lantern/moon in the play-within-a-play of *A Midsummer Night's Dream*). Major Yeates notes a similarity in the Irishman's ability both to perform (to act Irish) and to be critically aware of that fact (to be Irish):

> We sat there, and the moon and the round red Chinese lantern looked at each other across the evening, and had a certain resemblance, and I reflected on the fact that an Irishman is always a critic in the stalls, and is also, in spirit, behind the scenes.[11]

Theatrical scene-setting, pictorializing Irish life, and the self-conscious framing of events in Somerville and Ross's fiction become vehicles which demonstrate the process of acting Irish, whether that Irishness is pagan Celticism, Gaelicism, Anglo-Irishness, or Catholic nationalism. This process, in turn, gives rise to the uncomfortable suspicion that nothing (that is, no essential quality) might exist beneath the 'shifting face'. Nonetheless, the suggestion of a hidden dimension persisting somewhere beneath all this play-acting, the treasure in the landscape, lures the reader on.

Like their contemporaries Oscar Wilde and W.B. Yeats, Somerville and Ross draw attention to the possibilities of performance and masking in the creation of an Irish identity. This book addresses a range of aspects in relation to mask. It suggests that a mask can be an indicator of the performative nature of identity; how wearing an Irish mask, for example, can be an instance of adopting stereotyped notions of national character for an audience well versed in such notions. Masking might also suggest the deceptive practices established by the colonial situation that sees the wily peasant employing various pretences to mock or to fool the authorities. What becomes apparent in Somerville and Ross's writing is that being Irish can be a highly self-conscious performance depending on who is watching and what one wants to gain. Moreover, playing a role may involve an unspoken agreement between the performer and his audience. The kind of playful one-upmanship between a knowing audience and an adroit performer can become part of the masking process. In other words, just as important as the performer is the audience. Finally, mask can convey the sense that all representation is performative or borrowed and art is but a pastiche of collected images presented to the reader with the finesse of a circus ringmaster. Masking, of course, belongs to festival time and pertains to recurring figures that come to life whenever the circus is in town: the clown and harlequin, two significant figures in Somerville and Ross's work.

Though always aware of the scenic quality of Irish life, Somerville and Ross carefully detailed the immediate world in their fiction. They attempted to learn Irish, transcribed oral conversation (what they described as *obiter dicta*) into their fiction, and attended petty session courts to discover authentic material. They also put together a *Collection of Irish Anecdotes*, four full notebooks compiling phrases, letters, newspaper clippings, songs, jokes, and incidents gathered together from 1886 onwards.[12] They occasionally criticized their contemporaries for failing to write works true to Irish life. For example, Martin Ross did not much like Yeats and Moore's *Diarmid and Grania* when she saw it in 1901 because of its uneasy mix of material (modern French situation and Irish saga) and silly love scenes.[13] Four years later, she attacked Synge's use of dialect in *The Well of the Saints*, describing it as inauthentic. This same year, Augusta Gregory suggested that Martin Ross and her cousin write a play for the Irish Literary Theatre. Martin Ross seemed surprised and suspected in such a request a desire 'to drop politics and rope in the upper classes'.[14]

Somerville and Ross were not so much interested in taking peasant material and putting it on stage as they were intent to discover in Irish life a showmanship recalling a broader folk tradition. Martin Ross enjoyed Willie Fay's comic representation of Irishness because of the authenticity of his Dublin accent.[15] Lady Gregory, on the other hand, employed a dialogue in her plays which to Somerville and Ross did not ring true. It 'veered on the chant-like and the monotonous with its frequent "I to be" and "he to be" which failed to capture the fine sense of metre of the people'.[16] The cousins' preference for the theatre of the countryside, rather than the countryside in the theatre, had more in common with the visual artist Jack B. Yeats than his poet brother. Even though the women writers did not especially admire Jack Yeats's work, they shared with him a similar purpose – to render faithfully a life they perceived to be theatrical.

Somerville and Ross's reliance on folk material is most apparent in the Irish RM stories. These tales do not record the voices of marginal outsiders or isolated individuals. They celebrate the common people and employ types that recall the fables and fairytales that sustain a communal imagination. In his study of the modern short story, Frank O'Connor elevated the literary short story and neglected the popular kind.[17] His bias towards short fiction that expressed the 'lonely voice' rather than popular material leads to the assumption that writers like Somerville and Ross may be entertaining but have not contributed to the development of the modern Irish short story. This book argues that the strain of popular writing the women writers developed also responded to modern developments and did not merely revive the 'rollicking' tales of an Anglo-Irish past.

Somerville and Ross's comedy can be very serious, then, and the writers' attraction to the shadows of the Irish literary landscape may be ascribed in part to developments in European dark Romanticism.[18] Its modern inheritor, Charles Baudelaire, contends that concealment or mystery, as expressed in the Romantics, like the American Edgar Allan Poe, or the Irishman Charles Maturin, intensifies reality in the same way that shadow gives colour its strength and vividness:

> *Ce qu'on peut voir au soleil est toujours moins intéressant que ce qui se passe derrière une vitre. Dans ce trou noir ou lumineux vit la vie, rêve la vie, souffre la vie.*[19]

The revived interest in the sublime predominated in popular fiction of the late Victorian period. The dark side of German Romanticism, the *Nachseite*, appealed especially to some Irish writers. A specific instance of its attraction and one especially important in this study might be found in the works of a minor Irish playwright, William Gorman Wills, a kind of latter-day James Clarence Mangan and Martin Ross's second cousin. Wills worked with Henry Irving and Bram Stoker to launch a hugely popular version of Goethe's *Faust* on the London stage in the 1880s. The play adapted the darkly romantic material to suit popular taste. Bram Stoker's romance novel *The Snake's Pass*, and Somerville and Ross's *Naboth's Vineyard* transport the melodramatic effects onto Irish soil.

The romance or adventure novel, part of a 'literary current that began to overwhelm the domestic novel in the 1880s', developed alongside modernist fiction of the 1890s.[20] Thus although the romance revival as popularized by Robert Louis Stevenson, Bram Stoker, and H. Rider Haggard reflects earlier nineteenth-century romantic writing, its context within the growing publishing industry of the time makes it an entirely different phenomenon. Like Modernism, the popular romance negotiates the changes wrought by modernization: increased consumerism, the expansion of the professional middle-class, or 'new imperialism'.[21]

Recent criticism of Somerville and Ross's fiction sees the Irish writers as recreators of a gothic tradition of Irish literature. Like other writers of the Big House tradition such as Elizabeth Bowen or Molly Keane, Somerville and Ross are perceived as reinscribing the Anglo-Irish guilt encoded in Charles Maturin's *Melmoth the Wanderer* or Sheridan Le Fanu's *Uncle Silas*. Somerville and Ross's early novel, *An Irish Cousin*, has been described as 'a gothic landscape of the mind [which] anticipates future reworking of the tradition as a psychological rather than sociological literary form'.[22] Charlotte Mullen of *The Real Charlotte* has been compared to Sheridan Le Fanu's female vampire 'Carmilla', while Somerville's later *The Big House of Inver* (1925) has been seen as the psychological reworking of gothic convention that expresses the suppressed anxieties of the colonial élite in Ireland. However, as Nicholas Daly argues in his recontextualizing of the *fin-de-siècle* popular romance such as *Dracula* or *Dr Jekyll and Mr Hyde*, the 'invention of a Gothic tradition has tended to short-circuit historical inquiry'.[23] In the case of Somerville and Ross, research reveals that the echoes of Melmoth or Mephisto in the fiction have been channelled through modernist theory and popular treatment. More important than gothic material in Somerville and Ross's work is contemporary reality. For example, burlesque versions of Goethe's works or French theory on the nature of caricature as expressed in Baudelaire's treatment of Melmoth as the manifestation of modern caricature in 'De l'essence du rire' can be seen as conduits by which the earlier romantic material is conveyed. Somerville and Ross's texts are much more than psychological manifestations of the anxiety of empire. Such reduction of their highly artful works neglects factual record, ignores the writers' artistic self-awareness, and underestimates the impact of the consumer culture of the period.

The preoccupation with Ireland's colonial inheritance may lead critics to neglect the influence of Europe in Somerville and Ross's writing. For instance, the women writers have been placed within an English realist tradition, despite Somerville's art training in France.[24]

This study shares the view of critics like Charles Graves, who thought that the women writers did for Ireland what Honoré de Balzac did for France. In other words, the women writers profiled the types that emerged in the revolutionary changes to the social system of nine-teenth-century Ireland. For various critics Somerville and Ross were the 'creators of an Irish "Comédie Humaine"'.[25] Certainly, one could ascribe a French influence to Somerville and Ross's interest in the emerging Irish middle-class and their appreciation for the comic dis-play of character types whose greed and vanity results from the scramble for position in a changing world.

Somerville and Ross have been situated alternatively within two central discourses: first, a feminist/sexual argument, and second, the Anglo-Irish tradition of country-house writing. Early critical biogra-phies of the women writers established these two avenues of approach. Morris Collis speculated on the writers' sexual orientation in *Somerville and Ross* (1968). The response of Gifford Lewis in *Somerville and Ross: The World of the Irish RM* (1985) and *The Selected Letters of Somerville and Ross* (1989) relied on careful biog-raphical documentation to deny suggestions of homosexuality.[26] Literary criticism on Somerville and Ross confirms the writers' sexual or social significance. The writers are included in works that concen-trate on sexual politics, such as *Sex, Nation and Dissent in Irish Writing* (1997) edited by Eibhear Walshe, or in studies of Big House writing, such as Vera Kreilkamp's *The Anglo-Irish Novel and the Big House* (1998) or Malcolm Kelsall's *Literary Representations of the Irish Country House* (2003).[27] The last two volumes of *The Field Day Anthology of Irish Writing* by and about Irish women have confirmed these two approaches rather than offering new ways of studying the writers, largely because the treatment of Irish women's fiction in the *Anthology* follows along these self-same lines, the sexu-al and social.[28]

The publication of *The Edith Œnone Somerville Archive in Drishane House* by Otto Rauchbauer in 1995, and Declan Kiberd's inclusion of Somerville and Ross within a postcolonial framework in *Inventing Ireland* (1995) and *The Irish Classics* (2000), indicate the potential richness of Somerville and Ross's writings and Edith Somerville's art works.[29] Gifford Lewis's most recent book, *Edith Somerville, A Biography* (2005), introduces hitherto unknown biogra-phical facts that challenge both the sexual and social assumptions about the women writers.[30] Recent studies have thus widened the avenue by which a critic might approach Somerville and Ross's work.

The writers' interest in land matters or children's literature, for example, suggests the possibility of various ways of studying their work, using ecofeminist theory or beast fable and fairytale analysis, for instance, which will allow us to see the writing afresh.[31] Perhaps even more importantly, their regular visits to France, their inclusion of popular material in the writing and their negotiation of the demands of the English periodical press ask that the fiction and illustrations be considered in a wider context than has been the case thus far.

This book seeks to place Somerville and Ross more firmly within the Irish scene, to consider their work within a tradition of Irish writing. It asserts that the close attention given to Somerville and Ross's backgrounds and the consideration of their writings as social documents rather than imaginative constructs provide a one-sided view of the women writers. Writers live in their heads. Their lives are as much imaginary as they are material. Fictional stories can have as great an impact as real-life events. This book draws attention to the fact that Somerville and Ross are not just intent on drawing from real life to create an authentic picture of Irish life. They collect material of modern culture to create a pastiche of borrowed images and familiar tropes. Both history and fiction bear upon the characters and events of Somerville and Ross's work.

PART ONE:
THE COLONIAL VISION

CHAPTER 1

Land: Naboth's Vineyard *and the* Colonial Nightmare

The kingdom of heaven is like unto treasure hid in a field;
the which when a man hath found, he hideth, and for joy thereof
goeth and selleth all that he hath, and buyeth that field.

MATTHEW 13:44

NABOTH'S VINEYARD refers to an Old Testament account of kingly greed and female duplicity. King Ahab longs for the small plot of land owned by Naboth to create an unimpeded view of his domain. His queenly consort, Jezebel, takes it upon herself to have Naboth destroyed to obtain his field. The familiar tale of notorious high-handedness and the parable of greed it relates resonate within the Irish context. Dean Swift, for instance, commented ironically on his position in Dublin by naming his garden after that of Naboth. Distanced from the centres of power and influence, Swift suggests that position affects perspective: one's view of reality depends on where one stands.

Dean Swift maintained a three-acre garden near St Kevin's port in Dublin and called it 'Naboth's Vineyard'. The meagre parcel of land contrasted with England's broad, landscaped gardens and well-maintained estates. It provided Swift with an ironic comment on Ireland's 'postlapsarian' state, 'an arena for the flawed actions of fallen man'.[1] The cursed vineyard becomes a metaphor for Ireland, the antithesis of the garden of paradise, England, and the nightmare vision of the colonial world. In the Irish context, then, Naboth's vineyard suggests

more than coveted and conquered territory; it indicates an alteration
in place, the movement downwards into a nether world that operates
in opposition to the colonial dream. A prominent figure in this world
is the tradesman, the counter of pennies and half-pence and called
Marcus Brutus Drapier by Dean Swift in his Irish pamphlets. To step
into Naboth's vineyard is to enter the lower realms of the colonial
sleep and to gain thereby an ironic perception of the upper echelons.
This is the merchant's world, the world of the counting-house, as
W.B. Yeats would later describe the New Ireland.[2]

Somerville and Ross's selection of title for their second novel,
Naboth's Vineyard (1891), recalls both the Christian and colonial
context of the land issue. Like Swift, they are interested in the importance of position in a changing world, a world governed not by blood
but by market concerns. Their concentration on the gombeen man, a
modern-day Marcus Drapier, suggests that the study of place in
Naboth's world has as much to do with class and position as it does
land. Of course they would have been aware of the loaded significance of their title. Only the year before Bram Stoker had published
The Snake's Pass and employed the biblical account of Ahab in a West
of Ireland setting. In fact Stoker played out Naboth's story on the
Mayo coast, in Martin territory. In choosing as the title of their book
an obvious reference to land-grabbing, Somerville and Ross not only
promise to comment on the process of land acquisition in nineteenth-century Ireland but also indicate an ironic and self-conscious
treatment of place dependent on the narrator's distanced perspective
for effect. Somerville and Ross concentrate on the underside – a
colonial nightmare vision – of Irish life. The search for the kingdom
of heaven becomes a descent into hell. One piece of ground, one
field in the kingdom, conceals a treasure for which man will sell his
soul.

During the land wars of the 1880s desperate acts and terrible
murders emphasized the hellish aspect of the Irish countryside. Land
agitation directly affected land owners like George Moore and
Somerville and Ross or indirectly affected Dublin Castle officials like
Bram Stoker. A rash of fiction concentrating on the land wars emerged.
In 1886 Moore's *Drama in Muslin* and Emily Lawless's *Hurrish*
appeared. A significant difference between the two novels was their
approach: Moore concentrated on the wealthy land-owning class of
Galway and Mayo while Lawless studied the impoverished Irish peasantry in the Burren of Clare. Bram Stoker, then, followed Lawless's
example with what would turn out to be his only treatment of the Irish

peasantry, *The Snake's Pass*. The land wars thus provoked both Lawless and Stoker into a consideration of the peasant point of view.

In *Naboth's Vineyard* Somerville and Ross took up the argument raised by Emily Lawless and Bram Stoker by moving from the ascendancy world of their first novel, *An Irish Cousin* (1889), to concentrate on a Catholic nationalist population in West Cork. The violent Irish landscape is put to different uses in these land war novels, depending in part upon the burlesque, naturalist, or romantic elements of the authors' treatment. Their colonial perspective, a distanced and detached approach to the world they portray, is also used in different ways in the three novels.

Naboth's Vineyard can thus be seen as one of a number of land war novels. To assess its distinctive use of irony as expressed through perspective, we might compare it to other treatments of place and landscape of the period. Stoker's melodramatic *Snake's Pass* and Lawless's naturalistic *Hurrish* offer two very different treatments of the Irish countryside. The largely neglected land war novels of these writers provide a significant commentary on place which throws into relief Somerville and Ross's work. This study traces the impact of lesser known, popular writing on that of the Irish women writers to emphasize their self-conscious use of contemporary material. Thus in addition to the consideration of popular fiction by Stoker and Lawless, the latter half of this chapter introduces a minor painter and playwright of the period, Martin Ross's second cousin William Gorman Wills, to show an important point of contact between Irish matters and developments in popular culture.

A central preoccupation of the land war novels as they chart a revolutionary change in agricultural society must be the subject of time. The shift from the perception of a society and countryside not subject to modern notions of progress to one that has adapted new ideas is depicted as extreme. Somerville and Ross's novel, like its forerunners, is preoccupied with the ambiguity arising from the collision of different concepts of time – different chronotopes – stirred up by the 'seething pot' of Irish politics and made manifest in space. Modern concepts of progress, present time, confront what Martin Ross described as a 'largeness of time' arising from the impact of different periods evident in the monuments and ruins of specific places in the Irish landscape:

> Pagan altars & pagan forts overlook monastic ruins & crosses carved with the Irish decoration of interwoven lines. In this confusion of survivals, the present loses weight, the Baal worshipper is revealed with

the largeness of his time about him.[3]

For writers like Somerville and Ross, the romantic notion of timelessness or the 'largeness of time' belonging to a distant past coincides with a system of land management that relies on notions of inheritance rather than capitalist gain. The writers' interest lies in the tension provoked by the impact of the two different concepts of time and two different ideas of place.

Emily Lawless spells out the problem in *Hurrish*. Modern developments have distanced the younger generation of the Irish peasantry from their natural place in the world. Just as shop-bought clothing and whitewashed cottages look out of place in the Clare countryside, so too do newfangled ideas jar the ingrained thought patterns of a predominantly agricultural community. In *Hurrish*, the natural world dominates.

Like Somerville and Ross's second novel, *Hurrish* has suffered neglect, and although recent studies indicate a revived interest in Lawless's work, her land war novel continues to be overlooked.[4] Yet Lawless's most popular publication merits interest not least for its emphasis on the unique characteristics of the Burren's botany, geological formations and the richness of its archaeological remains. Lawless's novel had its great impact because of its environmental study of a unique Irish landscape. It examines the significance of landscape and reflects ongoing scientific interest in the Burren since the eighteenth century. It provides an important introduction to later studies of place by Irish writers such as Somerville and Ross.

Hurrish's lyrical beauty relies upon the author's exploration of the Burren. Lawless studies an Irish wasteland (impoverished and embattled) to investigate evolutionary discourse and notions of improvement and progress in Darwinian theory. Somerville and Ross continue to apply a Darwinian argument to their examination of place and character in *Naboth's Vineyard*. The later novel, however, self-consciously anticipates reader expectation and lays bare the discourse underlying romantic depictions of peasants and nature. Somerville and Ross's novel displays an artful and self-aware treatment that uses types and stage images to present an ever-shifting picture of Ireland, one that illustrates the social-cultural politics of the period as well as reflecting the significant growth of popular culture in the 1890s.

Considered alongside contemporary fictional treatments of the Irish peasant, Somerville and Ross's novel presents a grotesquely realistic view. Their political satire concentrates on a dark world of shady dealings and murderous intent. So although they follow Emily Lawless's lead by throwing themselves into the midst of Irish cultural politics, they are more like Bram Stoker in their interest in the dark side of reality, *Nachtseite*. Their darkly comic vision provoked writing that some critics would later describe as 'dirty Irish realism'.[5]

Somerville and Ross's *An Irish Cousin* avoided confrontation with the Irish situation and explored with ironic intent early nineteenth-century romantic concepts within the Big House setting. The 'Shocker', as they described their first experiment in fiction, addressed the revived romance of the period, adventure stories like those written by Robert Louis Stevenson and Bram Stoker that recalled gothic material but situated their events in a modern world to explore vital questions of the time. The adventures of Somerville and Ross's heroine in *An Irish Cousin*, however, are more like those that Catherine Morland enjoys in Jane Austen's *Northanger Abbey* than what Jonathan Harker endures in Dracula's Castle. Like Austen, Somerville and Ross provide a tongue-in-cheek review of the romance, but they do so in a troubled world and on a much darker landscape. *Naboth's Vineyard*, then, continues to examine a changing and modernized world and deliberately turns away from the crumbling decrepitude of the ineffectual ascendancy household to study the 'vulgar' struggles and desperate strategies of shop-folk, labourers, and small farmers. While their interest in elements of the revived romance continues in this second novel, it is directed by a modern impulse and a political intent.

Naboth's Vineyard responds to earlier accounts of the Irish land wars while offering a more direct political argument. The novel attacks the foundation supporting the Irish nationalist argument, which assumes the supposed unity of the Irish tenantry as it mobilizes itself as a national Land League. Set in autumn 1883, the work subverts the basic premise underlying the argument supporting the land agitation of the previous three years (1879–82): the Irish peasantry suffers a common suppression caused by a predatory landlord class. *Naboth's Vineyard* exposes the disunity of the Irish folk: it shows land greed masquerading as political strategy; it pits the land grazier against the small tenant farmer; it attacks the myth of Catholic unity in the face of Protestant oppression. The novel asserts that the proclaimed divisions of race, religion, and tradition between the landlord and his tenants, as emphasized by nationalist discourse, conceal the real power plays and the real struggles enacted in the towns and villages of Ireland.

The writers' resistance to popular nationalist perceptions of the Irish land wars becomes apparent in the opening pages of the novel. The usurpation of land indicated by the title does not arise from Ireland's colonization by England. The novel ignores past conquests and reviews only present-day land appropriation by successful farmers and wealthy shopkeepers. Thus the writers undercut any possible expectations raised by the text's provocative title.

Naboth's Vineyard deals with the basic process of colonization, the usurpation of the land, but concentrates on land-grabbing within the colonized state. As already suggested, Somerville and Ross may have been influenced by Stoker's use of the parable in his melodramatic study of land-grabbing in the West of Ireland. In the opening of *The Snake's Pass*, the priest warns the greedy gombeen man, Black Murdock, with the biblical tale. When Murdock ends up drowning in the bog, the Catholic cleric concludes the novel with the observation – in a language with strikingly Protestant overtones – that the gombeen man should have heeded his earlier warning:

> I told him what he should expect—that the fate of Ahab and Jezebel would be his. For Ahab coveted the vineyard of his neighbour Naboth, and as Jezebel wrought evil to aid him to his desire, so this man hath coveted his neighbour's goods and wrought evil to ruin him. And now behold his fate, even as the fate of Ahab and Jezebel![6]

Though Stoker frames his story with the biblical material, he neglects to include a Jezebel in the plans. His treatment of the land wars is incidental rather than central to a plot that focuses on the visiting Englishman's search for treasure in the Irish countryside. Somerville and Ross's choice of title could indicate their intention to correct Stoker's depiction of the violent Irish landscape of the early 1880s. They engage directly with the struggle for Irish land which the parable suggests, and they introduce an Irish Jezebel, Harriet Donovan.

The creation of a complex female character called Harriet Donovan, the forerunner of Charlotte Mullen in *The Real Charlotte*, did not dispel the view of Irish readers that Somerville and Ross did not really understand and thus could not write about the peasant heart. Despite their study of female passion in the character of Harriet Donovan, the novel's tendency to use caricature and stock situations led to criticism that the Protestant ascendancy could not comprehend Catholic Ireland. Undoubtedly, and like the land war novels of Lawless and Stoker, *Naboth's Vineyard* tends to resist critical study because of the authors' reliance on familiar Irish character types.

The reception of *Naboth's Vineyard* depended in part on its initial production and marketing. Somerville and Ross wrote the novel at the request of a clergyman and sold the rights for £30.[7] Its publishers treated the text as a sentimental novel, with the frontispiece presenting an idyllic illustration of the rustic lovers on a picturesque Irish hillside. The illustration gave no indication of the novel's satirical and self-conscious treatment of Irish life. The packaging of the novel did not anticipate, for instance, the narrator's insistence on pointing out how certain characters manifest stereotyped notions. Ellen Leonard is 'the realization of all pastoral romance';[8] like the other characters she is a familiar type in a self-aware study of violence in the Irish country-side. The novel sold, however, as social realism with a sentimental plot and was received as such. Ever since, the work has been treated as a document reporting on Irish affairs which tells the reader more about the authors' distance from the 'real' Ireland than it does their understanding of grassroots nationalism.

The 'deplorable over-simplification' of the characters in *Naboth's Vineyard* is subverted in part by Harriet Donovan's complex and compulsive passions,[9] but some critics believe that the work is weakened by the authors' inability 'to reveal the inner life of the simple people whom they claimed to know so well'. B.G. MacCarthy argues that Somerville and Ross were quite unable to portray 'the peasant per se' because 'their knowledge was confined to observations from above'. 'The inner life of the country people was outside their ken' concludes MacCarthy,[10] and John Cronin agrees when he notes that 'the people' of this work 'are observed from outside, without much real sympathy'.[11] He can only wonder at the improvement in their next novel (*The Real Charlotte*), believing that their movement 'from an Irish Catholic setting they scarcely understood to a Protestant Ascendancy world which nobody has understood better' accounts for such progress.[12] With *Naboth's Vineyard*, however, the writers may have been attempting, like Zola in *Nana*, which Martin Ross read in 1889, to 'pitch [their] story straight into the lowest possible strata of humanity, and make [one] feel nothing but how foul and terrific it is'.[13] The authors' distanced perspective strengthens the work's parody of the Irish land wars and shows all the more clearly that money, rather than religion or race, is the source of the bitterest conflicts in Ireland throughout the 1880s.

Naboth's Vineyard, like *Hurrish* and *The Snake's Pass*, appeared in the midst of a series of Irish novels of the 1880s about agrarian outrage. Margaret Kelleher has described these novels as 'factual

fictions', texts which offered themselves as vehicles for a better understanding of the Irish Question.[14] They frequently relied on journalistic
depiction of the land wars, fictionalized to present as particular acts
of violence. Gladstone admired Lawless's *Hurrish*,[15] and Stoker sent a
copy of his novel to the Prime Minister.[16] The seeking of Gladstone's
imprimatur indicates the authors' intent to reinterpret the Irish situation for English readers.

The land war novels rely on newspaper or magazine accounts to
record different kinds of agrarian outrage, but they do not depend
solely on written report and use visual as well as textual representation
of Irish affairs. The Caliban-like Mat O'Brady of Lawless's work calls
to mind simianized depiction of the Land Leaguers in English illustration. Stoker, then, puns on the notion of moonlighting in his novel,
obviously recalling representation of agrarian outrage as Captain
Moonlight while also suggesting the chiaroscuro effects of melodrama.
Somerville and Ross's satirical account of boycotting relies as much
on theatrical material as it does factual report. It may have been
inspired in part by *Punch*'s reviews of popular theatre production in
London – a farcical version of *The Tempest*, as well as William G.
Wills's version of Goethe's *Faust* – while also being influenced by
newspaper accounts of the investigation of forged letters supposedly
by Parnell that linked him to terrorism: the Parnell commission. The
land war novels employ various sources drawn from inside and outside Ireland to respond to popular accounts regarding land acquisition and to show how in Ireland the greed of the land-grabber from
among the folk provokes conflict. Consideration of Lawless's novel
emphasizes the significance of place, while the study of newspaper
and journal accounts of the early 1880s suggests the younger writers'
reliance upon popular material.

Both Edith Somerville and Martin Ross followed developments in
popular theatre and appear to have taken special interest in the revival
of the romantic irony of the Faust tradition. Later on in this chapter I
consider the women writers' involvement in popular theatricals; for
the moment, however, we might note that the story of Naboth also
appears in Goethe's *Faust*. In *Naboth's Vineyard*, Somerville and Ross
may well have had *Faust* in mind since they include a chapter entitled
'Mephistopheles' and allude throughout the work to satanic fires and
demonized violence. So it is worth observing, then, that in Goethe's
play the ironic devil, Mephistopheles, reminds his audience that the
usurpation of the land is an age-old process when he suggests to Faust
the need to destroy the small farm intruding upon his expansive

domain:

MEPHISTOPHELES:	Why should you scruple here and wince?
	Have you not colonized long since?
FAUST:	Go, then, and clear them from my sight!–
	The handsome little farm you know
	That I assigned them long ago.

....

| MEPHISTOPHELES: | [*ad spectatores*] What passes here is far from new; |
| | There once was Naboth's vineyard, too.[17] |

When Goethe's devil turns to his audience and comments ironically on the universal fact of colonization – 'There once was Naboth's vineyard, too' – he suggests the inevitability of human behaviour while drawing attention to the artifice of the action. The playful aside does double duty: it offers commentary on the action and its artifice. Mephistopheles' overarching perspective embraces the performance and its audience, the specific and the general. His distance from the action emphasizes the irony of the scene.

In Somerville and Ross's Irish novel, Naboth's world is claimed by hell's darkness and overlooked with playful self-awareness by Mephistopheles. At times in this text Faust's devil becomes Shakespeare's more benevolent sprite, Ariel. But throughout the novel, distance is maintained. To enter this world is to witness an ironic view of the Irish countryside, a view which not only sets itself up as the opposite of the idyllic, but also thrives on paradox, discontinuities, and ambivalence.

Naboth's Vineyard demonstrates Somerville and Ross's exploration of Irish reality as a complex and multi-layered tradition that mirrors modern aesthetic interests. Such a claim may seem a contradiction when we first look at the stage-Irish types who populate the novel and recall the figures of Lawless's and Stoker's works: the gombeen man, the innocent colleen, the violent peasant. However Somerville and Ross's use of perspective, which allows them to re-stage stage figures upon the Irish landscape, draws attention to the various masks employed to represent Irish reality. The authors' reliance upon multiple popular sources – magazines, melodrama and pantomime, the revived romance – creates a kind of pastiche of material reflecting multiple traditions.

The novel's focus, however, is on a rising middle class that originates in the ranks of an increasingly ambitious peasantry. Their primary compulsion, and the plot's motive, is to advance and to usurp. To usurp is to take someone else's place in the world. Usurpation in Naboth's world is to progress to some point of security in an unstable environment. The logic of the lower realms, the world of the merchant, assumes that one can move forward or backward according to possession of the land. John Donovan realizes that he must advance to some distant point 'up to which he felt his financial position quite assured',[18] and he will finagle the Widow Leonard out of her rightful inheritance to achieve this end. For the gombeen man, progress depends upon property ownership, and failure is its loss. To want too much is to go too far, like Ahab, who could not enjoy his vast realms because Naboth's land blighted his panoptic view – or like Faust, whose temptations included imperial dreams provoked by Mephisto's devilish logic.

THE 'QUAKING SOD',[19] IRELAND'S MIDDLE CLASS

From the beginning of *Naboth's Vineyard* the reader is placed at a remove from Irish life. The reader hovers on high, like Ariel, over the isolated island of the fishing village of Rossbrin, circled by water, shaken by storm, a place where rock and sea have battled for pre-eminence in a landscape which, as a result, has been transformed:

> Anyone who has glanced even cursorily at the map of Ireland, will have noticed how the south-west corner of it has suffered from being the furthest outpost of European resistance to the Atlantic. Winter after winter the fight between sea and rock has raged on, and now, after all these centuries of warfare, the ragged fringe of points and headlands, with long, winding inlets between them, look as though some hungry monster's sharp teeth had torn the soft, green land away, gnawing it out from between the uncompromising lines of rock that stand firm, indigestible and undefeated.[20]

The erosion of the land, like its usurpation, is an ongoing process. Rossbrin's surrounding mudflats, Scariff Bay, where the villains of the work meet their melodramatic end and are sucked down into its depths, stress this world's amorphous quality.[21] A place of shifting ground, the topography suggests a landscape undergoing transition over time. The perspective places readers on high; our gaze sweeps the landscape with what seems to be an imperial detachment as slowly, like some swooping gull, we approach the fishing town of Rossbrin, the plain utilitarian stores and the rising main street where two massive sycamore trees dominate as they once did in Castletownshend, Edith Somerville's home in County Cork. Our gaze moves closer still, and we view Donovan's Hotel with its garish, nationalist colours: a green and gold signboard on pink walls. We espy through its doorway (as if we are looking at a picture) John Donovan sitting atop a stool in his bar, counting money with snake-like speed:

> His fat finger travelled rapidly up and down the columns, and every now and then from between his thick lips came a sibilant murmur of multiplication and addition.[22]

The deliberate distancing of the readers from the life of the novel is furthered by the narrator's detachment from the characters whose caste is clearly lower than that of the narrator or implied readers. The narrative stresses their lowly distant rank just as the perspective emphasizes their geographically distant position, 'the furthest outpost of European resistance', a position not too far from hell itself.[23]

Naboth's Vineyard originates from Somerville and Ross's earlier short story 'Slide Number 42', a three-part story about Irish emigration, murder, and the corruption of the Irish peasant. The curious title refers to the story's plot device, a lantern slide that reveals with melodramatic coincidence the image of the dead man to the eye of the murderer, who sits in the audience watching the magic lantern show.[24] In the subsequent novel this self-conscious manipulation of representation becomes a play with perspective. We look downwards at the upheaval caused by Ireland's changing rural population as if we have the balcony seats in a theatre which makes all Ireland a stage. The ensuing fictional farce with its stage-Irish figures (pleasant Paddy, an Irish colleen, the simianized Fenian) focuses upon Parnellite tactics of the Land League, emphasizing agrarian violence which, as the novel appears to suggest, Parnell's policy tacitly condoned.

John Donovan's land greed propels the action of *Naboth's Vineyard*. As president of his local branch of the Land League, as proprietor of the most successful business in town, and as usurer or gombeen man, he has the power of a Prospero. Already he has disinherited the Irish Caliban of the novel, Dan Hurley, who has been reduced to working as a farmhand for the Widow Leonard and her pretty daughter, Ellen. Donovan now covets the small grazing farm of Drimnahoon whose tenancy belongs by right to the widow. John Donovan exploits the League's political aims under the mask of

President and calls for a boycott of the Leonards. Somerville and Ross suggest that Donovan's masking results from what some Irish critics consider to be the double-faced agenda of Parnellite strategy during the land wars.[25] However, masking, explored later on in this chapter, eventually becomes as important as politics in the text.

Naboth's Vineyard pays close attention to the details of land agitation. The novel includes boycotting, the killing of livestock and the attendant note from Captain Moonlight, arson and attempted murder, the influence of the *Freeman's Journal* and Parnell, whose oleograph hangs above the mantleshelf of the Donovans' parlour. John and Harriet Donovan are grotesque figures whose hunger for advancement becomes their undoing. They appear to epitomize the worst possibility of the Irish future, one which Somerville and Ross describe in 'An Irish Landlord of the Future: A Study From Life'. In the essay the narrator excoriates the rising middle class, especially the poorly educated 'land-grabbers' of the Irish countryside. Jeremiah Regan or 'Jerry the Gandher' (so called because of his mother's convictions for plucking live geese) will possess the understanding of a yahoo whose greed and cruelty is shown by the way he saves money by burying his mother 'with the primitive disregard of ritual' and by his manner of treating animals by beating his horse to death on the roadside. The landlord of the future will be a regularly drunk, superstitious lout who will reduce the land to the value at which it is sold to him under the land acts: 'prairie value'.[26]

Naboth's Vineyard concentrates on the power of the shopkeeper in small-town Ireland and his prominent position within the Land League as he amasses land for himself, a seeming contradiction which is subsumed by the national intents of the League. Irish historians have noted that the mobilization of Catholic Ireland not only excluded the landlord class but also 'transcended the differences and conflicts of interest between other rural classes'. The confrontation between large and small farmers (like the Donovans and the Leonards in *Naboth's Vineyard*) was overwhelmed by greater national interests:

> While the Land League condemned grazing as a misuse of land rightfully belonging to the tillage farmers, many graziers came to play an active role in its leadership and helped to establish and give credibility to the new 'collectivity' from which the landlords were being excluded.... The larger nationalist character which the movement was acquiring diminished the contradiction between their involvement and the declared opposition of the League to large-scale grazing, and the coexistence of groups with rival

economic interests further consolidated the League as a national rather than a merely agrarian body.[27]

By removing the main enemy of the people – the landlord – from their novel and by carefully ignoring the influence of the priest, Somerville and Ross shift focus upon the scramble for position and land among the folk. They show a whole variety of people: labourers, housewives, fishermen, shopkeepers, tenants, businessmen. All are driven by ambition and united out of a common fear of losing place in progressive Ireland.

The mobilization of Catholic Ireland would have been especially evident to land-owners and hunting advocates like Somerville and Ross with the anti-hunting protests of 1881 and 1882. Perry Curtis has pointed out that this movement 'deepened the divisions in Irish society and strengthened the conviction of landlords, already exposed to boycotting and ambush, that the League militants would stop at nothing – not even the poisoning of hounds – in their campaign to drive the gentry out of the country and expropriate their land'.[28] With Parnell's arrest in October 1881, and the outlawing of the Land League by Gladstone the same month, the anti-hunting campaign intensified. In November, hunts across the country were confronted by hundreds of demonstrators and stone-throwing protestors. Hounds were poisoned and hunting enthusiasts were dismayed by the vehemence of the popular protest. By January 1882 'at least a dozen packs of hounds and harriers' had been suspended indefinitely.[29] Throughout this period, says Curtis, the League staged its own 'people's hunts' which consisted of masses of people combing the countryside for game which was then given to the families of political prisoners. In County Clare, for instance, 'the people who had put the Kildysart harriers out of business celebrated their triumph by rounding up some dogs and old hounds, dubbed "the Parnell Pack", which they then took out hunting'.[30]

The staging of people's hunts reverses the order of things in the Irish countryside while dramatizing the power of the people as they mobilize themselves against a common enemy: the Protestant on a horse. The people's hunts parody the Sport of Kings with a politicized carnivalesque spirit and display a collective force. In *Naboth's Vineyard* Somerville and Ross adopt that sense of the land wars as a time of ever-threatening disorder and ferment issuing from inside the land itself. In their writing, Irish nationalism creates a topsy-turvy nightmare world edging on mayhem and madness.

Social upheaval gives opportunity for strange kinds of aberrations to emerge and for the progressive merchant to gain in power and prestige now that the old order has been overturned. Marcus Brutus Drapier's world of Swift's satirical pamphlets becomes the only alternative in *Naboth's Vineyard* and the reader slides downwards into the unsteady landscape of the merchant's world, where nothing can stop the gombeen man's advance. The movement of the novel changes from an upward/downwards model to a horizontal one, the model of progress.

In *Naboth's Vineyard* the free market rules, and everything is measured and assessed according to its standards. By removing the church and the gentry from the Irish scene, Somerville and Ross show that the weakest members of society fall prey to their own kind in a community which has adopted a *laissez-faire* economic ideology. Modern-day capitalism undermines the links between people while sabotaging their traditional relationship to the land. The 'counter-jumper' leaps beyond his rightful sphere to interfere with traditional land matters. With Swiftian satire, Somerville and Ross show how the land question becomes more a matter of capitalist venture than political play. Politics serves land opportunism. Competition replaces patronage with devastating effects on the Irish poor. The novel raises the question: Who will assist the weak in a world driven by market-place concerns?[31]

The swiftly shifting order of things in *Naboth's Vineyard* causes displacement and disarray. The weak or the vulnerable find themselves misplaced or out of place in the changing scheme of things. The torment in Naboth's world lies in the fact of placelessness in an unstructured society. Dispossessed Dan Hurley becomes a Caliban figure, thwarted and ridiculed. Frustrated Harriet Donovan becomes a Jezebel, manipulating and mocked. Yet another outcast, James Mahony, becomes an Irish Mephistopheles who assists John Donovan in his over-weening ambition. His sunken eyes with their 'hot sparkle', his 'long, gaunt figure', sanguine temperament, and invoking of the devil, 'Hon o maun dhiaoul!', deliberately recall Faust's demon.[32] He emerges out of the fractured and violent world created by the 'quaking sod' of Irish national consciousness.

The new Irish power base dips and rises along the social scale with the same volatility we discover in the central female's wilful character. Harriet Kelly married John Donovan to better her own situation, but she remains uneasy in her middle-class parlour, with furniture 'purchased at a forced sale of one of [Donovan's] numerous creditors',[33] and most of *Naboth's Vineyard* follows her as she roams restlessly the woods and fields surrounding Rossbrin. With this passionate character the deliberate distancing of the narrative collapses, as if overwhelmed by her tempestuous nature and the restlessness of her frustrated spirit. Indeed if the Irish land wars publicly manifest the shifting Catholic classes, then Harriet Donovan's internal tempests – and the violence they wreak – may be considered private manifestations of the same.[34]

Harriet's sex complicates her situation. Unable to tolerate the confines of married respectability, she flees her stifling parlour for the open fields. Both class and gender reasons influence her flight. She does not know her place, either as a married woman or as an upstart peasant. When Rick O'Grady looks at her, he remembers the country girl with a red plaid shawl around her dark hair. Now she speaks with disdain of country fashion, of the 'old shawl wisped over [the country girls'] heads'.[35] Her rarely used parlour is decorated with artificial flowers and books with 'gilded devotional exteriors'.[36] This brittle façade cannot conceal the torrential emotions of her nature. Like the Mephisto figure, James Mahony, she has no place in Naboth's world but dances back and forth between different positions.

Harriet Donovan ushers chaos and disorder into a world already unsteady with change. Her dangerous potential derives from her unrestrained attributes – an aggressive nature and an unmitigated social ambition. Her physical and mental ambivalence, the fine line she treads between good and evil or beauty and ugliness, make her a female demon struggling in the fires of her own making. With her character, Somerville and Ross create a figure who combines the crises of class and gender and who suggests a modern ambiguity, who suffers the violence of transition and wreaks violence herself in order to find peace. Harriet Donovan becomes much more than type; her complex nature includes taboo passions that do not coincide with popular notions of feminine feeling. At the same time her social ambitions and ability to dominate the narrative enable her character to resist the imperial perception of the indigenous woman as Other.

Harriet Donovan and Charlotte Mullen of Somerville and Ross's later work, Irish madwomen both, escape their attic confines and roam the whole house of the text. However primitive and wild Harriet appears, she dominates the novel. Her central position thrusts her concerns into the foreground. Unlike Bertha Mason who skirts Charlotte Brontë's narrative like a crazed figure of Jane Eyre's imagination, Somerville and Ross's madwoman has gained centre stage. Unlike Olive Schreiner's contemporaneous colonial novel, *The Story*

of an African Farm (1883), which does not even conceive of a
Hottentot intellect while arguing for women's rights, Somerville and
Ross's work presents a more complicated issue by uniting feminist
concerns and class and race matters in the one powerful character.[37]
There is no alternative reality to that of Harriet Donovan. Nothing
counters her shifting position, which remains central to the text and
provides its ambiguous core.

In the colonial nightmare demons and grotesques emerge. Let loose
upon the world, an ambitious peasant like Harriet uses one lover to
advance and then seeks another victim. She may appear to some to be
a fatal vampire woman,[38] but her origin can be traced more directly to
Somerville and Ross's involvement with a theatrical tradition and the
Mephisto figure emerging from nineteenth-century farce discussed
below. Harriet comes from the underworld of *Naboth's Vineyard*. She
is like a volcano waiting to erupt, 'tense with the strain of repressing
some wild speech or other', and her eyes when she looks at Rick have
'such intensity that a fire seemed to kindle in them'.[39] The evident
sexuality manifested in her pursuit of Rick O'Grady demonstrates distortion. Like the other unpleasant characters in the novel whose ugliness is detailed to suggest baseness, ignorance and enlarged sexual
appetites, Harriet is a grotesque.

The grotesque belongs in the underworld and might be considered
a kind of masking. The word comes from the Italian *grotta* (cave), and
the Latin of *grotta* is *crupta* (crypt). *Crupta* comes from the Greek for
vault, 'one of whose cognates is "to hide", thus implying that the
grotesque reveals the underground, the secret, the "buried".'[40] The
grotesque, says Baudelaire in 'De l'essence du rire', prompts a wild
hilarity in man. The grotesque is a creation rather than an imitation,
and man laughs to discover his superiority to nature which the
grotesque reveals.[41] So the grotesque is both a fantastic creation and a
sinister reflection of the chaotic forces of nature. It suggests a subterranean 'world in which the realms of the animate and the inani-
mate are no longer separate and the "normal" laws of symmetry and
proportion are no longer valid'.[42] A grotesque like Harriet conceals
something unknown. Half her figure lies shrouded in darkness.

The elusive truth of the grotesque figure lies in the suspicion of
a half-understood reality, and Harriet Donovan's power lies in her
mysterious ambiguity. Her vitality might be demonic but it energizes
the novel. The deformation of her character manifests a modern
ambivalence arising from abrupt social changes in late nineteenth-century Ireland. In Harriet Donovan, and, as argued in the next chapter,

to an even greater degree in Charlotte Mullen, character manifests the multiple tensions of the cultural politics of the period.

LITERARY CONTEXTS

Close attention to realistic detail confers a journal-like quality to *Naboth's Vineyard*. As already noted, the text relies on periodicals and newspapers for support. The intense violence, such as the killing of the Widow's prized heifer with 'a dozen gashes in her sleek skin' and which lies surrounded by a pool of congealing blood with the accompanying note from 'Captain Moonlight', is authentic. The note's message, 'Take notis, that this is the way I will sarve all Land-grabbers', is given point by a drawing of a coffin.[43] The threatening letter could be taken directly from nineteenth-century newspaper records of agrarian outrage.[44] It also recalls instances of threatening letters Edith Somerville observed close at hand in Castletownshend.[45] Precise details are accompanied by the use of distinct physiognomic coding of the characters' features. John Donovan has a cocked nose and heavy cheeks. His wife's dark beauty is marred by a heavy jaw and a projecting underlip. All the characters are separated from the narrator by class and generalized as types, at a firm distance from the novel's initial observational post. Even the more pleasant characters, such as Ellen Leonard, the Widow's daughter, are distanced by a gap of rank quite impossible to bridge:

> It cannot, of course, be supposed that [Ellen] explained her own emotions to herself very intelligibly; that luxury, or torment, whichever it is, is reserved for the cultured.[46]

Handsome Rick O'Grady may be the hero, but his appearance falls short of the implied reader's standard. He has good looks, but 'it must be confessed that they were not of a pre-eminently classical or intellectual type'. His hair curls too wildly, his brow dips too low, and his nose is 'put on at a more salient angle than is common in Greek art'. [47]

The physiognomic coding in *Naboth's Vineyard* suggests the writers' resistance to the demand for idealized figures in pictorial representations of Ireland.[48] Instead, the writers respond to familiar stereotypes from popular sources, such as contemporary Irish fiction or British periodical literature, and they incorporate or subvert these mainstream tropes. The deliberate appropriation of stage-Irish figures may thus indicate the authors' aesthetic intent as much as it reveals their class anxiety or possible alienation within the emerging Irish state.

Somerville and Ross's artful handling of popular images of Irishness becomes clearer when considered alongside Emily Lawless's earlier studies of character as it relates to place. Lawless's naturalistic treatment shows the impact of Darwinian thought on the handling of the Irish landscape and its people. Looking at Lawless next to the later female writers assists in the argument that there may be more than class-consciousness at work in the depiction of character in these land war novels.

Lawless's preoccupation with the Irish landscape as 'perfect mines and treasure-houses to the botanist' was established early on in her career with essays on Irish flora and fauna, including 'An Upland Bog' of 1881.[49] Her study of bogland echoes earlier nineteenth-century commentary on the Irish landscape as a manifestation of Irish character.[50] Lawless also suggests that nature offers a larger commentary on progress in Ireland. She speaks of passing a group of Scotch fir trees, 'a sorry-looking company, undersized and ill-disciplined; anything, evidently, but secure in their position'. She notes that these stunted firs are 'much domineered over by the original possessors of the soil, in the shape of big thistles and long wiry grasses and briers, which have their own views on agrarian matters, and have no notion of surrendering possession to new-comers – especially Scotch ones!'.[51] The Scottish Somerville family may well have appreciated Lawless's representation of the landscape as dramatic narrative echoing Irish history. Certainly Edith Somerville, who read Charles Darwin, would have been interested in Lawless's belief that the struggle for survival enacted on the Irish landscape follows Darwin's dictates, which Lawless invokes when describing the flesh-eating flora of the bogland: sundews, butterworts, and bladderworts.[52] She details the particular habits of the bog-flowers, which trap and devour insect life in their broad viscous leaves to enact the neutral – if grisly – process of adaptation and survival.

In a similar way Lawless's fiction gives witness to an environment, using place as the determining factor of narrative development so that the characters of *Hurrish* seem more like insects than active, thinking agents. Lawless's entomological interests and environmental determinism direct her treatment of the land wars. Like a thunderstorm or an avalanche, violence becomes part of a larger natural scheme that shapes its own development, not according to some progressive narrative but according to its own dictates. In a way, narrative serves nature; it appears to take its course from natural rather than artistic dictates.[53]

In her *Memoirs* of 1937, Elizabeth Burke Fingall described Emily Lawless as a 'staunch Unionist' who wrote her novels with an 'intensity of nationalist feeling'. Her passionate cultural nationalism, however, was well concealed. 'No one was ever less like her work than Emily Lawless,' says Countess Fingall. 'She was pale and flaccid, with half-closed, near-sighted eyes and limp white hands.'[54] Her decadent demeanour did not preclude her interest in British policy and an awareness of the '"lumbering absurdities" of national character as created by imperial conflict.'[55]

Somerville and Ross recall aspects of Lawless's determinism in their studies of bogland in various works, perhaps most obviously *The Silver Fox* of 1898.[56] They also echo Lawless in their decided rejection of stage-Irish conventions as 'over-blown blossom[s] of English humour'.[57] Such awareness suggests an ironic use of stereotyped traits in the writers' fiction, and the types that populate *Hurrish* and *Naboth's Vineyard* should be considered with such self-awareness in mind. However to appreciate Somerville and Ross's handling of character as it relates to place, a closer look at Lawless's novel is necessary.

In Lawless's *Hurrish* there is no further into the wilds that one can go, apparently, than the Burren in County Clare. 'Wilder regions there are few to be found, even in the wildest west of Ireland'[58] than this area of ancient history. Though the valley of Gortnacoppin dips within the desolate landscape, one has the impression of being on a height. 'Standing in it,' says the narrator, 'you may fairly believe yourself in the heart of some alpine region, high above the haunts of men, where only the eagle or marmot make their homes.' The valley has at its base a fertile oasis which results from the 'mass of detritus, borne down from the hills'. Sweet pockets of fertility arise out of the debris of the wasteland; opposites interact to create a landscape of complex parts. The artefacts of past traditions have 'melted into the surrounding stoniness'[59] and the diverse forces of seemingly good and bad interact in a constantly fluctuating cycle.

The novel's protagonist, Hurrish O'Brien, demonstrates a textbook Celtic temperament: 'poetic, excitable, emotionable [*sic*], unreasoning'. Half-farmer and half-fisherman, he comes from 'that amphibious part of the island', and as a 'contented giant' appears to be only halfway up the evolutionary ladder, not too far ahead in developmental terms to the resident 'human orang-utang or Caliban', Mat Brady.[60]

Violent Mat Brady manifests the traits of the worst type of Irish peasant as satirized by English cartoonists like John Tenniel for *Punch*.

He pursues Alley Sheehan, whose mind 'was too simple, too inherently limited, to admit of any large or complicated variety of emotions'. Like Somerville and Ross's colleen in *Naboth's Vineyard*, Lawless's simple lass 'was not given to introspection – that, happily, not being one of the vices of the class to which she belonged'.[61] Red-headed, drunken Brady hates his betters with the 'grotesque' brutality of a Caliban. He is the 'most obnoxious of Calibans', who has replaced the pike for the gun: 'Like every Irishman of his class – whether Coercion Acts are in force or whether they are not – he had an old gun hidden away in the thatch of his cabin.'[62]

Lawless's exaggeration of character, a perspective that enlarges the Irish world, relies upon familiar colonial stereotyping. The characters of *Hurrish* are carefully delineated as types. Somerville and Ross reverse the perspective in *Naboth's Vineyard*. Similar characters appear, but instead of looking up at them, we look down at the types on display. In both works, however, the characters demonstrate in their features and habits familiar categories of race and class. They are sorted into their groupings much as butterflies or beetles are arranged in glass cases in museums.

Lawless's treatment of Irish character is determined as much by her naturalist bent as her colonial eye. For instance, the distancing perspective deliberately recalls a revived Irish mythology that is closely linked to the environment, stories of Fomorian giants waging war across the island, which Lawless would incorporate in her history book, *Ireland* (1887), or later novel, *Maelcho* (1894). Mat Brady is not only a Caliban figure but also a 'man-mountain'[63] whose battle with gargantuan Hurrish becomes like a struggle of Irish mythological figures who have more in common with the rocks and soil of the Burren than they do with present-day events. Characters reflect the traits of their environment. Alley Sheehan's mind is compared to a clear mountain pool. Like the landscape, characters manifest both the brutal and benign forces of nature.

As types, the peasantry possesses both a scientific and religious significance in the narrative. On the one hand they are specimens scrutinized by a distanced narrator in the same way an entomologist studies insects under the microscope. On the other, their recognizable features prefigure a larger Christian meaning. For example, Alley Sheehan is a kind who appears as frequently in the Burren as does its purple gentian, and she has meaning in the story as both an individual and as a representative figure. Like the artefacts on the landscape she escapes the 'weight of the present' (Martin Ross) because of her larger significance as a type. 'Certain types repeat themselves eternally at all ages of the world,' explains the narrator, 'and hers was the type of all those gently ascetic natures which at every period and under all variations of circumstances have sprung up spontaneously'. Like the fertile oasis amidst the stony rocks of Gortnacoppin, Alley Sheehan is a repeatable figure of the landscape that balances out the natural order of things. Moreover, she seems but an earthly cast for the larger kind she worships, 'the mother who is the type of all motherhood,' the Virgin Mother.[64] Alley bears both a natural and Christian significance. Her type-casting issues from a colonial, scientific and religious sensibility, and her setting is all-important:

> The little dells where the grass grew rich and thick; the wells full of offerings to their respective saints; the rifts into which she could plunge her hands, and bring them up filled with flowers; the isles of Aran opposite, where the saints used to live, and at which she looked in consequence with such reverence; the wild clearness of the sea, and great environing arch of sky.[65]

In *Hurrish*, a world of extreme contrasts is set within a larger dimension of sea and sky to become at moments spiritualized. The Western bluish light transforms place, character, and action so that all appear to be enlarged and upon a different plane from that of ordinary reality.

In the novel, knowledge resides in the landscape itself and the writer looks to nature to discover patterns of reality. The close scrutiny of the Burren demands an acknowledgement on the part of the reader of the pre-eminence of place as a source of understanding. Nature tells the story. *Hurrish* is 'place-centred',[66] not only in terms of natural phenomena and topographical history but also in relation to its central argument which is based on land acquisition and social position. In other words, the driving force of the writer's analysis of Irish reality is place. Land-grabbing and social climbing – finding places – shape the plot, while the landscape's history tells a larger story of conquest and colonization. Thus the subject matter of the novel, the struggle for land and social prestige, determines its treatment. Lawless's naturalist methods of character depiction, for instance, demonstrate the natural dictates of the landscape. The humans are part of nature, and the deliberate selection of peasants allows the writer to emphasize the significance of the land in determining human behaviour. The supposed closeness of the peasantry to the natural world gives opportunity to explore the land as a primary source of meaning. Lawless's exploitation of this supposition, her depiction of the Irish peasantry as animal-like, must be understood within the larger argument of the novel where place 'function[s] as a cultural and textual paradigm'. [67]

As with Emily Lawless's work, *Naboth's Vineyard* situates its characters on various lower rungs of the evolutionary ladder, at the bottom of which lurks a simianized figure called Dan Hurley. As already noted, the descent into Naboth's nightmare world counters the narrator's ascent in *Hurrish*. Somerville and Ross satirize the violent Irish landscape by thrusting the perspective downwards. They reuse the Irish Caliban and cross him with other kinds of Calibans to create a burlesque yahoo with an Irish political dimension.

Somerville and Ross's satirical use of the Caliban figure reflects the fearful realities giving rise to the type. Dan Hurley, the Widow Leonard's illiterate and deformed farmhand, has a 'thatch of pale hair ... almost white' [68] and wears a white flannel coat. His propensity for violence, his epileptic fits, extreme ugliness and desire for Ellen, re-enact Caliban's role in a specifically Irish context – that of the Whiteboys. Somerville and Ross re-charge the appropriated *Tempest* material with a political edge. Their Irish Caliban targets the most popular peasant movement of the century. 'In a mind like his', the narrator assures us, 'thought is scarcely a coherent process, but resolves itself into a succession of more or less crude emotions.'[69] Dan Hurley fulfils the *Punch* reader's most extreme notions of the worst kind of Irish peasant: ignorant and ugly to the point of monstrosity, more animal than man, more vegetable than human:

> His face was that of a sullen, ugly young fellow of two or three and twenty; in colour a brick-dust pink; in shape, a pudding that has defied the restraining influence of the pudding cloth; in general effect, a remarkable confirmation of the theory that those who live on potatoes finally acquire a likeness to that vegetable. [70]

Dan Hurley – the disinherited tenant reduced to labouring by Prospero[us] John Donovan – bares his teeth at Rick O'Grady 'with the grin of a furious caged animal' and possesses a laugh 'that might have been taken from Caliban's *repertoire*'.[71] Dan Hurley lurks in the island's corners (which he knows better than anyone else), suffers his disinheritance by John Donovan, and accosts his beloved Ellen in a ludicrous parody of Caliban's postures in Shakespeare's *The Tempest*.

Somerville and Ross's satirical study of West Cork would have been directed in part by their immersion in a visual or theatrical arts tradition. Edith Somerville joined forces with Martin Ross only a few years before writing *Naboth's Vineyard* and brought to their joint efforts her painting and illustration training in Düsseldorf and Paris.[72] Martin Ross joined Somerville on some of her art training stints and the pair shared a love of the comic. Through her older brother Robert Martin, who wrote for the stage, Martin Ross was directly connected to popular theatrical productions in Dublin and London. The writers' treatment of the Irish land wars, then, is affected first by their European training and second by their comic sense. In writing *Naboth's Vineyard*, the two writers were redressing the balance. They admired Lawless's treatment of the Irish peasant but noted an absence of humour they enjoyed in Maria Edgeworth's representation of the Irish folk.[73]

Nonetheless, Somerville and Ross's emphasis on place as a defining factor in human behaviour readily recalls Lawless's environmental determinism. Somerville's interest in landscape (she painted the West Cork countryside throughout her career) directs attention in the novel to the slowly evolving nature of the Irish terrain and the jarring impact of sudden economic and political developments upon place and its human occupants. Somerville owned a copy of Darwin's *Expression of the Emotions in Man and Animals*.[74] The emphasis on behaviour patterns in *Naboth's Vineyard*, how people have evolved modes of behaviour that do not easily conform to sudden changes in position (leaping upwards on the social ladder, for instance), reflects Darwin's argument that human or animal behaviour patterns evolve just as surely, and just as slowly, as do their shape and form.[75]

At the same time Somerville and Ross's depictions of a greedy shopkeeper/Land Leaguer and his wife, John and Harriet Donovan, the despised Caliban figure, Dan Hurley, and the rustic hero, Rick O'Grady, recall popular theatre figures. Place in this novel also becomes a platform, a stage upon which the Irish peasant characters enact roles that recall well-known pantomime or melodrama figures. The writers demonstrate a self-conscious redeployment of stage masks in their depiction of agrarian agitation in West Cork. For example, John Donovan's cocked nose and heavy cheeks invert the exaggerated features of Mr. Punch, and both figures sport a paunch and carry a hefty stick to batter their wives. Their common pleasure in violence, the threat of cuckoldry in their marriages, and their courting of the Devil indicate that the Irish gombeen man owes something to the grotesque dimensions of the English clown.[76] Donovan's distinct facial features not only indicate his class; they also suggest the comic's grotesque mask. His ugliness is matched by his wife's brutal beauty, just as Judy rivals Punch in grotesqueness.[77] The Irish couple's violence, however, is internalized; their wars are psychological rather than physical. Harriet doesn't actually kill her husband, she merely allows his death to occur. John Donovan raises his stick to his wife, but his real torment of her is more insidious:

> Harriet rose to her feet with such a fire burning in her heart as she had never known before. The hidden raw that she scarcely owned to her own thought had been touched by her husband's coarse hand, and the torture was almost unendurable. She felt she could kill him as she looked down on him, stretched out in sodden comfort before the fire, with an egotistical smile on his heavy face, and his fat hand caressing his tumbler of whiskey and water.[78]

The indirect forms of violence waged between John and Harriet Donovan internalize the ludicrous, overt violence of the English pantomime.

The similarity of the pantomime characters to those in *Naboth's Vineyard* is paralleled by a similarity of content and method. Various elements of the Punch and Judy show are revived in the Irish context: the masks and violence, first of all, but also the elderly husband and his young wife who dallies with young men, marital abuse, the cuckold left holding the baby, allusions to topical issues, and the interweaving of literary and biblical material. Somerville and Ross, however, do not merely appropriate pantomime material, they restage it. So we have the pantomime masks redisplayed on the Irish land-scape which, in turn, becomes a platform. Ireland transforms the English material. Popular adaptations of the pantomime in Dublin at this time show a similar self-consciousness. The Christmas pantomime of 1888 at the National Music Hall called *Harlequin Bryan O'Lynn or the Sleeping Beauty of Erin* includes parodies of stage-Irish figures. There is Thomas Noddy, 'King of No Land', and Lord Factotum, who is described as 'Lord High Everything'. The agent of transformation, the harlequin, is Bryan O'Lynn, 'A Rale Irish Boy', and the heroine is Lady Bridget Casey, 'An Irish Woman to the Backbone'. The first of the ten scenes, before the 'Grand Transformation' and the Harlequinade, is set in Dublin. Then the entire cast is whisked off to an 'Irish and American Meat Market'. The pantomime format exploits Irish political-cultural interests, and we can easily imagine the nature of the 'Grand Transformation' when, perhaps, the 'King of No Land' will take over from 'Lord High Everything' in this nationalist material.[79]

The influence of popular farce and pantomime on Somerville and Ross's writing becomes more apparent when the significance of time in the novel is considered more closely. Unlike their other fiction, *Naboth's Vineyard* covers a short and specific time frame, October to December 1883. There are various reasons for the authors' detailing of exact dates. Because the action is firmly located in time, the novel's focus is upon the daily measure of minutes rather than that 'largeness of time' which Martin Ross perceived in the ancient ruins of the Irish landscape or Emily Lawless remarked in the stony fastnesses of the Burren. The subject matter thus addresses the significance of a modern concept of time as progress, as illustrated by the greedy gombeen man and his social-climbing wife. The dates provided also mark an especially active period of land agitation and unrest. 'By the end of 1882, the number of agrarian outrages had reached 11,320 (of which 62 percent were threatening letters' and in the early 1880s 'at least ten landlords and land agents were murdered'.[80] Specific acts of violence struck a note of horror for many: the Phoenix Park assassinations occurred in May 1882 and much more locally for Martin Ross, desperate acts such as the massacre of a family in Maamtrasna, County Mayo took place not far from Ross House.[81]

After Robert Martin's death in 1905, Martin Ross writes of her elder brother's involvement in the land wars in her essay 'The Martins of Ross'. Robert Martin's passion for pantomime and burlesque coincided with Parnell's leadership of the Irish Parliamentary Party. 'From 1877', says his sister, 'Parnell . . . carried the horn, a grim, disdainful Master, whose pack never dared to get closer to him than the length of his thong; but he laid them on the line and they ran it like wolves.'[82] Martin Ross's image recalls the 'Parnell Pack' of the people's hunts in County Clare in 1882. She also argues that the consecutive poor harvests of this period, increasing tenant discontent and random boycotting caused by Gladstone's Land Act of 1881, and a policy combining coercion and concession, led to the violence and murder epitomized by the terrible deaths of Maamtrasna: 'The stately mountains beheld the struggle and the slaughter, and the sweet waters of Lough Mask closed upon the victims.'[83] However, though Ross writes of the events of the early 1880s, and though the waters and hills of Rossbrin in *Naboth's Vineyard* witness violence originating from a similar mix of popular political agitation and personal vendetta, she does not isolate the autumn of 1883. The period does not appear to have any special significance. Why did the writers isolate October to December in their fiction? Why these months in particular?

John Donovan's reading material, the *Freeman's Journal*, which he hides behind while enacting the boycott by refusing to serve young

Ellen Leonard in his shop, could explain the authors' selection of this
time period. Throughout October in the *Freeman's Journal*, amidst
reports on Nationalist meetings and demonstrations, descriptions of
Land Commission court cases, and listings of the amounts accrued
through the Parnell National Tribute, ran a lengthy series of editorial
comment followed by letters to the editor on the convent education
of Irish girls.[84] The subject was immensely popular. So while Donovan
pores over articles on the Irish public's concern for the welfare of
Irish girlhood, his young and pretty victim waits in vain for food
(whatever about education). Harriet Donovan's punishment at the
end of the novel, banishment to the convent of the Sisters of Mercy,
gains significance when considered against the backdrop of the
Freeman's Journal.

Somerville and Ross read *Punch* magazine more frequently than
the *Freeman's Journal*, and a better indication of the authors' appropriation of sources might be found in the October to December issues
of the satirical British magazine. The writers' interest in pantomime
and burlesque would have directed their attention to the *Punch* material of October to December 1883, issues that also discussed Martin
Ross's cousin William G. Wills's plays.[85]

On 20 October 1883, *Punch* reviewed the 'triumphant
Shakesperian burlesque-fairy-drama', an extravaganza called *Ariel*,
performed in London's Gaiety theatre. The two accompanying illustrations of Ariel hovering above the waves and Caliban and Miranda
facing each other in harmless dance, the transformation of
Shakespeare's play into light-hearted burlesque, may have suggested
to Somerville and Ross similar manipulations in their fiction, an Irish
version of *The Tempest*.

FIGURE 1.1. Review of *Ariel*, *Punch*, 85 (20 October 1883).

FIGURE 1.2. John Tenniel, *Crowning the O'Caliban*, *Punch*, 85 (22 December 1883)

On 22 December 1883, *Punch* printed John Tenniel's notorious caricature of the Irish Fenian as O'Caliban and provided an entirely different version of the innocent dancing native of the earlier review.[86] O'Caliban is a brutal, frankly degenerate apeman representing the Irish Land League and a combination of the various images of previous issues. Perry Curtis describes him as 'the Celtic Caliban' in his study of the simianized Irish man of Victorian caricature.[87]

Somerville and Ross appropriate the *Punch* parodies and restage them on an Irish island that is like Prospero's world, tempest-tossed and subject to a patriarchal rule which both a Miranda-like Ellen and a Caliban-like Dan Hurley must endure. With O'Caliban in mind, the writers show a Whiteboy version lurking in the background, and the novel's tempests become the boycotts and fires conjured up by Donovan and his superior wizard, the absent Parnell.

Somerville and Ross's novel reflects a series of images of colonization or Irishness, rather than a particular Irish reality. It restages familiar burlesque material on a natural stage, the island of Ireland. At the same time it deliberately subverts picturesque versions of the Irish situation as advanced by romance adventure stories like Bram Stoker's *The Snake's Pass*.

Stoker provides an improving English landlord as the solution to Ireland's difficulties and promotes the idealized peasant girl – his future wife – as a natural lady, one who needs only to travel to Paris to attain 'high breeding – every stamp of the highest culture'.[88] Somerville and Ross's prognosis on the improvement of the Irish landscape in the hands of the English entrepreneur, or of the Irish peasantry, opposes Stoker's panacea for Ireland's ills. Nonetheless, like Stoker, they are concerned with the conflict generated between different notions of time which became evident with the success of late nineteenth-century capitalized venture. Earlier in this chapter, I argued that the tension between a vertical and a horizontal concept of the world reflected Irish cultural change. However, with an examination of Stoker's work, a further source for this conflict (and its use by Somerville and Ross) becomes apparent: German Romantic thought.

In Stoker's text, the gombeen man, Black Murdock, figures as a monster who appears in the hero's dreams as an enormous snake and who tricks his neighbour, Phelim Joyce, out of his land. Murdock wants to find a treasure supposedly hidden in the useless bog, which makes up most of the land on Knockcalltecrore, 'The Hill of the Lost Crown', also called Knocknanaher, 'The Hill of the Snake'. There is an ancient myth about St Patrick battling the snake for ascendancy in Ireland, and a more recent story about a lost chest of French gold coins buried in the bog at the end of the previous century. These old stories of the snake and the gold direct the action of the plot, for Murdock is determined to find the treasure, and the hero, an Englishman called Arthur Severn visiting Ireland for the first time, becomes haunted by the myths.

Stoker's text is more heavily weighted by the revived interest in the dark side – *Nachtseite* – of German Romanticism than is Somerville and Ross's work. The blackness of *The Snake's Pass* is matched by the unfathomable power of the shifting bog: swollen and bursting with weeks of rainfall, it eventually breaks its boundaries and sweeps across the land like an avalanche of quicksand. Black Murdock comes to an abrupt finish when the bog sucks him and his entire house down deep into its 'filth and wickedness'[89] and the whole lot of fetid water and evil derring-do is swept out to sea. In *Naboth's Vineyard*, Donovan's sordid death might be described as a realistic version of Murdock's incredible end, while Somerville and Ross's actual descriptions of agrarian warfare, led by Captain Moonlight, counter Stoker's determination to avoid the violent reality of the time. For instance, Stoker's lovelorn hero wanders restlessly at night and is accosted by the local policeman, who suspects some nefarious reason for Severn's nightly expeditions. But, Severn claims, his intent is moonlighting of another sort than that which the law might suspect: he walks at night 'to enjoy the effects of moonlight.' What he means is 'the view – the purely aesthetic effect – the chiaroscuro – the pretty pictures!'. [90]

The romantic quest, rather than local politics, predominates in Stoker's text.[91] Yet the larger picture, borrowing Severn's phraseology, originates in romance material that reflects interestingly on the troubled social terrain of the period. A possible source, Goethe's 'The Fairytale' of 1795, revived with other literary fairytales in the second half of the nineteenth century, might be considered as an example of the broader discourse informing the Anglo-Irish material. This highly symbolic tale offers a way of considering both Stoker and Somerville and Ross's *fin-de-siècle* sensibilities. It introduces into this discussion significant aesthetic material, the German *Kunstmärchen* or literary fairytale. Irish writers like Stoker or Wilde or Somerville and Ross took a particular interest in fairytales, and the romantic fairytale had a bearing on the development of Somerville and Ross's literary output throughout their career.

In Goethe's 'The Fairytale', a great river, swollen by rains, separates the East from the West and cannot be crossed by anyone other than an old ferryman and a female snake who turns herself into a bridge to access the beautiful East. This snake, however, lives in the caverns of the West and thrives on gold. She gobbles up gold which two travelling will-o'-the-wisps scatter onto the ground as they laugh and trick their way across the symbolic landscape. Various elements from Goethe's tale are echoed in the Irish writers' material; most interesting are the snake and the will-o'-the-wisps, who must assist each other in order that a new kingdom might be realized. The figures are presented as contrasting forces in Goethe's work:

> Exhausted, she [the snake] at last came upon a damp reedy marsh where our two will-o'-the-wisps were at play. She shot forwards to greet them and was delighted to find herself related to such pleasant gentlemen. The flickering lights sidled up to her, leaping to and fro and laughing in their usual manner. 'Dear Aunt,' they said, 'even though you do indeed belong to the horizontal line, it really means nothing; for we are related only through our shared brilliance, for, as you see' (at this point the two flames drew themselves in, discarding their full breadth and making themselves as long and as pointed as possible) 'a slender figure suits us gentlemen of vertical form quite beautifully; do not be offended, my friend, for what family can boast such a thing? Ever since the first will-o'-the-wisp was created, none of our kin has ever had to sit or lie down.'[92]

The forces that will eventually assist in bringing about an enlightened new order in Goethe's 'The Fairytale' take two directions: the horizontal and the vertical. The gold-gobbling snake – like Greedy Black Murdock, who appears as a snake in Severns's dreams, or the sibilantly murmuring money-counter, Donovan, in *Naboth's Vineyard* – belongs to the 'horizontal line' in the dark caverns of the earth. The progressive advance of the snake, however, becomes a much more ominous force in the Irish landscape of the late nineteenth century. Perhaps Ireland provides a suitable terrain to warn of the dangers of the horizontal line. In any case in the *Kunstmärchen* as well as the later Irish material, the snake perishes once union between the East and the West is achieved. The necessary progress of a gold-gobbling force, a movement which pushes forward in space and time, is countered by the vertical line, which in Goethe's tale is a timeless trickster who makes gold to feed the greedy snake her delightful meals.

The Irish writers' treatment of the greedy snake of modern progress questions its ability to realize a wondrous new order. In Ireland the reappraisal of the ideals of Enlightenment thought and early Romanticism provides ironic commentary on Irish events. In Stoker's work, the legendary snake coiling its length in the caverns of Knocknanaher perishes once and for all when his reincarnation, Black Murdock, is brought down by overweening ambition. In Somerville and Ross's novel, Donovan is laid low when he attempts to move from the horizontal line to the vertical, when he believes he can rise as well as progress. In short, the horizontal movement in the late nineteenth-century Irish novels – the modern Irish snake – believes it can adopt a vertical position, unlike Goethe's snake, who soon learns her place:

> The serpent felt most uneasy in the company of these relations, for no matter how high she tried to raise her head, she was still forced to lower it to the ground again in order to move, and whereas before she had felt so wonderfully at ease in the dark grove, here her glow seemed to diminish with every moment she spent in the presence of these cousins, so much so that she feared it would eventually extinguish altogether.[93]

Despite their different treatments of the violent Irish landscape of the early 1880s, Bram Stoker and Somerville and Ross question the notion of unlimited progress. Ambiguity results in Stoker's text when a benevolent English improver transforms the bleak wastes of Connemara (Martin territory) into 'a fairyland' of 'exquisite gardens' and elaborate waterworks.[94] In Somerville and Ross's revision of the theme, no such fantasy is realized. Instead Rick O'Grady, who never raises his head above the horizontal position, wins the day.

WILLIAM G. WILLS AND THE LONDON THEATRE

The various strands animating Somerville and Ross's second novel – pantomime material, periodical literature, and popular romance – might be given context by considering an earlier period of Martin Ross's life. Before the two women met, Martin Ross, or Violet Martin as she was then called, spent time with another second cousin on her mother's side, William Gorman Wills, the playwright. According to Martin Ross, Willie Wills had been a familiar presence at Ross during her childhood.[95] In 1885, when Violet Martin was 23 and Willie Wills 57, the young woman spent an extended visit to London in the playwright's company. That friendship, and what appears to have been a working relationship, continued up until 1890.

Violet Martin's friendship with Wills developed at the peak of the playwright's career. His first dramatic success, *Charles I*, had come about thirteen years earlier through collaboration with the actor-manager of the Lyceum theatre, Henry Irving. Based on an engraving, 'The Happy Days of Charles I' by F. Goodall, Wills's poetic interpretation was given melodramatic plotting through the encouragement of both Irving and the American showman Hezekiah Bateman.[96] Wills, known as a true Bohemian, wrote poetry, painted, and sported a dramatic cape, like Mangan and Maturin before him,[97] which Martin Ross described as *the* coat – 'an immense coachman's collar and cape'.[98] Not given to historical accuracy, as criticism of *Charles I* reveals, he nonetheless flattered Irving and pleased the Lyceum theatre-goers by adapting established texts for the stage. His *Olivia*, first performed by Ellen Terry in 1878, dramatized *The Vicar of Wakefield*. Oscar Wilde and W.B. Yeats both admired his work.[99] Ellen Terry described the playwright as 'Irish all over—the strangest mixture of the aristocrat and the sloven. He could eat a large raw onion every night like any peasant, yet his ideas were magnificent and instinct with refinement'.[100] Wills usually collaborated with others on his plays. For instance in spring 1892 the Dublin Gaiety put on *Claudian*, which was the work of Wills and Henry Herman, and then *A Royal Divorce*, a collaboration of Wills and Grace Hawthorne.

In 1885 when Violet Martin appears to have worked with Willie Wills, she was living in Bray, Co. Wicklow. According to her diary for this year, from January until July, when she left for London, she attended three plays (two pantomimes) with Robert in Dublin. During her first three months in England she did not see any theatre. Then on 14 September she met Willie Wills and over the next three months went to nine performances (twice to Wills's *Olivia*). Descriptions of her visits to Wills's studio (often alone) and their walks through Kew Gardens are punctuated in her diary by a list of popular plays: *Human Nature* and *The Japs* at the Novelty, *Loose Tiles* at the Vaudeville, *Hoodman Blind* at the Princess, *The Colleen Bawn* at the Adelphi.[101]

Willie Wills's letters to his 'amanuensis', as he repeatedly calls her, from 1885 to 1890, suggest that their friendship developed into some kind of working partnership. Certainly he read his verse to his 'pretty Violet'. One work in particular, a 6,000-line poem called 'Melchior', set in an imaginary town called Ort on the Rhine, and heavily influenced by German Romanticism with its Döppelganger, timelessness, and emphasis upon medieval romance, became especially important to both of them.[102] Wills's admiration for Violet Martin ('I don't think I have ever met any lady half so intellectual as you') led to a certain dependency on the part of 'the decrepit grandfather', the 'affectionate old cap & bells' on his 'dear maternal one', his 'Mother Jewel', his 'amanuensis'. He writes from the Fulham Road in London:

> Printers are out of mss & there is no one but you can find it – the last they had where proof breaks off is just after Melchior has seen the Döppelganger – now if you could send up the end of the second tavern scene – it will be printed at once.[103]

He sends her a cheque from the Garrick Club and speaks of giving her work and talking over some plots for various directors. 'Perhaps you might hereafter have some pride to have been in my boat again', he exults when all is going well.[104]

William Wills grew up in Dublin and Kilkenny. His father, James Wills, author of the eight-volume *Lives of Illustrious Irishmen* (1840–47), wrote for *Blackwood's* and *Dublin University Magazine* and was good friends with his neighbour, Dr Anster, the translator of Goethe's *Faust*, and Samuel Ferguson. Willie Wills graduated from Trinity College Dublin and departed for London to write for the stage. His interests were divided between painting and poetry, and from an early age he had become preoccupied with German Romanticism. He was known as an eccentric character about London, and insisted on devising all his poetry and plays in his bed: 'One consequence of the practice was that he soon found the convenience of having an amanuensis, to whom he dictated as fast as the pen in longhand could conveniently follow his thoughts.'[105] Various dramatic aspirants fulfilled this role, and Martin Ross evidently took on the job at a crucial period in 1885.[106] At this time Wills would have been finalizing work which had preoccupied him since the beginning of the decade, and up until Martin's departure at the end of November, he must have been working on this venture, which would open a few weeks later on 19 December 1885. This 'pantomime for adults', as some critics pejoratively described it, proved to be the grand success of Wills's career. It enjoyed an enormous popularity and it followed immediately after Violet Martin, his 'amanuensis', had departed for Dublin. The play, initially to have been called *Mephisto*,[107] was an expensive, electrifying reworking of Goethe's *Faust*.(Plate 1)

Bram Stoker worked as Acting Manager. An organ provided music. Real electricity gave sparks to the dueling foils, and real steam enveloped Irving's Mephistopheles. His slim and mocking devil, as red and as long as the vertical burning will-o'-the-wisps of Goethe's 'Fairy Tale' and the inspiration of Stoker's *Dracula*, thrilled audiences who flocked to the production. One hundred thousand translations of *Faust* were sold in the first month of the run.[108] The play was described as 'mediaevalism incarnate',[109] a re-enactment of diabolism that had been worked from a German version of Goethe's *Faust*.[110]

Especially significant in the reworked material was the depiction of evil. In Willie Wills's version, Mephistopheles describes himself with chilling ambiguity as 'an exemplary Christian' and hardly needs to tempt Faust to his doom.[111] According to a contemporary reviewer, watching this play shows 'how little temptation besides devilish opportunity is needed to draw men into sin'. One of the central scenes is the witches' Walpurgis night revel when 'forms weird but squalid begin to congregate and jibber' and 'their language . . . is daringly idiomatic and common'. The hellish Brocken scene 'is created by . . . strange wild creatures, who yet bear traces and give proofs that when not revelling they frequent the haunts of men'. The reviewer concludes that it is an 'over true tale' because its depiction of evil coincides with the ordinariness of everyday modern life.[112]

To what extent Martin Ross actually contributed to Willie Wills's work, whether she merely listened to his verse and sorted his material or whether she advised and suggested change, remains unknown. However given Wills's delight in his own work as evinced in his correspondence, the discussion of his next production during their various conversations over this three-month period probably occurred. As a result, the reworking of German romance material preoccupied the playwright and his amanuensis, and establishes a link in the Wills/Martin friendship between the Faustian material and Somerville and Ross's use of that tradition over the next thirty years.

In October 1885, while Martin Ross worked as Wills's amanuensis and Bram Stoker became involved in the forthcoming production of *Faust*, *Punch* published John Tenniel's provocative illustration on Irish agrarian outrage, 'The Open Door!'. In the illustration an Irish peasant hides his face with a paper mask with the word 'boycotting' written across its front. The boycotting mask (like that used by Donovan in *Naboth's Vineyard*) is clearly meant as a cover for the violent intents of the intruder, well indicated by his rifle and the pistol and knife thrust into a belt proclaiming his title, 'Captn. Moonlight'. At his feet and just inside the open door lies a plank of wood, what should be the bar holding shut the gaping aperture. 'Crimes Act' is written across the plank and the accompanying verse to Tenniel's illustration argues the necessity for legal restraint in Ireland:

> True, stern restraint on Freedom jars;
> We have no fondness, even at need,
> For those stone walls and iron bars
> Which form no part of freemen's creed.
> But that's a creed that's shaped for men,
> Not human-visaged beasts of prey;

FIGURE 1.3. John Tenniel, *The Open Door!*, *Punch*, 89 (10 October 1885)

For these the shackle and the den,
Not mastery in the public way.[113]

For Irish writers in London in 1885 – writers like Bram Stoker and
Martin Ross – a potent mix of Irish land politics and British policy,
Irish appropriation of German Romanticism, and the dynamic effect
of popular theatre created a nexus of discourse which would have
a far-reaching effect.

The early Wills/Martin friendship, as it coincided with Irish cultural politics, provides a context for Somerville and Ross's development
of character and experiment with form throughout their writing
career. In the early days, with *Naboth's Vineyard*, they plotted their
story with both Mephistopheles and popular burlesque in mind. The
writers' initial exploration of grotesque realism demonstrates their
awareness of the importance of perspective and place in the treatment
of the Irish landscape.

Three years later with the publication of *The Real Charlotte*,
Somerville and Ross developed a female Irish character that incorporates the extreme dimensions of a Harlequin/Mephistophelian figure.
When Charlotte Mullen speaks with 'Mephistophelian gaiety'[114] to
her enemy Mrs Lambert, we are given a clue as to the source of her
nature. Like Mephisto, Charlotte tempts her victims. She avails of
'devilish opportunity' to 'open doors'. Curiosity, excitement, and fear
overwhelm Mrs Lambert's weak heart. Charlotte doesn't kill Emily
Lambert; she merely allows her death to occur. Charlotte doesn't
destroy Roderick Lambert; she provides him with ample opportunity
to destroy himself and then refuses to save him. In the words of
Mephistopheles, Charlotte Mullen is an 'exemplary Christian'.

The Faustian material of Willie Wills's revived German Romanticism and *Kunstmärchen* like Goethe's 'The Fairy Tale' or, as dealt with
in Chapter 2, Friedrich de la Motte Fouqué's *Undine*, prevail throughout *The Real Charlotte*. Roderick Lambert initially meets Francie
Fitzpatrick when she is 14, Margaret's age when Faust first meets his
doomed love. In Willie Wills's adaptation of *Faust*, Margaret emerges
into Faust's view 'shrived, pure and white, [to] pass like a sunbeam
from the church' in Nurnberg[115] just as Francie leaves Christ Church
in Bray, her hair 'like a mist of golden threads',[116] to be met by
Lambert. The influence of the Anglican Church as it intersects with
revived stage romance, as shown in the next chapter, has particular
significance in Somerville and Ross's third novel.

By the end of the decade Somerville and Ross had turned their attention to form; with some reluctance they more or less discarded the novel in favour of comic and unrealistic short fiction. Echoes of *Faust* linger. In their darkly satirical study of Catholic Ireland, 'Holy Island' (1899), Dr Hickey resembles Mephistopheles. In 'Oweneen the Sprat' (1907) drunken Christmas celebrations in Skebawn become a scene from the Brocken of *Faust*.[117] More importantly, however, they gave full rein to the darkly comic vision of adult pantomime with this developing and fluid genre, and both *Some Experiences of an Irish RM* (1899) and *Further Experiences of an Irish RM* (1908) find congruence with the serious jesting of Mephisto, the acrobatics of harlequin and company, the Irish material, and the short story form.

CHAPTER 2

Religion: The Real Charlotte and the Colonial Dream

Christian! dost thou see them
On the holy ground
How the hosts of darkness
Compass thee around?
Christian! up and smite them,
Counting gain but loss;
Smite them by the merit
Of Christ's holy Cross.

JOHN MASON NEALE

It must be wonderful to have a soul, but at the same time it must
be a terrible thing to bear. I ask, in the Lord's name, would it not
be better never to have had one at all? . . . The soul must bear a
terrible burden . . . most terrible! For even as it approaches, it
overshadows me with such fear and sadness. Oh, I was so free, so
happy before!

FRIEDRICH DE LA MOTTE FOUQUÉ, 'UNDINE'

The two most prominent features of Somerville and Ross's land-scapes are the Church and the theatre. Even a cursory scanning of their letters or diaries reveals the constant presence of the rites and celebrations of Anglicanism or the inevitable participation in some form of theatre. The 'Irish Church', in particular, carves out the background of their lives and education, and although their politics or their sexuality may be open to question, their religion remains firm.[1] Their landmark novel, *The Real Charlotte*, written sporadically over a three-year period from 1890 to 1893 and published in 1894, sets itself within this world. It initially appears to investigate the social rather than the spiritual preoccupations of Anglicanism: a Protestant cast of characters comes together to pursue the largely secularized activities of the Church. Despite the dominance of the Church within the novel, activity remains at a material rather than a spiritual level. Nonetheless, through satire, largely drawn from burlesque, the novel explores the ramifications of the crisis of religious thought in late nineteenth-century Ireland, and the text might be viewed as an imaginative construct of the Irish Protestant world view. Not only does the content deal with a secularized Protestant landscape, the form also issues from an Anglican ethos.

The main action of *The Real Charlotte* takes place during a hot summer in the West of Ireland of the early 1890s. Charlotte Mullen invites her second cousin, Francie Fitzpatrick, to Tally Ho Lodge to fulfil the last request of her dying aunt.[2] Brief scenes of dubious respectability in Dublin, Francie's home, give way to lively social scenes in the country town of Lismoyle and the somewhat more secure middle-class homes of the Lamberts and the Beatties, which are dominated by Sir Benjamin Dysart's estate of Bruff and enlivened by red-coated English officers stationed nearby. The young woman's vivid charm and 'modern' daring, coupled with Charlotte's manipulation, gain Francie access not only to the Big House, but also to Christopher Dysart's favour. Sunday school, the choir and the bazaar give opportunities for the mingling of different classes. The Church brings together different Protestant ranks and provides the central platform on which the events of the novel are enacted.

Fin-de-siècle discourse – revived romance, New Woman thought, social Darwinism, and colonial expansion – is interwoven throughout the novel's treatment of the Irish Protestant ethos. So while *The Real Charlotte* reflects an exclusively Irish Protestant reality, as numerous critics point out, it does so in a complex manner. The novel traces the effects of a sublimated evangelical impulse in the novel's hero, Christopher Dysart, as it intersects with the influence of the art and poetry of the Pre-Raphaelites or the impact of the discussion on gender roles in New Woman writing. Nevertheless, the critical condition of the Anglican Church in late nineteenth-century Ireland bears heavily upon the novel's treatment of Irish reality. Especially interesting is the connection of the Protestant subject matter to the form of the work in a consideration of the manner in which the authors handle the text's essential argument: saving souls in a secularized Ireland. At the same time a critically neglected dimension of the novel influences this discussion and might also be drawn from the writers' back-grounds. The novel immerses itself as much in popular theatrics as it does in the Protestant world. The two traditions are inextricably con-nected, and the very conception of the text – a work of grotesque realism which turns everything upside down or, more appropriately given the influence of the pantomime, topsy-turvy – draws upon pop-ular burlesque. The work both reflects and parodies romantic come-dy; it draws attention to the tension generated between romantic con-cepts (which are linked to the evangelical impulses in Christopher Dysart) and realistic concerns (which appear most clearly in the char-acter of Charlotte Mullen) in the Irish landscape of the period.

Though land issues play a part in *The Real Charlotte*, especially the nineteenth-century argument of land improvement versus land rights, the main subject of Somerville and Ross's satire is of a spiritual nature – as befits a Protestant text. The saving or making of a soul, Francie Fitzpatrick's soul, in an increasingly secular and highly contested landscape propels the action of the plot. A romantic notion, a 'form-less and unquestioned dream',[3] energizes the missionary zeal of the Irish Protestant *Weltanschauung* of the novel. Christopher Dysart's determination to reform Francie Fitzpatrick's soul springs in part from his childhood reading of the Sunday-school books of Mrs Mary Sherwood, but continues to be inspired by Pre-Raphaelite imagery and the romantic comedies in Dublin's Gaiety Theatre or the Theatre Royal. Of colonial stock, the Dysart heir has been shaped by a secu-larized evangelical fantasy. His position as leader of the imperial quest, however, has been subverted in this topsy-turvy Irish world. Instead of hunter, he becomes the hunted, the prey of Charlotte Mullen, who occupies for the first half of the novel the aptly named Tally Ho Lodge.

On another level, Christopher's blazing white trousers and self-con-scious romanticism symbolize the struggle against the hosts of darkness led by a pragmatic troglodyte in black alpaca, Charlotte Mullen. This argument not only appears within a colonial/evangelical framework as demonstrated by Christopher Dysart's attempts to save Francie's soul, but also occurs as a manifestation of the revived romance as popular-ized by Robert Louis Stevenson in works like *The Master of Ballantrae*. In Somerville and Ross's text the dominant romance material derives from traces of the *Kunstmärchen*, 'Undine', and its version of soul-making deepens this study of human improvement in Ireland. At the same time the text's burlesque of these various traditions transforms the Church of Ireland into a kind of playhouse. This comic stage set

comes charged in the work with a tragic Manichaean vision, a
Protestant world view which determines the apocalyptic fears and
Faustian warnings of the novel's conclusion.

PROTESTANT PERSPECTIVES

In February 1890, Edith Somerville and Martin Ross read Stevenson's
recently published Scottish tale of the two Durisdeer brothers: James,
the Master of Ballantrae and supporter of Charles Stuart during the
Jacobite rebellion of 1745, and Henry, who stays at home to run the
estate. Their interest in the novel may have been provoked by a
Scottish review in *The Old Saloon*, published the previous November,
that compared Stevenson's novel with Somerville and Ross's first
work, *An Irish Cousin*. Though admiring the Irish writers' pleasant
treatment of the Irish landscape, the reviewer implied that the novel
did not demonstrate the same skilful handling of national affairs evident in the Scotsman's work. In Somerville and Ross's novel, 'there is
not a word of politics from beginning to end, and the events of the
story might be going on in Somersetshire or the Isle of Wight . . .
instead of in the most agitated part of an agitated country'.[4] The Irish
writers immediately read Stevenson's novel. Martin Ross admitted it
was 'first rate in parts', and Edith sent off Stevenson's 'Studies of Men
and Books' to her brother Cameron the following April. The same
month they finished writing their picturesquely political *Naboth's
Vineyard* and, by May, had written two chapters of a new book they
called 'The Welsh Aunt', their working title of *The Real Charlotte*.[5]
Although *Naboth's Vineyard* and *The Real Charlotte* are realistic novels, they both concentrate on characters similar to Sir Henry of
Stevenson's romance, 'a skinflint and a sneckdraw [a sly person], sitting, with his nose in an account book, to persecute poor tenants'.[6]
The women writers look to the middle ranks, however, to explore this
type: the gombeen man or woman and the land agent. Moreover, they
contemporize their accounts, setting both novels during the 1880s
and 1890s, and satirizing the socio-political culture of the time. The
Catholic colonial nightmare of the Irish land wars in West Cork of
Naboth's Vineyard becomes the colonial dream of a Protestant population in the West of Ireland in *The Real Charlotte*.

In *The Master of Ballantrae* Stevenson explores duality and shows
among other things how position affects perspective. A central incident of the text demonstrates the kind of self-consciousness which

becomes central to Somerville and Ross's comic sense in *The Real Charlotte*. Stevenson's romantic adventure story highlights a modernist awareness which pervades the Irish writers' grotesque realism and explains a primary impulse of romantic irony.

Stevenson demonstrates how the narrator's view of evil alters depending on where he stands in relation to his objects of study: the two brothers, James, who supports the Catholic Young Pretender, and Henry, who follows the foreign Protestant monarch. In the first half of the novel, the narrator Mr MacKellar, Sir Henry's steward, can only see his skinflint employer as good and the older brother as some 'insidious devil'. Yet in the course of the narrative it becomes apparent that one picture may not be the entire truth. MacKellar witnesses the emergence of an entirely different reality in the course of the story.

Stevenson uses the movement between two locations, Scotland and America, to activate Mr MacKellar's change of view. In Scotland, the narrator sees Henry as the hard-working and much maligned hero of the piece. In America's wilderness, however, James appears to MacKellar as truly heroic and brave. Both realities exist. The altered landscape changes the picture so that MacKellar perceives a layered reality, different truths instead of one.

En route to America, on board the *Nonesuch* and during a tremendous storm, the Master of Ballantrae (wild and courageous James) tells MacKellar an ambivalent tale of evil. The pair sit on 'a high, raised poop' with the Master 'betwixt [MacKellar] and the side' and in this position in the middle of the storm (and the middle of the novel) with the boat rearing up and down across the monstrous waves, MacKellar comments on the Master's alternating position:

> Now his head would be in the zenith and his shadow fall quite beyond the *Nonesuch* on the further side; and now he would swing down till he was underneath my feet, and the line of the sea leaped high above him like the ceiling of a room.[7]

This topsy-turvy position, where extremes of movement allow for a rapidly successive occupation of polarized locations, occurs halfway to America, when the characters are situated in between specific locations, in a kind of no man's land. In a late nineteenth-century novel preoccupied with duality and sectarian conflict, such extreme shifting may demonstrate, on one hand, modern ambiguity, and, on the other, the situation of the split identity, of a person negotiating the polarized positions of a hybrid culture, what Homi Bhabha calls an 'interstitial perspective', one which allows a person to see from the outside as well as the inside, 'identities that "split" – are estranged unto themselves'. Such a perspective originates from the 'interstitial passage between fixed identifications', says Bhabha, and 'opens up the possibility of a cultural hybridity'.[8] In Stevenson's novel divided loyalties and the positions they demand (as much as the storm-tossed sea) appear to cause MacKellar's extraordinary split perspective.

Topsy-turvydom also allows one to see oneself; it displays the self. Stevenson's boat on a stormy sea creates a swift reversal of perspective which allows MacKellar to see through the Master's eyes. The quick-change demonstrates the arbitrary nature of one particular viewpoint. This display of perspective recalls the extremely popular nineteenth-century pantomime which figures so largely in the Irish writers' work. In the manner of a Gilbert and Sullivan burlesque, then, turning things inside out and upside down draws attention to the process of performance itself. This self-consciousness, and its portrayal in a sectarian landscape in Stevenson's tale, introduces an intersection of popular discourse which helps to clarify the Protestant perspective in Somerville and Ross's text.

Stevenson's romantic treatment of the Jacobite rebellion may have been of particular interest to Martin Ross, whose own family marked a hybrid course in its conversion from Roman Catholicism and Jacobism to Low Church Protestantism in the late eighteenth century.[9] The Martin household remained somewhat mixed in its affiliations, but the young Violet, like Edith Somerville, participated fully in a Victorian Anglican upbringing. For much of their early lives, they attended church twice on a Sunday. Violet Martin won prizes at Sunday school in Dublin,[10] and her later letters to Edith Somerville frequently include comic descriptions of prayers or church services.[11] Edith Somerville played the organ in St Barrahane's Church, Castletownshend, for seventy years, and occupied dull stretches of the sermon by drawing sketches and caricatures of the rector and his congregation.[12]

The High Church Somervilles maintained a 'strong service tradition',[13] and nowhere is this fact clearer than in St Barrahane's, where the admirals, brigadiers, and soldiers of the realm, who frequently died in service to Great Britain, have their names inlaid in brass on the lectern, inscribed in stone on the tombs, and covering the plaques mounted on marble walls. St Barrahane's appears to be as much a memorial as a church; the names have greater presence than the religious artefacts decorating the altar and nave. In Castletownshend the

Anglo-Irish families, the Somervilles, Coghills and Townshends, do not merely head the congregation, they *are* the Church.[14] In St Barrahane's the clergy come and go, but the gentry remain. There is a sense in such a place that the names of the pre-eminent families of the area are being served and commemorated by transient parsons in the same way that local poets eulogized their landowners. The Protestant parsons, however, appear to have been more loyal. For instance when Edith Somerville's grandfather returned home from the Crimean war in 1856, Jeremiah O'Donovan Rossa composed for him an acrostic poem inscribing the Major's name in a 'flowing Italianate hand' on blue paper. The poet's Fenian activities at this time would seem to contradict his apparent loyalty:

M artial child of Erin and brilliant son of Mars
A ll hail and welcome thee to home, from the Crimean Wars.
J oined hands and hearts are creed and class this meed of praise to shower
O n one of Ireland's gallant sons, who braved the Russian Power
R egarding nought but honour bright, no coward thought appalled him
T o make him shrink before the foe when Martial duty called him.
H ow oft you read the fatal lists, with joy our hearts oft bounded
O n finding that *one name* was not among the killed or wounded.
M uch pleasure beamed from every face (and happy felt the Muse)
A s a respected Father's life depended on the news,
S o fondly did he love that child, a true and only son,
S o fatal would the tidings be to *read that he was gone.*
O h could you picture his despair, thank God 'tis different far,
M uch joy and peace await him now, as ended is the War.
E xpected shortly is that son, a worthy one of Erin,
R eturning to his peaceful home from battling with the Alien.
V alour's representative Skibbereen will proudly greet him
I nclined with feelings of respect she joyfully will meet him,
L oudly to home we'll welcome him, old friends, old scenes – say rather
L ike one arisen from the dead around him we will gather
E njoyed to see that he again has met his honoured Father.[15]

O'Donovan Rossa's paean depicts a loyal and respectful Skibbereen. Perhaps the poem's lavish praise seeks to conceal a growing anger caused by the divisions of 'creed and class' that simmered beneath surface platitudes. After all, this same year O'Donovan Rossa founded the revolutionary Phoenix National and Literary Society in Skibbereen, and two years later, the year of Edith Somerville's birth, he established an Irish Republican Brotherhood centre.[16] Pride, 'feelings of respect' and loud welcome for those of the Big House would become quite different emotions in the ensuing years, culminating in the shocking murder of the grandson of the 'Martial child of Erin' at the hands of the IRA in 1936. Things had been reversed and Vice-Admiral Boyle Somerville suffered a more brutal welcome at the door of Drishane House, his attackers leaving bullets rather than blessings to mark their regard.[17]

In the 1870s and 80s, however, agrarian agitation or political losses did not affect the gentry as strongly, says Edith Somerville, as the government's attack on their religion. In her autobiographical sketches she claims that the 1869 Act, which disestablished the Church of Ireland, weighed more heavily on the Castletownshend ascendancy than any later political grievances. It was a death blow:

> To my grandfather, and to my father and mother, and my uncles and aunts, strong Churchmen and women all, Mr Gladstone's Irish Church Act was an almost incredible sacrilege, a felon stab that hit them harder, even than the measures that, thenceforward following, ended by stripping them not only of their property, but also of the political and civic influence that their consciences could assure them they had exercised only for good.[18]

With the disestablishment of the Church of Ireland, a significant source of ascendancy employment within Ireland was eroded. Younger sons who had often found positions within their Church now travelled abroad.[19] More insidiously for Anglicans in the south of the island was the removal of an 'obstacle to the spread of Catholicism'; henceforward the undermining of the Protestant community would inevitably occur.[20]

Ascendancy power within the Anglican Church discovered its greatest challenge in the Roman Catholic priest, and Somerville and Ross's suspicion of the peasantry's spiritual leaders must be considered in this context. Martin Ross's political bias when finishing *The Real Charlotte* in 1893 becomes apparent in her explanation to the English electorate of the dangerous power of the Irish Catholic priest. She argues with polemical point that 'the priests can do as they like with the Roman Catholic lower classes . . . they direct them how to vote at every election.' The power of the priests for the peasantry, says Ross, is a supernatural one; a 'Roman Catholic has said in my hearing that his priest would make horns grow out of his head if he disobeyed him, & yet another man wondered why a certain priest did not turn Mr Balfour into a goat.'[21]   Martin Ross demonstrates the awesome authority of the peasantry's religious leaders. Their power, she suggests, appears to the Roman Catholic masses to be the power of God. The women writers' suspicion of priests would erupt at different points in their career. In the writers' *Collected Irish Anecdotes* further instance is provided of the Irish peasantry's dangerous superstition. 'What would you do if you hadn't the comforts of the RC church', asks a local man, 'supposin that afther your death ye met the Dog with the seven heads?' In 1899, then, Edith Somerville asks a fellow Irish artist, 'I wonder if the English will ever believe that Irish self-government simply means strengthening the power of the Priests'.[22]

In *The Real Charlotte* the Roman Catholic priest lurks in the background as a preying figure, ready to snap up lost souls. The Anglican clergyman, on the other hand, fulfils a social rather than a religious role. Instead of acting as a spiritual director of the community, he appears as a cypher to those in command. At Lady Dysart's garden party, at the opening of the novel, a 'representative trio' of the male Protestant population includes a loud-voiced country gentleman, a 'dejected-looking clergyman', and a self-satisfied land agent. The clergyman ranks lowest of the group, his contribution to a conversation on politics a mere 'echo in the cathedral aisle'.[23]

Terence Brown notes that Irish writing of the modern period tends to present Irish Anglicanism as 'a series of clichés and programmatic responses'. The Church of Ireland typically represents one of three things, either the privileged Ascendancy, or the good priest, or an 'irresistible decay'.[24] The crumbling face of the Anglican Church alongside the decrepit ascendancy house features most prominently as a symbol of Irish Protestant maginalization. Martin Ross's description in 1912 of a decaying Protestant church and a crumbling ascendancy household (Tyrone House) that Edith Somerville claimed to be the source of her later novel, *The Big House of Inver*, has been considered a more general example of Protestant identity.[25] Yet Martin Ross was particularly interested in the contrast of a sparsely attended Anglican service in the midst of Irish Catholic mobilization. In the 1890s especially, she was much more fascinated by paradox and incongruity than the theme of loss. Witness an earlier letter she writes to Edith in 1896 when she travels to Oughterard, County Galway to attend an Anglican service of six people but is held up by a barely controlled election meeting in the town. The contrast of the priest-led masses and the subdued Protestant service provides a striking incongruity which Martin Ross appreciated.[26]

The Real Charlotte, published only two years earlier, initially appears to deny any notion of decay, or special privilege, or even good clergymen in its portrayal of Irish Anglicanism. The novel deliberately includes Protestants of all sorts and of all classes. It does not reflect Irish Protestant reality in the 1890s.[27] Indeed if *Naboth's Vineyard* has been criticized for its disparagement of Catholic Ireland, [28] *The Real Charlotte* might be criticized for its marginalization of the same and the comic handling of the few Catholic characters who appear. Yet such treatment emphasizes Irish Protestant reality: the whole point of a primarily Protestant list of characters, and the victimization and violence within their ranks, lies in its comment on the effects of colonialism in this section of the Irish population.[29] By establishing a mainly Protestant community in *The Real Charlotte*, the authors show how its different levels (from servant to gentry) suffer and enact violent measures, as though violence were an inherited condition. Somerville and Ross may have removed the Catholic element from the Irish equation to demonstrate the dynamics of class relations in Ireland, to show that class consciousness, as much as religious bias, may give rise to discontent. Most importantly, by concentrating on a Protestant population Somerville and Ross continue an attack introduced in *Naboth's Vineyard* on the basic premise supporting political nationalist thought, that a dominant, monolithic Protestant ascendancy suppresses the Irish Catholic tenantry. The novel demonstrates the disunity and differences among the Protestant population in southern Ireland.

Further reason for Somerville and Ross's concentration on an Irish Protestant cast of characters becomes apparent as the plot proceeds. The novel traces, as already indicated, the process whereby Christopher Dysart comes to believe that he can save Francie's soul. His particular brand of Protestantism opposes the distanced kindliness of his sister, Pamela, a High Church advocate. Francie Fitzpatrick, then, is accustomed to the scripture reading and rote learning of the Dublin Sunday schools and demonstrates a competent knowledge of the visiting evangelicals to her Low Church congregations. The novel shows the characters' religious backgrounds influencing their worldly roles. One could argue then that the novel addresses the 'surrogate religiosity' of Victorian literature, 'a transference of evangelical preoccupation, rendered theologically unsustainable by scepticism, to social and aesthetic dimensions'.[30] The process recalls the transformation of religious metaphor in earlier Victorian painting, what John Turpin points out in Daniel Maclise's historical studies such as 'Strongbow' or 'Wellington'. According to

Turpin, 'religious transposition' in Maclise's work 'is a feature of an age when orthodox religious subject matter almost totally disappeared'.[31] Yet contrarily, as the study of religious revivalism in nineteenth-century Ireland has shown, decline also reveals the struggle of religion to resurface and revive amidst scepticism and change. For Protestant women in particular who often found a significant outlet in the Church – whether it might be something like Lady Dysart's charity work or Mrs Gascoigne's organ recitals in The Real Charlotte – revivalism in the face of decline may be more marked.[32] So although Somerville and Ross's late nineteenth-century novel displays the process whereby religious postures become secular poses, one could also claim that religious revival in the face of decline energizes the plot and character development. In any case, the lasting significance of The Real Charlotte is its portrayal of an Irish Anglican ethos as it is secularized and faces modernization in the British colonial world.

The Real Charlotte is most frequently described as a portrayal of 'the twilight of the Big House'.[33] The distance of the landed gentry, the Dysarts, from their tenants and their consequent susceptibility to the shrewd dealings of their underlings has indicated the writers' intent to provide reasons for the demise of the Irish Gentleman. Somerville and Ross were aware of the loss and their third novel is typically seen to be on the cusp between some period when the landlord system actually worked in Ireland and its fall with gradual decolonization.[34]

The attention devoted to the demise of the Anglo-Irish ascendancy in The Real Charlotte, however, leads readers to neglect the main matter of the text: Protestantism. The novel deals with the face of Irish Protestantism within a range of classes on the social ladder. While the alienation of its top rung manifests the disenfranchisement of the tradition within the Irish state, the main focus rests upon the religious crisis of an entire society.

A source of Anglican alienation in the novel lies within a troubled awareness of the Church's élitism. The underlying fear that the Irish Church has severed its links with the past and has been cast adrift by its own reformative tradition destabilizes its position on the Irish landscape. Unlike Irish Catholicism, which the peasantry embraces, Irish Protestantism appears to some of the characters to have broken away from a continuous tradition. So concludes Eliza Hackett, Mrs Lambert's Protestant servant, when she explains her reasons for attending Sunday Mass. Charlotte Mullen, an anti-Catholic, is furious when she hears that the apparently solid Protestantism of the cook has

succumbed to the blandishments of Father Heffernan. The Church of
Ireland, complains Eliza when Mrs.Lambert questions her, has not the
Apostolic succession which connects the Catholic priest to his spiritual forbears.[35] The defecting cook discovers in the Catholic faith a
belief system which asserts a continuity and wholeness as complete
and rounded as the Catholic host. Mrs Lambert's and Charlotte's horror at the cook's turn indicates two things. First, it demonstrates the
determination of a minority religion to maintain its ranks in the face
of national Catholicism. Second, it suggests a fear that the peasantry's
religion possesses a prior right to the spiritual pool, a greater con-
nectedness to the country's past (and the country's future) which only
exacerbates Protestant dislocation.

Something of that fear is indicated later on in George
Birmingham's observations on the difference between the Protestant
and Catholic positions in Ireland. Birmingham emphasizes the consequent reactionary nature of the Protestant position in the face of a
Catholic majority:

> Perhaps the difference between Catholic and Protestant is really one of
> temper. If so, it is something real and important. In Catholicism there
> seems to be a certain suavity, the result of a feeling of security.
> Protestantism is another name for aggression in religion. The Catholic
> spirit belongs to the man who is comfortably aware of being one of an
> unassailable majority. The Protestant is forced to assert himself and his
> position. His spirit is the vice – or perhaps the virtue – of active minori-
> ties. The Catholic is conscious of being a member of that universal,
> time-transcending Church which is the blessed company of all faithful
> people. He does not want to say so and is quietly tolerant of people
> who do not understand. The Protestant is eager to proclaim an evangel
> of some kind, and therefore must be aggressive.[36]

In the 1890s, as demonstrated in Somerville and Ross's novel, the
evangelical Protestant trope of the master/servant relationship, the
mistress's responsibility for the servant's soul as well as her body, has
been overturned. The evangelical spirit of Protestantism has been
thwarted.

Intermarriage between Catholic and Protestant, which indicates a
union across class divides as well as religious ones, furthers the alienation of the Protestant tradition in *The Real Charlotte*. Even though
Julia Duffy's Protestant gentleman father introduced his Catholic
dairymaid wife and their hybrid daughter to his own Church (a
circumstance that we assume results from the father's superior social

status because a female offspring was generally reared in her mother's religion), the daughter defects. Social rather than spiritual reasons account for Julia Duffy's alienation. No longer able to afford a handsome bonnet for church and despising her mother's chapel, she decides that she 'would have nothing of either chapel or church, and stayed sombrely at home'.[37] Julia Duffy turns to science and becomes a kind of witch doctor, an outsider who knows charms and herbal cures but who remains estranged from both parents' religions. For Julia Duffy, to enter the Catholic Church is to admit to social failure: class and religious affiliations are inextricably linked.

In the landscape of Lismoyle, 'the rival towers of church and chapel' battle for the souls of Ireland. Of course ostensible soul-saving may be dying out; nonetheless, a secularized form continues to be practised. Evangelists and missionaries scour the Irish terrain, and while one religion boasts continuity of tradition, the other asserts class superiority. Souls are lost on the wayside, such as Julia Duffy, who hoards her Protestant acres like a dog its bone, or Charlotte Mullen's tenants in Ferry Row, the dirtiest and most squalid part of Lismoyle, where 'slatternly' washerwomen ply their trade and where Dinny Lydon, the tailor, lurks like a troll in his 'disreputable abode'. The Lydons have little time for authority of any kind, much less priests. 'If I couldn't knock the stone out of the gap for meself, the priest couldn't do it for me', claims Dinny, and his wife's drinking and violence, her greasy face and unctuous manner belong to some darker region of the Irish landscape.[38] Their use of Irish (which Charlotte appears to understand), their ready lies and their blatant poverty conceal subterranean and hidden desires which have escaped the broad beam of religious enlightenment in Ireland.

The Real Charlotte reveals the different strains of Irish Protestantism and highlights the social dimension of its church. Perceived as the religion of the land-owning ascendancy, Protestantism becomes a means of access to that world. The novel also demonstrates, primarily through Charlotte, anti-Catholic tendencies within that tradition. The fear of defection, caused by intermarriage or isolation, and sharpened, perhaps, by the suspicion of what Birmingham would describe later as the 'universal, time-transcending' assumptions of Irish Catholicism, gives rise to a fundamental antagonism. Perceived to be the religion of an inferior class, Catholicism becomes the path to social disgrace. It also contains traces of near-demonic attributes. When Norry-the-Boat crosses herself, for instance, the casual Catholic gesture acquires significance because Norry happens to be holding a paper taper to light the fire in her kitchen hearth. The gaunt and grizzled housekeeper makes the sign of the cross with her fiery torch and inflammatory images of past Protestant martyrs spring to mind.

SAINT CHRISTOPHER DYSART, SOUL SAVER

The project of saving souls occurs within church and chapel in the Ireland of *The Real Charlotte*, but nowhere does this project become more susceptible to distortion than when it is driven by the reformative zeal deriving from evangelicalism. In Christopher Dysart, the colonial dream comes interlaced with a 'missionary resolve to let the light of culture illuminate [Francie Fitzpatrick's] darkness',[39] so that he not only believes that the Dublin jackeen's soul needs saving but that he is the one to do it. Eventually he sees himself as a kind of imperial saviour. He aspires to be Christ-like, his ascension to glory unchecked by the intercession of man or priest. He becomes besotted by a Protestant colonial dream.

Lady Dysart of Bruff, an English Anglican and cousin of Mrs Gascogne, wife of the Archdeacon, has raised a son and daughter who manifest the two strands of Irish Anglicanism. Pamela Dysart's pleasure in the rites of the Church, her 'High Church tendencies', indicates a 'Romanizing' bent, while Christopher's fastidiousness and missionary impulses reveal an evangelical frame of mind.[40] His leanings may well have been fashioned by a childhood steeped in the Sunday-school reading of Mrs Mary Sherwood and her stories of evangelical family life. Although Christopher's family falls short of the Sunday-school ideal, their *modus vivendi* appears to have been inspired by Sherwood's moral tales. Lady Dysart and Pamela work hard at gardening in Bruff, for instance, but Lady Dysart cannot tell chickweed from asters, and plants the former where the latter belong, 'an imbecility', the narrator tells us, 'that Mrs. Sherwood would never have permitted in a parent'.[41]

Mary Sherwood's didactic tales on appropriate behaviour included biblical quotations and religious maxims summarizing the action of the plots. Her best-selling *History of Little Henry and his Bearer* (1814) tells of 'the conversion of a little boy of five or six and of his attempts . . . to convert his Indian servant'.[42] Other early books like *The Ayah and Lady* and *The Indian Pilgrim* continue to stress the importance of the Christian mission and the dangers of heathen contact. Mrs Sherwood's *History of the Fairchild Family* (1818) represented the ideal evangelical family which 'helped to create the Victorian belief in the family'.[43] Mr and Mrs Fairchild taught their children to face death, resist evil, and recognize the consequence of sin.[44]

Upon closer consideration, Pamela and Lady Dysart's industry in the garden – 'a scene worthy in its domestic simplicity of the Fairchild Family'[45] – becomes a parody. Not only is Lady Dysart's labour utterly useless (she plants weeds instead of flowers), but also her husband, the doting Sir Benjamin, fails entirely as a Protestant patriarch. Nonetheless the allusion to Mrs Sherwood's Fairchilds recalls the religious missionary zeal that fuels the Dysart engine, however poorly they might operate the train. Evangelical purpose will eventually inspire Christopher to attempt to educate Francie and to save her soul; he has inherited (or learned in the nursery) Mrs Sherwood's notions of patronage and imperial condescension. He will give Francie inspirational texts like Rossetti's mock-medieval poetry and John Henry Shorthouse's Anglican novel, *John Inglesant*.[46] Unfortunately, like his well-meaning mother in her garden, Christopher's seed is the wrong sort for Irish soil. The Dysart heir recalls the sower who 'went out ... to sow' of the New Testament, but his secularized sowing is wasted on the Dublin jackeen.[47]

Christopher Dysart's concern for 'Miss Fitzpatrick's problematic soul' addresses her cultural rather than her spiritual development.[48] His evangelical models, like those provided by Mrs Sherwood, inspire his actions in a worldly context. Christopher attempts to reform Francie's taste. The English servants at Bruff who discuss Francie's abysmal table etiquette indicate, literally, the need to reform her manners. Francie's bad manners and vulgar tastes, her preference for a poached egg rather than the Bruff Scotch woodcock, or, to put it in romantic terms, Hawkins's kisses rather than Christopher's poetry, and the latter's consequent determination to demonstrate the pleasure of Scotch woodcock, directly recall the comedy of manners.[49] In Ireland, as Francie concludes with some sarcasm in her final meeting with Christopher, 'You couldn't expect any manners from a Dublin Jackeen'.[50] The reformation of manners in eighteenth-century Irish drama becomes a literal exploration of that theme in Somerville and Ross's late nineteenth-century fiction.

Perhaps even more specifically, Francie's simple tastes and disregard for what the English visitor Miss Hope-Drummond describes as the *convenances* of civilized life recall another blow-in to Irish life one hundred years earlier. In 1793/94 Edward Fitzgerald wrote to his mother of the natural and simple delights of Frescati in Blackrock, Co. Dublin, where he and his new wife, 'Lady *Egalité*' – Pamela Simms, presumed to be the secret daughter of the Duc d'Orléans, enjoyed the bucolic activities in the *ferme ornée* in preference to the opulent rooms of Castletown House. 'Gay and giddy' Pamela did not ascribe to Dublin fashion and suffered public censure as a result.[51] Flighty Francie Fitzpatrick, who wears the *bonnet rouge* and plays the Boulanger March, also exposes the stilted manners of an outdated Anglo-Irish society.

However Christopher's interest lies not in Francie's manners but in her mind. The event triggering his missionary impulse is when Roddy Lambert's boat, the *Daphne*, overturns. Like the see-saw motion of Stevenson's *Nonesuch* in *The Master of Ballantrae* which alters MacKellar's perspective, the upending of the *Daphne* turns the world of *The Real Charlotte* topsy-turvy; the plot is reversed when Christopher saves Francie from the waves of Lough Moyle. Like St Christopher, 'the great giant Christopher', who, according to Tennyson, 'stands upon the brink of the tempestuous wave' and carries pilgrims to safer ground, Christopher Dysart is transformed from dabbling amateur to committed reformer, one who has saved Francie's body and is thus inspired to save her soul. The sudden squall on Lough Moyle transforms the gentle *Daphne* into a rearing beast that 'snatch[es] at the tiller like a horse at its bit'. Young and pretty Francie with her red sailor cap is flung into the waves, 'a white figure with a red cap', that Christopher desperately strives to rescue.[52] For a moment, then, the romantic icons of late eighteenth-century Ireland flicker to life in this storm-tossed scene as the 'dear little pale pretty wife'[53] with her revolutionary connections and dubious background, Lady Fitzgerald, seems to be outlined in the tragic figure of the modern Miss Fitzpatrick. Christopher's 'old-fashioned, eighteenth-century look'[54] and clean-shaven face allow him to play the romantic lead when he saves – this time at least – the charming but doomed victim of the piece.

Christopher's desire to rescue Francie's inner life as much as her outer derives from a romantic dream which seduces him to love an 'Aboriginee' he has refashioned with his inner eye. Like a secular Church Militant with pygmalion tendencies, Christopher sees his beautiful statue as pure and somehow untouched by her environment; she has 'some limpid quality that kept her transparent and fresh like a running stream' and gives him reason to believe that 'she really must have a soul to be saved'.[55] When Francie Fitzpatrick visits Bruff, the colonial view falls victim to its own myopia and we see Christopher falling in love with an idealized version of the Dubliner. Christopher 'clothes [Francie] with his own refinement, as with a garment' and thus masks her real self.[56]

Christopher and Pamela Dysart, with their English contacts and their colonial education and lifestyle, see Ireland and its inhabitants with the imperialist's vision. In other words, their perspective – one of a number in *The Real Charlotte* – is that given to the narrator and the implied reader in *Naboth's Vineyard*: the distanced and detached bird's-eye view. In fact their viewpoint (and we must remember that Christopher is short-sighted) is limited and partial, even dangerously blind, as we discover when Christopher 'sees' Francie Fitzpatrick not for what she is but for what he can make her. Moreover, Christopher's main occupation and only passion is photography, an art which distances him even further from actual life.[57] He is a latter-day Horatio Mortimer, spying upon the wild Irish girl with his artist's eye. His distance forbids full participation in Irish affairs, just as his self-criticism prohibits true artistic development. His English mother, Oxford education and initial placement in the West Indies – in Barbados where 'all the blacks bow down to him' – make him very much a colonial hybrid. His objectivity, this ability to see things as a 'dispassionate onlooker', is marred by a myopia which literally and figuratively distorts his perception. Hybridity has created within him a kind of exaggerated apathy which stifles his ability to act. He also epitomizes modern ambivalence. His lethargy is a 'modern malady of exhausted enthusiasm' issuing from self-consciousness. He possesses a 'super-sensitive mind', primed by Pre-Raphaelite romanticism and reform literature. Yet he fails as an artist because he cannot truly 'see.' His ideal of perfection has thwarted his creative impulse – photography alone can capture life in perfectly executed (and detached) pieces. He is 'intellectually effete' and overly civilized with 'a little more culture than [he can] hold'.[58]

Christopher Dysart cannot see either the full picture or *behind* the picture of Ireland because of his distance from the object of his gaze. Christopher's eye, peering from behind his old-fashioned eyeglass or camera lens, capturing picturesque scenes of 'groups of old women and donkeys' is, ultimately, the sight of 'the observer whose impressions are only eye-deep', a perspective which the narrator at the beginning of the novel warns us against.[59] Thus when Christopher initially looks at Francie Fitzpatrick and thinks to himself, 'how vast was the chasm between her ideal of life and his own', his 'patronizing criticism' is suspect.[60]

When Francie arrives at Bruff House, Pamela Dysart searches out her brother to ask that he entertain their latest visitor. Christopher has hidden himself from family and guests in the attic, and he develops film amongst ancient trunks, broken furniture, and 'three old ball skirts [which] hung like ghosts of Bluebeard's wives upon the door'. Amongst these theatrical-like props, the daughter of the estate discovers a big case and sits 'gingerly down in the darkness on an old imperial, a relic of the period when Sir Benjamin posted to Dublin in his own carriage'.[61] Pamela's imperial seat in *The Real Charlotte* is the imperial of a carriage, a trunk for luggage which was fitted on the roof of a coach or carriage. The imperial of a coach, situated as it is next to the conductor, would afford a wonderful panoramic view of the countryside and this ancient prop reminds readers of the Dysarts' colonial status and the viewpoint it affords.[62]

Christopher's imperial view is reinforced by daydreams which divert his attention from a changing world. He looks backwards rather than forwards and recalls with idle comparisons of Inisochery island to 'the enchanted country through which King Arthur's knights rode', some vague feudal age.[63] When Julia Duffy is threatened by Lambert with eviction from Gurthnamuckla, she flees her dirty nest like the rat that earlier in the novel had been routed from its lair and coolly executed by the ex-hedgeschoolmaster, James Canavan. Half-dead with fever, she staggers across the miles to Bruff to remind the landlord's son of a verbal contract, but Christopher is too busy reading Rossetti's poetry to Francie to give sufficient heed to the old woman's reminder of her traditional hold upon the land. He is too besotted with the ideal glories of a feudal age to give consideration to present realities. Moreover, Christopher's reading emphasizes once more the gulf existing between himself and Francie, whose only interest in 'The Staff and Scrip' from which Christopher reads is the description of the beautiful queen. For Christopher, however, the pilgrim knight's idealized love for his Lady, his devotion, courage, eventual death for her stolen lands, and their reunion in Heaven, is nothing less than a dream. When Christopher stops reading Rossetti's poem, he feels as though he has 'stepped suddenly to the ground out of a dream of flying'.[64] Christopher flies high and sees far within the colonial dream; in so doing, he overlooks both Francie's practical view and the destruction of traditional land rights by modern notions of progress and improvement. He does not see how Julia Duffy's situation echoes with grotesque overtones the plight of Queen Blanchely in the Rossetti poem:

> 'Who rules these lands?' the Pilgrim said.
>   'Stranger, Queen Blanchelys'.
> 'And who has thus harried them?' he said.
>   'It was Duke Luke did this:
>   God's ban be his!' [65]

Those familiar with Rossetti's poetry realize that Somerville and Ross's reference to the revived medieval material offers further ironic reflection on Christopher's character and situation. Duke Luke harries the Queen's estate in 'The Staff and the Scrip', just as Charlotte Mullen's tool, Roddy Lambert, threatens Julia Duffy with eviction and Garry Dysart's ferret bolts a rat. Here is a marvellous opportunity for Christopher to pick up the staff and scrip. The event poses itself between extreme comparisons, and the irony of the land issue is nicely doubled.

Christopher's character demonstrates most clearly the sublimated evangelical Anglican discourse of *The Real Charlotte*. His particular interest in Pre-Raphaelite poetry indicates the aesthetic dimension of his thought. Closer consideration of the impact of the nineteenth-century movement on the form of Somerville and Ross's novel might be achieved by addressing popular Protestant iconography in Pre-Raphaelite paintings. Francie's character, which unites in its manifestation a complex amalgam of romantic and Protestant imagery, provides the most important source.

FRANCIE FITZPATRICK, THE DUBLIN ABORIGINEE

Somerville and Ross considered a series of titles for their study of land-grabbing and soul-making amongst Ireland's Protestant population of the early 1890s. One of these titles, 'A Dublin Aboriginee', emphasized wild and beautiful Francie Fitzpatrick, rather than her nasty relative, Charlotte Mullen, who eventually took centre stage when the novel was published as *The Real Charlotte*. Early critics preferred Francie to Charlotte. Francie's questionable origins could not diminish the spunk and brilliance of the fair-headed Dubliner. She directly recalled popular romantic female images like Daphne or Undine.[66] Her awakening conscience in the course of the novel also reflects and parodies the evangelical discourse of William Holman

Hunt's popular paintings, *The Light of the World* and *The Awakening Conscience*. Examination of both the Protestant iconography of the Pre-Raphaelite painter and the revived romance tradition in the shape of the German fairytale 'Undine' in the treatment of Francie suggests an attempt to come to terms with Protestant thought in a secularized language.

Francie first appears in the opening of the novel in Dublin's north side. The tedious lessons of Sunday school have not dampened the 14-year-old's liveliness. Her tricks and mischief, as well as her golden hair and sunny spirits, captivate her 29-year-old admirer, Roderick Lambert. Fortune appears to favour Francie when six years later she becomes the guest of her second cousin, Charlotte Mullen. In the limited society of Ireland's Protestant community, a pretty girl like Francie travels well, and Mr Lambert, despite his complacent marriage to a 'woman of the turkey-hen type',[67] finds himself contending with a series of admirers. First the ne'er-do-well English soldier, Gerald Hawkins, pursues Francie; later Christopher Dysart becomes a surprising addition to Charlotte's cat-infested lair.

Francie prefers the evident affections of the English soldier. She falls in love with Hawkins and, like Undine, gains a soul but loses everything else. Because of misplaced love, she loses Charlotte's favour. Because of love's betrayal – for Hawkins is betrothed to a rich English girl – she loses face and ends up marrying the widowed Lambert. Because of love and an awakened conscience, Francie eventually loses her life when, in a last-bid attempt to be true to herself, she flees on horseback and is thrown to her death.

References to Rossetti, Tennyson, and medieval romance abound in the text, and the detailed descriptions of the Irish landscape and the emphasis on domestic life, such as Francie's sewing, recall the heightened naturalism of the Pre-Raphaelite painters. Two well-known paintings by William Holman Hunt provide a visual counterpart to Francie's fortunes in *The Real Charlotte*. Painted in the early 1850s, they earned John Ruskin's approval for their religious content and faithful depiction from nature. Both *The Light of the World* and *The Awakening Conscience* have frames inscribed by biblical text, and their titles suggest the possibility of spiritual enlightenment. In the first painting the crowned Christ stands and knocks on a closed door. He holds a lamp which lights up the brambles and weeds tangled around the door and highlights the delicate filigree of the gold cloth of the cloak. There is no handle on the door; it must be opened from within.[68] In the second painting a young woman rises from the lap of

FIGURE 2.1. William Holman Hunt, *The Light of the World* (first exhibited in 1854)

her singing lover. Something has stirred her, perhaps the song her lover sings, and she stares out into the green trees of the garden, reflected in the mirror behind her, as if nature contains the source of her startled understanding.[69] The lover sings on, unaware that some change, some kind of enlightenment, has been wrought in the heart and soul of his pretty mistress. Like *The Light of the World*, the painting of secular life suggests the hope of a spiritual awakening. Redemption is promised to the fallen woman in her material world. Beneath a table beside her, a cat stalks a bird, and the question the painting poses is whether or not the bird, like the young woman, will escape the embrace of its pursuer. A spiritual liberation beckons outside the open window of the richly decorated love nest.

Holman Hunt's religious vision as demonstrated by these two paintings is reversed in the Irish landscape of Somerville and Ross's novel. In the course of the narrative Christopher begins to see himself as the man with the lamp, bringing the light of educated taste to the Dublin jackeen. However, the awakening of Francie's heart is caused not by the inspirational reading he suggests but by the daring kisses of her charming and heedless lover, Gerald Hawkins, a man not unlike the careless singer in Hunt's second painting. Francie's escape to freedom, compared to the flight of a wild bird in the text, never takes place. Charlotte Mullen snares her victim before any redemption can

FIGURE 2.2. William Holman Hunt, *The Awakening Conscience* (first exhibited in 1854)

occur. The 'old cat' Charlotte, as Francie calls her cousin, destroys her flighty prey; in this way the Irish novel suggests a much darker conclusion for the awakened female conscience than that suggested by the Hunt painting.

The narrative of Francie's history is complicated by the romance discourse which develops further the notion of soullessness in the novel. The absence of soul (transformed into a lack of taste) in the Christian world, the world of Bruff House, is not necessarily an absence of light, for Francie shines with a natural glory of no man's making. As a 'Dublin Aboriginee', she comes from the landscape itself. She is, as the narrative tells us, Undine. The reference to the popular nineteenth-century fairytale deliberately revives romance material in *The Real Charlotte*. The story of Undine, painted most notably by Daniel Maclise in 1844, tells a tale of a mermaid who can possess a soul only when she loves and is loved by a man. This is also Francie's story. Her enchanting charm and delight in tricks and mischief are the qualities of Undine. The wild jackeen, like the mermaid, 'could not possibly be weighted with the responsibility of a soul'.[70] Unfortunately Francie, like Undine, loves a fickle human being and in gaining a soul through love is sacrificed to the gods of a materialistic Ireland. In the

German story, Undine's soullessness aligns her to nature. She has knowledge of the powers of the seas and sky which frightens her Christian companions. She challenges the notion of a Christian awakening. Francie, through her connection to the Queen of the Underworld, Charlotte Mullen, also manifests the dark unknown.

In *The Real Charlotte* the broad beam of enlightened thought has not quite reached the darkened corners of a troubled landscape. Francie stands poised between two worlds. She sees the immediate world and can dimly envisage a grander prospect beyond. Her perspective contrasts with that of Christopher. When she visits the Dysart home everything seems too big. When Christopher and she look at his photographs, they actually see different things: what Christopher explains to be a Sunday-school feast, Francie sees as a waterfall in the grounds of Bruff. Christopher's Christian material becomes to Francie a natural scene, and the waterfall she perceives is like the god of the water who takes the shape of a waterfall in the story of Undine. Francie and Christopher's views – and the narrative portrays both and shows both as limited – oppose each other. When Christopher takes Francie to witness his favorite panoramic view of Lismoyle and its environs, all Francie can see is the English officers' boat on Lough Moyle. Short-sighted Christopher sees only the distant landscape, while 'keen-sighted' Francie sees only the boat.[71]

While Somerville and Ross's text draws attention to the dangers of Pre-Raphaelite and evangelical thought by dramatizing its inability to realize modern Irish realities, it also relies in part upon the kind of symbolic realism employed by Victorian painters like Holman Hunt. *The Real Charlotte* exploits a similar typological symbolism to that which scripture readers such as John Ruskin or Holman Hunt advocated in painting. Typological interpretation is the 'reading in terms of symbols not only of the Bible, but of God's word made manifest in his creation of the natural world'.[72] So in Hunt's paintings, for instance, the various details of the work might be interpreted to tell a story of spiritual change. There is, as a result, the actual narrative of the painting (which is not allegorical because it exists on its own terms) and the spiritual meaning which the various details of the painting reveal. Details, like the absent door handle in *The Light of the World*, are clues to the overall spiritual meaning of the work. Figures, like the fallen woman of *The Awakening Conscience*, are types that might be read for spiritual meaning.[73]

Evangelical Anglicans – such as Christopher Dysart – apply typological interpretation to the natural world. Francie might thus be seen as a type, as a being who has a soul to be saved or one who possesses another reality beyond the material presence. Christopher himself is described in the text as a type whom the socially conscious inhabitants of Lismoyle cannot recognize. For Francie as well, he is a 'wholly unknown type'.[74] Of course, as an aesthete who stands outside of the social and moral dictates of a pragmatic Irish world, Christopher may be unrecognizable. But perhaps the Protestant congregation cannot recognize Christopher's type, his symbolic significance as a Christ-like figure, because of their materialistic world-view. Francie Fitzpatrick is also a type according to Martin Ross, who soon after completion of the novel wrote to her second cousin Cameron Somerville:

> I am in hopes that as you have to some extent sounded the depths of Dublin, you will have a feeling for our young woman – not that I indeed sympathise altogether with the demand for extra charm in a heroine. I think she ought to be in some way striking or the most typical of her type, but not necessarily with leanings towards perfection. [75]

Martin Ross's language here could suggest that Francie is a type in the theological sense and that the authors' method in the writing of their third novel owes more to typological symbolism than has been realized.

The stylized patterning of the details of the text complemented by the biblical imagery and reinforced by the various church settings lends itself to typological interpretation. A swift review of such patterning in the novel suggests symbolic significance.

The ring that Francie's childhood sweetheart thrusts upon her finger, a symbol of future material constraints, parallels the bracelet with its pearl horseshoe which Roddy Lambert later clasps around her wrist 'like a policeman putting on a handcuff' to lay his claim.[76] Francie's dress, her pink horseshoe dress, silver horseshoe brooch and gold horseshoe bracelet, foretell her tragic end. A more insistent pattern of black and white imagery, represented starkly in Charlotte and Christopher's opposition, runs throughout the novel as a kind of Manichaean motif. The photographer Christopher Dysart in particular calls up this imagery. His first words set in train a pattern which will be sustained throughout the work. At Lady Dysart's garden party he apologizes to Charlotte for his social absences by explaining that work on the officers' new steam launch has taken up so much of his time that he 'can't call [his] soul [his] own'. He is too busy 'with a nail-brush trying to get the blacks off'. The link between the evangelical and colonial discourse is achieved by Charlotte's quick response, her punning of 'blacks' when she refers to Christopher's stint in the West Indies and his 'deserting . . . old friends for the blacks a second time'.[77] The introduction of Christopher's character sets up a black/white contrast which identifies him throughout the narrative: his white trousers underneath the black pall of his camera, his black and white photography, his tall, white figure alongside Charlotte's squat black shape. Such patterning is reinforced by reversals and doublings in the background details, characters and plot. The tomcat bears a female name, Susan. The cockatoo snares a kitten. These initial reversals anticipate Charlotte's masculine and Christopher's feminine attributes, or the servant James Canavan's role in the Bruff theatrics as Queen Elizabeth. Events also mirror each other back and forth across the text. Francie fleeing on a milk cart led by a white horse in the opening scene contrasts with her drastic flight upon a black mare at the novel's dark conclusion. James Canavan's execution of the rat which Garry Dysart's terrier has worried from the earth parodies Julia Duffy's eviction by Roddy Lambert and her consequent death later on in the story.

The central event of the novel – Christopher's rescue of Francie from the dangerous waters of Lough Moyle – might thus be construed as a significant Protestant evangelical trope: the fishing for souls. Adriaen van der Venne's early seventeenth-century painting *Fishing for Souls*, which depicts Protestant and Catholic leaders fishing for new followers on the River of Life, comes to mind.[78] In the Dutch painting the Protestants have won a lively gathering on their side of the river, including some prominent political figures. In Somerville and Ross's self-conscious novel, however, Protestant politics are subverted and proselytism has little effect. Christopher's misguided attempt to cast out his net and to gather up a lost soul mirrors his mother's ineffectual sowing of seeds at Bruff House. The Dysarts, ensnared in a colonial, secularized Protestant dream, mistake the kingdom of heaven for the actual world of Ireland.

The Anglican Church provides the clue to the cluster of carefully patterned details in the text. While such unobtrusive stylization might subtly call attention to the mask-like nature of the representation, it also builds up a picture which offers commentary on the action and the characters of the novel. The black and white imagery, the series of reversals and inversions and the parallel events offer an alternative reading to *The Real Charlotte*. Such details in their entirety can be interpreted typologically, as symbols prefiguring Christian meaning. In the manner of the Bible, the action of the narrative and the introduction of the characters herald the 'Good News'. In the Protestant novel the prefiguration of Christ is indicated in the collection of symbolic details which possess a hermeneutic role. To understand their full significance, however, the forces of darkness in the novel must be dealt with in the character of Charlotte.

QUEEN OF THE UNDERWORLD: CHARLOTTE MULLEN

Charlotte Mullen, the face of modern progress in the Irish landscape, seeks to reign as a kind of Queen of the New Irish World. Her soul, like her ugly face, is truly benighted. Just as beauty has directed Francie's fortunes, so has ugliness guided Charlotte's star. The reason for her worst acts and cruellest deeds, her physical appearance, lies at the source, the narrator tells us, of Miss Mullen's pathology:

> There is pathos as well as humiliation in the thought that such a thing as a soul can be stunted by the trivialities of personal appearance, and it is a fact and beyond the reach of sympathy that each time Charlotte stood before her glass her ugliness spoke to her of failure, and goaded her to revenge.[79]

Charlotte's stunted soul results from features remarkably Caliban-like in appearance. Described by a contemporary reviewer as a sort of *lusus naturae*,[80] Charlotte appears as freakish with her short arms and legs, large jaw and thick lips. Her hands are broad, her feet big, and her brown hair grows so low on her forehead that she appears to be wearing a wig 'pulled too far over the turn of the brow'.[81] Charlotte Mullen's squat, troll-like appearance, her black clothing and shabby black horses contrast especially with Christopher Dysart's slim, white elegance, his long hands, long nose, and white flannel trousers. So, too, do Charlotte's coarse energy, her hot or warm face, her outbursts of passion oppose Christopher's reflective lethargy and his drooping supine figure. As Captain Cursiter steers his boat across Bruff Bay, he sees in the distance 'two incongruous figures on the turf quay, one short, black, and powerful, the other tall, white, and passive'.[82] Charlotte Mullen shadows the Anglo-Irish landlord. She acts as a landlord in her own right with a tenantry made up of the bedraggled inmates of Ferry Row, Lismoyle's underworld. In Charlotte's domain the washerwomen ply their trade and 'clouds of steam from the cauldrons of boiling clothes ascend from morning till night'.[83] Ferry Row appears to lead to the witch's kitchen of *Faust* rather than the country cottages of Lough Moyle. Charlotte Mullen's ugliness roots her character in the soulless domain of a supernatural world.[84]

Charlotte's masculine attributes and Christopher's feminine characteristics emphasize the opposition of the two central characters.[85] Contemporary readers who compared Somerville and Ross's novel to Honoré de Balzac's *Cousin Bette* (1846) may have noted a similar reversal of both class and gender roles in the pairing of opposing types.[86] Indeed, the origin of Balzac's character types in *Cousin Bette*, the turmoil caused by the French Revolution, reveals a possible cause for the development of similar types in Ireland and is worth some consideration at this point.

Balzac's *Cousin Bette* features the dangerous and frightening Lisbeth Fischer whose black dress, heavy eyebrows, 'long simian face', terrible jealousy and vindictive revenge on the beautiful cousin who steals her only love anticipates Charlotte in startling detail.[87] Cousin Bette loves an impoverished artist and aristocrat and supports him with her hard-earned cash. Together this odd couple displays an 'alliance of feminine energy and masculine weakness'[88] that anticipates the gender reversal of Charlotte and Christopher in Somerville and Ross's novel. In *Cousin Bette* this relationship reverses a central power play in Western consciousness: 'The situation, in fact, was that of Shakespeare's *Tempest* in reverse, with Caliban master of Ariel and Prospero'.[89] The female Caliban Bette has the savage primitiveness of the common people barely suppressed by a veneer of civilized behaviour; her dissimulation and ingratiating manner are caused by her subservient position. New types such as Bette and her male counterpart, the up-start shopkeeper Monsieur Crevel, have come about because of the rise of an order that gauges things in terms of money rather than blood:

> In revolutions as in storms at sea solid worth goes to the bottom, while the current brings light trash floating to the surface. Cesar Birotteau, a royalist and in favour, was an object of envy, and became a target for bourgeois hostility, while the bourgeoisie triumphant saw its own face mirrored in Crevel.[90]

Like Monsieur Crevel, Cousin Bette's ability to rise occurs in an unstable environment. Cousin Charlotte's unchecked advancement comes about because of similar conditions.

In the 1890s the inversion of gender roles became an important device in both the New Woman novel and decadent discourse.[91] Sarah Grand's immensely popular *The Heavenly Twins*, published the year before Somerville and Ross's novel appeared and the source of much discussion in the Somerville household, reversed masculine and feminine attributes in the aptly named twins, Diavolo and Angelica.[92] In Somerville and Ross's novel Charlotte's devilish nature and masculine appearance – her black or red clothing, her 'gentlemanly glass of Marsala with Mr. Beattie and other heads of families', her 'workman's eye' or 'general's eye'[93] – enable her to look down or up, to see deep into the cabins of her tenants or right up into the houses of the landed gentry. Wearing the New Woman mask of the time, Charlotte Mullen manages to overcome both gender and class limitations, while her evident sexuality provides a grotesque reflection of George Egerton's exploration of female sexuality in her provocative story collection *Keynotes* of 1893.

In 1890 and 1891, the years Somerville and Ross were writing up their 'Welsh Aunt', *Punch* ran a series called 'Modern Types' and included in December 1890 a figure called the Manly Maiden. 'She conceives the idea that she can earn the proud title of "a good fellow" by emulating the fashions and the habits of the robuster sex.' This newfangled type, says *Punch*, 'consciously apes the manly model'.[94] Charlotte fulfils such notions of the New Woman, although she manages to break the mould of *Punch*'s stereotype. She does much more than act the gentleman farmer or 'ape' his manly attributes like some female Irish Caliban. Charlotte owns and runs the gentleman's farm; she pays his accounts and out-manoeuvres his competitors; she has not only replaced her male counterparts, such as Lambert, but also runs neck and neck with her social male superior, Christopher Dysart. Thus Charlotte defies the limitations of her prototype and uses the New Woman cover to conceal much more than tender feminine sentiment.

Charlotte Mullen's complex character may have some of its source in the authors' ambiguous position. Somerville and Ross's suffragism in the 1890s expressed itself against Ireland's political situation. In a letter Edith Somerville wrote to her brother in 1892 she questions the right of 'priestridden savages' to vote when well-educated women must remain dumb: 'It certainly is a maddening thing', she tells her brother, 'that these cowardly illiterate priestridden savages are given votes when [gentlewomen] . . . are not considered fit to exercise such a responsibility.'[95] Somerville sees one inequity but wilfully ignores another. Thus Charlotte Mullen evinces an independent capability Somerville would have admired, but the character's inferior rank compromises such advantages. Her admirable intellect and dominant will are freakish aberrations rather than manifestations of female strength.

Charlotte's character, and in particular her ability to wear masks, may also result from the colonial conditions of Irish life. Charlotte Mullen camouflages her intent, conceals her purpose, and wears a pleasant mask in order that she might not startle or provoke fear and hatred. She wants to blend herself within the different ranks of Irish society. However the distinct difference between the impoverished peasant huts of Ferry Row and the Anglicized comforts of Bruff demands an elasticity of presence, an extreme adaptability of character. Much of the humour of Charlotte's camouflaging tactics is the partial revelation of one side or another of her various selves. She slips from grand tones to shrill shrieks as swiftly as she reckons the cost of a pig or a lamb. She presents a strangely incongruous and mobile character, an ugly mottling of mood and face as she mimes imperial postures.

Charlotte Mullen's character parodies the landlord/tenant relationship and calls into question Christopher Dysart's role as landlord in Lismoyle. Her exaggerated claims to the gentleman's position – his seat and his imperial view – parody Christopher's position as 'mimic man' of colonial Britain.

The mimic man, with his English education and English ways, says Homi Bhabha, repeats rather than re-presents the formats and structures of the dominant culture. He is 'almost the same but not quite', and his partial presence creates an ambivalence that disrupts the authority of the colonial discourse.[96] Christopher Dysart's ambivalence is manifested in his hesitant speech and paralysing apathy and might be seen as an expression of an 'ironic compromise' resulting from a 'panoptical vision of domination' and 'the counterpressure of the diachrony of history – change, difference' which progressive entrepreneurs like Charlotte suggest. Christopher Dysart's ambivalence undermines his knowledge and power. It brings into question the belief systems of the colonial project since his mimicry is 'a discourse uttered between the lines and as such both against the rules and within them'.[97]

Charlotte Mullen's gross gestures, then, her peculiar, topsy-turvy position and hybrid appearance reinforce Christopher's clownish figure as colonial mimic man. She also represents a threatening and unstoppable force: modernism. She is a type that originates in the same revolutionary upheaval that created Balzac's Lisbeth Fischer. But she has come so much further than the French peasant and now dominates in the new Irish world. Like Sarah Grand's 'heavenly twins', she manifests the fearful genius of her age, 'the ineffectual genius of the nineteenth century . . . which betrays itself by strange incongruities and contrasts of a violent kind'.[98] Her taste for French novels may suggest a French background. More specifically, the 'yellow paper-covered volumes', like those Dorian Gray reads in Oscar Wilde's novel, could indicate degenerate tendencies.[99] Her suspect but progressive tastes counter Christopher's romantic dreams. Their opposition creates a tension between a horizontal, snake-like movement (Charlotte) and a static, vertical posture (Christopher).

Charlotte Mullen's black force facing Christopher Dysart's white elegance recalls the popular treatment of carnival figures in French art that Aubrey Beardsley employed in his stylized illustrations, such as his black cat and pale-faced Pierrot. The black and white imagery of *The Real Charlotte* culminates in a scene when Captain Cursiter's steamer, the *Serpolette*, approaches two figures across the water on the opposite bank; from this distance, as already noted, the Captain sees in stark relief the white and black which the idealistic Christopher and the nefarious Charlotte present.[100] Christopher occupies his idle hours dabbling in black and white photography, while Charlotte's black dress, and her kitchen in Tally Ho – a 'cavern of darkness' – contrast with the crisp white dress of the Englishwoman, Miss Hope-Drummond, and the Dysart's 'white stone double staircase'.[101]

The black and white effects of the novel complement the self-transformation of a complex female character to an Irish caricature; Charlotte Mullen becomes a simplified version of herself. Charlotte's powerful ugliness – her simianized appearance, which can be fully appreciated only in contrast with Christopher's lanky and feminine effeteness – distorts her character traits. Circumstances force Charlotte to become an exaggeration of herself. The novel records how she reduces herself to a caricature. Her ability to play two hands at one time, to anticipate the needs of Norry the Boat and Lady Dysart, allows her to transform herself swiftly, effectively, and frequently. One moment she is quaintly clever Miss Mullen, and the next she is a shrieking termagant. Most of the time she is any person's equal, able to slip in and out of male or female circles; occasionally she is weakly feminine when faced by the man she loves, Mr Lambert. Affability and good humour fall from Charlotte 'like a garment'.[102] Moving from one extreme position to another, she slips on and off masks with such rapidity that we can no longer discern her real face.

Charlotte turns somersaults between the various camps she visits: the upper and lower classes, the male and female domains. She is an acrobat, a tumbler, and, because it is the only way she can embrace opposite points, she is also a mimic.

Charlotte Mullen might be conceived of as a kind of harlequin figure. Her grimacing face, half-concealed purposes and shadowed desires anticipate Picasso's 1915 painting, *Harlequin*. Picasso's harlequin is 'the "her-lequin" of medieval legend – a soul escaped from hell'.[103] One arm is white and one arm is black; half the head is black and half white while a toothy grin stretches across both, much as Charlotte's jocular smile spans the gap between hell and heaven in *The Real Charlotte*. In the case of the Irish character, however, it is living in Ireland which causes her distortion.

FIGURE 2.3. Pablo Picasso, *Harlequin* (1915)

The project of soul-saving in the novel reflects different discourses. First, it recalls the purpose of the Protestant evangelical movement or the Catholic missions. Second, it serves as a code for the education of taste deriving from the eighteenth-century comedy of manners. The religious project becomes a worldly pursuit. Third, in the context of its time and place, it carries overtones of scientific, feminist, aesthetic, and colonial argument. Social Darwinism of the Victorian period makes soul-saving a means of ranking man along a new kind of Jacob's ladder, where the hierarchy remains but the devil becomes an ape and

God appears as a Caucasian male. Soul-saving becomes a means of refashioning the human being within a world which challenges fixed notions of gender (as propagated by New Woman fiction or decadent thought). Finally, in the colonial world soul-saving can be a means of instilling a dominant way of thinking upon the colonized mind.

The Real Charlotte satirizes soul-saving in all its dimensions by parodying Christopher Dysart's mission. Because Christopher fails, the novel questions the validity of such an enterprise in the modern world. Education, money and art cannot tame Francie's headstrong heart. The romantic outcome promised by an Irish Anglican childhood and encouraged by the revived romance of the Pre-Raphaelites has been exposed as false. At the same time the symbolic narrative sets up a pattern of imagery which suggests a meditation on the question of enlightenment in a changing Ireland. The novel attempts to reconcile the tropes of a Protestant heritage with the demands of a secularized world.

The display of the colonial dream as illusion – romantic irony – relies in particular upon stage material as a means of showing the mechanics of the romantic illusion. Central to the novel's study of Irish Protestantism, for instance, is the amateur theatricals at Bruff House. The play within the novel invites comparison with Jane Austen's *Mansfield Park*,[104] but Somerville and Ross's treatment of 'nightmare snatches of "Kenilworth" '[105] recalls more than anything else the comic display of the real and the ideal in *A Midsummer Night's Dream*. As in Shakespeare's comedy, the inner play's parody calls attention to the artifice of the entire work. (Indeed the novel's indirect allusions to Shakespeare's *The Tempest* and *A Midsummer Night's Dream* recall Goethe's nightmare vision in his Walpurgis Night's Dream in *Faust* where both Ariel and Puck appear.[106])

To appreciate the treatment of theatrics in *The Real Charlotte*, a closer look at the theatre in Somerville and Ross's lives is necessary. Already the suggestion has been made in relation to *Naboth's Vineyard* that the women writers owed much of their treatment of the Irish landscape to nineteenth-century popular Irish theatrics. In *The Real Charlotte*, then, Miss Mullen's postures suggest the popular harlequin figure of French and Italian farce. Her black dress and malevolent intents, her acrobatic social skills, her masked face and androgynous traits suggest a character who incorporates extremes and who recalls in a literary text the visual dimensions of harlequin. Later on in this study, the harlequin figure in Somerville and Ross's short fiction will become important. At this point, however, the writers' involvement with pantomime and burlesque reveals the extent of their impact on their writing at this time.

Robert Martin (1846–1905), Martin Ross's elder brother, was better known for his writing of pantomimes and popular songs like 'Ballyhooly' (his pen name and the title of his most popular song) than his capacities as landlord of Ross House. He spent his Dublin years in the late 1870s and 80s acting in and writing for pantomime in the old Theatre Royal and the Gaiety. In 1878 he wrote a three-act play for the Gaiety called *Midge*. He took part in *HMS Pinafore* at the Castle, and he contributed 'songs of the hour' to various pantomimes in the old Theatre Royal (narrowly missing death by fire when the place burned to the ground in 1880). In 1883 Robert Martin wrote various songs, including the popular 'Ballyborough Bridge Brigade', and he continued to be involved in pantomime throughout the 1880s.[107] He introduced his youngest sister to the Dublin theatre. She frequently attended pantomimes and burlesques at her brother's side.

Dublin's Gaiety Theatre staged popular farcical comedies from London, light opera, pantomimes and burlesques. Theatre programmes of the period tell us that the D'Oyly Carte Opera Company performed a series of Gilbert and Sullivan works in the 1880s and the 1890s. Henry Irving and Ellen Terry appeared frequently in Shakespearian productions. Beerbohm Tree starred on numerous occasions with London's Haymarket Theatre Company. *Faust* came out in different forms: Gounod's Opera Company staged its version in 1888, as did the Carl Rosa Company in 1888 and 1893. *Faust Up to Date* was performed as a Gaiety burlesque in 1890. Most likely Robert Martin wrote the words of *Little Doctor Faust* during this period.[108]

The Christmas pantomime at the Dublin Gaiety in 1886, as the *Irish Times* announced in early December, was Robert Martin's *Bluebeard*. According to the newspaper, Robert Martin had already co-authored with Lieutenant Hobday, RHA, a series of burlesques: *Faust and Margherita*, *The Forty Thieves*, *Sinbad*, and *Jack and the Beanstalk*. *Bluebeard*, however, was Robert Martin's work alone and included a series of novelties: a Turkish bazaar, a Parisian black and white ballet, the acrobatics of the brothers Griffiths, and the harlequinade.

In late December, amidst notices of land agitation, eviction, and tenant collective bargaining of the Plan of Campaign, the *Irish Times* reviewed *BlueBeard Repaired, or the old Hare in a new form*. The descriptions of Robert Martin's sumptuous costumes and scenery, the elaborate stage machinery and variety of acts give startling contrast to the reports on tenant rights, a contrast as stark as the black type of the paper on its white newsprint.

Robert Martin's burlesque comments flippantly on Irish affairs. As the reviewer notes: 'The Widow Musphata proceed[ing] to repel the bailiffs with boiling water recalls a recent circumstance in Ireland.' BlueBeard deliberately refers to *Othello* in relation to Irish matters when he states that 'he who steals his purse steals trash, for he is an Irish landlord.' But the comic ditties ('Tim M'Carthy of Tralee') and charming turns are the stuff of fun and nonsense rather than satire. The pantomime ends with the familiar harlequinade, the antics of clown, pantaloon, and policeman. The reviewer reports finally that, 'A winter farmyard scene is made to suddenly transform into a flowery summer landscape, where the Harlequin, Columbine and their attendant mischief-makers have merry undertakings'.[109] The description anticipates the world of the Irish RM short stories: Harlequin (Flurry Knox), Columbine (Sally Knox), the policeman (Major Yeates), the clown (Slipper), and Pantaloon (Bernard Shute).

In 1886 Robert Martin amused his family and Dublin theatre-goers with pantomime and its harlequinade. He retells Bluebeard's story and includes glancing reference to the Irish context. He prefers using the stock characters of the harlequinade for the immediacy of the form. He prefers, as his younger sister tells us in 'Memoir of Robert', burlesque 'set in gorgeous absurdity' to the real bite of parody. Realism does not appeal to him, and Martin Ross concludes that 'writing a play was a task too heavy for Robert's light hand . . . nor was his sunshiny nature drawn to the problems of life's shady side'.[110] The 'shady side' and all its chiaroscuro effects, however, attracted Martin Ross, so that a decade later, when she and her writing partner had begun to realize their potential with *The Real Charlotte* but had not yet started writing farcical short fiction, she meditates on how to unite the extreme realities of life. She is in Paris and watches absurd Monsieur Guignol and his screeching baby in a Punch and Judy show in the Luxembourg Gardens. She reflects on the paradox of the scene. This same place the previous May saw the shooting of men and women, all Communists, in front of the Palace. 'It is incredible', states the narrator, 'many of the ears now strained to catch the witticisms of

Guignol must have heard the fusillade, and worse things than it.'[111] How can such an immense contrast between past horrors and present gaieties be realized?

Edith Somerville's interest in pantomime rivalled that of her cousin. In 1885, while Robert Martin wrote songs and pantomimes for Dublin's Gaiety, she played the widow, Mrs Partlet, in an amateur production of Gilbert and Sullivan's *Sorcerer*. She also revised and added music to a farce called *Poor Pillicoddy* and she played Miss Maria Noodle Poodle in a sketch adapted from the German by her uncle, Sir Joscelyn Coghill. In 1891, while writing *The Real Charlotte*, she and her Martin cousins presented *Ballyhooly's Troupe of Wax-Works*.[112] Like Robert Martin, Somerville performed and wrote pantomime;[113] both acted in Gilbert and Sullivan's *HMS Pinafore*. In 1888 Somerville played Buttercup in an amateur production by the Bedale Musical Society in Yorkshire,[114] and according to her letter to Martin Ross great fun ensued throughout the performances with Dick Deadeye, who sported an eyeglass, and a stuttering Captain Corcoran.[115] The eyeglass and the stutter reappear in the character of Christopher Dysart in *The Real Charlotte*. The emphasis upon class division and the possibility of love across class divides in the novel also recalls the musical's romantic plot, but the indebtedness of the novel to *Pinafore* is suggested primarily by Francie Fitzpatrick's mention of watching the musical comedy in the Gaiety with the Lamberts on one of their visits to Dublin.

On 9 April 1888, while Edith Somerville was performing as Buttercup in Yorkshire, the D'Oyly Carte Opera Company amused Dublin audiences in the Gaiety with the nautical opera, *HMS Pinafore or The Lass that Loved a Sailor*. Most likely this is the performance that Francie mentions in *The Real Charlotte*, for on the back of the theatre programme is a brief notice of a forthcoming engagement, and it is one which becomes the central parody of the novel. 'The celebrated burlesque' by Moncrieff, *Little Amy Robsart*, is advertised in the Gaiety programme,[116] and in the Somerville and Ross novel, the Dysart's amateur production retells Amy Robsart's story. Both burlesques – the real one and the fictional one – are based on Sir Walter Scott's *Kenilworth*. The theatrical material, then, is more than a backdrop to the fiction; rather, the fiction includes the theatrical sources for parodic purposes. After all, the mayhem resulting from the Dysart theatricals, 'nightmare snatches' as they are described, turns romantic farce into a kind of mad harlequinade. Poor Amy Robsart is nearly smashed to pieces in her ottoman/coffin by a bewhiskered Queen

Elizabeth. In the nature of the harlequinade the illusion of reality is ridiculed, with young Garry Dysart making such comments to his co-star as, 'Talk about Queen Elizabeth, you ass!'.[117] As in *A Midsummer Night's Dream*, the crazy antics of the clowns make fun of (and display) the process of play-making, and we know that in *The Real Charlotte* there were two Gaiety productions the authors had in mind: *Amy Robsart* and *Pinafore*.

The central theatrical piece of *The Real Charlotte* is a home-brewed performance of Amy Robsart's tragic death which brings together the dominant concerns of the novel while questioning the 'truth' of the main action. Garry Dysart's production concentrates on the jealousy of Queen Elizabeth (played by the talented James Canavan) and Amy Robsart's death. Beautiful Amy Robsart marries Queen Elizabeth's favourite, the Earl of Leicester, who conceals the marriage to keep the Queen's love. Elizabeth becomes suspicious when Amy Robsart seeks out her husband and begs him to reveal their connection. The Queen discovers Leicester's marriage (betrayal) and Leicester sends away his supposedly unfaithful wife to be murdered. The plot of *Kenilworth* provides immediate comment on Francie's position in Bruff as she hides from Lady Dysart's queenly eye in the carriage with Hawkins. More broadly, however, the historical material summarizes the main impetus of the action of the novel: Queen Charlotte's jealousy of pretty Francie Fitzpatrick who steals the favourite's heart and who is eventually destroyed because of the Queen's sexual jealousy.

Garry's production of the imperial majesty of the English court and the political machinations of its royal subjects parodies the regalia and pomp of the monarchy in pantomime fashion while drawing connections between the English Queen's authority and Charlotte's dangerous powers. The spirit of farce is most felt, however, in the figure of James Canavan as Queen Elizabeth. With a ridiculous 'mincing amble' the ex-hedgeschoolmaster takes the stage. His whiskery face and stooping Irish physique, half-masked by the bedraggled left-over military clothing of Sir Benjamin, calls up in his ludicrous display as Queen Elizabeth the central concerns of *The Real Charlotte*. Crossing discourse of colonial and feminine tropes becomes most apparent in the cross-dressing of the theatricals at the centre of the novel:

> James Canavan had from time immemorial been the leading lady in Garry's theatricals, and his appearance as Queen Elizabeth was such as to satisfy his old admirers. He wore a skirt which was instantly recognized

by the household as belonging to Mrs Brady the cook, a crown made of gold paper inadequately restrained his iron-grey locks, a ham-frill ruff concealed his whiskers, and the deputy-lieutenant's red coat, with the old-fashioned long tails and silver epaulettes, completed his equipment.[118]

James Canavan's startling appearance makes sly comment on Charlotte Mullen's gender reversal in the main action of the novel while displaying with ludicrous fun her ultimate intent – to be a new kind of Protestant Queen in Ireland. His transformation, however, from the masculine to the feminine role, from servitude to rulership, demonstrates the primary impulse of pantomime: to subvert normality. The appearance of a transformation scene in the amateur theatrics of the novel, moreover, calls attention to such masking and role playing throughout the text.

The ludicrous play-acting in Bruff House indicates a central preoccupation of this Protestant text: burlesque. The characters of *The Real Charlotte*, like the farcical historical figures of the Dysart theatrics, owe their origins as much to the playhouse as they do to real life. Roddy Lambert, for instance, is named after Dr Cantwell's dupe in *The Hypocrite*. In Bickerstaff's play the doctor tries to make his resistant daughter, Charlotte, marry Lambert, a situation which Somerville and Ross's novel turns round when their Charlotte longs to marry Lambert. The English soldiers in *The Real Charlotte* act more like stage sailors than British authority; compare, for example, Captain Cursiter to Captain Corcoran of *HMS Pinafore*, or Gerald Hawkins to the boatswain Hawkins of Scott's *The Pirate*. Even minor characters, like Francie's childhood beau, Tom Whitty, or Charlotte's housekeeper, Norry the Boat, appear to be upside-down versions of English stage figures: the silly old lover, Thomas Whittle, in Garrick's *The Irish Widow*, or Buttercup, the 'Portsmouth Bumboat Woman', of *Pinafore*.

Somerville and Ross's reuse of these popular stage figures occasions the deliberate upending of such roles upon an Irish platform. They turn topsy-turvydom upside down and, as a result, a queer version of reality might be said to exist.

THE MODERN ABYSS: THE WHIRLPOOL

And the fifth angel sounded, and I saw a star fall from heaven unto the earth: and to him was given the key of the bottomless pit. And he opened the bottomless pit; and there arose a smoke out of

> *the pit, as the smoke of a great furnace; and the sun and the*
> *air were darkened by reason of the smoke of the pit.*
>
> Revelation 9:1–2

The forces driving the queer character types of Somerville and Ross's novel are larger than the characters' individual traits and derive from social and political realities of the time. In Ireland during the late nineteenth century critical conditions regarding land and religion intensified the dramas of everyday life. The novel offers a dark warning about these conditions, a kind of doomsday declamation that recalls no less than the apocalyptic predictions of the bottomless pit in Revelation. In the modern context the romantic sublime is perceived not so much as an abyss as a whirlpool caused by the confrontation of traditional and contemporary impulses, what George Gissing described as a 'ghastly whirlpool which roars over the bottomless pit'.[119] Francie's ruin at the end of the novel, the collapse of the light into the darkness, into a kind of whirlpool generated by the horizontal force in confrontation with the vertical line, progress in the face of traditional rights, reveals the ambiguity at the heart of the novel. Francie Fitzpatrick is the sacrifice in this study of agricultural improvement and cultural enlightenment in colonial Ireland.

Andrew Lang recognized the innovative qualities of the Irish novel. When he met Martin Ross in Scotland in 1895 he told her that he thought the work 'treated of quite a new phase – and seemed to think that that was its chiefest merit'. The Scotsman urged the Irish writers to include in their future work 'more of the sort of people one is likely to meet in everyday life'.[120] Andrew Lang shared with Martin Ross a love of 'ruins, old churches and the like' and while showing her the sights of St Andrews, he cursed John Knox's influence on the city's architecture.[121] Lang may have recognized in *The Real Charlotte* the attempt to address an Irish Anglican heritage infused with Calvinistic undertones within a secular language. He would also have appreciated the confrontation in the novel between the romantic impulse and the realist tradition. Charlotte Mullen, Christopher Dysart, and Francie Fitzpatrick, characters from everyday Irish life, according to Andrew Lang, not only demonstrate the complex discourse of the day but also might be read as symbolic types who propose a meditation on the nature of enlightenment in the modern world.

The Real Charlotte is embedded in two inseparable traditions which determine its black humour: the workings of the Anglican faith in a secular world and popular farce in the Dublin and London

theatres. Although significant issues of contemporary discourse interact with these two traditions – colonialism and feminism in particular
– the novel's mainspring originates in the writers' backgrounds. To
what extent, then, does the novel demonstrate the failure of
Protestantism in southern Ireland? Though the concrete manifestation
of the Church fails Francie in her attempts to find help, Anglican tradition determines her outcome. The novel records a Protestant ethos,
and certain unexplainable things, like Francie's death at the end of the
novel, are understood within the 'light' of the Protestant world view.
Francie's tragic end results not just from 'the psychological dynamic of
Anglo-Ireland in the nineteenth century, of a people who swung
between disintegration and intermittent comedy'.[122] It also derives
from the text's Manichaean perspective infused by romantic irony. A
Protestant perspective drives Francie to her doom and the novel to a
conclusion haunted by apocalyptic tremors and Faustian warnings.

In the latter half of the novel Lady Dysart is on the Irish mailboat
heading into Dun Laoghaire, and she cannot complete her acrostic
puzzle. There is one final word missing for which she has two letters,
a C and an H. She asks Pamela for assistance: 'I shall go mad, Pamela,
perfectly mad, if you cannot think of any word for that tenth light. C
and H – can't you think of anything with C and H?'[123] The reader
immediately thinks of Christopher and Charlotte until Lady Dysart
says that the word ends in H. 'Church' may be the missing link of
Lady Dysart's and the novel's puzzle. When Lady Dysart asks Pamela
the word for the tenth light of her acrostic, she ironically provides her
own answer, for the Church *is* the light to the soul in darkness.
Ironically, the Dysarts remain unenlightened and unable to recognize
the brilliant possibilities provided by an uneducated Dublin jackeen,
the light-hearted and light-headed Francie Fitzpatrick. This is the
Dysarts' failure, however – not the embracing Anglican tradition.
When Roddy Lambert first sees Francie at 14 (as already mentioned,
Margaret's age when Faust first meets her), her high spirits and gold-
en hair brighten Dublin's north side while her giddy exploits, running
off on a milk cart with its white horse, delight her Sunday-school pals.
Such glorious light is utterly doused by the end of the novel when the
black mare, frightened by Julia Duffy's funeral procession, throws her
to her death. Anglican thought could explain Francie's undeserved
end, a doomsday scenario manifesting the 'eschatological note' which
is 'intensely familiar from the evangelical homiletic tradition'.[124] The
description of the passing funeral procession, with its keening women
and Norry's sepulchral posture as she flings her arms wide under a

billowing black cloak so that she appears as 'a great vulture',[125] con-
jures up a scene which suggests an Irish Protestant perspective on an
Irish Catholic event. Throughout the novel, the Manichaean conflict
posed by Francie's fate or Christopher and Charlotte's opposition
indicates the essential tension of man's worldly position.

Mephistopheles, like Somerville and Ross who were accused by
some critics of heartlessly destroying Francie, faces questions of blame
when grief-stricken Faust witnesses Margaret's tragic end. Faust cries
out to the demon to save his beloved, and Mephisto coolly replies,
'"Save her!" Who was it that plunged her to her ruin? I or you?'[126] We
might receive a similar response from Somerville and Ross. Francie's
ruin, her ultimate fall to her death, the light into the darkness, reveals
the ambiguity of modern Irish reality at the heart of the novel.

Why did Somerville and Ross not write another novel to match the
quality of *The Real Charlotte*? Their study of the colonial dream in
the Irish landscape, a dream which reveals a heart of darkness anticipated in their earlier novel, *Naboth's Vineyard*, disturbs readers to this
day. Since its publication in 1894, the novel has gradually come to be
recognized as an Irish tour de force. Andrew Lang's admiration was
soon followed by the sympathetic support of Lady Gregory and Yeats.
Stephen Gwynn described it as 'the best novel ever written about
Ireland',[127] and more recent criticism tends to concur with James
Cahalan's observation in *The Irish Novel* that *The Real Charlotte* is
'the greatest Irish novel of the nineteenth century'.[128] For Elizabeth
Bowen, it was a 'masterpiece' which determined the writers' artistry;
in this novel 'they made their own a terrain of outrageousness,
obliquity, unsavoury tragedy, sexual no less than ambitious passion'.[129]

The writers' increasing interest in form, however, is shown by their
involvement in the issues of their day – artistic or otherwise – during
this period. Their ironic sensibilities peaked during a period of vigorous change in the publishing industry, and they found themselves in
the mid-1890s in the advantageous position of being at the forefront
of popular taste. At the same time their extended trips to England and
France, their involvement in the visual arts and their ongoing struggle
as representative Anglo-Irish landowners brought together a unique
combination of interests which would determine the increasingly
political and ambivalent nature of their writing. As the following
chapters reveal, after 1894 Somerville and Ross turned their attention
to form as it expressed the Anglo-Irish landscape, its places and people, in fiction and illustration.

PART TWO
CONTEXTS OF *THE IRISH RM*

CHAPTER 3

Money: The Business of Being Irish in the Periodical Press

Irish writers publishing in the late nineteenth-century popular English press negotiated demands between the expectation that they avoid unpleasant realities while creating works that were 'racy of the soil', distinctively Irish. Although inclusion of incidents of violence or scenes of poverty may have been welcomed, such agitation or desperation had to be 'properly managed' and worked to evoke pathos or a picturesque background rather than discomfort or disgust. In the words of one of Somerville and Ross's reviewers, the point of Irish politics in Irish fiction was not whether or not it should be included but how best it might be controlled: 'Novelists satiated with the intricacies of London society or the matchless sunsets of the Scottish Highlands are beginning to find that Ireland with her smiles and tears can, when properly managed, make excellent "copy"'.[1]

As women writers, Somerville and Ross struggled to gain professional recognition of their work while also achieving commercial success that would guarantee their continued employment. They sought to publish in the best magazines. At times market interests conflicted with artistic intents. However, they gained enough popularity to fall prey to plagiarism[2] and they published in enough magazines to know their market. Somerville and Ross's successful entry into the English marketplace produced its own pitfalls. While the pair may never have reached the 'great English middle class reading public – the readers of Marie Corelli & Hall Caine',[3] they created a reputation in Britain for writing artful and witty stories about Ireland. Their commercial success resulted from an able handling of the magazine

business and the great appeal of their treatment of the Irish countryside
and its people. Popularity led to the creation of a formula story that
repeated certain kinds of situations and included familiar characters.
This comic material sold very well as the Irish RM series, which in its
entirety gave a particular impression of Ireland as 'comic Arcadia'.[4]
Somerville and Ross pleased their public by returning again and again
to the 'World of the Irish RM', but they understood at the same time
the difficulties in depicting poverty, ignorance and corruption as
charming. Alongside their comic short fiction they published material
that included incisive comment on Irish matters. Stories such as 'At
the River's Edge' (1914) or articles such as 'An Irish Problem' (1901),
dealt with later in this chapter, demonstrate the writers' interest in a
range of social and political issues. Thus the superficial charm of the
Irish RM stories can be misleading. The women writers were keenly
aware of the darker side of Irish life and did not hesitate to write
about episodes that 'lie far below the surface of that Ireland which
comes to English breakfast-tables in special correspondence and party
speeches'. They may have published comic stories but their humour
often concealed a submerged reality, one that Martin Ross compared
to those vanished ships on Irish waters that unsuspecting visitors to
Ireland could never imagine: '[an Irish reality] almost as deep as the
shadowy wrecks and memorials of human death agony that lie below
the feet of the tourist while he reads his paper on the deck of
a Channel steamer, and feels pleasantly aware of his position and
general advantages'.[5]

Somerville and Ross's biggest artistic challenge lay with their comic
material, and particularly with the reader demand that they reuse
familiar types and stock situations. Perhaps their true success, then,
rested in their ability to energize the types and scenes that make up
the Irish RM stories, as well as the subtle manner in which they handle reader expectation and avoid simplifying a complex countryside.
They negotiated a line between predefined concepts of representing a
landscape and its people and new ways of representing reality that
paid attention to multiple perspectives. The resulting ambiguities and
tensions in their writing reflect the multi-layered tradition within
which they worked.

In addition to facing the challenge of writing saleable material that
addressed a complex Irish reality, Somerville and Ross introduced
visual material, Edith Somerville's illustrations, which negotiated the
visual language propagated by the magazine industry. Both writers
were sensitive to the conventions established by the periodical press,

in particular a nineteenth-century pictorial tradition that relied upon both high and low art and traded in a visual language to convey concepts of gender, class and national identity.

Somerville and Ross's immersion in a visual arts tradition and Edith Somerville's illustrative work demand that a consideration of their magazine work pays attention to how pictures interact with text. Indeed, the discussion of Somerville's pictures gives an opportunity here to consider the significance of the picturesque in relation to Somerville and Ross's work. Concentration on Somerville's illustrations reveals her frequent use of familiar Irish tropes: crumbling cottages amidst a rough and varied countryside and peasant types, especially old women with long cloaks or ragged shawls. The evident poverty of both the landscape and its people in these pictures introduces discussion on the political problems of the picturesque. Somerville and Ross's position within the larger discourse of the picturesque raises questions regarding the implications of picturing Ireland – land, economics and language – in the late nineteenth and early twentieth centuries.

The widely used notion of the picturesque, a concept originating in the eighteenth century and an established shorthand by the end of the next century, possesses various meanings. It refers most commonly to the countryside, and like the pastoral suggests an idealized view. The pastoral, however, usually incorporates a specific kind of writing about the countryside, while the picturesque is a descriptive term ranked between the beautiful and the sublime to suggest scenes of diversity and charm that might be successfully contained or framed like a picture. In the nineteenth century the picturesque was largely associated with tourism in the countryside, discovering views that were reminiscent of pictures. However the picturesque also referred to a landscape style, improving the estate along the lines of art. As estate owners and gardeners, Somerville and Ross would have been aware of the picturesque landscape style introduced in the great Irish estates of the eighteenth century. Moreover as writers and artist from Ireland, they would have recognized the political significance of the picturesque in modes of representation. To be Irish and to represent poverty and ignorance as charming for an English reader becomes a politically fraught exercise. To be Irish and aware of the contested nature of the land being portrayed as charming – and the question of who owns that land being debatable – gives additional irony to the solely aesthetic appeal of the picturesque.[6] Various aspects of the picturesque as they relate to the Irish land and its people were inherited by late nineteenth-century Irish writers. Satirists such as Somerville and Ross exploit preconceptions of a picturesque Ireland by directing attention in their magazine publications to the deceptively charming nature of the Irish scene and the performative nature of the Irish identity, to the fact that being charming and dishevelled and colourful can be a way of hoodwinking the observer. Somerville and Ross explore what might be described as the mask-like potential of Irishness. They show that being Irish can be an act and a way of getting business – for both themselves and for the characters in their stories. By emphasizing the business of being Irish, they achieve two ends: they parody the picturesque and they question notions of national identity.

SOMERVILLE AND ROSS AND THE PERIODICAL PRESS

Somerville and Ross enjoyed an easy familiarity with the periodical press in Britain. Martin Ross knew Mr Watson, editor of *Sporting and Dramatic*, through her brother, Robert Martin, and became friends with Edmund Yates, editor of *The World* and Charles Graves of *The Spectator* and *Punch*.[7] Edith Somerville's childhood pastimes included reading and copying material from her grandfather's collection of *Punch*.[8] Hunting pictures, such as those by John Leech, John Tenniel and Georgina Bowers, were her preferred models.[9] Because of her background in illustration, she gravitated naturally towards illustrated magazines. Most of the Irish RM stories were first published in illustrated newspapers and magazines.

The thriving magazine business at the end of the nineteenth century had established a readership that understood the shorthand of the form. Not only did the British audience recognize immediately the features of a well-conceived landscape, for instance, it also identified the character traits indicated by physiognomic coding and enjoyed the satirical ends caused by the exaggeration of features. Somerville and Ross's treatment of the Irish landscape and its occupants in the periodicals demonstrates an awareness of the British audience's expectations regarding the picturesque. They anticipated the visual language with which the reader or viewer confronts the descriptions or illustrations in popular magazines.

Writers like Somerville and Ross worked within a flourishing industry that constantly reassessed and traded on popular images and types. Their currency, fast-moving and of-the-moment, embraced with equal enthusiasm classical set pieces and more popular sentimental scenes. Perhaps the most significant difference between early nine-teenth-century romantic nationalist treatment of the picturesque and later nineteenth-century use of familiar visual language lay with the kind of images at hand. From childhood onwards, writers and artists in the latter half of the nineteenth century collected a store of well-traded popular images.

Edith Somerville's early art education tracing pictures from *Punch* as well as her own and Martin Ross's involvement in amateur theatri-cals would have provided the second cousins with what Robert Louis Stevenson describes as a 'gallery of scenes and characters' collected in the playgrounds of childhood. Stevenson is speaking of the miniature theatre figures and scenery that excited his early imagination. From these cut-out plays, a popular children's game called Skelt's Juvenile drama, Stevenson constructed a range of mental pictures which he carried on into adulthood. His first visit to England merely confirmed his childhood games, verified the imagined landscape and national iconography of the miniature theatre:

> England, the hedgerow elms, the thin brick houses, windmills, glimpses of the navigable Thames – England when at last I came to visit, was only Skelt made evident: to cross the border was, for the Scotsman, to come home to Skelt; there was the inn-sign and there the horse trough, all foreshadowed in the faithful Skelt.[10]

Stevenson applies a ready set of images to the English landscape. In Ireland visual artists such as Jack B. Yeats, who read the Scotsman's essay and shared his enthusiasm for miniature theatres, applied similar imagined scenes of childhood to the Irish landscape of adulthood.[11] Pirates, black-mustachioed adventurers and dare-devil acrobats popu-late his pictures of the Irish countryside. As with Stevenson, theatrical images vivify the landscape that the artist imaginatively reconstructs.

Both Robert Louis Stevenson and Jack Yeats rely upon the miniature theatre as a kind of shaping-house of the artist's imagination. As a result, the remembered scenes possess a degree of theatricality, of display. Just as important as the collection of a variety of features identifying a place for the young Stevenson is their performative nature. Scenes and characters have not only been framed, they also have been staged in the playhouse of the imagination. A difference thus becomes apparent between the visual language of the picturesque, which relies upon established visual tropes of high art, and the visual language sug-gested by certain late nineteenth-century writers/artists. Performance is as important as framing. Like their contemporaries, Somerville and

Ross portray self-consciously picturesque material which is often just as intent on displaying its masks as representing a nation.

The application of a series of visual images to the natural scene recalls the touring artist of the previous century who looked for appropriate details in the topography which repeated the classical, idealized landscapes of Poussin, Claude, or Veronese. The eighteenth-century discourse on the picturesque argued that an appreciation of landscape as a picture depends upon the viewer's knowledge of Arcadian myth and classical landscape. Established images were carried in the imagination to be produced when exploring new territory in the same way that Stevenson would later describe seeing anew the intense mental dramas from his childhood play when he finally views the English scenery. In Ireland the early nineteenth-century touring aesthete could be bitterly disappointed in his or her search for the arranged variety of the picturesque in what one of Maria Edgeworth's characters describes slightingly as the 'black bricks' and 'black swamps' of the Irish landscape.[12] Yet romantic writers in search of the picturesque managed to discover it if they looked hard enough. When James Clarence Mangan describes a landscape painting of the Irish countryside by Daniel Maclise[13] in 'The Lovely Land', for example, he finally perceives the aesthetic possibilities of his 'sire-land':

> But—what spy I?. . . Oh, by noonlight!
>   'Tis the same!—the pillar tower
>   I have oft passed thrice an hour,
> Twilight, sunlight, moonlight!
>
> Shame to me, my own, my sire-land,
>   Not to know thy soil and skies!
>   Shame, that through Maclise's eyes
> I first see thee, Ireland![14]

The speaker rediscovers Ireland when Maclise clothes the countryside in the visual language of Veronese and Poussin. If it were not for the unique pillar tower, the speaker could believe this idyllic place to be sixteenth-century Italy or seventeenth-century France, hardly nineteenth-century Ireland. The speaker realizes the beauty of the Irish scene through Maclise's rendition. It is not just that he sees something new, but that he sees the countryside's suitability to artistic arrangement.

At the end of the century Somerville and Ross depicted the Irish landscape in illustration or text for a readership well accustomed to visual

FIGURE 3.1. Lady Butler, 'Scotland For Ever!' and Tom Merry, 'Ireland For Ever', *Strand Magazine*, 24 (1902)

arrangements like 'Renaissance Holy Families', 'Counter-Reformation altarpieces', or 'idealized classical landscapes'. Fintan Cullen defines this visual language as 'the variety of stylistic traditions at the disposal of the artist' and employed in the representation of the nation.[15] Comic writers and artists did not hesitate to parody the visual language of high art for their own purposes. For example, in 1902, two years before Somerville and Ross published in the immensely popular *Strand Magazine*, the periodical included, in a running feature on 'Pictures and Parodies', Lady Butler's painting *Scotland For Ever!* 'Tom Merry' alters the stridently nationalist vision of the Scottish subject matter – the Scots Greys at Waterloo – in his comic Irish version.

In the parody the thundering line of horses becomes a disorderly stampede of pigs carrying members of the Irish Separatist Party who wield shillelaghs and hurley sticks.[16] The easy switch from Scottish to Irish politics, from character to caricature, from fine art to popular parody, and from nationalist idealization to its demonization indicates *Strand*'s fascination with the possibilities of the visual image as shown in its pairing of high art and low farce. Somerville and Ross naturally gravitated towards such a journal, though they eventually became disquieted by its 'vulgar' tone.

Magazines such as *Strand* show the awareness of late nineteenth-century writers and artists of the pool of images and types they had at their disposal as well as the potential for parody which romantic nationalist iconography afforded. The expansion of the publishing industry at this time may explain in part the blurred boundaries between high and low art that is evident in the casual deployment of both popular material and established images. At the same time a flourishing popular theatre and the self-awareness of writers and artists of the modern period contributed to their self-conscious appreciation of identity. Certainly these realities directed Somerville and Ross's treatment of the troubled Irish landscape and its potentially picturesque people. The Irish writers were as much interested in the art of appearing Irish, of theatrical self-display, as they were in presenting a picturesque Ireland.

As the launching pad and site of publication for their short fiction, then, the British periodical press allowed Somerville and Ross opportunity to engage with Irish socio-political topics and to develop a comic formula for the Irish RM stories. Edith Somerville's illustrative work, Martin Ross's essays, and the pair's travelogues and stories appeared in a range of magazines from sporting journals (*Badminton Magazine*) and ladies' magazines (*The Lady's Pictorial*) to illustrated newspapers (*Graphic, Strand Magazine*) and the established family miscellany and political periodicals (*Blackwood's Magazine, The National Review*). The more serious magazines, *Blackwood's, National Review, Cornhill*, were the authors' preference – *The Spectator* and *Punch* held less appeal because of their cheaper rates. Occasionally they contributed to Irish magazines for reasons other than money. As Somerville points out when speaking of 'drawing a couple of stupid . . . or would-be comic things for a paper called the Irish Homestead', it is 'for love & not money'. [17] The immediacy and swift economic returns of English magazine publication – the demands by editors for ready material, the commercial potential for the 'racy' type of story (that is 'racy of the soil', characteristic of a country or a people), the necessity of continuing regularly to publish popular material – provide a crucial site for airing ongoing concerns of the day. The magazine, increasingly ephemeral and of-the-moment with the technical improvements of the 1890s, was especially adept at relating popular interests to the different sectors of society.

Somerville and Ross's experience with popular theatre probably helped them to accommodate the shorthand of magazine writing in their stories. Pantomime's light-hearted incorporation of numerous topics of the day, a method which led Goethe to describe the theatre of Pulcinella as 'a sort of living newspaper',[18] would have sharpened the writers' appreciation for abbreviated form and innuendo. The women writers also had connections in the magazine industry, and initially Martin Ross used her contacts with editors and publishers of various English magazines to promote and publish material. Then, in 1897, Somerville and Ross appointed as their literary agent James Pinker, a Scotsman with little formal education but much business savvy. Pinker had worked as assistant editor of the ladies' magazine, *Black and White*, and briefly edited the popular *Pearson's Magazine*. In 1896 he became a literary agent, and his early clients included Arnold Bennett, Oscar Wilde, H.G. Wells, Joseph Conrad, Henry James, and Stephen Crane. When Somerville and Ross took up with Pinker he was a powerful figure in the publishing industry, who 'knew the monetary secrets of authors and the weaknesses of publishers'.[19]

James Pinker favoured Somerville and Ross's comic stories – what he described as a 'comic Irish business' – which appealed to a range of magazines. These stories had hunting and shooting for the sporting magazines, light-hearted romance for the ladies' journals, Somerville's vivid Irish character drawings for the illustrated newspapers, and ironic Anglo-Irish commentary on British foreign policy for the political periodicals.

By the time the women writers started working with James Pinker, Somerville had already acquired significant experience creating comic strips. In 1886 *Graphic Magazine* commissioned her to illustrate three comic serials. 'A Mule Ride in Trinidad' appeared in 1888 and shows not only her wry comic sense and ability to tell a story with pictures but also her consummate ease within an imperialist masculine domain. The Somervilles' background in the British military, their pride in the 'undaunted pluck' and fighting spirit of numerous male relatives, like Edith's uncle, Colonel Kendall Coghill, commander of the XIXth Hussars in the 1880s, provided the young artist with a comprehensive understanding of the hero-making project of an imperialist discourse. The venerable aspect and white mustachioed face of the wealthy planter in 'A Mule Ride in Trinidad' may have been modelled on that of Uncle Kendall Coghill, an old soldier type.[20] The ludicrous dismounting of Lieutenant F. in the illustrated narrative, like Robert Louis Stevenson's struggle with Modestine in *Travels with a Donkey*, may poke fun at male valour but ultimately reveals Somerville's fascination with a British male preserve. (Plate 2)

No wonder, then, that the first story that sparked most enthusiasm in Somerville and Ross's agent and publishers appeared in the British periodical *The Badminton Magazine of Sports & Pastimes* in April 1897, alongside articles such as 'A Day's Duck-Shooting in Kashmir' and 'Pig-Shooting in Albania'. Somerville and Ross's short story 'A Grand Filly' suited the colonial sporting world of the British soldier evidently so familiar to them. Its narrator announces his identity and occupation right away – an English touring sportsman – and the tale's deliberate recalling of Rudyard Kipling's stories provides a tongue-in-cheek commentary on British colonial discourse:

> I am an Englishman. I say this without either truculence or vainglorying, rather with humility – a mere Englishman, who submits his Plain Tale from the Western Hills with the conviction that the Kelt [*sic*] who may read it will think him more mere than ever.[21]

The English touring sportsman, a familiar figure of the travel-book pattern,[22] arrives in Ireland to be confounded and amused by a 'Half-sir' called Robert Trinder, the forerunner of Flurry Knox of the Irish RM series. Trinder lives in Lisangle House with an aunt who resembles 'a badly preserved Egyptian mummy with a brogue' – none other than Mrs Knox-to-be.[23] The dubious respectability of Lisangle House and its wild servants reaches outrageous proportions in this highly farcical tale of the Irish hunt. The Englishman is met at the front of Lisangle House by a frantic dog with a plucked turkey in its mouth.[24] Screaming servants chase the dog; the turkey turns out to be dinner. Disorder prevails throughout the story, which culminates in the Englishman – on the grand filly – jumping a bank to descend onto the thatched roof of a barn: The roof 'gave way with a crash of rafters, the mare's forelegs went in, and I was shot over her head, rolled over the edge of the roof, and fell on my face into a manure heap'.[25]

The tumbling and toppling of the self-satisfied Englishman or the dapper lieutenant in Somerville and Ross's comic material occur during holiday time (on leave from normal soldiering duty and on a sporting tour of Ireland) – what Mikhail Bakhtin describes as carnival time. The rogue, the fool, and the clown who 'live life in the chronotope of the *entr'acte*, the chronotope of theatrical space' are granted 'the right to rip off masks'.[26] Robust humiliations test the mettle of the tumbler and prove his nerve and good sportsmanship. These rather cruel profanations of hardy and vigorous types are like the initiation rites of a boy's boarding school and recall the rough justice of the battlefield. If nothing else, the 'mere Englishman' is a good sport. *Badminton Magazine* depicted Ireland as the site of such testing ground, England's holiday camp and playing field. Its cover design during the 1890s displayed a shamrock with three horseshoes outlining the trefoil and a hunting crop replacing the stem. Tiny figures engaged in fox-hunting, grouse-shooting, and cricket sported inside the three leaflets of the shamrock.

FIGURE 3.2. Cover of *Badminton Magazine* (1897).

Badminton's editor, Hedley Peek, loved Somerville and Ross's comic turn on hunting. Edith writes to Martin from London about Peek and Pinker's enthusiasm for 'the Bad Mag stories' and 'especially the "Grand Filly"'. Somerville tells her cousin that Pinker believes the 'serio-comic hunting business' is their ' "own stuff" & no one else does anything like it', though Peek advises the addition to such stories of 'plenty of love making'. What Peek wants, says Somerville, is 'plenty of love & plenty of comic Irish business' and he asks for a series of stories like 'A Grand Filly' divided up into twelve parts – each with its own curtain – and plenty of illustrations. Somerville urges her partner to consider the proposition and its potential, claiming that 'some other Irish Devil who can hunt and write will rise up & knock the wind out of our sails, & we can't afford to be jockeyed like that'.[27] Unlike their Englishman, they had landed on a good thing. Their new male voice with its wondering tone and underlying sense of humour would soon become their English Irish Resident Magistrate.

At this time, the latter half of 1897, Somerville and Ross were working on a novel they would never finish called *A Man of the People*. The novel includes characters, scenes, plot lines, and entire episodes that would reappear in *Some Experiences of an Irish RM*, which *Badminton* first published.[28] Though Somerville claims that the invention of the Irish RM characters occurred while she and Martin Ross were in Étaples, France, in the summer of 1898,[29] 'A Grand Filly' had already introduced the essential figures of the Irish RM stories. Clearly, the enthusiastic response of the English publishers to this story directed the writers to develop the embryonic formula.

Somerville and Ross were less at ease within the intensely feminine world of *The Lady's Pictorial* or *Black and White*. When publishing for such magazines, they were well aware of a reading public made up of 'young unmarried women who are supposed to know but one side of life'. Literature, as George Moore had already claimed in 1885, '[was being] sacrificed on the altar of Hymen'.[30] Edith Somerville was not so much concerned with moral censorship as she was impatient with depictions of 'the Eternal Feminine in crinoline and silk'.[31] The Ireland she knew paid less regard to the ladylike type, perhaps because, as noted in her memoirs, Irish women had the reputation of enjoying greater social freedom than their English counterparts.[32] Somerville and Ross took advantage of the notion of the wild Irish girl and through humour explored different kinds of femaleness. Although aware that being funny might lessen their credibility, they also realized that comic material gave opportunity to display humanity, especially female humanity, in a variety of ways. So while Irish women writers and artists like Somerville and Ross may have struggled to be recognized as professionals (bound as they were by family and social responsibilities), they also had access in the relatively freer Irish countryside to material that challenged the limitations that prevailed in England. The alterations and censorship of early work by the English ladies' magazines indicate how Somerville's pictures of Irish women challenged popular notions of femininity.

Despite censorship, Somerville and Ross published in the ladies' magazines because of their copious illustrations and appeal to women of the leisured class. Somerville in particular would have been attracted to magazines such as *The Lady's Pictorial* for its reputation of being one of the best illustrated papers in England and bought frequently for its drawings alone.[33] Like *Black and White* or *The Gentlewoman* it used the image-based format of the *Illustrated London News* and followed the successful style introduced by *Queen* in 1861. Such magazines featured pictures of fashionable and (frequently) titled women as central material. Publishing in such magazines, however, could compromise artistic integrity.[34] Somerville's naturalistic and comic illustrations, for instance, suffered alteration in the early years of her career when her sense of humour did not accord with notions of femininity and Irishness as perceived in the popular ladies' magazines. The original illustrations for her and Martin Ross's first series of touring articles, 'Through Connemara in a Governess Cart', published by *The Lady's Pictorial* in 1891, were either altered or omitted because they might 'shock delicate ladies'.[35] The magazine illustrator, W.W. Russell, copied and changed significantly the originals. Comparison of Somerville's original sketches from life and the published version show that Martin Ross's pince-nez has been removed and her ungainly gestures have become graceful and feminine postures. A grotesque dwarf does not merit inclusion in the magazine and comic action pictures have disappeared. 'A Gentle Angler' with his wrinkled face and hooked nose has become 'A Fisherman at Recess', a perfectly ordinary chap. The reformed pictures excise any suggestion of politics and insist on generic types: a rather inflammatory picture by Somerville, 'Donkey with Cropped Ears', becomes the ubiquitous boy with donkey, and various grotesque female faces with massive noses and missing teeth do not appear at all.[36]

In 1900 Somerville endured yet another occasion when the ladies' magazines deliberately controlled her material. She published 'High Tea at McKeown's' in *Black and White*, a magazine that typified its

FIGURE 3.3. Max Cowper, 'Rattle of a Falling Coal Box',
from 'High Tea at McKeown's' by Edith Somerville, *Black and White* (1900)

FIGURE 3.4. Edith Somerville, sketch of 'The Grey-Haired Kitchen Maid' from 'High Tea at McKeown's', *All on the Irish Shore* by Somerville and Ross (1903)

class and where illustrations and photographs of pastoral views and Christian-colonial subject matter dominated over the written text. Light-hearted romantic stories, such as Somerville's story in the Christmas edition, occasionally provided humour and love interest in a colonial setting. 'High Tea at McKeown's' anticipates Somerville's later novels *Mount Music* and *French Leave*: a strong-minded young girl, one of an 'Amazon brood' of Anglo-Irish, gets into various scrapes such as falling off horses into muck or running from rats, rustic adventures that stretch the boundaries of ladylike behaviour.[37] The *Black and White* illustrator, Max Cowper, provided a series of conventional pictures that normalized the comic action of Somerville's story.

Cowper's central illustration presents the usual charming forms and faces of romantic lovers. The picture regularizes the story and challenges Somerville's artistic autonomy. A less important sketch, 'Rattle of a Falling Coal Box', re-enacts the moment when a large rat surprises the lady of the house and the 'grey-haired kitchen-maid', Julia Connolly. Cowper emphasizes action, a careful repetition of what happens in Somerville's narrative, rather than character: Julia Connolly is merely a rougher version of her mistress and both figures serve as a foil for the bland prettiness of feminine beauty in the main picture.

Somerville redressed the balance and wrested control of her material when she republished the story in *All on the Irish Shore* three years later. Julia Connolly becomes Mary Ann Whooly, 'a grey-haired kitchen maid who milked cows and made the beds, and at a distance in the backyard was scarcely distinguishable from the surrounding heaps of manure'.[38] Somerville's preparatory character sketch of 'The Grey-Haired Kitchen-Maid' enhances rather than repeats the narrative of her story. The drawing focuses on the incongruity of the character – the kitchen-maid's antiquity is unexpected in itself. Then, her thick scarf and wool shawl, her tray of steaming hot whiskeys – unlike the ordinary details of Cowper's picture – elaborate upon character. Most importantly the servant looks conspiratorially at the reader. Somerville's illustration focuses upon the paradox of the type. It also emphasizes the disorderly dress, the wrinkled features and scant grey hair of the elderly woman; it provides a picturesque and self-aware version of the shawled old Irish woman.

The difference Somerville's illustration effects stresses the impact of illustration on the written text. The *Black and White* version focuses upon the conventional action of the story and the 'glib faces' of late-Victorian depiction of woman.[39] The romantic plot dominates. In the later version the illustration draws attention to the paradox of character, and a hitherto minor character dominates. The romantic plot recedes. Somerville's picturesque rendition is not necessarily any more 'true' than Cowper's version. However Somerville's work – the conjunction of illustration and text – subverts romantic convention of the feminine discourse. More specifically, the intent of the picturesque (which Somerville's illustration fulfils) clashes with the demands of a commercial, feminine sentimentality developed and propagated by magazines like *Black and White*.

Somerville saw illustration as an essential addition to the written text and argued that the successful depiction of Irish character depended on the artist's connection to place. Although she illustrated Somerville and Ross's writing with some typical action scenes, especially of the hunt, she preferred her character illustrations because they added to the narrative. Her correspondence with James Pinker shows her constant awareness of the importance of illustration in its own right:

> I have the greatest dislike – as I think I have told you before – for little line drawings repeating facts sufficiently expounded in the text. My cousin agrees with me in thinking that character studies of the more important or interesting people in the stories . . . are both more interesting and more suited to my capabilities. I detest, with but few exceptions, my drawings in the 'Irish RM', but I fear my cousin and I would both detest any other artist's attempts to realise our people even more! [40]

Keeping in mind the increasing popularity of the illustrated magazine, we might note that Somerville's illustrations – which represent her best art work[41] – form an essential aspect of Somerville and Ross's magazine publications.

Somerville's approach to illustration is indicated further in a story published in *Strand Magazine,* a publication that appealed to a wider audience than *Badminton* or *Black and White.* Launched in 1891, 'its editor's insistence on a picture on every page earn[ed] it a circulation of 300,000 for the first number'.[42] Its use of new journalistic techniques and its populist appeal is evident in the monthly feature, 'Curiosities', with accompanying photographs, or the lightweight articles on science ('Things that Get in Our Eyes') and art ('Which is the Best Painting of a Child?'). The visual image as both subject and medium dominates. A legend on the 1904 cover boasts '120 Literary Pages. 150 Illustrations', and its editor, George Newnes, claimed at the end of the tenth year of publication that 'a new era in magazines was created by [*Strand*'s] appearance' with its 17,000 illustrations which employed no less than twenty leading artists in black and white.[43]

Writers for *Strand* included Jules Verne, H.G. Wells, Rudyard Kipling, Bret Harte, and George Gissing. Most prominent of the writers, however, was Arthur Conan Doyle with his Sherlock Holmes stories. Mysteries, visual curiosities, developments in popular science as it related to perception, and anything to do with art shaped the features of the magazine in the early 1900s, and it was naturally drawn to film by the second decade. Throughout the period of Somerville and Ross's involvement, *Strand* paid particular attention to advancements

FIGURE 3.5. Edith Somerville, 'Mrs. Honora Brickley, a Sacred Picture', *Strand Magazine*, 39 (1905)

FIGURE 3.6. Edith Somerville, 'Kate Keohane', 'The Boat's Share', *Strand Magazine*, 39 (1905)

in art and published articles on 'Finest Views' and 'Beauties in Painting'. Though attentive to aspects of Fine Art, the magazine's main interest veered towards popular art, especially caricature and parody.

Strand Magazine, then, showed a special interest in the making of pictures: the question of beauty, the significance of scale, the importance of perspective, and so on. Somerville and Ross responded to the magazine's central interest with a story called 'The Boat's Share' from *Further Experiences of an Irish RM*, published in *Strand* in 1905. The narrative deals with the visual· image, with 'a face and its fortunes' – the face of the peasant woman, Mrs Honora Brickley, whose appearance, 'a sacred picture', belies a savage greed that wins her a small fortune.

The interaction of illustration and text in 'The Boat's Share' demonstrates the manner in which the authors negotiate the claims of the picturesque and the feminine. Honora Brickley fulfils readers' expectations of the picturesque in that her wrinkled skin and hunched figure in its long cloak have a charm that age and hardship have bestowed. She recalls an earlier study by Somerville entitled *Mrs Kerr* (probably 1888) that shows the artist's sensitive appreciation for Irish character. (Plate 5) The later black and white illustrations also emphasize the venerable dignity of age, what Ruskin would have described as the 'unconscious suffering' of the picturesque,[44] as in both sketches Mrs Brickley disdains the viewer's eye while the careless folds of her cloak and the rough texture of her worn hands and face give interest and appeal to her depiction. The caption in *Strand*, however, suggests something quite different to the dignity depicted with the old woman's appearance. The line reads, ' " 'Twas all I done," she concluded, *looking like a sacred picture*; "I gave a shtroke of a Pollock on them." ' [my italics]. Mrs Brickley looks like rather than is a sacred picture; the character wears a mask. Picture and text work together in this instance to mock the sanctified notion of the Old Irish woman and to emphasize the object's self-awareness. A final illustration of this story, a comic sketch rather than a life drawing, of Mrs. Brickley's foe Kate Keohane, stresses the wild woman at the heart of the matter. The third sketch thus presents yet another picture of Irish peasant womanhood: fierce, strong, and crude.

The story's text also overturns audience expectations regarding dignified old age. Mrs Brickley carries herself with a 'nunlike severity' in her 'stately blue cloth cloak'; she is 'an example of the rarely blended qualities of picturesqueness and respectability'[45] with her 'rippling grey hair', and her 'straight-browed and pale face'.[46] Yet the woman who 'might have been Deborah the prophetess, or the mother of the Gracchi' reports on female behaviour that is distinctly undignified and outrageous, of women brawling and where 'the faymales is as manly as the men! Sure the polis theirselves does be in dhread o' thim women! The day-and-night screeching porpoises!'[47] Mrs Brickley's knowledge suggests her enthusiastic participation in the lively action of her female compatriots. The text responds not only to the picturesque discourse, reacting to the stereotyped Irish peasant and offering a more truly picturesque version, but also to that of venerable femininity, exploding the surface appearance with a supposedly more authentic reality. At the same time, text and illustration draw attention to the object's self-conscious pose. Mrs Brickley's posture and appearance are false, deliberately manufactured for the public's benefit. The reader may smile at the picture of Mrs. Brickley looking like a picture, but she is quite aware of what her performance will gain her. She has the last laugh.[48]

Somerville and Ross learned how to handle the demands of the British popular press through careful assessment and adroit management of general notions of Irish or feminine tropes. At times they pandered to the expectations of the editors of the periodicals. However they also resisted the same through humour. Somerville's pictures in *Strand Magazine* show an important aspect of the artist/writers' comic treatment of Irish character. The willingness and the ability to slip in and out of being 'a sacred picture' distinguishes the artist's illustrations in general and identifies Somerville and Ross's treatment of both Irish character and landscape. Moreover, the representation of poor Irish women as noted in the treatment of the elderly servant maid or the feisty old woman shows a deliberate challenge to the limitations imposed on female representation by the popular ladies' magazines.

The women writers' determination to represent the Irish people, and especially Irish women, in a naturalistic or comic manner could be confounded by what Somerville described as the narrowed interests of the ladies' magazines. In a speech addressed to the Munster Women's Franchise League in 1911, Somerville's argument for the reform of these publications was based on experience as a writer and illustrator who had to tailor the crude realities of Irish life to the limiting demands of these popular magazines:

> The Editors of the Ladies' Papers seem to have agreed that though Lookers-on may see most of the game, they cannot be expected to

regard it with any enthusiasm. And so they narrow down their topics to the arbitrary estimate of women's intelligence, & narrow down women's intelligence to the contemptible level of their topics. There are columns in many papers, generally near the end and imbedded in advertisements, headed 'things interesting to Ladies'. We know the class of fact that we shall probably find under that heading.[49]

Despite frustrating obstacles, Somerville and Ross's work challenged the limited space of the ladies' magazines by using the comparative freedom of the Irish scene.

Turning briefly to Martin Ross's treatments of Irish womanhood in her individual magazine publications, we see an equally determined overturning of romantic notions of feminine behaviour and idealistic attitudes towards love. Her studies of women in the West of Ireland, for instance, provide a comparative treatment to that of Synge's depiction in *The Aran Islands*: natural and frank in their expression, these women resist idealization. However Martin Ross goes a step further than Synge in that she refuses to exoticize Irish peasant women. 'In Sickness and in Health', published in *Blackwood's* in 1890 (which appeared as 'For Better, For Worse' in *Cornhill Magazine* in 1906), and 'At the River's Edge' published in the suffragistic magazine *The Englishwoman* in 1914, concentrate on the harsh realities of life amongst the hard-working women of the West. Unlike Somerville's chosen milieu of the casual gentry in stories like 'High Tea at McKeown's', Martin Ross concentrates on the cottages and small farms of the Irish countryside to make it quite clear that romance has little place in that kind of setting. In the first story practical matters, a life of poverty, small land holdings, and frequent childhood mortality, leave little room for sentimental notions of romantic love:

> Writers of novels, and readers of novels, had better shut their eyes to the fact, the inexorable fact, that such marriages are rushed into every day; loveless, sordid marriages, such as we are taught to hold in abhorrence, and that from them springs, like a flower from a dust heap, the unsullied, uneventful home life of Western Ireland.[50]

Economics rather than love-making lies at the heart of a marriage transaction in the small cottages of the West. Ironically, the picturesque countryside conceals the fact that marriage must be a commercial business that thrives on common sense and that poor women tend to ignore love if it glances by. Ordinary Irish life contrasts with the fanciful stuff of sentimental novels or the 'material of the accepted sort for a playwright'; unlike popular romance, the Irish short story by Martin Ross yields no 'unsatisfied yearnings and shattered ideals', just an ironic realism.[51] Gifford Lewis sees Martin Ross's treatment of love and romance as embittered in this story, possibly reflecting the writer's past failures in love and romance.[52] But as illustrated here, the context of the ladies' magazines shows Martin Ross responding directly to popular notions of love and female behaviour and she looks to Ireland as a site of possible resistance. The Irish situation gives Martin Ross an opportunity to question popular romantic beliefs upon which the ladies' magazines structured their readership.[53]

Martin Ross's studies of women and poverty in the midst of a beautiful Irish countryside inevitably raise a central issue for Irish writers publishing in English magazines: the political problem of the picturesque and its relationship to development and improvement in the Irish countryside. To what extent did Irish writers adopt a distanced view of the impoverished landscape they depicted in text and pictures for the English magazines? As a visual artist Edith Somerville did not hesitate to rely upon stereotype to emphasize the immense suitability of the Irish countryside and its 'charming peasantry' in the making of pictures. As a commercial artist, her awareness of the possibilities of the picturesque becomes clear in a 1900 article, 'West Carbery as Sketching Ground'. She depicts the topography of West Cork as 'sea and sky and distant headlands which make pictures whichever way you turn'. She describes Castletownshend with its 'irregular horde of grey, slated cottages' and the market crowds of Skibbereen who are 'the most picturesque peasants in the Three Kingdoms':

> Do not believe the common fable of the Irish cocked nose, the illimitable Irish upper lip. You find both, of course – and very amusing to draw they generally are – but oftener, . . . the Spanish type recurs . . . [or] women with heavy blue-hooded cloaks and kerchiefs of many colours.[54]

Somerville emphasizes the variety of form and colour, the ever-changing scene and the 'rough and fierce' coastline.[55] These qualities of the picturesque, qualities that also indicate poverty and neglect, enable the artist to provide 'variety within a controlled design'.[56] Somerville's detached perspective of her neighbours when writing for the readers of *International Art Notes* affords an advantageous viewpoint. From a distance the artist not only sees the play of light on the land or the seductive veiling of mist around the trees, she also does not see certain things, such as inadequate farming methods or the poverty inside the crumbling cottages. For touring artists wishing to capture an unsullied landscape, distance was vital, and in Somerville's Castletownshend fewer developments provide better possibilities for picturesque scenery.

At the same time that she exploited Ireland's picturesqueness, Edith Somerville ostensibly rejected stereotype and stage-Irish buffoonery. She agreed with her cousin in *Some Irish Yesterdays* in 1906, for instance, that the Irish experience in England suffered because of its typecasting.[57] The captive 'Children of Erin' have sold their songs in the London drawing-rooms and now must listen to the English strumming the Irish harp, as Somerville and Ross observe: 'They must smile, however galvanically, when friends, otherwise irreproachable, regale them with the Irish story in all its stale exuberance of Pat and the Pig'.[58] The captive race is doubly bound, first by its domination and second by its humiliation, the mirroring of its image in the feeble jokes of the 'tormentors'.

The issue for Somerville and Ross was not so much whether or not stereotypes or a picturesque countryside existed but who had the right (and the knowledge) to depict the Irish world. The same year that Somerville and Ross objected to England's reliance on Irish stereotypes, Edith Somerville was writing to James Pinker about her illustrations of Irish types as 'a class of drawing not easily come by as they are all from real Irish country people, & are typical of their class' (30 April 1906). Somerville stressed the genuine quality of her pictures while noting that she represented particular types. From 1904 until 1907 Somerville and Ross published six stories of *Further Experiences of an Irish RM* in *Strand Magazine*, and Somerville wrote frequently to Pinker about her illustrations of these stories, arguing that her work was unique, 'not illustrations in the ordinary sense of the word, but supplements [to] the text' (21 April 1906). Like the stories themselves, Somerville's pictures presented 'sketches of the more salient of the peasant & lower class people', although her work would add to the writing, not merely repeat 'facts already recorded in the text' (13 November 1902). Somerville's illustrations were not only true-to-life, even though typical; they also operated as a significant aspect of the work. As a result Somerville had no interest in drawing the usual generic pictures of 'struggling gentlemen in evening clothes' (25 September 1904) but saw herself as one who could best depict the Irish: 'Our Irish characters require to be done by someone who knows them intimately', Somerville wrote to Pinker on 8 October 1904.[59]

Somerville and Ross's success was assured by their work's publication in the most popular British illustrated journals of the time. The first half-dozen stories of *Further Experiences of an Irish RM* appeared in *Strand Magazine* from December 1904 to December 1907. The second six came out in *The Graphic* from 4 July 1908 to 15 August 1908. Both publications emphasized visual representations and provided a forum for popular developments in visual techniques.

THE PARADOX OF THE PICTURESQUE

Perspective, as its inventor remarked, is a beautiful thing. What horrors of damp huts, where human beings languish, may not become picturesque through aerial distance! What hymning of cancerous vices may we not languish over as sublimest art in the safe remoteness of a strange language and artificial phrase!

GEORGE ELIOT, *DANIEL DERONDA*[60]

Somerville and Ross inherited a complex notion of the picturesque and the sublime within the Irish landscape. As an estate manager, Edith Somerville would have appreciated the importance of utility as much as pleasure in landscape design. At the same time she and Martin Ross would have been aware of the political significance of the landscaping of the Irish estates. Some of the great estates at the beginning of the nineteenth century were improved along the lines of French rather than English models, and incorporated egalitarian ideals of the French Revolution which reflected their owners' patriotic intents.[61] The romantic hopes that fuelled the ideals of Somerville and Ross's great-grandparents and their friends, however, also inspired a taste for the wild and exotic parts of the island rather than the more settled gardens of the inland areas and their great houses. Touring books concentrated on the western wilds or the mountains of Killarney. Early national tales by Lady Morgan and Charles Maturin, such as *Florence Macarthy* (1818) and *The Milesian Chief* (1812), discovered in the Irish wilds the extreme and varied conditions of a picturesque sublime.

Somerville and Ross would have appreciated both the aesthetic potential and the practical realities of the Irish countryside. Their farming background, Somerville's artistic training and Martin Ross's connection to the romantic landscapes of the West of Ireland provided them with an informed understanding of the ambiguity inherent in picturing a troubled and destitute countryside. As comic writers they were especially attracted to the tension arising out of what is described as the paradox of the picturesque. A consideration of the nineteenth-century discourse on the picturesque demonstrates the continuation of this tradition and its ambiguities up until Somerville and Ross's time.

The picturesque has been described as the 'aesthetics of improvement'.[62] Tensions arose when improvements to an unruly landscape did not accord with aesthetic demands. In a study of the Scottish Highlands, for example, Peter Womack suggests that the aspects of reality that did not fit within the economic framework of improvement shaped a 'coherent counter-image'. What appears to be the opposing picturesque sublime of the romance is in fact the other side of an argument on land management. Womack claims that 'the ideological function of the romance [is] that it removes the contradictory elements from the scope of material life altogether; that it marks out a kind of reservation in which the values which improvement provokes and suppresses can be contained – that is preserved, but also imprisoned'.[63] Such confinement recalls the significant role of framing within the picturesque, the containing of the wilderness.

Womack believes that 'socialised scenic taste' – the picturesque – has a 'latent context' of political economy.[64] The accommodation of extreme variations of mountains and forests 'in a unity of contrasting but interdependent parts' within the picturesque shows that 'nature has the intelligible diversity of commercial society, and by the same token society exhibits the harmony of nature'. So the disparities of class, for instance, might be conceived as an inevitable part of the larger whole. Thus 'a truly pleasing landscape', says Womack, was 'one which reflect[ed] in a single prospect the success of the land's productive use and the extra-social integrity of its being'.[65]

The economic ramifications of the picturesque, its compliance with rather than resistance to the policies of *laissez-faire*, and – implicitly – its furthering of Britain's industrialization, were not ignored by its practitioners. Ruskin's mid-century re-evaluation of the concept 'Of the Turnerian Picturesque', from *Modern Painters*, investigated what he described as 'the modern feeling of the picturesque'.[66] Ruskin's approach to the tradition halfway through the nineteenth century not only illustrates its continued popularity but also reveals the need to expand the eighteenth-century cult of the picturesque to embrace Victorian moral attitudes towards social responsibility.

'The essence of the picturesque', says Ruskin, is 'a sublimity not inherent in the nature of the thing, but caused by something external to it; as the ruggedness of a cottage roof possesses something of a mountain aspect, not belonging to the cottage as such'. There is a detached carelessness in the picturesque ruin, says Ruskin, a disregard 'of what any one thinks or feels about it, putting forth no claim' on the viewer. Its contribution to a scene is the manner in which it links the present to the past. It shows in its aspect and its continued usefulness the living past, the continuity of tradition, and it does so in an England where history is 'names in school-books'. The decrepit ruins found abroad are not the carefully restored objects or isolated museum pieces that one finds in England but, instead, part of people's lives. England's affluence has deadened the past for its people. The 'border and order', the 'spikiness and spruceness' of an English people who 'neglect nothing' opposes the rugged variety of colour and form, the complexity of light and shade seen in 'suffering, poverty, or decay, nobly endured by unpretending strength of heart' in what Ruskin describes as the noble picturesque. There are two kinds of picturesque, he claims: the surface picturesque, which is an 'outward sublimity', and the noble picturesque, which reveals the inner as much as the outer character of the object. The viewer's 'tender sympathy' and understanding will enable him or her to render the object with a dignity and care the mere surface picturesque cannot achieve: 'One painter has communion of heart with his subject . . . the other only casts his eye upon it feelinglessly'.[67] Nonetheless, both views, and especially that of the noble picturesque, must be distanced from the object being viewed in order to give it dignity conferred by remoteness. As George Eliot's narrator notes with some irony in *Daniel Deronda* of 1876, 'What horrors of damp huts, where human beings languish, may not become picturesque through aerial distance!'

Ruskin's reconsideration of the picturesque provides 'an ethical response to scenes of poverty and decay' which George Eliot's wry commentary on the picturesque suggests. Thus Ruskin provides a means of apprehending destitution – feeling it – with an understanding that invests greater depth in the object being viewed.[68] Furthermore, Ruskin points out that restoration effectively erases the natural record of the past and replaces it 'with the present age's versions of the past', a kind of rewritten history.[69] This aspect of his argument directs the picturesque discourse, as Malcolm Andrews points out, into the fields of conservation and heritage. Ruskin claims that if the traces of the past are either reconstructed (renovated) or isolated like rarefied objects in museums, they are effectively changed. The picturesque provides a means of animating the past, of linking today's developments with yesterday's ventures in one unbroken strand. His argument resonates within Irish national cultural discourse of the nineteenth century. What Enlightenment reclamation programmes of the previous century saw as boundless wastes signified to cultural nationalists hidden treasure troves of the past.[70] By the end of the century what appeared as decay and destitution to the middle-class expansionist signified the traces of the past which had merged in the landscape like outgrowths of the ages and had become increasingly vulnerable to the compulsive tidiness of English industrial housewives.

Ruskin's mid-century defence of the picturesque complicates a tradition which retained vital connections to eighteenth-century arguments on improvement and which in Ireland continued to loom large in the depiction of the national terrain. Enlightenment reclamation programmes of improving the countryside vied with cultural longings to discover the past in its ruins. A range of contradictory significances emerges in the Irish landscape, and a brief reconsideration of early nineteenth-century literary treatment of the picturesque as it relates to the idea of improvement indicates the interaction of some of those meanings. In particular, we might note Lady Morgan addressing directly the immorality of an exclusively artistic appreciation of the Irish world. She challenges the aesthetic perspective of the Irish scene in *Florence Macarthy* (a name Somerville and Ross would borrow for Florence McCarthy Knox of the Irish RM series); she also offers an alternative series of pictures of the Irish world along the lines of the sublime as employed by Italian painters such as Salvator Rosa.

The touring English 'aesthetiquarian' in *Florence Macarthy* admires the 'poetic misery' of the destitute Dublin streets, where 'rags well draped, misery well chiselled' give opportunity for the 'painter's pencil' and a model for the 'poet's eye'. The nationalist hero challenges this perspective when he asks the Englishman, who 'can see such wretchedness as this, with a *man's eye*, and not feel it with a *man's heart*?' The aesthete searches for the images that books and paintings have erected in his mind's eye. He is like one of those touring painters mentioned earlier in this chapter who carries a stock of images, a visual language, in his mind's eye to assess the aesthetic potential of a cityscape or a landscape and its people. He is only satisfied with what he sees when it reflects the picture he believes it should shape. Thus Lady Morgan's narrative suggests that England's crime against Ireland is doubled by its representation as a picturesque site. Not only has England neglected Ireland but also its tourists, who relish the poverty such neglect has caused, are unable to see things as they really are.[71]

Writers like Lady Morgan, intent on creating a national novel, knew that visiting painters to Ireland, such as the Scottish artist David Wilkie in 1835, delighted in the country's backwardness since it provided material especially suited to a popular sense of picturesqueness. 'The whole economy of the [Connaught] people', claims the artist, 'furnishes the elements of the picturesque'.[72] Yet while Lady Morgan stresses the unconscionable taste of the touring aesthete, she also cordons off wilderness areas as a kind of catch-all for that which does not sit comfortably within an improved landscape. Her romantic western landscapes, for example, can be considered as sublime and picturesque backdrops, like that of the Scottish Highlands, which actually accommodate the larger agenda of land improvement.

Perhaps more important for writers at the end of the nineteenth century was the notion that the picturesque, as Ruskin had shown, attempted to contain the past in the present, to draw a line between what was and what is. The picture of the ancient cottage, where crumbling stone merges with outgrowths of ivy, displays the effects of time while existing in the present moment. The tension within this discourse as it affects Irish writers like Somerville and Ross lies in the possible discrepancy between appearance and reality in a layered landscape. What something looks like does not always reveal what happened to it. False appearances may indicate a troubled past. After all, masking is a sine qua non condition of the colonial state. Somerville and Ross show the Irish peasant embracing notions of the picturesque with suspect enthusiasm. In so doing, they demonstrate the essential artifice of the convention in the manner of the romantic ironist. At the same time they demonstrate instances of the picturesque, which allows them to incorporate the past in the present time as one particular vision of the Irish landscape. Ultimately, however, in their magazine stories and articles especially, Somerville and Ross explore the way in which what you see is not always what you get in Ireland. Things may appear to be one thing, but the appearance is not necessarily the truth. Seeming connections to the past can be fabrications in what is really a more complex reality. Both Edith Somerville's illustrations and Somerville and Ross's written text reveal a common interest in picture-making in Ireland.

As already noted, the painter and illustrator Somerville was aware of Ireland's picturesque potential. Her writing with Martin Ross, however, reveals the inevitable ambiguity of depicting poverty as charming. The Irish cousins may have understood that 'progress and picturesqueness', as Thomas Hardy comments, 'do not harmonise',[73] but they still relied upon the ironic possibilities of their conjunction. In 1901 they question easy stereotyping by urban tourists from Dublin and abroad of

Irish rural conditions in an essay entitled 'An Irish Problem', published in the political journal *The National Review*. They present the piece as a journalistic report on the working of the law in an Irish-speaking district in the West of Ireland, a particularly problematic area that was being assessed at this time by the Congested Districts Board. The writers base their narrative on their visit to a petty sessions court in Carna, Co. Mayo in August of that year.[74] Three months later the essay appeared amid articles on the British parliament and the South African War, and it reflected the journal's interests by addressing language and identity as they might be influenced by colonial policy and economic conditions. On one hand, the essay attacks the largely Laputan theory (Swift's long-sighted view) of English newspapers and magazines on the so-called Irish Problem by studying a specific case of two Irish farmers involved in a dispute over a drowned sheep. This approach shifts the discussion from theoretical argument as employed by most essayists on Irish land issues in the *National Review* to concrete example in Ireland, so that the colonial conundrum might be considered among 'anaemic patches of oats and barley, pale and thin, like the hair of a starving baby'.[75] On the other hand, the essay dramatizes the comic self-parody and rough-hewn humour of an impoverished community. Martin Ross thought 'An Irish Problem' one of the best pieces of writing in their 1903 collection, *All On an Irish Shore*.[76] The examination of Irish local dealings and British colonial policy provides a good example of the writers' self-conscious treatment of the picturesque Irish landscape and its people.

The essay concentrates on a court case where every participant plays a given role. The narrators, like many of the 'actors' in the court room, are not what they seem. They travel with a mixed group of tourists and Irish people into the West. As silent listeners to a knowing conversation on game laws, they appear to be English. But the narrators really are 'Irish wolves in the clothing of English tourists': visitors to a world they already know well.[77] Their destination is the small village of Letterbeg, an Irish-speaking community where they discover a curious communion with the common folk based on the necessity of disguise. The essay deliberates on the donning and discarding of roles in an Irish-speaking community that conducts procedures under an English law.

Finding themselves with a few hours to spare between journeys, the narrators linger outside the premises of Heraty's shop cum public house. Like Jack Yeats's drawings of porter-houses and shops along the western seaboard, Heraty's offers the basic requirements of a small community's needs. Everyone welcomes a timely distraction when it arrives. A court case is about to commence. The two visitors quickly join the fun in a performance involving both the actors in the case and its appreciative audience. Indeed, the whole point of the petty sessions court case, which all the villagers attend, is to demonstrate the art by which the various characters manipulate the system. This Irish court-room scene provides more entertainment for its audience than Heraty's pub, which is speedily vacated when Sweeny's case starts.

Sweeny's case is a simple one and everyone, except for the visitors, already knows the truth of the situation (and its history), just as every-one understands the Irish of the plaintiff, which the government official attempts to interpret. The fun of the situation arises from the mock court that ensues: the interpreter's Irish-English can be as incom-prehensible as the Irish he interprets and the schoolmaster is called up from the audience to interpret words like *gorsoon* or *ullán*. Not only is the English interpreter ridiculed in this all-Irish court, but also the chairman – the publican, Mr Heraty – constantly disrupts court proce-dures by calling up various members of the audience to offer their con-tributions. Meanwhile the other magistrate, clever Dr Lyden, whose appreciation for getting the most out of the incongruity of a situation anticipates George Birmingham's playful Dr Whitty, offers a running commentary. Most importantly, as the narrators point out at the end of their report, everyone knows and expects that a series of lies will uphold Sweeny's case. To lie and to get away with it, however much one promises to tell the truth in an English court, is the art of the situation. As Birmingham observes in his later comic stories: 'In Ireland the guardians of law and order have to be suspicious'.[78] Indeed they do. The litigious nature of the Irish peasant, carefully documented at the begin-ning of the century in Maria Edgeworth's *Castle Rackrent*,[79] becomes an artful display of one-upmanship and playing the fool in Somerville and Ross's or George Birmingham's early twentieth-century writing.

The playful subversion of an imposed civil order by the characters in Somerville and Ross's narrative is explained by the surrounding desolate, but picturesque, countryside and the economic stranglehold that it implies. The 'hungry hillsides' of 'An Irish Problem', with their 'brown solitudes and windy silences',[80] admit the charm of incongruity and the unexpected, which is revealed, for instance, by the contents of Mr Heraty's front window:

> It was very small, about two feet square, but made its appeal to all the needs of humanity from the cradle to the grave. A feeding-bottle, a rosary, a picture of Mr Kruger, a peg-top, a case of salmon-flies,

an artistic letter-weight, consisting of a pigeon's egg carved in Connemara marble, two seductively small bottles of castor oil – these, mounted on an embankment of packets of cornflour and rat poison, crowded the four little panes. Inside the shop the assortment ranged from bundles of reaping-hooks on the earthen floor to bottles of champagne in the murk of the top shelf. A few men leaned against the tin-covered counter, gravely drinking porter. As we stood dubiously at the door there was a padding of bare feet in the roadway, and a very small boy with a red head, dressed in a long flannel frock of a rich madder shade, fluttered past us into the shop.[81]

Mr Heraty's window is an inside-out version of Thackeray's window in the Shelbourne Hotel in the *Irish Sketchbook*. The visiting tourist looks out through an aperture propped open with a broomstick and offering a complete miniaturized view of Irish society: 'A person with an allegorical turn', claims the narrator, 'might examine the whole country through this window'.[82] Looking in through Mr. Heraty's window, a peculiar mix of material tells the countryside's story while also demonstrating the picturesque. The framed depiction of incongruous things continues when the viewers hesitate at the threshold of the shop and see from this outline further absorbing instances of difference and variety that inform the picturesque. The shop's contents charm and provide a rich effect, but the listing of its objects also reinforces an unavoidable fact: the limited pool of goods to be sold or bartered within the community. One of these items – one that would be most familiar to readers of *The National Review*, a point of contact in alien terrain, a 'picture of Mr Kruger' – suggests that 'An Irish Problem' hints at an underlying Irish nationalist sympathy for the Boers. The petty sessions court case in Letterbeg may thus provide commentary on British foreign policy.[83]

The mention of the Boer statesman Paul Kruger suggests an added dimension to the Irish situation. The community of Letterbeg, arguing half in Irish and half in English, the official language, debate for half a day the value of a drowned sheep: a half-sovereign. The feuding of the community is contained within a tiny in-bred populace and concerns an even tinier amount of money. While one admires the abilities of a people who can stretch a half-sovereign so far, one must also wonder at the waste of such talent within a system of this nature. A xenophobic society like Letterbeg, comparable to that of the Boers perhaps, knows the game and the players too well and, instead of improving the situation, merely invents new tricks. It reshuffles the few cards remaining in the

pack rather than adding to the deck. The Irish problem is as much the
self-absorption of an impoverished nationalist community, one that
folds in on itself, as it is the ignorance of a distant English authority. In
the framework of *The National Review* the text tackles not just Irish
affairs but – indirectly – British colonial discourse.

The problem of the picturesque, as outlined by Somerville and
Ross in *The National Review*, becomes more complex when the difficult issue of language is examined. The topic was of vital interest to
the readers of the periodical, and Somerville and Ross responded to
this aspect of colonial discourse with an example from Ireland. The
Irish situation gave opportunity to explore in a concrete manner an
abstract discussion in the magazine.

The previous June, *The National Review* published 'Our Next
Blunder in South Africa' by Sydney Brooks, a Canadian who argued
that Britain's decision to allow both the Dutch and English languages
to be used in the Transvaal schools and courts invited the continuation of divided politics and resulted from a dangerous leniency which
would continue the establishment of South Africa as 'a museum of
Imperial blunders'. Brooks argues that the 'reckless liberalism in fos-
tering a plurality of tongues' in colonies such as Canada or Ireland
encourages separate and distinctive cultures; for the French-speaking
Canadian 'the permission to speak French is an invitation to preserve
his French individuality'. How much wiser are the Americans, who
'take hold of the immigrant's children and flatten out whatever may
be too un-American in their mental make-up beneath the steam-roller
of the English language'. In Ireland the most divisive force might well
be the popular Gaelic League. The power of the Empire, stresses
Brooks, 'will not be assured till English is the only language permitted in the schools, law courts, legislature and government offices of
the Transvaal, Orange River, and Cape Colonies'.[84]

The following November, Somerville and Ross published 'An Irish
Problem', a piece that shows a people who move easily from Irish to
a version of English invigorated by the mother tongue. As part of a
larger discourse on language in the British colonies, the essay demonstrates the process of creating an alternative way of communicating,
one that marries two languages to create a hybrid tongue. This same
year Martin Ross celebrated the artful possibilities of Irish-English in
her comic book illustrated by Somerville and called *A Patrick's Day
Hunt*.[85] Even though English readers would hardly understand the
Hiberno-English of the story as told by a local lad, Martin Ross insisted on publishing the piece. The story demonstrates how English

renews itself by working with another language to create a powerful means of expression. It also provides a good example of how Somerville and Ross did not always seek to 'ingratiate themselves with their English readers' as John Wilson Foster claims.[86]

'An Irish Problem' shows the artful evasion of the law through the confusion wrought by using an interpreter. Language becomes a means of evasion, a way of playing the system. Nonetheless, Somerville and Ross show that it is not the difference of identity as expressed through different languages that incites the people. It is lack of money. It is insularity. Brooks's argument for the suppression of separate languages as the most effective means of colonial control posits only two positions: a people united by speaking one language or a people rebellious and divided by speaking many tongues. Somerville and Ross proffer an alternative option and suggest that different languages such as Irish and English can marry to become a new and vital means of communication.[87] At the same time they provide the reader with a way of speaking that demonstrates with its variations the charm of the picturesque. Hiberno-English does not follow the patterns of speech found in the Queen's English. It disrupts conventional English usage and its hybridity allows for play amongst those – the Irish-speaking villagers – who must conduct Irish affairs in a British court.

But Somerville and Ross have a double purpose in this essay. They captivate readers with a picturesque Irish scene and a lively use of language, and they also suggest the problem underlying such charm. Let us return once more to the description of the small shop window which introduces Somerville and Ross's observations on depicting poverty in Ireland. The paradox of the picturesque becomes clear, as clear as glass, in Mr Heraty's window in 'An Irish Problem'. Its appearance is as remarkable for the variety of the goods on offer as for the scarcity of their numbers. As the visitors look at the odd mix of things – rat poison, rosary beads, and champagne – they are drawn by the vitality in the scene, an appeal absent in the monotony of order (and order, of course, is most required when there is plenty). On one hand, the appeal of the scene, its charm and humour, relies upon the economic stranglehold of local politics and a history of impoverished conditions, a fact which the authors acknowledge throughout the essay. The symbolic contents of the window – the rosary, Paul Kruger's portrait (the forces of religion and nationalism within this impoverished state) – contradict the pretty appeal of their representation. The window illustrates the ambiguity of the picturesque. On the other hand, Heraty's shop window, just like the mock court case, is merely a picture or a mask which conceals as much as it reveals. In the same way, the villagers (acting as the audience), the publican (acting as the judge), the doctor, and even the narrators wear masks. The essay calls attention to the art of being a picture.

A visual alternative to Somerville and Ross's shop window in 'An Irish Problem' is found in Jack Yeats's *The Country Shop* (ca. 1912). Yeats's watercolour is based on his 1905 trip to the West of Ireland with Synge, who was commissioned by the *Manchester Guardian* to write a series of articles on the Congested Districts. In Yeats's picture, the viewer is placed inside the shop (instead of at its threshold as in Somerville and Ross's work) and faces a medley of goods hanging from the ceiling. Smack dab in the middle of boots and fishing tackle is a mirror which reflects the scene outside the shop. The window frame and the chimney and roof of a cottage behind the viewer are reflected in the mirror. The reflection hints at the actual life beyond the pictured composition of the shop's contents. And yet that 'real life' is also part of the picture. The mirror not only emphasizes the viewer's position and perspective but also draws attention to the framing of Irish reality. Like a *mise en abyme*, it ironically displays the artifice of picture-making. As in Somerville and Ross's shop-window 'picture', Irish life, with its picturesque arrangement and symbolic accoutrements (the rosary beads and harp), is self-consciously framed.[88]

Late nineteenth- and early twentieth-century Irish writers/artists appropriate the visual language of the picturesque to explore its artifice. The paradox of the picturesque, as outlined in Somerville and Ross's study of 'the Irish problem', admits of the significance of economic conditions in the portrayal of the Irish landscape. To what extent, then, do the writers actually facilitate the economic programme they appear to resist? Do Somerville and Ross – one of them a committed unionist and both writing for a British audience while living in Ireland – utilize the picturesque as a politicized discourse? While close consideration of the satirical treatment of picturesque Ireland in 'An Irish Problem' reveals the writers' ambivalent self-awareness of picturing economic destitution, other instances of framing an impoverished state, however 'noble' or empathetic they might be, suggest a compliance in the use of the picturesque as a means of including and preserving the 'dysfunctional ideological traces' of a conservative programme. Yet what dominates Somerville and Ross's treatment of what many British readers expect to be picturesque Ireland, is an artful display of the same. The illustrations of the shawled old Irish women draw attention to the act of being

FIGURE 3.7. Jack Butler Yeats, *The Country Shop* (ca. 1912)

picturesque. Such amusing depictions demand that we question the truth of their reality. If the old women are not as they appear or if the characters in the Irish courtroom of 'An Irish Problem' are not what they say they are, then what might they be? What *is* Irishness? Ultimately, Somerville and Ross call attention to the art of masking on the part of those who have been handled in the British magazines as picturesque. In other words, the Irish writers parody the picturesque while questioning notions of national identity.

The writers' awareness of the business of being Irish, then, may in part have been a response to market concerns but also was swayed by changing attitudes to the role of art in the modern world. Like their contemporaries, Somerville and Ross would have noted new ways of considering old issues. After all, Ruskin's emphasis on meaning and morality in the visual arts faced a public contretemps in London during the period that Edith Somerville was training as a visual artist at the South Kensington School of Art. Although only 19, her interest in the Whistler/Ruskin trial may have been provoked by an Irishman's involvement in the well-publicized event. James Whistler exhibited *Nocturne in Black and Gold: The Falling Rocket* (1875) in the Grosvenor Gallery in 1877 and Ruskin famously criticized the artist's 'impudence' in asking for 200 guineas 'for flinging a pot of paint in the public's face'. Whistler sued for libel but had some trouble finding significant witnesses to testify publicly as to the quality of his work. On 25 November 1878, the day that art went on trial, his third and final witness was none other than the minor Irish playwright and portrait painter William Gorman Wills, the only painter other than Albert Moore whom Whistler could persuade to come to court. Wills was full-hearted in his praise for the impressionist style:

> I have affirmed that Mr Whistler's works are artistic masterpieces. Allow me to go further. They have been painted by a man of genius. Mr Whistler looks at nature in a poetical light and has a native feeling for colour.[89]

The eccentric Willie Wills, whose friendship with Martin Ross's eldest brother Robert occurred around this time[90] and who, as noted in an earlier chapter, worked closely with the young Martin Ross, committed himself with enthusiasm to the new kind of painting that Whistler advocated and the rising interest in art for art's sake. Somerville and Ross's appreciation for new ways of considering reality in picture and text would have been influenced by such developments and accentuated by their travel and studies in France over the next few decades.

CHAPTER 4

Law: Harlequin in Ireland

Thou believest that there is one God;
thou doest well: the devils also believe, and tremble.

JAMES 2:19

From 1884 onwards Edith Somerville was one of numerous female artists enjoying *la vie de Bohème* in the ateliers of Paris, leaving Ireland whenever she could to work in the ladies' studios of the French capital.[1] By the end of the century she was studying black-and-white art with the American illustrator Cyrus Cuneo, a student of James Whistler. Martin Ross also attended some of these classes and watched her cousin draw gladiators, monks and swordsmen in black crayon.[2] Posted on the studio walls were Whistler's *Propositions*, and the Irish writers would have been familiar with Whistler's emphasis on art as a matter of form, line and colour, demanding that a work of art be independent of all 'clap-trap' that distracts a viewer from the artistic arrangement itself.[3] Somerville carefully copied some of Whistler's dictates in 1899 and in *Irish Memories* she stresses his commentary on the significance of art – as opposed to nature – in the making of pictures:

> People never look at Nature with any sense of its pictorial appearance, for which reason, by the way, they also never look at a picture with any sense of Nature, but unconsciously, from habit, with reference to what they have seen in other pictures.[4]

The indirect influence of Whistler and the Parisian studios on the work of Somerville and Ross demands that we reconsider the apparent realism of their treatment of Ireland. Although Somerville constantly drew from real life in both her artwork and collaborative fiction, she was aware of the significance of art as much as nature in the representation of reality. Such self-consciousness would have increased Somerville and Ross's understanding of the possibilities of viewpoint in both fiction and art: what may appear to be a straightforward depiction can be but one version of a multifaceted reality. Paul Henry, who remembered meeting the 'two Irish girls' on the Boulevard du Montparnasse, points out in *An Irish Portrait* that the most important lesson of his training in France was his realization that there may be more than one way to look at a subject.[5] For artists and writers in Paris, the vibrant art scene called attention to perspective and the importance of art in the representation of reality. As Oscar Wilde would note in his story about a painting that takes on a life of its own, *The Picture of Dorian Gray*, it is an enticing French novel with a Parisian hero that shows young Dorian how fiction can prefigure life. Wilde's protagonist discovers himself in a work of fiction and learns from the French how a person can invent himself as one thing or another, adopt various roles so that his identity shifts and changes accordingly. For 'two Irish girls' in France, young women who could just as easily be described as two British tourists in Ireland (as noted already in Somerville and Ross's essay 'An Irish Problem'), the deceptive nature of appearance would have been concretely realized in their own case. Somerville and Ross's Anglo-Irish background and their time in Paris would have drawn the writers' attention to the slippery nature of race and identity.

As editor of *The Woman's World* in the late 1880s, Oscar Wilde promoted material by Irish women writers and artists. Yet when Edith Somerville brought him some of her drawings for possible publication he rejected them because Somerville had included French images and Wilde thought that 'French scenes should be drawn by French artists'. Wilde obviously thought his compatriot should stick to representing Irish material.[6] At this time Wilde's assessment of contemporary Irish fiction in the magazine praised in particular a 'faithful' rendition of Irish life, especially Irish peasant life, because the 'note of realism in dealing with national types of character' is a 'distinguishing characteristic of Irish fiction, from the days of Miss Edgeworth down to our own days'.[7] Wilde's posturing as an advocate of realistic and nationally aware fiction for the readers of *The Woman's World* did not impress Edith Somerville. Like Dorian Gray, Somerville and Ross appreciated the complexity of character types, that 'man was a being with myriad lives and myriad sensations, a complex multiform creature that bore within itself strange legacies of thought and passion'. Man could create himself as one thing or another, wear different masks, and his origins could be as much fictional as fact: 'Yet one had ancestors in literature, as well as in one's own race, nearer perhaps in type and temperament, many of them, and certainly with an influence of which one was more absolutely conscious.'[8]

Somerville and Ross, like Oscar Wilde, demonstrated a strong awareness of type. Undoubtedly the expectations of a British audience influenced Irish writers' production. Reviewers rated the truthfulness of character types according to established notions of Irishness. Somerville and Ross's self-conscious framing of conventions regarding 'national types of character' succeeded because of the familiarity of such types. However, equally influential in Somerville and Ross's magazine publications was the impact of French thought on the treatment of character.

Yet when we turn to the Irish RM stories, we find a range of figures with stereotyped Irish qualities. They appear to come close to the stage buffoonery the writers despised. First, the trickster and charming ne'er-do-well, Flurry Knox, a half-sir, enters the scene. He introduces the Resident Magistrate (symbol of British law and order) to the Irish countryside. Flurry, an Anglo-Irish squireen who knows horses and dogs better than he knows his own family, loves his second cousin Sally Knox. The initial collection of stories deals in part with the various obstacles Flurry must overcome in pursuit of Sally. Second, an Irish clown, the tipsy storyteller, Slipper, provides further observations on Irish manners. Finally the peasantry fight, evade the law, love to drink, sing, and make mischief.

Common to all the Irish characters is a picturesque vivacity considered to be a defining quality of Irishness throughout the century, and as much an aspect of the landscape as it is of the people. In *Researches in the South of Ireland* of 1824, for instance, Thomas Crofton Croker discovers an overriding characteristic in the Irish peasantry. The peasantry possess, says Croker, digging deep into history by quoting Giraldus Cambrensis to support his point, 'extremes of temperament': ' "When they . . . be bad, you shall no where meet with worse, if they be good, you can hardly find better" '.[9] Though Flurry Knox is no peasant, he too demonstrates such extremes of temperament in his chameleon-like nature; one moment he appears to be in the highest of spirits and the next he sinks into dark irritation and despair. Unlike placid and unchanging Major Yeates, Flurry tends to adapt his mood to suit his environment, and the elastic possibilities of his character match his ability to mix with the highest and lowest of the land. Flurry Knox occupies a 'shifting position';[10]

he mingles as easily with stable-boys as he does with gentlemen; like an acrobat, he turns somersaults across the Irish social terrain and, like a magician, he manages to effect transformations within his domain of the Irish hunt.

As Master of the Hounds, Flurry Knox can convert a sedate pastoral scene into a site of chaos with a flick of his whip: Lady Knox turns fool and Slipper becomes king. The orderly way of the world reverses when Flurry leads his followers after the fox and carnival ensues. So Flurry not only manifests extremes of temperament, he also introduces Major Yeates and his English wife, Philippa, to a different kind of world discoverable in the Irish countryside, the Bakhtinian chronotope of festival time.[11] Flurry belongs to this in-between time; he demonstrates the attributes of a stock theatrical figure – harlequin – and his quicksilver qualities issue as much from popular pantomime as they do from colonial stereotyping.

Cultural-political readings of the Irish RM stories tend to ignore the writers' absorption of a tradition complicating colonial concerns. The European dimension of Somerville and Ross's fiction, especially the French fascination with the artificial masks of carnival, cannot be ignored. However Somerville and Ross's colonial background has frequently been seen as determining their superficial treatment of character in the Irish RM stories. Maureen Waters argues that the ascendancy writers' racism gave rise to their creation of characters who are a 'comic exposition of Arnold's thesis as outlined in his *Study of Celtic Literature*': their treatment of Irish character sees Major Yeates as the manifestation of Saxon dullness opposing the 'unpredictable countrymen' and rustic clowns of Celtic Ireland. More recently Joep Leerssen describes Flurry Knox as a positive stage-Irish male type, what he describes as the 'pleasant peasant' of nineteenth-century fiction whose boyish traits counter English stereotyping of itself as adult male.[12] Flurry, however, ranks higher on the social ladder than Leerssen admits, a half-sir rather than a peasant. He also recalls more than one tradition. Somerville and Ross's use of carnival figures and awareness of a pictorial tradition, their self-conscious framing of conventions regarding nationality, derives from a broader European context, as well as from the Irish romantic production of national character or the demands of the English periodical press.[13] The writers' treatment of Irish caricature might thus be considered in connection to developments of modern caricature in France. Popular theatre – burlesque and pantomime – and caricature (based on the French model as it intersects with the creation of the nineteenth-century Irish national character) help to shape the kinds of figures developed in Somerville and Ross's short fiction. In other words, popular form and modern aesthetic, as much as a colonial perspective, determine the creation of certain characters in the Anglo-Irish fiction of the period.

Of course Somerville and Ross's use of stage types like the tipsy servant, the half-sir or the bumbling official in text and illustration immediately recalls the conditions of colonial life. These versions of Irish national character derived from a colonial rhetoric that defined Irishness to support and argue methods of policing in the 'sister colony'. Perceptions of Irishness originated in a larger political agenda: the management of the Irish countryside. Major Yeates's position as British authority is an inescapable fact of the Irish RM stories. His presence, however ineffectual, is an immutable one upon the Irish landscape. He recalls earlier authority figures, such as the hero of a collection of sketches which anticipate Somerville and Ross's short fiction, Henry Robert Addison's *Recollections of an Irish Police Magistrate* of 1862.[14] Addison based his tales on the real-life exploits of an early nineteenth-century police magistrate, Thomas Vokes. However, even more significant than the fictional and factual antecedents of the Resident Magistrate of Somerville and Ross's stories is how Major Yeates reminds us of the officious bumpkins of farce. Robert Martin of Ross House played the role of the foolish authority type on stage more than a decade before his youngest sister and her collaborator had devised their version.

Somerville and Ross would have been influenced indirectly by developments on the Continent in their creation of the Irish RM characters. Already I have noted how the profiling of character types from different classes in *The Real Charlotte* reminded Somerville and Ross's readers of Honoré de Balzac's display of all human nature in *La Comédie humaine*. In this chapter, I will look more closely at Balzac's treatment of character and Charles Baudelaire's later theory of caricature, to show the extreme dimensions of late nineteenth-century caricature in another light. Especially significant in relation to Somerville and Ross's short fiction is the French writers' fascination for a figure who originates in Ireland: John Melmoth, the trembling devil and Irish Mephisto created by Charles Maturin. Maturin's 1820 novel, *Melmoth the Wanderer*, made a lasting impact on both Balzac and Baudelaire's thought. In 1835 Balzac took Protestant John Melmoth and set him amongst the tawdry business concerns of Catholic Paris in *Melmoth réconcilié*. Three years later James Clarence Mangan poached Balzac's version of Maturin's tale for the *Dublin University Magazine* with a story called 'The Man in the Cloak'. Then Baudelaire used the Anglo-Irish Mephistopheles as his main example to explain modern caricature in 'De l'essence du rire'. The wandering path of this romantic Irish-European figure makes possible the connection drawn in this chapter between the discourse on Irish national character and French theory on modern caricature. Because John Melmoth transcends borders delineating generations, classes, religions and countries, he reveals a much wider network of influences that support his construction.

The characters of the Irish RM stories, then, suggest a range of traditions related to colonial discourse, modern French theory on the nature of the comic, genre development, and the short story form. Ultimately Flurry, Slipper, Major Yeates, and Mrs. Cadogan are masks of masks. They are generic stage types transported with self-conscious aplomb onto a stylized Irish landscape. Somerville and Ross's short fiction does not merely represent Irish people; it frames the characters of the Irish landscape in the romantic ironist fashion. These characters' origin may indeed be the stage, but to say that they are merely stage-Irish (and to dismiss them as such) is to ignore the vitality of the world theatre that gives them shape.

CARICATURE: THE ART OF THE CENTURY

Edith Somerville's art education, pursued mainly in Paris, emphasized illustration during a period when the effects of the law on the liberty of expression (1881) were being enjoyed by a dynamic and increasingly liberal French press. While the young Martin Ross gravitated towards the theatre in London in the 1880s, her cousin preferred the art studios of Paris. After a term in South Kensington School of Art and two terms with private masters in Düsseldorf, Edith Somerville persuaded her reluctant parents to let her go to France. Like other Irish women artists of the period, including Sarah Purser, Helen Mabel Trevor and Rose Barton, Somerville was attracted by the opportunity for a broader training in Paris, easy access to life drawing and an international mix of art students.[15] She first started working in Colarossi's studio for young ladies in 1884. She returned to Colarossi and Délécluse's art studios for three more stints in the 1880s. During this time she may have come across a recently launched periodical called *Chat Noir* (1883). The paper revived popular interest in carnivals, and Adolphe Willette's illustrations of a malevolent Harlequin (who could transform himself into a black cat) and an effete, white-garbed Pierrot ('the needy bohemian')[16] may have caught Somerville's eye and influenced the contrasting black and white figures of Charlotte Mullen and Christopher Dysart in *The Real Charlotte*. Squat Miss Mullen with her black dress and cat-infested house shadows the long, white-suited figure of Christopher throughout Somerville and Ross's carefully patterned novel.

The vibrant poster art of Paris in the 1890s dominated the city streets. Toulouse-Lautrec's vivid figures and Théophile-Alexandre Steinlen's social realism, heavily influenced by the work of the former, stressed ordinary daily life in the French capital and its environs.[17] Edith Somerville enjoyed reading the French magazine *Gil Blas*, in which Steinlen's work featured prominently.[18] Martin Ross joined her cousin in Paris at different stages in the 1890s, and her familiarity with Steinlen's work becomes apparent when she compares Jack Yeats's Irish sketches in an exhibition in Dublin in 1901 to the work of the French illustrator.[19] Somerville and Ross's later admiration for the black and white artwork of Aubrey Beardsley and Harry Clarke may have originated in the *cafés* and *crêmeries* of Paris, and Somerville's preference for drawing exaggerated single figures against empty backgrounds recalls the poster art of the period. For instance, two chalk pastels depicting characters from the Irish RM stories, the owner of the Mountain Hare and Mrs Cadogan, show figures that fill the page space and nearly seem to leap out of the frame so direct and vital are their expressions and gestures. In these pictures character dominates. (Plate 4)

Caricature, a public form of satire (what Baudelaire described as '*la satire générale des citoyens*'), might be described as the art of the century.[20] Early French censorship laws changed the nature of caricature from political to social satire. This development moved caricature into a more general realm so that it became a means of mirroring the crowd. In Paris, where six thousand papers flourished by 1900, it provided vigorous commentary.[21] Henry James described the art form around this time as 'journalism made doubly vivid'.[22] Its success depended on an appreciative and knowing audience, one that derives, says Baudelaire, from '*une civilisation perspicace et ennuyée*'. In 1855 Baudelaire considered the significance of the images of French and foreign caricaturists of the nineteenth century in three essays. The first of these, 'De l'essence du rire', advanced comic theory.[23] To explain the nature of modern caricature, he refers to the Irishman John Melmoth's essential ambiguity. The devil's ambivalent laughter, so clearly demonstrated in the Irish novel, expresses the contradictory nature of caricature: '*Le rire est satanique, il est donc profondément humain*'.[24]

Somerville and Ross were well positioned to appreciate the social and political satire of the French press. In 1899, for instance, Martin Ross wrote home about the French papers' attitudes to Britain's involvement in the Boer War. The 'better' papers admitted their error in initially attacking Queen Victoria while *Patrie* and *Libre Parole*, the halfpenny papers, continued to use the opportunity to attack the French government's support of Britain. A satirical newspaper called *Rire* deserved special mention for its 'horrible' and 'disgusting' caricatures from British history. Despite her distaste, Martin Ross read them all and obviously studied the subversive material before 'consigning the whole thing to the stove'.[25]

To understand caricature, Baudelaire suggests that one must comprehend the darker side of human nature to have an ability to see the vice caricature unmasks. When Martin Ross studies the French parody of an English tradition and describes it as 'horrible', her elaborate disgust could indicate more than British loyalty or ladylike distaste. She may also appreciate – as someone living among artists in Paris in 1899 – the troubling duality of caricature: its peculiar mix of beauty and ugliness and its acknowledgement of the grotesque and sinister in the crowded modern city. Looking at the caricatures of the British, she sees herself as the object of parody, but she also sees the demonic distortion that her Irish sensibility may have allowed her to appreciate. With some self-consciousness, then, she assigns the latter to its infernal source – the fire.

Somerville and Ross's appreciation for the ambiguous nature of modern caricature becomes apparent in their treatment of Irishness in the social satire, *A Patrick's Day Hunt* (1902). A comparison of two of Edith Somerville's illustrations of Martin Ross's text and John Leech's 1859 watercolour of the old fishing village on the estuary of the River Corrib, the Claddagh in Galway, points up the uneasy perspective of Somerville's pictures. Though Leech's work in this instance reflects the gently comic intent of its context, *A Little Tour in Ireland*,[26] and while Somerville's pictures reinforce the madcap nature of Martin Ross's narrative, significant differences in point of view emerge. Leech's picturesque scene of the Spanish faces and red skirts of the Claddagh contains subdued comic elements recalling his political satires for *Punch* (a grotesque old woman being fed from a tea kettle; a wild-eyed boy chasing a pig). The comic additions, however, remain on the edges of the depiction of an exclusively peasant gathering. This group, self-absorbed and distanced by obvious signs of poverty and exoticism, never disturbs the viewer. (Plate 6)

John Leech provided the young Edith with various models. However Somerville's modern illustrations of the mad Irish hunt strike a different note to that of the work of the Victorian illustrator. In Somerville's crowd scenes, a range of ordinary figures fill the pictorial space – farmers, huntsmen, and peasants – while the children at the centre of 'When the Hunt's in it on a Holyday' stare directly at the viewer as if he/she is included in the picture, a part of this hectic world. In a similar way Martin Ross's text does not translate its Hiberno-English dialect; no intermediary explains the lively language of the story as related by a local lad:

> With that he gives the yella pony a salamandher of a belt, and he coorsed him about three turns around the field the way he'd knock the wind out o' him, in regard of he being out on grass always, and when he thought he felt him jaded it's then he faced him in at the wall. But in spite of all he jumped it very sevare and very ugly. Them Shan Buies is very piggish that way.[27]

Edith Somerville feared the text's dialect would be too 'idiomatic' for English readers,[28] but the paradoxical twists of meaning in the Irish expression, like the upending of normal reality in the pictures, conveys a general impression of life in the Irish countryside. We are thrust into the middle of mayhem. In 'The Villyan Wheeled into the Yard as Nate as a Bicycle', the brutally comic farmyard scene prominently displays the crazed behaviour of its human and animal figures.[29] The scene opposes Leech's distant vision of Irish humanity. It disturbs the viewer because the main female figure remains just on the edge of caricature, her features exaggerated only slightly so that she avoids becoming a distanced object. She does not invoke amusement or pity so much as discomfort. She mirrors the viewer. (Plate 7) She might even mirror Martin Ross, who often modelled for her cousin and learned how to ride a bicycle that year. She was 39 and experienced at wheeling neatly across the Irish roads. Somerville and Ross's work may recall particular notions of Irish national character, but their modern use of perspective allows for audience participation. The result is not entirely comfortable and asks that we consider more carefully the origins of national types.

THE PICTURESQUE AND THE IRISH NATIONAL CHARACTER

> *It has been remarked by more than one artist of eminence, as a*
> *comment on the Irish landscape, that the forms of the trees are*
> *more graceful and capricious than in England. 'Your trees,' said a*
> *gentleman to me, 'partake of your national character, wild and*
> *irregular they both assume extraordinary ramifications, that treat-*
> *ed with justice by a master hand appear noble features but of*
> *which an unskilful delineator produces only clumsy caricature.*
>
> THOMAS CROFTON CROKER, *RESEARCHES IN THE SOUTH OF IRELAND*[30]

Thomas Crofton Croker's 'observations on the manners and superstitions of the Irish peasantry' in 1824 seeks to trace the 'national
distinctions' of a people. The peasantry, says Croker, manifest
observable characteristics which distinguish the Irish from other
races. His list of the manners and customs of the Irish lower classes
(their hospitality, hyperbole, fondness for drink and faction fighting, their means of courtship and marriage, and so on), as he guides
his reader through the picturesque spots of the south of the island,
finds its basis in one over-riding feature: 'extremes of temperament'.[31] The extraordinary dimensions of the Irish national character
might be discerned in the landscape itself, where Irish trees take one
of two forms, dependent upon the landscape artist's treatment:
nobility or 'clumsy caricature'. Not only does character apparently
manifest itself in the land but also such character is distinguished by
similar qualities: malleability, duality, and extremeness. Croker thus
deliberately connects his discussion of national character with the
land while aestheticizing both. The artist's comment that nature
reveals the national character emphasizes the process of turning
nature into culture and applies this process to both the Irish world
and its occupants: both are framed in the manner of the picturesque.

Different impulses shape the construction of the Irish national
character at the beginning of the nineteenth century. First, a distanced perspective originated in both an emerging scientific view of
reality and a picturesque discourse. Second, this perspective led to
the discrimination of pattern and similarity. Types of people, like
kinds of animals or insects, might be categorized. Third, the privi-
leging of the peasant and his or her construction in reaction to
English stereotypes became important. Particularly interesting in this
process, because of its connection to caricature, is the insistence

throughout such studies of national character that the Irish nature incorporates extremes. Such extraordinary dimensions, as Croker suggests, require an artist's touch, a 'master hand' which will bring out the best of the cultural landscape and its occupants. Extreme realities require expert control.

The eighteenth-century cult of the picturesque, the transformation of nature into culture, has been described as a means of reclaiming a disappearing way of life in Britain. Aestheticizing the traditional, rural, and local – presenting natural scenes of varied detail – determined a specifically British way of perceiving nature from that of the French or the Dutch with their formally arranged landscapes and gardens.[32] In his discussion of the unique qualities of Ireland, Croker applies the aesthetic discourse of the British picturesque. The Corkman's casual reference in his second chapter, 'Scenery and Travelling', to Dr Syntax (a spoof of picturesque tourism called 'The Tour of Dr Syntax in Search of the Picturesque' by William Combe in 1809) suggests that *Researches in the South of Ireland* might be read as part of a more general trend of assuring national identity through objective means.

The conflation of nature and nation during the eighteenth and early nineteenth centuries emphasized the increasing awareness of Man's detachment from nature. Tabulating national characteristics, like the ordering of knowledge in histories and dictionaries, reflects a sense of distance from the natural world. For the scientific observer, nature became a stage or picture whence patterns and laws emerged. Collecting, distinguishing, and arranging types allowed one to perceive pattern in a nature clearly set apart from the gazer. Similarity rather than difference became significant: 'uniformity, not oddity, became the important feature of nature'.[33] Croker's observations, his list of the characteristics of the Irish peasants and his categorizing of their behaviour, follow scientific methods of sorting and arranging the natural world, in this case Ireland.

By the time Croker was publishing his folk material, the picturesque had acquired a political charge. The previous chapter has already noted how landscaping of some of the great Irish estates incorporated French models to reflect political beliefs at the end of the eighteenth century. Edward Fitzgerald of Frescati House and Valentine Lawless of Lyons House, for instance, 'looked to French rather than English landscape for inspiration; this choice was made from patriotic, and ultimately revolutionary loyalty'.[34] The French *ferme ornée*, which was adapted in Blackrock, Co. Dublin and the

Lyons demesne, Co. Kildare, expressed the 'radical enlightenment ideals of the French Revolution' and demonstrated how the 'correct management of a demesne made it beautiful, and not the reverse'.[35] In a similar way, description of the national landscape could express either a conservative or a radical view. After the French Revolution recuperating the loyal peasant retainer became a means of distinguishing the 'antique values – feudal fealty rather than commercial contract' of Jacobin ideology.[36] Thus, though Croker assures his reader that 'politics have been carefully avoided' in his researches, and that the establishment of national identity stands separate from political ideology, he still emphasizes a fierce patriotism and innate love of freedom in the Irish peasant. His emphasis suggests the Irishman's rebellious potential as much as it marks a trait of his character. In fact the main reason for the malleability of the Irish character, suggests Croker, might be accounted for by considering the weight of his unjust subjugation in the past. Croker's appendix of a frightening account of piked Protestants and murderous Catholic mobs of 1798 demonstrates the present-day effects of past oppression. The concluding narrative of peasant rebellion seems to contradict Croker's benign observations of peasant fairy belief and Irish hospitality. Yet the appendix reveals both extreme cruelty and extraordinary kindness on the part of the Irish rebels, thus exemplifying Croker's fundamental thesis on the national character. Croker does not merely distinguish racial differences; he directs attention to traits of the Irish Catholic national character that reflect a deep-seated fear in Protestant consciousness arising from the 1798 rebellion.[37] His evaluation of the extreme dimensions of the Irish national character depends upon a politically charged notion of the picturesque.

In Ireland, then, the observation of the peasant folk and the collection of their stories go further than social commentary. The peasant acted as 'a reservoir of raw material to be mined and cultivated: to be retrieved from its illiterate repository'.[38] The peasant provided national character and, as Joep Leerssen points out, was one of two cherished founts of Irish nationalist identity, the second being the myths of a pre-Norman past. The 'past and the peasant' were identified throughout the nineteenth century as aspects of Irish culture 'most distinctively un-English' and therefore privileged.[39] From the Irish peasant masses, whose traits are figured repeatedly throughout the nineteenth century, negative and positive stereotypes emerge. Moreover, the Irish peasant's central quality – an extreme of temperament – required equally extraordinary measures of control, and from the extreme manifestations of the Irish national character arises a figure that mirrors the peasantry's nature.

One version of this extraordinary authority type appears to have been a kind of folk legend in his time, a police magistrate called Thomas Vokes. While Croker conducted his researches in various parts of Ireland, Vokes exercised harsh measures of control in Limerick and Clare. The severity of his measures against crime, he claimed, was based on the extreme nature of the criminals, mainly agrarian agitators of the secret societies. Vokes would become the hero of a later fictionalized account of crime control in the Irish countryside, Henry Addison's *Recollections of an Irish Police Magistrate* (1862), which anticipates Somerville and Ross's Irish RM stories.

The evolution of the police magistrate type, his mirroring of the Irish folk and his movement from fact into fiction, shows us one possible source for the creation of the resident magistrate figure while also suggesting a connection between developing fiction and colonial policy in Ireland. In 1824, when Croker's *Researches* first appeared, Thomas Vokes was writing to Dublin Castle about the state of the country and how best to manage its character. His letters attest to swift reckonings of justice. In January he writes to the under-secretary, William Gregory (Sir William Gregory's grandfather and an opponent of Catholic emancipation), that 'as the crime of taking arms has been so often committed at and near this place I think any person charged with it ought to be held over for the assizes and if convicted, executed on the spot'. The next month he claims his measures to be effective: 'It will therefore appear to His Excellency that the Spirit of Insurrection is checked in this County and that in almost every instance the immediate apprehension of the offenders follows the Commission of Crime.' In June, Vokes speaks of the murder of a man by one 'who struck him with a stone and with a spade handle' over 'a dispute they had some time ago at a hurling match'. Then, in August, Vokes writes in some detail to a Castle official about the execution of members of the Whiteboys. He speaks of their remorse at the gallows, when surrounded by 'seven or eight priests', one of its leaders told the attendant audience that 'those ropes and scaffolds and gallows would be all idle if the people attended to the advice of their Priests and . . . it was not evidence nor information nor Laws that restored the Country to quiet but the influence of the Priests'.[40]

Thomas Vokes operated as 'a maverick figure within police circles . . . at the very edges of the law', and was feared by the people and disliked by fellow magistrates.[41] Nonetheless, forty years later, the Irish dragoon and playwright Henry Addison enthusiastically record-ed his hero's strong-arm strategies. Most likely Addison's stories appeared as a response to increased Fenian agitation of the 1860s. These narratives the author insists to be true. They bear witness to the early 1820s when Thomas Vokes successfully managed crime and thus provide examples of crime management. Addison published his work to provide incentive for the present-day police force in 'the sister country'.

Recollections of an Irish Police Magistrate is part of a more general discussion throughout the 1860s about the need to reform the police force in Ireland. It might be considered more closely here for two reasons. First, it raises a central question in relation to the Irish RM stories: does the later fiction also contribute to a more general dis-cussion on colonial policy and policing in late nineteenth-century Ireland? Second, it demonstrates a curious combination of fact and fiction which illustrates the developing nature of Irish short fiction.

In the 1860s the position of the resident magistrate, frequently occu-pied by country gentlemen who acted as head of that force, was under particular scrutiny because of Fenian unrest.[42] In *Recollections*, Addison argues for a vigorous and military-trained leader to occupy such a posi-tion. He believes that the successful handling of agrarian outrage depends upon the knowledge of Ireland possessed by the magistrates and landowners of that country. Vokes, whose hard-headedness and understanding of the Irish terrain and the 'bloodthirsty nature of the Irish peasantry'[43] enable him to capture Captain Rock single-handedly after pursuing him for three days and nights in 1822, demonstrates the significance of extraordinary ability in stamping out crime in Ireland. This fearsome figure provokes a dreadful hatred in the people:

> I must needs admit I would have willingly dissuaded Vokes from enter-ing the crowd, who, as he approached, gave three *groans* for him – a welcome they poured forth with all the venom of their souls, for many among them had reason to dread his power. The major took off his hat with a smile, and laughingly thanked them, then plunged into the midst of them.[44]

The violent undercurrent in descriptions of Vokes and the magis-trate's demonic attributes give a gothic dimension to the stories in

Addison's collection. Yet violence is contained and controlled in the stories. The 'blood-thirsty' peasantry is matched by a hard-hearted administration. In any case, the author stresses that these sketches are not fiction; the reader is asked to peruse them as a kind of manual of effective rule in the Irish countryside. The soldier/writer mounts a strategic attack on contemporary British colonial policy by observing crime management in relation to social behaviour in the past.

In a story called 'The Terry Alts', an instance of the government's mismanagement of outrage demonstrates the need for local administration. The sketch records how the secret society protests the diminishment of conacre by digging up thousands of acres of land in County Clare in 1830. The Lord Lieutenant arrives to address the people and reprimand the landowners in a bid for popular support. However, though the people laud the speaker, they defy his authority. That night members of the agrarian protest society arrive and dig up the four hundred acres surrounding the estate where the Viceroy has lodged. Vokes, who knew all along that 'blarney' would do little to effect change, urges the local magistrates to double their efforts. The story demonstrates the comic ineffectuality of Dublin Castle in appealing to the folk and the effectiveness of 'a proper degree of severity, mingled with strict justice' by the local magistrates in suppressing agrarian outrage.[45]

While Addison's sketches may be true to the spirit and intent of Vokes's administration in Limerick, the dramatist's inclinations influenced their form. According to the *Dublin University Magazine* in 1841, Henry Addison was 'as much adjutant as author: equally ready to improvise punch or poetry, to devise a devil or a drama'.[46] Major Vokes fulfils in part a dramatic role. Half-fiction and half-fact he faces agrarian outrage – dastardly deeds such as clocking a comrade with a spade handle or murdering a landowner over arms – and high farce, of actual historical fact and melodramatic device. Both character and action demonstrate the interplay of generic form.

Addison and his prolific farces have nearly vanished from literary view while the Draconian measures of Major Vokes are forgotten. Yet the fictionalization of social record in nineteenth-century Ireland attests to that heritage. Addison's sketches might be seen as part of British administrative reform of the mid-nineteenth century advocating a strong military presence while utilizing Vokes's violent measures for dramatic effect. They are as much historical records as they are fiction. Somerville and Ross's Irish RM stories might be seen in part as a response to this tradition.

Various types of incidents referred to in Vokes's letters reappear
regularly in nineteenth-century writing. The internecine violence
between sporting factions noted in Vokes's 1824 letter becomes
central in Addison's 1862 sketch and Somerville and Ross's 1898
'The Waters of Strife'. The similarity of the conception of peasant
behaviour in both public record and fiction may suggest a similarity
of intent on the part of the writers. Major Yeates also attempts to
maintain order among the unruly Irish (though, unlike Vokes, he
never succeeds). One might assume that Somerville and Ross (like
Addison perhaps – 'as much adjutant as author') also advocate British
involvement and argue the necessity of Anglo-Irish mediation, their
reason made even more acute by the Local Government Act of 1898
which significantly decreased unionist powers.[47] However, while
Somerville and Ross rely upon colonial discourse in their fiction,
they utilize it with a self-awareness encouraged by dynamic change
and genre development. In their own families they saw fiction over-
take fact. An interesting example of self-parody, a self-conscious representation of the self as caricature, might be drawn from the Martin
household when Robert Martin collaborated with E.A.P. Hobday on
a pantomime called *The Forty Thieves*, performed in the Queen's
Royal Theatre, Dublin on 23 August 1886. The work included a
police figure, and the late nineteenth-century burlesque version gives
an added dimension to the resident magistrate type. Martin Ross's
elder brother actually performed this character on stage in 1886. It
seems likely that Robert Martin's self-parody of colonial authority, as
much as Addison's violent Vokes, would have inspired Flurry Knox
or Major Yeates of Somerville and Ross's fiction.

Robert Martin played Cassim, an authority figure of multiple
roles:

> Mayor and Chief of the Police, Lord of the Manor,
>   Justice of the Peace . . .
> I fill a lot of offices, and what is more, I can,
>   Though it's needless perhaps to be told ye;
> I'm chief of the home service, I'm a grand militiaman,
>   Though I'm not very much of a soldier.
> I'm the chief Robert here – head policeman I am made –
>   . . . .
>
> A soldier and a peeler and civilian all in one.[48]

Robert Martin plays the fool. He is chopped into two pieces, sewn
back together again, and miraculously revives. The head policeman

manifests the clownish possibilities of the harlequinade. The humour of Chief Robert's address is doubled for his Anglo-Irish audience by the basis of his claims in reality. Robert Martin really *was* at one time a Justice of the Peace, 'a soldier and a peeler and civilian all in one'. However, as his youngest sister realized, he performed his role more successfully on stage in Dublin than he did at Ross House in Galway. Robert Martin may once have been lord of the manor, but when he died in 1905, aged 58, he left neither house nor heir and, as Gifford Lewis points out, his death marked 'the end of the line that connected the family of Martin with the house and lands of Ross'.[49] Robert Martin's fall showed acutely how times had changed, and the only place left for a landlord's posturing, it appears, was the comic stage. Reality had become fiction. The Anglo-Irish landlord had become a parody of himself. The re-enactment suggests that Robert Martin did not fade from the Irish landscape; rather, he reduced the postures of his inheritance to caricature.

The real Thomas Vokes of the early nineteenth century, Addison's half-fictional portrayal of the police magistrate, the real Robert Martin of Ross House, and his own self-parody provide a constellation of sources which suggests a dynamic of historical record as it works with artistic development. This network indicates that the kind of short fiction Somerville and Ross wrote in Ireland at the beginning of the new century reflects a complex tradition indebted to social conditions, political erosion, and generic transformation.[50] The Irish RM stories reflect both an aesthetic and a historical reality.

CARICATURE

> *Charge (Peinture & Belles-Lettr.) c'est la représentation sur la toile ou le papier, par le moyen des couleurs, d'une personne, d'une action, ou plus généralement d'un sujet, dans laquelle la vérité & la ressemblance exactes ne sont altérées que par l'excès du ridicule. L'art consiste à démêler* [unmasking] *le vice réel ou d'opinion qui était déjà dans quelque partie, et à le porter par l'expression jusqu'à ce point d'exagération où l'on reconnaît encore la chose, & au-delà duquel on ne la reconnaîtrait plus: alors la charge est la plus forte qu'il soit possible . . .*
>
> Diderot Encyclopédie, 3:202 (1751)[51]

The conception of Irish national character, then, appears to have been influenced by revolutionary change at the end of the eighteenth century. We might note, however, that the dates 1789 and 1798, indicators of French and Irish foment, also signify periods of change of another sort that would bear heavily on how character might be handled in the future. Champfleury (Jules Fleury) in *Histoire de la Caricature (1865–85)* dates modern caricature from the French Revolution.[52] Lithography, the art of printing form with ink and thus providing an immediate effect, was invented in 1798. During the early decades of the 1800s Balzac was working on his studies of physiognomic coding and character types in *La Comédie humaine*. Like a scientist, the detached observer applies a bird's-eye view to survey human nature:

> Newton, and also the great painter and the great musician, all are observers . . . those sublime birds of prey who, while rising to high regions, have the gift of seeing clearly in matters here below, who can at the same time abstract and specify, make exact analysis and just synthesis.[53]

A 'sublime bird of prey' achieves a panoramic view but with eagle-eyed vision can still distinguish difference. He is the 'doctor of social medicine'[54] and he is the artist: someone who sorts through all varieties of life and creates categories and divisions in nature. His perspective, as Balzac points out, is vital.

For Charles Baudelaire, the French Revolution introduced the conscious spectator, the *flâneur*, who sees his own reflection in the city scene. The man in the crowd participates in the action while observing it. His ability to immerse himself in the human comedy while noting its parts suggests his self-awareness. In Baudelaire's prose poem 'Le Miroir', *'un homme épouvantable'* looks at himself in the mirror, and when questioned about how he can endure to perceive his own ugliness answers that the Revolution of 1789 has given men the right to observe their own reflection, horrifying or otherwise:

> *L'homme épouvantable me répond: '–Monsieur, d'après les immortels principes de 89, tous les hommes sont égaux en droits; donc je possède le droit de me mirer; avec plaisir ou déplaisir, cela ne regarde que ma conscience.*[55]

Balzac's sublime bird of prey had become Baudelaire's private eye. The shift in perspective suggested by this comparison of the French writers might be usefully considered in the analysis of the development of modern caricature. However, before analysing modern caricature as it relates to the discussion on Somerville and Ross's use of Irish nation-

1 Henry Irving as Mephistopheles.

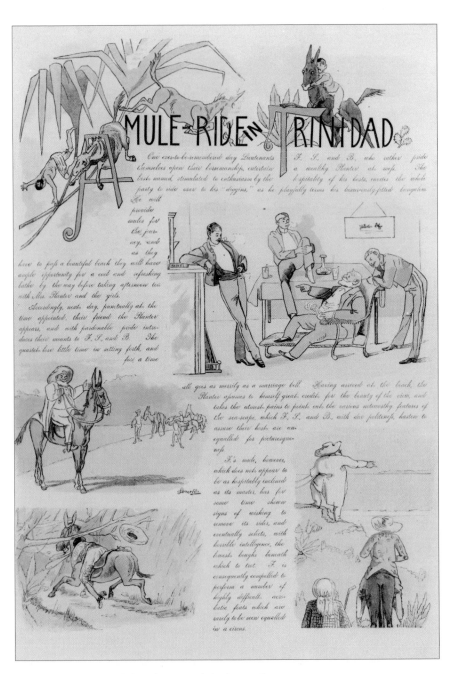

2 Edith Somerville, *A Mule Ride in Trinidad*, *The Graphic* (1888).

After their own dip the Planter suggests to Messrs. J., S., and B. that they should "swim the mules." His visitors comply with alacrity, but unfortunately J.'s mule very distinctly intimates that he would rather not. For some time it appears as though patience and perseverance were to have their due reward. J. is temporarily triumphant, but, having forced his mule into the water, the wily animal suddenly changes its tactics, and rolls.

The British soldier never accepts a defeat, and, acting upon this unalterable military axiom, J. mounts again, but even then entertains grave doubts as to the permanency of his position.

The mule's bridle and headstall having come off, the animal finds itself complete master of the situation; and determined to make the most of its victory, bolts for its own stable, and conveys the reluctant J. past the scene of his prospective tea-party, where his appearance excites hilarity rather than the sympathy which its owner doubtedly deserved.

This is the general aspect of affairs as J. dashes by the Planter's "diggins," where he had hoped to have been so hospitably and pleasantly entertained. His sufferings are considerably augmented by the unexpected presence of his hated rival, already installed at the tea table. At the stable door the mule stops abruptly, in its wild career, and J.'s Mazeppa-like ride comes to an end, his spirited finish being hailed with great delight by the grinning stable boy, who, however, is most profuse in his expression of concern at the gallant officer's ill fortune.

Next the serious question of costume presents itself to J. and our last sketch will give some idea of the humiliating appearance of J. dressed like a heathen in a vest by "voluntary subscriptions."

N.B. The boots are a kind loan from Mrs Planter.

He goes home by the shortest possible cut, without waiting for tea.

3 Edith Somerville, cover design of *The Kerry Recruit* (1889).

4 Edith Somerville, 'Owner of the Mare, the Mountain Hare' and 'Mrs. Cadogan' from *Some Experiences of an Irish RM*.

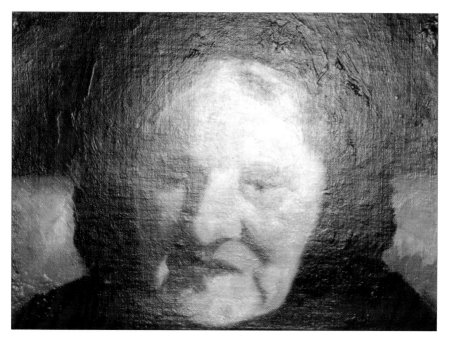

5 Edith Somerville, *Mrs. Kerr* (ca. 1888).

6 John Leech, 'The Claddagh—Galway', frontispiece, *A Little Tour in Ireland* by 'An Oxonian' (1859).

7 Edith Somerville, illustrations from *A Patrick's Day Hunt* by Martin Ross (1902).

8 Edith Somerville, Study of a Cow (no date).

9 Edith Somerville, illustration from *The Story of the Discontented Little Elephant* (1912).

10 Jack Butler Yeats, *This Grand Conversation Was Under the Rose* (1943).

al character, we might look more closely at the nature of caricature itself.

Caricature is related to the concept of unmasking. *Charge*, a synonym of 'caricature' in eighteenth-century France, depends upon the revelation of real or reputed vice for its effect. *Charge* or caricature differs from the grotesque in that the grotesque does not distort something already inherent but instead creates deformities. Caricature merely lifts the veil masking a distortion, real or imagined. Edith Somerville's caricatures include drawings of faces with exaggerated features or pictures of shuffling old men in bedraggled dress and crooked old women in shawls who suggest the lesser conditions of Irish life. Somerville and Ross's writing also indicates the troubling realities at the heart of Irish matters. *Démêler*, unmasking, is the essential component of *The Real Charlotte* and becomes increasingly important in Somerville and Ross's short fiction, where the plots frequently revolve around the unveiling of a character's mask (the Widow's deception in the courtroom in 'The Waters of Strife', James Canty's elaborate pretence in 'Holy Island', or the various costumes employed by characters in 'A Royal Command' or 'The Comte De Pralines').

Freud says that unmasking occurs 'where someone has attached to himself dignity and authority which in reality should be taken from him'.[56] He sees unmasking as the 'practical counterpart' of caricature, which he describes as exaggerated imitation; both unmasking and caricature 'range themselves against persons and objects who command authority and respect and who are exalted in some sense – these are procedures tending towards degradation'. Unmasking brings us down to earth; it reminds us, says Freud, that 'this or that one who is admired like a demigod is only a human being like you and me after all'.[57] The elongated nose of some well-known caricatured face allows us to see the weakness of humanity, and this process also occurs in comic writing. In Somerville and Ross's magazine stories the Irish rustics swiftly unmask pompous English visitors like the 'mere Englishman' of 'The Grand Filly' who lands in a pile of manure. In an early Irish RM story, 'Lisheen Races, Second-Hand', Slipper the clown and Driscoll his fool expose the utter vacuity and vanity of the Honourable Basil Leigh Kelway. By the end of the story the sanctimonious Basil Kelway ends up doused by the rain and as 'scuttered' as Slipper, as vulnerable as any other man to the effects of the Irish weather and Irish drink.

The exaggerated depiction of character apparent in nineteenth-century Irish writing has also been ascribed to the conditions of Irish life. Charles Robert Maturin, like his contemporary Lady Morgan, noted that extreme realities determined his method of 'painting life'. In his opening dedication in *The Milesian Chief* (1812), Maturin claimed that his chiaroscuro techniques suited the sublime Irish landscape:

> If I possess any talent, it is that of darkening the gloomy, and of deepening the sad; of painting life in the extremes, and representing those struggles of passion when the soul *trembles on the verge* of the unlawful and the unhallowed.
>
>   In the following pages I have tried to apply these powers to the scenes of actual life: and I have chosen my own country for the scene, because I believe it the only country on earth, where, from the strange existing opposition of religion, politics, and manners, the extremes of refinement and barbarism are united, and the most wild and incredible situations of romantic story are hourly passing before modern eyes. [my italics][58]

A key word for Maturin, one that becomes especially important in *Melmoth the Wanderer* (and one that Baudelaire takes up fifty years later in his study on caricature) is the word 'trembles'. Wavering between extremes, the position of existing in two places at one time fascinates Maturin. In the same way, Lady Morgan in *Florence Macarthy* (1818) and Sheridan Le Fanu in *Uncle Silas* (1864) are enthralled by their characters' 'shifting faces', faces that slip in and out of different masks. Lady Morgan ascribes the ever-changing identity of her heroine to Irish conditions. As Florence Macarthy points out,

> I sometimes almost lose my own identity for I am absolutely beyond my own control, and the mere creature of circumstances, giving out properties of certain plants, according to the region in which I am placed; and resembling in blossom that of the Chinese shrub, which is red in the sunshine and white in the shade, and fades and revives under the influence of the peculiar atmosphere in which it is accidentally placed. The strong extremes and wild vicissitudes of my life have perhaps given a variegated tone to my character, and a versatility to my mind, not its natural endowments.[59]

Irish novelists note how the extreme conditions of Irish life affect characterization. Emphasis rests on a trembling or wavering position that can manifest itself as a masking/unmasking process.

Maturin most successfully depicts a character trembling on the edge of an abyss, forever posed between extreme conditions, with

Melmoth. This extraordinary character, like James Clarence Mangan's Wandering Jew, is 'prohibited repose from life'. As Mangan tells us, such a figure remains outside the dictates of time and is never 'to be vouchsafed the boon of Death'.[60] Having sold his soul to the devil, Maturin's Melmoth leaves Ireland to range the world in search of some desperate man or woman who will take his place. Neither time nor space impedes his journey; he wanders across Europe, recognized by all men, and he wanders across time, never changing or growing old. His manifestation results from the wild and extreme contradictions of Irish life that bring forth a trembling or wavering position best demonstrated by ambivalence.

Maturin's novel appeared two years after Lady Morgan's national tale, *Florence Macarthy*. Both works employ Enlightenment philosophy on the Nature of the Sublime and the Beautiful as it relates to character or race;[61] they superimpose the sublime scenery of the Italian painter Salvator Rosa upon Irish scenery. The writers translate Salvator Rosa's visual language – groups of *banditti* half-hidden under dark masses of looming rock, for example – into the elaborate descriptions of their novels. Both rely upon the heightened dramatic effects of chiaroscuro in their descriptions of moonlit crumbling abbeys and night-time storms at sea. In Maturin's *Melmoth*, chiaroscuro as a writerly technique emphasizes the Manichaean vision of the text. Similarly national character becomes a site of extraordinary dimensions manifested by the sublime.[62] For Maturin the extremities of Melmoth's nature recalled the Irish national character.

For Charles Baudelaire, however, Melmoth manifested the paradoxical nature of caricature. Baudelaire saw Melmoth's in-between position as illustrative of emerging concepts of art. In 'De l'essence du rire', a wavering or trembling position identifies caricature: '*Le Sage ne rit qu'en tremblant*'.[63] The Sage laughs while trembling only in the full knowledge of the evil his humour courts. It is as though he stands on the edge of a cliff, contemplating his inevitable fall and forever wavering. Knowledge, like the demon's shuddering comprehension of God, produces his wild laughter. Caricature results from knowledge. A knowing art, self-conscious and self-reflective, caricature reveals a progression from innocent realism to experienced exaggeration.

Baudelaire's description of the 'essence of laughter' identifies the primary ingredient of caricature as an anxious or trembling knowledge of the ways of the world. The child or the pure innocent – the whole person – cannot laugh. Only those like Melmoth, the '*célèbre voyageur . . . la grande création satanique du révérend Maturin*',[64] possess this 'mask which hides the convulsed and distorted features of agony', and a laugh 'which never yet was the expression of rapture . . . [being] the only intelligible language of madness and misery'.[65] Laughter, says Baudelaire, can be, on one hand, a sure sign of man's inherent evil. On the other hand, it merely indicates one's supposed superiority. It demonstrates an unconscious, arrogant pride at the heart of him who laughs which causes mirth, a belief that '*ce n'est pas* moi *qui commetrais la sottise de ne pas voir un trottoir interrompu ou un pavé qui barre le chemin*'.[66]

The best exemplar of the mixed nature of laughter and its source in pride is Melmoth, an Irish Mephisto, who laughs because of 'his dual and contradictory nature, which is infinitely great in relation to man, infinitely vile and base in relation to absolute truth and righteousness. Melmoth is a living contradiction.'[67] Melmoth's anguished laughter does not spring from gaiety or joy. Its ambivalence represents a knowing apprehension of the world in its entirety, both innocence and experience; it conceals underlying pain.

Like caricature, stereotype originates in knowledge. Homi Bhabha identifies stereotype, the repeated 'articulation of difference', as deriving from fear produced by the awareness of difference in the Other which threatens a sense of purity or wholeness.[68] Anxiety determines the repetition of the stereotype. The colonizer, says Bhabha, fixates upon a trait of difference such as skin or nose and repeatedly visualizes that difference to establish his own purity. This 'anxiety associated with lack or difference' is based on 'the desire for an originality which is . . . threatened by the differences of race, colour and culture'.[69] The ambivalence of the stereotype lies in its constancy of something known and its need for repetition.

Both Baudelaire's nineteenth-century analysis of caricature and Bhabha's recent study of stereotype describe such forms of the comic as based on the lack of wholeness or purity. We laugh anxiously at caricature because we have sinned (Baudelaire), or we use stereotype because we fear sinning and the consequent loss of wholeness (Bhabha). Both conditions are predicated on an understanding of loss. With the second condition, Bhabha stresses race difference and the threatened colonial identity as energizing the stereotyping process. Undoubtedly racial, economic and religious stereotyping determines caricature, what might be described as 'symbolic violence: the negative portrayal of another sub-group or group for the purpose of defining the self group in a positive way'.[70] While French theory on caricature and the development of genre show that other considerations inform this method of depicting character, race-politics, in particular the simianization of the Irish character in the British periodicals, adds to our understanding of Somerville and Ross's treatment of caricature.

To consider race as it relates to the aesthetics of caricature reveals more than what Perry Curtis has described as 'Hibernophobia' in Victorian caricature of the Irish.[71] Curtis demonstrates how popular English illustration depicted the Irish in an idealized or demonized way. He argues that the simianization of the Irish, indicated through physiognomic coding and influenced by social Darwinism, works as a form of cultural imperialism.[72] Equally significant, however, is the peculiar suitability of the Irish national character to the extremes of black and white effect. Curtis has shown how Victorian caricaturists co-opted race and politics as a means of deploying such extremes. But what worked better in the late nineteenth century as a figuration of binary extremes of black and white than Irish politics and colonial policy?[73] Moreover, the transformation of the Irishman into what Curtis has described as the 'white negro' suggests a paradox we also find in chiaroscuro.[74] Race, and especially the apparent difference of the black and white races – the 'fact of blackness' in the face of whiteness[75] – suggests that the play of black and white in visual terms found appropriate subject matter in the extreme situations posed by Irish conditions.

As already noted, the contrast of black and white works like a Manichaean paradox; it is its visual equivalent. The darkness of the sublime and the light of beauty stand in eternal opposition. Chiaroscuro (bright–dark) utilizes this visual paradox. Chiaroscuro is the distribution of light and shade in a composition: light emphasizes the dark just as the deep tones of the latter highlight the former. In black and white caricature, chiaroscuro is utilized for dramatic effect and the extremes deliberately play one upon the other. The term, like an elaborate conceit, yokes polarities as one. Blackness renders light.

Black and white illustration inevitably relies on the chiaroscuro style, an abbreviated and nuanced technique of rendering reality. In France at the end of the century, black and white art developed alongside Impressionism. Thus while George Moore argued that modern French painters had 'dispense[d] altogether with shadow' and had 'scattered' 'veil after veil' that had darkened a landscape still shrouded in medieval belief, he did not consider developments in illustration.[76] Edith Somerville, however, was as much influenced by developments in illustration as in painting while she was in Paris. The new black and white style interested her especially, and her first illustration using the carbon pencil method appeared in *The Irish Homestead* in 1899.

Developments in illustration coincided with the growing interest in a form that the periodical press preferred at this time: the short story. The highly suggestive nature of chiaroscuro, a technique that relies upon the viewer's ability to discern in the darkness everything which is not depicted, anticipates the use of implication in modern short fiction, the reliance upon the reader to imagine in the spaces of the text all else that has happened in the story. Depictions of Irishness, with its black and white national traits – 'extremes of refinement and barbarism'[77] – translate well into this particular shorthand. In the same way, and as Henry James in an echo of Baudelaire concludes, caricature requires a discriminating viewer/reader who can recognize the shorthand of the technique:

> A society has to be old before it becomes critical, and it has to become critical before it can take pleasure in the reproduction of its incongruities by an instrument as impertinent as the indefatigable crayon. Irony, scepticism, pessimism are, in any particular soil, plants of gradual growth, and it is in the art of caricature that they flower most aggressively. Furthermore they must be watered by education – I mean the education of the eye and the hand – all of which takes time. The soil must be rich too, the incongruities must swarm.[78]

The vast outpouring of nineteenth-century periodical literature, its illustrations and text, educated readers in the appreciation of new forms and increased their knowledge of types.

In addition to market developments and a knowing audience appeared an equally aware artist or writer alert to the fact that the frequent trading of types and borrowing of masks in a fast-moving industry challenged notions of originality and authorship. Irish writers who worked closely with the periodical press, like Somerville and Ross or Oscar Wilde, would also have been aware of an Anglo-Irish tradition that questioned the idea of authenticity in the manner of the romantic ironist. To demonstrate we might turn one final time to Charles Maturin's *Melmoth* and Clarence Mangan's ensuing revival of the Irish devil to show how this demonic figure is refracted in different ways by the Irish writers of the *fin de siècle* period.

As already noted, Maturin's Melmoth illustrated the strange ambiguities emerging in a changing world dominated by middle-class interest for Honoré de Balzac. The French writer situated the wandering figure amid crass materialist venture and consequent forgery in

Paris. In 1838 Mangan plagiarized Balzac's version of Melmoth's story for the *Dublin University Magazine*.[79] Slight but significant changes in 'The Man in the Cloak: A Very German Story' serve to make Melmoth more Irish, nearly as if he is being rehabilitated as much as reconciled. However, like Balzac, Mangan situates his story in a bank to allow for the protagonist's attempted forgery. Thus Mangan's forgery about forgery provides a playful mirror version while staking a prior claim. Mangan 'sees through his author, as through glass, but corrects all the distortions produced by the refraction of the substance through which he looks'. The plagiarism revivifies the translated material; the translator has 'created a soul under the ribs of . . . Death' and has become no less than the 'real author' of Melmoth.[80]

In a similar way, and at the end of the century, a Protestant version of Melmoth returns to France when the wandering homosexual outcast Oscar Wilde converts to Catholicism and dies in Paris. Oscar Wilde/Sebastian Melmoth follows the fate of his fictional predecessor and becomes reconciled to a Catholic fate. If we turn to Somerville and Ross, we see yet another recreation of Melmoth's story. In this instance an unreconciled version of the wandering Anglo-Irishman can be located in the Protestant comic world of the Irish RM stories. The Irish devil, as shown overleaf, is reduced to the harlequin figure in the comic material.

Somerville and Ross's self-consciousness broadly reflects the satanic school that influenced the developments in fiction and the visual art of the *fin de siècle*. Both Somerville and Ross enjoyed Beardsley's stylized illustrations of clowns and harlequins published in *The Yellow Book* and *The Savoy*. Somerville thought *The Savoy* especially interesting and Martin Ross praised 'two awfully good pictures of Aubrey B.' in its last issue.[81] These black and white pictures of theatrical productions, like Yeats's 'poems concerning peasant visionaries', retrieve a popular, non-literary tradition.[82] The viewer/reader, however, is twice removed from that tradition by the artists' distancing devices. Beardsley's design cover for the first issue shows Pierrot on stage (in the published version, Pierrot is changed into a simpering John Bull), the curtain lowered behind him in wait for the opening 'scenes' of the periodical: Yeats's highly stylized 'Rosa Alchemica', Arthur Symons's 'In Carnival' and essays on Millais and Verlaine, George Moore's translation of Stéphane Mallarmé – a series of artful displays of art. Beardsley's illustrations are pictures of figures framed by the draping sweep of a plush theatre curtain. Pierrot and

FIGURE 4.1. Aubrey Beardsley, *The Death of Pierrot*, *The Savoy*, 6 (October 1896)

Harlequin are masque characters masked.

The caricaturist Max Beerbohm describes conversation at the dinner launching *The Savoy* as a display of seemingly self-contradictory
interests. Yeats monopolizes Beardsley in conversation on French
diabolism. Symons, interrupting his enjoyment of *Bombe glacée à la
Vénitienne*, comments on the importance of travel and change in the
artist's life. Yeats, 'in a pause in his own music', swiftly rebuts
Symons and recalls Wilde when he says that the artist works best
'among his own folk and in the land of his fathers'.[83] Beerbohm pin-
points the main interests (other than the French menu) at the Savoy
dining table: French diabolism and Irish folk material – hell and
hearth. Thus the final number Martin Ross mentions includes

Symons's translation of Mallarmé's 'Hérodiade' and his travel essay, 'The Isles of Aran'. Beardsley's black and white illustrations also incorporate popular folk material and the French diabolism of symbolic decadence. His pictures span two worlds, the earthy comedy of carnival and the aesthetic vision of symbolism. The flat black line delineating white space demonstrates the extreme limits which the material straddles.

Beardsley's harlequin, clown, and pierrot, depicted on a theatre platform as stylized groups of black and white effect, appear to be the stage figures of the popular pantomime. They are that, of course, but they are something more, as a closer look reveals. Concealed in Columbine's skirt is an over-sized penis, while Pierrot's imminent death foreshadows a grim end to the ensuing farce. While these figures appear to be those we readily identify with pantomime, they actually manifest something new. Similarly Somerville and Ross's comic figures may appear to continue a tradition of stage-Irish figures. Yet the antics of Flurry and his mob owe more to the playful realm that Beardsley explored – the harlequinade – than they do to Handy Andy and Mickey Free. Their Irish caricatures are modern versions of stage types. Harlequin's history in particular indicates a central comic source for Somerville and Ross. Already in previous chapters I have noted the importance of burlesque and pantomime in the writers' novels. Closer study of pantomime's key figure reveals its workings in their short fiction.

Harlequin is a hybrid figure whose background mixes malevolent forces and comic fun. He appeared first in popular legend as a devil 'leading that ghostly nocturnal cortege known as the Wild Hunt'.[84] His original devilish aspect never quite faded when he later appeared in the *commedia dell'arte* in the guise of a comic acrobat dressed in motley with a black mask, carrying a bat and wearing a hat with a fox's tail. He was of uncertain nationality and possessed a chameleon-like nature.[85] Bakhtin speaks of a late sixteenth-century work performed in Paris called *The Gay Story of the Feats and Adventures of the Italian Comedian, Harlequin*. Harlequin's descent into hell is mirrored by his acrobatic postures down below:

> In hell Harlequin turns somersaults, leaps and skips, sticks out his tongue and makes Charon and Pluto laugh. All these gay leaps and bounds are as ambivalent as the underworld itself. Harlequin's somersaults are topographical; their points of orientation are heaven, earth, the underworld, the top and the bottom. They present an interplay, a

substitution of the face by the buttocks; in other words, the theme of
the descent into hell is implicit in this simple acrobatic feat.[86]

In later French works of the eighteenth century the servant Arlequin
is transformed in Arcadia into the natural man (one who can teach his
master many lessons based on his natural experience). In England
during this period the comic John Rich developed a form of
pantomime which became its basic structure: the first part of the pantomime contained a serious theme from mythology or legend, while
the second part dealt with Harlequin and Columbine's love affair.
Obstacles, such as attentions from the rival suitor, Pantaloon, obstruct
the successful course of love. Harlequin must use his magic bat to
effect transformations and enchantments to secure his Columbine.[87]
The harlequinade involves the antics, tricks and acrobatics of familiar
figures, which reappear essentially unchanged in different pantomimes.[88]

Unlike comedy, which tends to focus on a specific subject to satirize or burlesque, a precise 'quarry' to bring down, pantomime
prefers to pursue or 'hunt' multiple topics: a mixed bag of issues and
matters of the day.[89] The hunt always used the same characters:
Harlequin (Flurry), Columbine (Sally Knox), Clown (Slipper), and
Pantaloon (Bernard Shute). In pantomime after pantomime (just as
in story after story of the Irish RM series) these figures appear, and
their familiar antics introduce unfamiliar game or quarry. The pantomime is a particularly useful means of bringing together a rattle-
bag of material.

Harlequin's pervasive presence in the early nineteenth century
attests to his ability to adapt to all sorts of material; his versatility and
mixed background make him both a stock comic character and a
strangely fluid cypher that spans in his nature extreme differences.
Like Melmoth in Maturin's novel, Harlequin wanders Europe, a figure in every play, the culprit on every stage. He is the devil and he is
our comic saviour. He wavers between extremes and his motley costume never admits allegiance to any dimension. He trembles forever
in between. Unlike Melmoth, however, he comes from a world of
greasepaint and farce.

Harlequin is a stage figure and, like the festival fool, is part of carnival time, when normality collapses and the *Prince des Sots* reigns
supreme. Everything is topsy-turvy so that the hierarchy reverses itself
and all is in disarray. The Lord of Misrule or the festival fool is another kind of middleman, one who combines the foolishness of the

buffoon with the wit of the satirist.[90] But Harlequin 'is wholly a creature of make-believe'. He does not possess 'religious significance or subversive tendencies' because he emerges from nowhere and has no allegiance to any domain.[91] Harlequin is a figure of the stage, the product of the theatre rather than the popular imagination. He is the stuff of pure artifice.

In many of the Irish RM stories Flurry Knox plays Harlequin. He dances, fools, and falls in love. He introduces a madcap world not unlike that which Baudelaire describes in 'De l'essence du rire' as *'la frontière du merveilleux'*, which is the delirium of the harlequinade.[92] More insidiously, he rides like a madman across the precarious landscape of the Irish RM stories where 'boggy holes of any depth, ranging between two feet and half-way to Australia' await his foolish followers.[93] Leading the wild Irish hunt Flurry creates a kind of madness with his whirling whip and unpredictable temper. Like an acrobat he leaps stone walls and grassy banks, and like a chameleon he waits attendance on the highest and lowest of the land. He is the natural man, the man of the people, who teaches his master/tenant a thing or two about the real world. He is eminently adaptable and cannot be described as a stage Irishman – he is much less, a mask reflecting distorted versions of Anglo-Irish life. He is the product of pantomime and the result of caricature.

Story after story of the Irish RM series employs pantomime material. In 'A Royal Command' in *Further Experiences*, Slipper appears to the half-blind Yeates as 'a coloured potentate, the Sultan of X—', and a funeral group in black and with weepered hats ends up chasing an escaped filly in harlequinade fashion. In 'Sharper than a Ferret's Tooth' in the same collection, the boat carrying a picnic party capsizes and Major Yeates, Philippa, and Sally Knox are transformed by the McRory's fabulous clothes. Sally Knox's slight figure appears foolish in a heavily brocaded purple gown, and the dismayed picnickers dine on trifle swimming in whiskey and a 'soup tureen full of custard'.[94] The stories' mythological allusions, such as Flurry's possible incarnation as the 'Lord of Animals', Dionysus, that Roz Cowman notes,[95] come mixed with political references and topical material that can be best appreciated when perceived as issuing from a pantomime tradition.

In the same way, the caricatures of the Irish RM stories gain in significance if compared to the clowns of carnival. The Irish RM characters do not reflect reality, they distort it. They serve as easily recognized ciphers that recall the figures of the circus or the public

FIGURE 4.2. Edith Somerville, illustrations from *The Irish RM*

square. As Bakhtin notes, these timeless carnival figures work as universal symbols that cannot be translated literally:

> The rogue, the clown and the fool create around themselves their own special little world, their own chronotope . . . . These characters carry with them into literature first a vital connection with the theatrical trappings of the public square, with the mask of the public spectacle; they are connected with that highly specific, extremely important area of the square where the common people congregate; second . . . the very being of these figures does not have a direct, but rather a metaphorical, significance. Their very appearance, everything they do and say, cannot be understood in a direct and unmediated way but must be grasped metaphorically. Sometimes their significance can be reversed – but one cannot take them literally, because they are not what they seem. Third . . . their existence is a reflection of some other's mode of being – and even then, not a direct reflection. They are life's maskers; their being coincides with their role, and outside this role they simply do not exist.[96]

The members of the harlequinade are masks that act as distorted reflections of the world. They are warped mirrors (like Beardsley's grotesques or like Jack Yeats's circus figures). They issue from popular theatre and cannot be understood as simple characters. Moreover, Harlequin, the leader of the harlequinade, brings with his mask a modern ambiguity and lends to Somerville and Ross's comic writing an elusive dimension.

If Flurry Knox is Harlequin, both a mask of carnival and a modern theatrical figure, he heralds both popular farce and the idea itself of modern caricature. His courtship of Sally Knox in *Some Experiences* repeats the familiar pattern of the harlequinade. Their reign as a married couple in *Further Experiences* establishes their position. The Knoxes introduce a suspended time zone where clowns and fools ring the changes. By using exaggerated movements and masked appearances they transform character to caricature. Their high jinks and humour are accompanied by Somerville's seventy black and white illustrations. These pictures of clowns and carnival not only assist in the storytelling but also indicate with their use of graphic art the nature of Harlequin (or Flurry Knox).

Baudelaire describes pantomime as the essence of the comic in 'De l'essence du rire', its *'l'épuration'* or distillation: *'La pantomime est l'épuration de la comédie; c'en est la quintessence; c'est l'élément comique pur, dégagé et concentré'.*[97] If pantomime is the distillation of comedy, then Harlequin as the leader of that form might be described as a distillation of Melmoth, the manifestation of the comic sense. In Ireland his features come charged with a colonial and a political significance. In the Irish RM stories he calls himself Flurry Knox.

PART THREE
LANDSCAPING IN *THE IRISH RM*

CHAPTER 5

History: Picturing the Past

When something like a decade has been expended in explaining Ireland by skilful newspaper writing, by writing less skilful but more direct, by speeches diplomatic & fine, & by coarser declamatory bellowings, that she is oppressed of the oppressor, who can wonder, or very much blame, if the hearers of such things believe England's only role *in history to be that of Ireland's tyrant.*

MARTIN ROSS, 1889

In 1889 Martin Ross lamented the absence of History in Ireland's national schools. She argued that popular polemics had replaced factual record and consequently reduced the Irish–English relationship to only one kind of interaction, that of oppressor and oppressed.[1] A decade later she and her cousin lampooned romanticized versions of the past that stood in the place of historical record in a series of short stories called *Some Experiences of an Irish RM*. Somerville and Ross directed their satire at the notion that only one point of view or one image/myth might represent the Irish landscape. Their suggestion that more than one perspective might exist in the representation of reality coincided with new treatments of perspective in the arts.

Somerville and Ross's agent, James Pinker, represented at least two writers (Joseph Conrad and Stephen Crane) who have been situated as modernists working to develop fiction, including the modern short story. Somerville and Ross, however, tend to be seen as Victorians whose venture into short fiction was motivated by commercial interests alone. Yet the Irish writers published at the same time as Conrad and in similar periodicals like *Blackwood's Magazine*, and their interests included combining textual and visual material in new ways. So even though Somerville and Ross may not be described as modernist they still were intent on developing the magazine story and took special interest in a pictorial tradition, self-consciously incorporating into short fiction techniques of the visual arts. They published in prominent English periodicals and wrote stories that satisfied their readers in one sitting, to achieve a 'single effect', which Edgar Allan Poe described as vital to the shorter form.[2] However the Irish women writers' popular and anecdotal short stories were quite different to the so-called literary story that Frank O'Connor would later identify as 'modern' in *The Lonely Voice*.[3] Somerville and Ross were more interested in the collective than the lonely voice, but they also paid attention to modern developments. Their work drew attention to picture-making by exploring point of view (as employed with impressionistic effect in Stephen Crane's 'The Open Boat', a work Martin Ross especially enjoyed),[4] or using both text and illustration to tell a story (as in their Irish RM stories), or demanding like Conrad that 'fiction – if it at all aspires to be art . . . must strenuously aspire to the plasticity of sculpture, to the colour of painting, and to the magic suggestiveness of music'.[5] They took special interest in using visual techniques in literary form.

As already argued, Somerville and Ross employed a pictorial aesthetic in the text as well as in the illustrations of the Irish RM stories. Flurry Knox might be seen as a kind of harlequin figure, and the simple lines of his character, like black and white illustration, suggest modern notions of caricature as propagated in French theory. Just as interesting as Flurry's character, however, is the world he introduces in various Irish RM stories, especially in the first series from *Badminton Magazine*, where we see the extent to which the authors play with perspective. Their attack on single-faceted versions of the past as conveyed by the monument, the ballad, or the portrait becomes especially evident if we consider their approach not just to Ireland but across the water to Scotland. Somerville and Ross resist a particular sense of history, a sense demonstrated in *Ulysses*, when Michelangelo's Moses is described as a 'stone effigy in frozen music'. The man describing Michelangelo's marble statue as 'horned and terrible, of the human form divine, that eternal symbol of wisdom and prophecy' is Seymour Bushe, grandson of Charles Kendal Bushe, who presided as Lord Chief Justice of Ireland at the end of the eighteenth century. Somerville and Ross were also descended from the Lord Chief Justice; Seymour was their cousin. The last was renowned for his magnificent rhetorical flourishes. In Aeolus of *Ulysses*, the failed solicitor and occasional contributor to the newspapers, J.J. O'Molloy, quotes the lawyer's description of the statue. It is, he tells Stephen Dedalus, a 'most polished period', and his rendition of silver-tongued Bushe's oratory arouses to admiration the young Dedalus:

> The stone effigy in frozen music, horned and terrible, of the human form divine, that eternal symbol of wisdom and of prophecy which, if aught that the imagination or the hand of sculptor has wrought in marble of soultransfigured and of soultransfiguring deserves to live, deserves to live.[6]

The idea that the artistic representation – the statue, the portrait, the ballad – somehow freezes the soul in flight and isolates in one, epiphanic moment the essential spirit of the time and place is an idea which the grandchildren of Ninety-eight inherited.

The months leading up to the centennial year of the 1798 rebellion were marked for Somerville and Ross by an increasing awareness of Irish revivalism fostered by Douglas Hyde and Lady Gregory. Douglas Hyde encouraged the writers to collect folk material from Irish-speaking storytellers of the Cork region. In January 1897 Hyde wrote to Edith Somerville to draw her attention to a local Cork storyteller named Curly Minihane. He urged her to collect stories and to learn Irish using grammar booklets by his friend, professor of Irish at Maynooth, St. Patrick's College, Father Eugene O'Growney.[7] From February until June, Somerville and Ross studied Irish at home in Castletownshend, and during this time Hyde sent them his folk stories and a lecture on Irish folklore.[8] Lady Gregory also started learning Irish this year, and in the summer Douglas Hyde visited her at Coole where she assisted him in collecting folk material.[9]

Business in London interrupted Somerville and Ross's Irish lessons that spring. Edith Somerville met with Pinker, the editors of *Badminton Magazine*, and publishers Lawrence and Bullen to discuss their forthcoming novel, *The Silver Fox*, and some recent magazine stories. As already noted, the Englishmen 'raved' about a piece called 'The Grand Filly'; they loved this 'comic Irish business'.[10] That summer Somerville and Ross gave up Irish and left for France where Edith Somerville painted and they both devised the characters and situations of *Some Experiences of an Irish RM*.

Somerville and Ross would return to study Irish in later years, but in 1897 they chose to pursue their interests in art and short fiction. While Lady Gregory and Yeats, inspired in part by Douglas Hyde's enthusiasm, conspired to create a Celtic Mecca in Dublin that summer with the Irish Literary Theatre,[11] Somerville and Ross channelled their energies into comic short stories. Their concentration on satire may have been encouraged in part by the Local Government Act of 1898, which altered significantly the balance of power in southern Ireland. Control shifted from the grand juries to local government through county councils, rural district councils, and boards of guardians. Nationalists began to replace unionists as the elections of March 1899 indicated: nationalists won about 75 per cent of county council seats and southern landlords lost out.[12] By the 1900s Martin Ross associated the Gaelic League with divisive nationalist factions, although she and Edith Somerville kept up correspondence with Douglas Hyde and maintained contact with those involved with the developing Irish Literary Theatre. Instead of concentrating on Irish, they continued to record overheard stories, expressions and sayings in their *Collected Irish Anecdotes*. Although they had started this collection as a basis for their writing in 1886, the extensive use of Irish-English in their fiction did not become fully apparent until the Irish RM stories appeared.[13] Their increasing interest in incorporating in their fiction a language they describe as 'a fabric built by Irish architects with English bricks',[14] in other words, a hybrid tongue resulting from transculturation in Ireland, might be seen as a reaction to the politicization of the language question. Their increased concentration on the peasantry and the subversion of their idealization in the Irish RM stories might also be seen as a reaction to the politicization of the Irish scene.

The year the Irish RM stories appeared in *Badminton Magazine*, Lady Gregory published 'Ireland, Real and Ideal' in *The Nineteenth Century*. The article defends the Irish peasant who for too long has worn the mask of 'boastful adventurer' or 'rollicking buffoon' conferred by stage and literary tradition. Lady Gregory reveals to English readers the *true* Irish peasant by showing that his involvement in the co-operatives demonstrates a practical sense while the growth of the Gaelic League indicates an ideological purpose. The materialistic Irish co-ops might be likened to an Irish Sancho, and the idealistic Gaelic League to Quixote. In place of the absent Parnell, these two growths, the Irish Agricultural Organization Society and the Gaelic League, have become powerful grass-root forces in Ireland. (Augusta Gregory thus identifies the political significance of the Gaelic League, a significance which repulsed the unionist Martin Ross.)

Lady Gregory's article has been identified as a 'seminal piece' in its focus on self-help movements to bring about change in Ireland.[15]

Somerville and Ross show equal interest in local development but are alert to its comic potential. They ridicule the po-faced collectors of Irish folklore and the earnest students of the Irish language, suggesting that the discovery of the real Ireland is an impossible task, not unlike the quest of Sancho Panza and Quixote in Cervantes's work that Lady Gregory alludes to in her writing.

Lady Gregory focuses her discussion on language and argues that colonization has suppressed an unrecovered cultural mine at the heart of the Irish peasant. The loss of language, caused by English penal laws, the Famine, and National schools in Irish-speaking areas, is a loss of culture. Echoing Douglas Hyde in 'The De-Anglicization of Ireland' Lady Gregory argues that language 'expresses the spirit of the race', and without his Gaelic past the Irish peasant finds himself stranded in a linguistic and cultural limbo. Douglas Hyde's translations of Irish songs reveal this hidden tradition. In fact, Augusta Gregory claims, such carefully collected songs show more than anything else the Irish peasant's imagination, dignity, and spirituality. One of her numerous examples in 'Ireland, Real and Ideal', a 'merry' song, as she describes it, might be considered with the sacrilegious Irish RM parodies in mind:

> The Irish songs I have heard sung in the cottages are for the most part sad, but I have heard a girl last year sing a merry one, in a jubilant mocking tone, about a boy on the mountain, who neglected the girls of his village to run after a strange girl from Galway that came here. And the girls of the village were vexed, and they made a song about him. And he went to Galway after her, and there she laughed at him, and said he had never gone to school or to the priest, and she would have nothing to do with him. So then he went back to the village and asked the smith's daughter to marry him, but she said she would not, and that he might go back to the strange girl from Galway.[16]

Although Lady Gregory successfully displayed the humour of the Irish countryside in some of her writings (her play *The Spreading of the News* springs to mind) her pedantic description for the readers of *The Nineteenth Century* falls short of capturing the merry carnival spirit so evident in Somerville and Ross's short fiction. Such serious treatment of light-hearted material invites the kind of parody Somerville and Ross would later employ in a satire on the recuperation of the past in 'The Last Day of Shraft' discussed below.

In quite a different way and using Hiberno-English and anecdotal material, Somerville and Ross also addressed questions concerning the real and the ideal in the Irish countryside with their *Badminton* stories. Despite suggestions that the Irish RM stories reintroduce the 'rollicking buffoon' which Lady Gregory and Yeats deplored, Somerville and Ross used comic fools and rogues 'to rip off masks' concealing the private interests of public patriotism.[17] They employed parody to reveal what might lurk behind the picture frames enclosing the romantic scenery or venerable portraiture of nineteenth-century Ireland. They subverted a romantic vision which is as much Protestant as it is Catholic, as much Scottish as it is Irish, by considering both sides' propensity for making monuments out of molehills.

Somerville and Ross's sly send-up of romanticized notions of Irishness appears in two stories dealing with story-telling and language, 'Lisheen Races, Second Hand' and the 'Last Day of Shraft'. The writers' parody, however, does not confine itself to Irish Catholic romantic imagery. A study of the background of the main Irish character, Florence McCarthy Knox, reveals that the stories' treatment of memory includes Protestant myth-making. The first part of Flurry's surname suggests a response to Catholic-nationalist versions of the past in ballads from *The Nation* with emphasis on the Cork name McCarthy. The second part of Flurry's name suggests a subversion of a Protestant tradition made manifest by portrait painting and indicated by the Cork painter Daniel Maclise. The Protestant discourse extends discussion to Scotland; it necessitates the inclusion of a wider range of material to appreciate the comprehensive nature of the Somerville and Ross parody. Two of the most striking examples of the authors' parody must be 'Waters of Strife', a story which focuses on popular commemoration of 1798, and 'Holy Island', which attacks Catholic Ireland.

Somerville and Ross's involvement with Irish political discourse in their short fiction emphasizes the wide range of the writers' Irish interests. Of particular interest is the playful treatment of nineteenth-century antiquarian discourse, and we might keep in mind that Edith Somerville's brother, Boyle Somerville, 'was the first archaeologist mathematically to measure and survey stone circles'.[18] As noted earlier Vice-Admiral Boyle Somerville's assassination by political extremists in 1936 demonstrates the harsh political reality confronting the Anglo-Irish population. Somerville and Ross's comic fiction, developed and produced over a period of seventeen years, the final years of their collaboration, exploits most fully the ideologies of race and nation to provide a series of modern short stories attacking grand ideologies of nation and providing alternative visions of a picturesque

Ireland. Thus we might ask (in an echo of W.B. Yeats) if Somerville and Ross's satire contributed to the feelings of resentment and hatred that produced those fatal shots in later years.

ORAL STORIES AND SONGS: 'LISHEEN RACES, SECOND HAND' AND 'THE LAST DAY OF SHRAFT'

The first three stories of *Some Experiences*, 'Great-Uncle McCarthy' (October 1898), 'Trinket's Colt' (November 1898), and 'In the Curranhilty County' (December 1898) ('When I First Met Dr Hickey' was first published in the final series of Irish RM stories, *In Mr Knox's Country*) set the picturesque backdrop of Shreelane and Aussolas and establish its hybrid mix of characters: Anglo-Irish Mrs Knox and her Irish servant, 'Robinson Crusoe', her grandson, Flurry Knox, whom she nicknames Tony Lumpkin after the spoilt practical joker of Goldsmith's *She Stoops to Conquer*, the English Major Yeates with his Irish background and English wife, Philippa, and the Irish peasantry including Mrs Cadogan and Slipper.

The next nine stories continue to provide a series of madcap adventures while taking potshots at a mix of material relating to topics as diverse as New Woman attitudes and Irish nationalist ideology. 'The Waters of Strife' and 'Lisheen Races, Second-Hand', for instance, parody the exaggerated tropes of current perceptions of Irish rebellion, especially the mythologized Wexford Rising of 1798. 'Philippa's Fox-Hunt' and 'A Misdeal', on the other hand, develop the feminine discourse (women in sport, women in love) and the romantic plot between the Irish cousins, Flurry and Sally Knox. 'Holy Island' satirizes the role of Catholicism in Ireland, while 'The Policy of the Closed Door' returns to love and subversive female behaviour in the Irish countryside.

Two strands run through the twelve *Badminton* stories which unite in the aptly named finale, 'Oh Love! Oh Fire!' (December 1899). The love in the title indicates the harlequinesque union of Flurry and Sally. They emerge as the king and queen of misrule, bringing mayhem to its successful end – marriage. The fire suggests the nationalist flame in the tower of Aussolas which is successfully doused by the combined efforts of the Anglo-Irish and the country folk. Throughout this first series of Irish RM stories the nationalist flame is fed by idealized pictures of the past and fanned by a love of storytelling and a playing to the audience which pervades Irish rhetoric and is especially apparent in the fifth *Badminton* story, 'Lisheen Races, Second-Hand'.

Major Yeates's first discovery in 'Lisheen Races' is that things are not as they appear, especially the 'enshrined portraits of the friends of [his] youth' captured in the photographs of Oxford days in England. His old pal, Leigh Kelway, has become the Honourable Basil Leigh Kelway whose political ascent is matched by an insufferable rise in self-esteem. As the private secretary to Lord Waterbury he has come to Ireland to collect information on 'the Liquor Question in Ireland'. Gone is the youthful curl of hair and an insipid romanticism which drew the young Sinclair Yeates to his side. Now all has changed, muses Major Yeates as he studies his younger self and Leigh in a 'David and Jonathan memorial portrait', side by side in the photograph picture frame, like some newly married couple.[19] By the end of the story the Oxford portrait will be cruelly ridiculed when Leigh Kelway is discovered clasped in the arms of the drunkest and most disreputable Irishman one might possibly meet at the country races – the loser.

A later story from *Further Experiences*, 'The Last Day of Shraft', repeats the successful satirical formula of 'Lisheen Races' but strikes closer to the bone. The English visitor to Ireland this time knows quite a bit about Celtic studies, and his earnest collecting of Irish folklore recalls the seriousness of revivalists throughout Britain. Ironically this story is one of a pair of stories drafted in August and September 1903, and the first draft, 'The Boat's Share', uses as its principal matter 'a verbatim report of a court-room scene, a dispute about fishing heard before J.P.s, attended and reported by E. Œ. S.'[20] 'Lisheen Races' also relies upon the authors' transcripts of Irish raw material. Slipper's anecdote at the centre of the story, his narration of the Lisheen races which the Oxford graduates never manage to attend, is included in Somerville and Ross's *Collection of Irish Anecdotes*. Martin Ross transcribed the material as early as May 1893 as 'The Story of Owld Bocock's Mare'. So while the stories parody the earnest and overly serious collection of Irish material by English visitors, they rely at the same time on various overheard stories of the Irish folk. Obviously, and as noted before, the question for Somerville and Ross was not if one can successfully collect and transcribe Irish material but who would be best qualified to do so.

The retelling of events that occurs in 'Lisheen Races' is by the best and least reliable storyteller of the Irish RM series – Slipper. His enthusiasm for his story is encouraged by a good few drinks and a gullible listener, the visiting English parliamentarian. Slipper's second-hand version of the races, however, follows the general breakdown into mayhem which Flurry Knox introduces. 'Like a clown at a pantomime' who climbs out of windows rather than exits out of doors,[21] Flurry also manages to employ three horses and two articles of conveyance *not* to arrive at the Lisheen races. Kelway, 'a writer of thoughtful articles' who intends 'to popularize the subject [of Irish drinking] in a novel', soon finds himself in the middle of the action of a harlequinade, no longer the observer but the observed, no longer the statesman but the ridiculous fool.[22] Kelway's only thirst is for statistics, and so he is swiftly and surely chastised for imagining he might retell the Irish story by the greatest drinker of the Irish RM series, Slipper, whose 'brogue' flummoxes the Englishman and whose story, a blatant exaggeration of reality, seduces him into belief. The drunkard, Leigh Kelway's object of study, outdoes the politician on all fronts. The sot reigns supreme.

Slipper's story, a performance as much as a narration and full of exaggeration and downright lies (and enjoyed by its Irish pub audience for that very fact), also parodies a certain type of Irish historicizing which relies on general effect rather than truthful record. The story of Driscoll, his horse – Owld Bocock's mare – and the race, an Irish skirmish performed with the aid of much 'porther and whiskey' and 'the Sons of Liberty's piffler and dhrum band from Skebawn', climaxes with the frightful death of Driscoll. With the ready assistance of Slipper's stick, Driscoll's mount bolts, throws his rider, and rolls on him 'as cosy as if he was meadow grass'. With relish Slipper describes 'the blood [that] was dhruv out through his nose and ears, . . . his bones crackin' on the ground!'.[23] The story (or what he understands of it) horrifies Leigh Kelway. He believes Slipper.

Slipper's story is a great lie, as Kelway must realize when a well-bandaged Driscoll breaks through the pub audience to find and destroy his tormenter. Leigh Kelway's humiliation continues further as indignity follows indignity, and he is finally discovered by his superior, the Right Honourable the Earl of Waterbury, in the embrace of the very same (and now very drunk) Driscoll singing the 1798 rebellion ballad 'The Wearing of the Green'.

The satire in 'Lisheen Races' has a double barb. It ridicules the pomposity of the colonial who makes a study of Irish culture and believes he can summarize the story of Ireland by taking notes and earnestly observing its habits. It also parodies the folk story so popular in its retelling in national balladry like 'The Wearing of the Green', its deliberate romanticizing and fudging of events. The retelling of the Lisheen Races displays the art of the storyteller rather than the truth of his telling. The final insertion of an instance of this kind of myth-making, the popular Irish ballad, as well as the Englishman's ultimate humiliation, manages to unveil two different kinds of pictures of Irish reality: the colonial dream and the nationalist nightmare.

'The Last Day of Shraft', published in *Strand Magazine* seven years later and collected in *Further Experiences*, does not mock folk memory so much as burlesque the idealization of the people and their native tongue. Major Yeates's wife, Philippa, has become an Irish language enthusiast and after five Irish lessons can say good morning to her teacher. She invites her stepbrother, Maxwell Bruce, a serious collector of ancient Irish stories and desiring to practise the tongue on native Irish speakers, to visit Hare Island, 'an unworked mine' of Irish folk-lore where Major Yeates is going to shoot ducks.[24] Though Maxwell Bruce speaks Irish, he does not understand the language of commerce which is the real means of communication on the island. His visit to Mrs Brickley's illicit drinking house to collect authentic folklore from the local poet Shemus Ruadth becomes opportunity for shebeen shenanigans of the liquid kind. Meanwhile, Major Yeates's shooting expedition becomes a laborious struggle through mud which renders nothing, except for Mrs Brickley's fine drake.

Like many of the Irish RM stories, 'The Last Day of Shraft' includes comical changes of dress reminiscent of the transformation to the harlequinade of nineteenth-century pantomime. Peter Cadogan dresses himself in the fine left-over clothing of his employer, a striped blue suit and yellow boots. Major Yeates, drenched during his shoot-ing expedition, must change into one-legged Con Brickley's one-legged trousers. The costume changes transform lovesick Peter into a figure closely resembling the bagged drake that the Major has acci-dentally (and shamefacedly) shot down while Yeates's new clothes reduce him to playing the fool.

It soon becomes apparent that Mrs Brickley's charming appear-ance masks a hustler's heart. Similarly her charming, white-washed thatched cottage conceals an illicit business, selling poitín. The arrival of 'neighbours' (the clients) to listen to the Irish singer entertaining Maxwell Bruce becomes an opportunity to fool the police and to drink the day away, the day before Lent which is, of course, carnival time. Sharpening both the performers' and the audience's pleasure is the performative nature of the event. Everyone wears a mask and con-tributes to fooling the serious folklore collector and the representative of English law in Ireland, Major Yeates. Everyone is on stage.

The show reaches its hilarious apex (the masks begin to become apparent) when the audience pushes forward a young singer named

Paddy, the picture of timid ineptitude: 'an incredibly freckled youth . . . with eyes fixed on the ground and arms hanging limply at his sides, like a prisoner awaiting sentence'. Again appearances deceive for Paddy delivers a bold commentary on the day's adventures in a ballad satirizing the solemn songs of Shemus Ruadth. The song relates the capture of a drake, a 'poor little fella' / His legs were yella' / His bosom was blue, he could swim like a hake'.[25] With an air of gloom young Paddy breaks out into a brief stomping jig before continuing his song. Maxwell Bruce realizes he is being fooled but does not understand the clever subtext of the ballad that Major Yeates uncomfortably suspects. The audience is delighted. They know the joke and are thinking of blue-chested, yellow-legged Peter Cadogan fleeing across the water this moment with the Brickley daughter. Paddy's comic song satirizes Shemus Ruadth's dignified ballads, Major Yeates's inexpert marksmanship, and earnest Peter's elopement with Bridget Brickley in one fell swoop. Best of all when the 'polis' arrive to search for illicit drink (tipped off by Flurry Knox) they find in the centre of the action the Resident Magistrate in half a pair of trousers and a full glass of whiskey at hand.

Like the parody in 'Lisheen Races', 'The Last Day of Shraft' shows that a romanticized version of reality (the remnants of ancient Ireland lurking in the Irish oral tradition) does not convey the whole truth. Paddy's parody of Irish tradition exploits the tools of the past to comment on the present; he provides a subversive picture of Ireland. This shows another 'truth.' In 'Lisheen Races', also, the formal memorial portrait and Slipper's exaggerated anecdote give versions of reality which possess as much 'truth' as other versions, like the one provided by Somerville and Ross's story. Song, oral tale and portrait are versions of reality. The so-called truth of Ireland, the real Ireland, is not necessarily discoverable in one or another of these versions.

SUBVERSION OF ROMANTIC IMAGERY: MCCARTHY AND THE NATIONALIST DISCOURSE

The resounding spell-words of mid-nineteenth century Irish balladry from *The Nation* – 'Watch and Wait', 'Bide Your Time', 'Stand Together', 'Step Together', 'Brothers Arise', 'The Sword', 'Advance' – find a mocking echo in Somerville and Ross's short stories.[26] These stories resist the striking poses, the inflated imagery, the martial overtones of Irish nationalist thought.[27] They subvert the grand vision by introducing the monocular perspective of Major Yeates, the new Resident Magistrate to West Cork, who peers at Irish life through his monocle, and is frequently thrust right down into its messy dealings by Flurry Knox.

Florence McCarthy Knox, the Resident Magistrate's landlord and grandson of old Mrs Knox of Aussolas, suggests with his name two cultural strands: the Catholic McCarthy family and the Protestant Knoxes. As a squireen, a half-gentleman and hybrid, Flurry, as noted earlier, 'occupies a shifting position' in between these two camps.[28] Despite his land ownership he does not quite merit the hand of Sally Knox. He stands as 'a man of the people',[29] more at home with the farmers and horses than the visiting English or the local gentry. Nonetheless his connection to the better families dignifies his character and allows him access to their homes. Flurry's name reveals a network of influences that suggest the backdrop to the stories in which he figures.

The first part of Flurry's name recalls Lady Morgan's romantic nationalist heroine, Florence Macarthy, the 'grand-daughter and heir of old Denis Macarthy' whose ancient Irish aristocracy makes her the '*Bhan Tierna*' and true mistress of the land, a kind of 'woman of the people'. *Florence Macarthy* (1818) revolves around the lost birthright of the ancient Irish-Catholic Macarthy family, once kings of Munster but now a fallen race.[30] However, a more recent connection to Flurry's maternal half becomes immediately apparent in the first Irish RM story. Flurry's great-uncle Denis or 'Great-Uncle McCarthy' suggests that one part of Flurry's family may descend from the mid-nineteenth-century poet Denis Florence McCarthy, collector of Irish ballads and regular contributor to *The Nation*.

Of course McCarthy is a common Cork name, but Denis Florence McCarthy – the conspicuous signature of 'Great-Uncle McCarthy' – features less frequently. The first story of the Irish RM series is set in Great-Uncle McCarthy's decrepit house of Shreelane. In fact, Shreelane, which Major Yeates rents as Irish Resident Magistrate, is the site of Denis McCarthy's death. Shreelane, 'a tall, ugly house of three stories high, its wall faced with weather-beaten slates, its windows staring, narrow, and vacant' rears itself high up in ruined destitution like one of the monuments of the Irish past, a tower house or, more significantly, a romantic Round Tower of popular Irish poetry. The building's supposed ghostly haunting by Uncle Denis is assisted by a sense that one has slipped back in time to a 'prehistoric age' where, according to Mrs Cadogan, a Turk would not endure the filth that the real ghosts, the squatting McCarthys relish. Flurry's relatives' nightly perambulations and banging of doors sound to Major Yeates like 'the priests of Baal call[ing] upon their god'.[31] The story's Oriental overtones evoke a vaguely ancient world that recalls the ruined Round Towers of the nineteenth-century poetry by the *Nation*'s regular contributor, Denis Florence McCarthy.[32]

The ghost of great-uncle McCarthy and the Catholic-Irish nationalist tradition he represents suggest Denis Florence McCarthy's vision of Ireland, his contribution to the construction of a half-fabricated 'towering' family lineage, and provide part of the background to the Irish RM stories. Particularly important within this background is McCarthy's involvement with the Irish ballad, material which Somerville and Ross's short stories parody. The first dozen Irish RM stories respond to nationalist discourse and work to expose its shibboleths as vainglorious posturing while attempting to establish a truer and yet ultimately saleable picture of the land and its people.

In Charles Gavan Duffy's *Ballad Poetry of Ireland*, first published in 1845 and 'one of the greatest best-sellers of the entire century',[33] Denis Florence McCarthy presents his elegy on the McCarthy clan. 'The Clan of the MacCaura' recalls Timothy Sullivan's earlier work, 'Elegy on the Death of Denis McCarthy' in Hardiman's *Irish Minstrelsy*,[34] but the later poet parallels his family's illustrious past with the romantic history of the Irish Round Towers. The first and fourth verses of the ballad combine the history of the family with the poet's interest in Irish antiquities:

> Oh! bright are the names of the chieftains and sages,
> That shine like the stars through the darkness of ages,
> Whose deeds are inscribed on the pages of story,
> There for ever to live in the sunshine of glory—
> Heroes of history, phantoms of fable,
> Charlemagne's champions, and Arthur's Round Table,
> Oh! but they all a new lustre could borrow
> From the glory that hangs round the name of MacCaura.
> ....
> Proud should thy heart beat, descendant of Heber
> Lofty thy head as the shrines of the Guebre [the Round Towers],
> Like *them* are the halls of thy forefathers shattered,
> Like *theirs* is the wealth of thy palaces scattered.
> *Their* fire is extinguished—*your* flag long unfurled—
> But how proud were ye both in the dawn of the world!

> And should they both fade away, oh! what heart would not sorrow
> O'er the towers of the Guebre—the name of McCaura![35]

The Irish Round Towers, which McCarthy invests with eastern con-
notations (the Guebre fled Persia for India in the seventh and eighth
centuries to escape Muslim persecution), represent the McCarthy
family with its equally ancient (and equally vague) background. The
poet sees both hailing from 'the dawn of the world', possessing the
status of myth and a sense of timelessness that French and English histories might envy. The McCarthys are a hidden – an unknown – Irish
royalty, and their grandeur is all the more wondrous for its tenuous
and shadowy connections. Both family and edifice prop up each
other's aspiring reputations, and just as the pagan flame no longer
burns in the Round Towers of Ireland so too does the McCarthy flag
no longer fly.

The real Denis McCarthy, the poet, died in Blackrock, Co. Dublin
in 1882. Thus Shreelane might be considered Somerville and Ross's
response to McCarthy's creative (and crumbling) house of fiction
which the popular poet constructed in his ballads and criticism. In his
introduction to *The Poets and Dramatists of Ireland*, for instance,
Denis Florence McCarthy sets about establishing a questionable foundation of Irish literature. 'Early Religion and Literature of the Irish
People' persuades readers of Ireland's glorious and ancient past, a
noble Phoenician heritage introduced in pre-Christian times whence
Irish culture, language, and religion derive. The poet sees the past as
a series of events that may be distorted in their retelling but from
which an essential truth can be extracted. McCarthy argues that
Ireland's first colonizers were 'princely merchants' from Phoenicia,
but more important than any facts for McCarthy is how past truths
might be established. He believes that present-day Irish spectators
prefer to view the past – indeed, prefer the past to the present – as a
series of pictures:

> It is not to be wondered at, that Irishmen are fond of recalling the
> ancient glories of their country, and that they live more in the past than
> in the present; for the past, such as it was in fact, and such as it is
> presented to us in the traditions of the people and the songs of the
> bards, is indeed a pleasing picture to behold.[36]

The 'pleasing pictures' of the past constructed by writers and poets
such as Denis McCarthy counter the scientific view of George Petrie
in the 1830s who claimed the Round Towers were of Christian date,

had a monastic origin, and were used for defensive purposes. The popular, romantic view prevailed in a public debate regarding the origins of the Round Towers that endured throughout the nineteenth century.[37]

To read McCarthy's poetry under the shadow cast by Somerville and Ross's Shreelane is to acknowledge the heavily ironic underscoring of the later writers' work. Somerville and Ross's first story in the Irish RM series recalls the Round Tower debate – the eastern, pre-Christian hauntings of the ruined house/tower, the picturesque scene, the overwhelming sense of a lost grandeur – and introduces the format from which these subversively picturesque tales originate. The humour of the first story and those that follow depends in part on looking behind the 'pleasing picture' of the past so that the ghostly haunting of Shreelane by Denis McCarthy and his priests of Baal turns out to be nothing more than the mundane squatting of a degenerate great-niece, Mrs McCarthy Gannon.

Some Experiences of an Irish RM reinvents nineteenth-century discourse by deliberately recalling Denis Florence McCarthy in the first story and returning to his thesis in the last. The collection both begins and ends with the historical symbol of the Irish Round Tower. The pagan fire of these mysterious edifices becomes a reality when in the final story, 'Oh Love! Oh Fire!', the tower of Aussolas erupts into real and dangerous flame. In a dramatic finale to the *Badminton* series, on 'the hottest day of a hot August', Major Yeates attends the tenants' dance held by old Mrs Knox of Aussolas. The 'unknown age' of the castle, with its rusty suit of armour, 'mouldering pictures', and 'pre-historic mirrors', recalls the anachronic decrepitude of Shreelane.[38] Here, at the height of the festivities, 'a heavy stack of chimneys in a tower that stood up against the grey and pink of the morning sky'[39] ignites for no particular reason other than to recall the McCarthy heritage (and the romantic nationalist subtext) of these stories. The tenants and the Anglo-Irish eventually douse the red sparks of fire, but the incident bears little relevance to the plot and so its significance appears to be symbolic. Thus the frame of the *Badminton* series includes the McCarthy/Irish nationalist discourse, an underlying argument which enriches a seemingly superficial yarn in the British sporting magazine.

The Denis Florence McCarthy name works like a signature tune accompanying the various movements of the Irish RM stories and especially the *Badminton* series. The name introduces an Irish symphony of argument and counter-argument revolving around questions of iden-

tity and place in nineteenth-century debate. The text subverts patriotic pretensions of an ancient grandeur by placing the McCarthy's
present-day antics against the romantic nationalist discourse. The
other part of Flurry's name, the Protestant Knox part, complicates the
nationalist discourse by introducing external influences.

SUBVERSION OF ROMANTIC IMAGERY: KNOX AND PROTESTANTISM

The only indication we have of the origins of the paternal side
of Flurry's family is a portrait of Grandfather Knox hanging in the
dining room of the Butler-Knoxes' family home, Garden Mount
House. This venerable picture appears briefly in a later Irish RM
story, 'A Horse! A Horse!' (published in two parts in *The Graphic* in
1908 and eventually collected in *Further Experiences*). Grandfather
Knox's likeness – this frozen record of character – gains significance
when considered within contemporary discussion on portraiture.

As descendants of Cromwell and a soldiering breed, the 'dingily
respectable' black coats and hats[40] and the dour dullness of the Knoxes
seem far indeed from the green blaze of Irish nationalism which the
McCarthy family colourfully evokes. The Butler-Knoxes represent a
more prosperous and respectable branch of the Protestant clan. They
are more interested in singing church hymns than Irish ballads; they
are 'rich, godly, low church, and consistently and contentedly dull',
and their serious religiosity gives opportunity for much clowning by
the disrespectful cousins, Flurry and Sally Knox.[41] Because the Butler-
Knoxes enjoy their comforts just as much, if not more, than their
prayers, they become easy targets for the hard-living Anglo-Irish.[42]
The settled side of Flurry's family becomes material for Somerville
and Ross's attack on religious hypocrisy. Just as the nationalist
McCarthy clan erects a towering family lineage out of the past,
the Knox family maintains a belief system that calls attention to its
religiosity. Thus these stories suggest that if late nineteenth-century
Catholic nationalism requires an appropriate past to bolster its claim
to the land, Protestant unionism needs a stronger faith to maintain its
hold. In any case, playful Sally Knox gives us some clue to the source
of the Protestant discourse. Unable to consume the bounties of the
Knox table, she distracts attention from her disposal of a brimming
glass of claret by pointing to a portrait of their collective great-grandfather and asking if it is the work of Daniel Maclise.

The Knox family adds a curious note in stories that tend to focus on the Catholic-McCarthy side of the equation, but their inclusion and its significance within the nationalist discourse is vital. They upset the notion that patriotic sentiment and ethnic pride might be exclusively Catholic or, indeed, exclusively Irish. They make complex Somerville and Ross's subversion of the nationalist discourse, and they open up the stories to the possibility of external influences. The portrait of Knox, which reminds the Irish RM readers of the Scottish Presbyterian line of inheritance trickling its 'black blood' through these stories, suggests two possible origins.[43] The first possibility rests with Daniel Maclise, a Cork painter of Scottish-Presbyterian background, renowned for historical paintings and illustrator of Thomas Moore's *Irish Melodies*. Maclise painted numerous portraits: while living in Cork as a young man, he sketched Sir Walter Scott in 1825, and Colonel John Townshend of Castletownshend the following year.[44] The portrait Sally Knox singles out for notice in 'A Horse! A Horse!' may refer to Maclise's portrait of Edith Somerville's relation Colonel John Townshend.[45]

A second possible origin also relates to Maclise and the subject of portrait painting. A rather circuitous route from the Cork painter to Thomas Carlyle in Scotland (and his ideas on portrait painting) provides further commentary not only on the Knox family but also their tradition and its idealized portrayal.

In the 1830s Maclise published a series of portrait drawings for *Fraser's Magazine*, including in 1832 a picture of Thomas Carlyle. Maclise's sketch of a young and dapper Carlyle as one of the Fraserians contrasts strikingly with later venerable images of the influential Scotsman by Millais, Sargent, and others. Carlyle figures in numerous guises in different paintings, including Ford Madox Brown's painting, *Work*, which positions Carlyle alongside destitute Irish immigrants. The variability of Carlyle's image, the fact that he appears as quite different in each painting, intrigues us when we consider Carlyle's strong interest in portraiture as historical record. How ironic that the man who believed the portrait acted like a 'lighted candle' by which one read the biography of a historical figure appears himself in visual history as a multi-faced figure whose portrait presents a series of guises of which no two are alike.[46] Carlyle possessed the Victorian sense of portraiture as a means of 'translat[ing] history into character'. This form of representation had become 'art's sole link with eternity'.[47] Thomas Carlyle professed a strong interest in portrait painting as valid historical record up until the end of his life.

One portrait, the picture which connects him to the Irish RM stories, dominated Carlyle's imagination in the 1870s. He became obsessed by a work he called the 'Somerville Picture', and in attempting to prove its subject he published an extensive and inevitably fruitless account in *Fraser's Magazine* in April 1875. This was Carlyle's last work: he called the essay 'The Portrait of John Knox'.

Sally Knox's reference to her ancestor's picture, a portrait of Knox, the dubious nature of its authority and authenticity, the possibility that it could be the work of Daniel Maclise, gives us some idea of the Scottish-Presbyterian connection of the Knox family name as well as, perhaps, further indication of the background of myth-making which the Irish RM stories resist. The portrait of Knox and the possible involvement of Maclise resonate within nineteenth-century argument on historical portraiture emanating from Scotland and, more specifically, from the ideas of Thomas Carlyle. Carlyle's views on the 'Somerville Picture' demonstrate the conflation of myth and historical fact in the Scotsman's vision.

In 'The Portrait of John Knox' Carlyle argues that the accepted version of the Presbyterian Scottish reformer by Theodore Beza is not genuine. Carlyle finds unbelievable that Beza's portrait honestly depicts this heroic figure, this 'most Scottish of Scots', a 'national specimen' whose face must surely reveal the characteristics inherent in the place and its people. 'No feature of a Scottish man' appears in Beza's icon. The portrait seems 'entirely insipid. . . . more like the wooden Figure-head of a ship than a living and working man'. It is 'highly unacceptable to every physiognomic reader'. There is, however, an engraving of Knox, claims Carlyle, which does resemble the heroic figure of Scottish Protestantism. That picture – the Knox Portrait – belongs to the Irish branch of the Somerville family and is owned by Mrs Ralph Smyth of Gaybrook near Mullingar. The 'Somerville Picture', as Carlyle terms this work, he believes erroneously to be a copy of a painting by the sixteenth-century artist Francis Probus.[48]

Carlyle's attempt 'to prove the authenticity of the Somerville portrait' demonstrates his effort to make 'the fact . . . support the vision'.[49] We know already how the Irish poet Denis McCarthy sought to create eternal myths from half-truths. Evidently such a tendency can be traced in a Scottish Protestant discourse on portraiture as witnessed by Thomas Carlyle. John Knox represented a priest-hero for Carlyle, and his god-like stature and Scottish background prove a potent combination perhaps equal in its patriotism to Irish romantic nationalism. In his 1840 lecture 'The Hero as Priest', Carlyle claims that John Knox resurrected the Scottish nation. Before Knox, 'the bravest of all Scotchmen', Scotland was 'a poor barren country, full of continual broils, dissensions, massacrings; a people in the last state of rudeness and destitution, little better than Ireland at this day'. After Knox, says Carlyle, 'the people began to live ... Scotch Literature and Thought, Scotch Industry; James Watt, David Hume, Walter Scott, Robert Burns: I find Knox and the Reformation acting in the heart's core of every one of these persons and phenomena; I find that without the Reformation they would not have been'.[50] Carlyle's determination to establish the Somerville-owned portrait as the suitable version of his priest-hero flies in the face of the conclusions of art experts and contradicts the reality of facts.

Thomas Carlyle visited Ireland in 1846 and 1849. His friendship with the editor of the *Nation*, Charles Gavan Duffy, and their dialogue concerning the Irish situation in the 40s and 50s replicate in history the fictional dialogue of Knox and McCarthy in the Irish RM stories.[51] Duffy sought to persuade his friend to support the Irish nationalist cause. Carlyle could not be persuaded, despite his admiration for Duffy and his reading of *The Nation* (courtesy of the editor who placed the Scotsman on its mailing list). According to James Froude, who possessed firm Anglocentric views himself, Carlyle saw England and Ireland as inseparable, and only asked that England admit its responsibilities to its poorer sister-nation.[52] Carlyle believed that 'English stupidity and selfishness on the one hand and Irish superstition and sloth on the other' had sabotaged the Irish economy and caused the nation's problems.[53]

Despite the polarized opinions of the Irish nationalists of *The Nation* and the Scottish historian regarding 'the Irish situation', a concordance of ideology and sentiment becomes discernible in their world view as demonstrated in either Irish romantic balladry as dealt with by Denis Florence McCarthy or in the portrait of Knox as perceived by Carlyle. Somerville and Ross's stories satirize this world view.

Somerville and Ross's Irish RM stories and in particular their hybrid McCarthy-Knox hero join in fiction the seemingly polarized perspectives of Catholic and Protestant factions. By tracing these two lines of descent and dissent, a similar conjunction of interests in history becomes apparent. Thomas Carlyle, Scottish Presbyterian and staunch unionist, and Charles Gavan Duffy, Irish nationalist and editor of *The Nation*, meet in fact and implicitly in Somerville and Ross's fiction. Thus the investigation of Flurry's two halves brings this

discussion full circle. The McCarthy interests and the network of connections which the name Denis Florence McCarthy unveils lead in the
same direction as that of Knox.

The comic form of the Irish RM stories enables the writers to make
sly digs at various romantic notions of both Irish nationalist ideology
and Scottish ethnic pride. The stories attack grand ideologies and
self-consciously reveal a series of fabrications while, in their own way,
creating yet another version of the 'real' Ireland. Martin Ross admired
especially Thomas Carlyle's writing, however, and may in the end have
imbibed some of his biases.[54] Certainly *Some Experiences of an Irish
RM* pays special attention to what has been described as the McCarthy
version of Irish history. A number of tales, such as 'The Waters of
Strife' or 'Holy Island', satirize romantic nationalistic pieties. The first
of these two stories, a grim parody of the 1798 commemoration of the
Wexford rebellion, concerns itself with the memory of the Irish past
by restaging key myths in the Irish RM countryside. The second story
shows Somerville and Ross's manner of exposing various idealized
pictures of Ireland, pictures that often mask a dangerous reality.

IRELAND, PAST AND FUTURE, IN 'THE WATERS OF STRIFE' AND 'HOLY ISLAND'

The third story of the *Badminton* series introduces the darker under-
currents of Somerville and Ross's humour. 'The Waters of Strife',
published in January 1899 and thus offering a commentary on the
previous year, quickly establishes itself as a work which attends to
Irish politics and their dangerous mix of personal vendetta and
national sentiment against a sublime backdrop of Irish scenery. The
scenery is important. With self-conscious irony the narrator claims
that 'the president of the Royal Academy could scarcely have chosen
more picturesque surroundings': a towering mountain, dark woods
alongside a lake, purple heather.[55] Close up, however, the hectic variety
of scene, the disorganization and roughness, the comical chaos and
eventual violence contradict the picture-like setting. Once again the
reader is directed to look behind the picture frame. The Irish sublime
is subverted, just as nationalist propaganda will be debunked.

The story focuses on the fortunes of a fighter called Bat Callaghan,
a local lad who murders a member of the green-clad football club
'The Sons of Liberty', and with the help of his widowed mother flees
to England to enlist in the British army. Callaghan becomes the

element of self-destruction within Irish nationalism. His purposeless act of murder flies in the face of popular accounts of patriotic assassination and heroic sacrifice.

As patron of the 'Sons of Liberty's' regatta, Major Yeates attends the rowdy festivities held on the picturesque banks of Lough Lonen. The brass band plays 'The Boys of Wexford' while boats race across the lake. The Major recognizes the familiar white face of Bat Callaghan among the shouting supporters, and very quickly the charming scene becomes a rough and ready battleground with Callaghan at its centre. When the shirt-sleeved crew beats the 'Sons of Liberty' crew (both teams making up the rules as they advance to the finishing line), fighting among the supporters breaks out: a green-jerseyed figure called James Foley attacks Bat Callaghan, who will later murder his challenger in vicious revenge.

The comic festivities become ugly when, the next day, Foley is discovered murdered and Bat Callaghan disappears. His mother, a grey-haired widow looking the image of restrained grief when she appears at the Resident Magistrate's door, attempts to bribe Yeates with a fat goose while swearing her son's innocence. Eventually the Widow Callaghan appears on the stand as a witness, maintaining under oath a series of scurrilous lies to protect her son.

The waters of strife turn even darker at the end of the story when Major Yeates comes across the absconded Irishman in England. Yeates is dining with his old regiment when a sentry on guard shoots into the night and then collapses into a fit. The sentry, Yeates discovers, thought he saw a ghost, and when he dies the next day the Major realizes a strange coincidence. The guard was Callaghan and the letter in his pocket from his mother provides clear evidence as to his guilt. White-faced Bat Callaghan's terror in the English night had obviously been provoked by his guilt.

The mayhem and vivacity of the Irish regatta (far indeed from Major Yeates's Oxford memories) reflect the political violence energizing local nationalist movements. The significantly named 'Sons of Liberty', their band's chosen tune, 'The Boys of Wexford', the mob violence, and the resulting murder suggest that the story parodies romantic nationalist memory of Ninety-eight. In an historical study of the position of the Resident Magistrate in Ireland, Penny Bonsall briefly considers the political significance of 'The Waters of Strife', suggesting that the green-jerseyed crew recall the United Irish League, founded by William O'Brien in County Mayo in January 1898.[56] Its slogan, 'the land for the people', challenged ascendancy landowners, and its popularity helped to bring about Wyndham's Land Act of 1903.[57] Somerville and Ross's black humour in 'The Waters of Strife', however, is more sweeping than Bonsall suggests. It parodies a tradition, a way of looking backwards to determine present-day politics and the future of Ireland, rather than any particular organization.

For instance, when Major Yeates eventually escapes the dubious pleasures of the regatta, his last view of the scene is the sight of Bat Callaghan climbing the greased pole to capture the pig hanging in a sack at its end: 'Callaghan's lithe figure, sleek and dripping, against the yellow sky, as he poised on the swaying pole with the broken gold of the water beneath him'.[58] This miniaturized view of a human standard could suggest different things. Through his monocle and from a distance, Yeates sees in Callaghan's figure an alternative banner to the 'immortal green' of Irish nationalism, the green flag of the Sons of Liberty and of *The Nation*'s songs.[59] At the same time, and much more ominously, Callaghan's swaying body suggests the gibbeted martyr of popular nationalist balladry.

As already mentioned, Bat Callaghan's co-conspirator, his means of escape and his chief character witness, is his lying widowed mother. On the stand the Widow Callaghan is 'deaf, imbecile, garrulously candid, and furiously abusive of [the] principal witness, a frightened lad of seventeen'. The result of the trial is 'complete moral certainty in the minds of all concerned as to the guilt of the accused, and entire impotence on the part of the law to prove it'.[60] Mrs Callaghan demonstrates an utter disregard for the law and a craven cleverness revealed in her final letter to her son: 'God help one that's alone with himself I had not a days luck since ye went away. I am thinkin' them that wants ye is tired of lookin' for ye'.[61] Somerville and Ross's widow opposes popular nationalist notions of Irish motherhood because her defence of her son's deed has little to do with Irish patriotism. Her depiction contests the idealized versions of Irish motherhood/widowhood praised by the poetry of *The Nation*.

In *Irish Penny Readings*, a compilation of extracts by the editor of *The Nation*, published in 1879, there are two variations on a Ninety-eight story, whose sentiment Somerville and Ross's work appears to mock. Both pieces focus on the love and sacrifice of a widow who has already lost her husband to the English forces and now faces the death of her son. The prose extract tells of the vicious flogging of the mother by the English soldiers when she dares to challenge their verdict. The second piece, a poem called 'Ninety-Eight' by J.T. Campion, also shows the wicked means of subjugation by the English when a mother attempts to defend her 'white-faced son' and is hanged alongside him as a result:

> They were hanging a young lad—a rebel—
>   On a gibbet before the old jail,
> And they marked his weak spirit to falter,
>   And his *white face* to quiver and quail;
> And he spoke of his mother, whose dwelling
>   Was but a short distance away—
> A poor, lorn, heart-broken widow—
>   And he her sole solace and stay. [my italics][62]

The dignified old woman kisses her son's 'pallid and wan' face (and this white-faced son recalls white-faced Bat Callaghan) and, speaking 'with the air of a queen', tells the 'vile yeoman' that her son will not inform against his country. The widow's courageous defence and her son's tragic end become in the Irish RM parody a cowardly woman's cunning trickery and a fighter's vicious revenge.

An approach to the Wexford rebellion that echoes Somerville and Ross's view in 'The Waters of Strife' might be found in J.C. Beckett's argument that though '"the boys of Wexford" often figure as the champions of national freedom' in Irish nationalist discourse (as propagated in popular ballad form), the actual cause of their rebellion might be summed up as 'local grievances'. Their connection to the United Irishmen, Beckett claims, was accidental rather than indicative of any common belief.[63] In Somerville and Ross's version of the events of Ninety-eight Bat Callaghan's actions parallel this view of the rebellion. Ironically Callaghan finds some safety with an English regiment. The next time Yeates meets him, however, he is dead, mysteriously collapsing while on sentry duty and probably overwhelmed by his own fear of the ghosts he shoots at in the night. Callaghan's deathly white face posed against the green of popular Irish nationalism throughout 'The Waters of Strife' is a means of resisting the heroising of Irish balladry, such as *The Nation*'s 'The Memory of the Dead':

> Then here's their memory—may it be
>   For us a guiding light,
> To cheer our strife for liberty,
>   And teach us to unite.
> Through good and ill, be Ireland's still,
>   Though sad as theirs your fate;
>   And true men be you, men,

                    Like those of Ninety-Eight.[64]

Unlike the cohort of the dead of Ninety-eight, the rebels in Somerville
and Ross's story are divided by internal feuding which has little to do
with patriotic intents. The story provides an ironic alternative to the
concept of the 'united Irishmen'. 'The Waters of Strife' contests
popular nationalist propaganda published in the Irish journals and
subverts the notion of the heroic folk, the idealized Irish widow and
her courageous son.

   'The Waters of Strife' satirizes official records of the nation. The
mad fooling of the regatta carnival becomes demonic murder which
lays bare the mask or the front of the romantic nationalist cause.
David Lloyd has noted that the writers of *The Nation* countered actual dislocation and disintegration of their numbers by discovering a
'transcendental unity' through an 'obscured but common origin' of
the Irish people. A ballad history of Ireland 'produces a unity that
transcends actual division', while the martyr incarnates the essential
spirit of the nation.[65] Somerville and Ross's story displays the actual
disunity of the fighting Irish and the sham status of the martyr. The
writers parody both the national historical record and its symbolic
manifestation.

   Somerville and Ross may have reserved their most savagely humor-
ous attack, however, for the dreams of the Irish future rather than the
memories of the Irish past. In a later novel by Edith Somerville, *An
Enthusiast* (1921), a Catholic priest describes his dream of Ireland's
future as 'the Sanctuary of Religion': 'to be the one country in the
world that cherishes our Holy Church!'.[66] 'Holy Island', first published in May 1899, attempts to turn that dream on its head. It attacks
the power base of the rising middle class, the Catholic Church. It
shows influential farmers using the chapel as a front to conceal their
various conspiracies against a weakened British authority. It moves
from the troubled waters of Lough Lonen in 'The Waters of Strife' in
September to the savage and wild waves of the Atlantic in November.
At the beginning of the story a storm rages, and the reader enters a
dark and troubled Catholic landscape where 'foul and ugly mists' (like
the 'base contagious clouds' of Falstaff's dominion in *Henry IV, Part
One*) shroud the outlaw activities of the tricky Irish, and where 'gentlemen of the shade, minions of the moon' overwhelm entirely the
proper order of things.[67]

   When an American ship carrying barrels of rum and butter capsizes
on the rocks of Cork's rugged coastline, all hell breaks loose. Major

Yeates, the local police, and the British coastguard try to salvage the booty from the waiting hordes of Irish. The shipwreck, the storm, and the possible loss of life become in this dark night a feverishly festive occasion, a Catholic drink-fest:

> The long strand was crowded with black groups of people, from the bank of heavy shingle that had been hurled over on to the road, down to the slope where the waves pitched themselves and climbed and fought and tore the gravel back with them, as though they had dug their fingers in. The people were nearly all men dressed solemnly and hideously in their Sunday clothes; most of them had come straight from Mass without any dinner, true to the Irish instinct that places its fun before its food. That the wreck was regarded as a spree of the largest kind was sufficiently obvious.[68]

The attempts of the authority to salvage the barrels of contraband goods are as ineffectual as the sailors' efforts to save their yacht from the rocks at Yokahn Point. Rum flows in bounteous founts across Tralagough strand as a piper plays a light-hearted jig 'The Irish Washerwoman' in celebration:

> The people, shouting with laughter, stove in the casks, and drank rum at 34 degrees above proof, out of their hands, out of their hats, out of their boots. Women came fluttering over the hillsides through the twilight, carrying jugs, milk-pails, anything that would hold the liquor; I saw one of them, roaring with laughter, tilt a filthy zinc bucket to an old man's lips.[69]

By nightfall, bodies of drunken Irish lie strewn across the sand while a suspiciously large number of unopened barrels have disappeared. James Canty, a well-established farmer and 'noted member of the Skebawn Board of Guardians' (possibly elected the previous March when the 1898 Local Government Act took effect), distracts attention from his smuggling of rum by treating the police and Yeates to his exaggerated and fulsome attentions. James Canty's 'Falstaffian figure'[70] indicates the kind of authority he represents in Catholic Ireland.

'Holy Island' shows the empty pieties and, indeed, the veil over action such pieties cast, of the Irish middle-class. The story responds to idyllic pictures of Catholic Ireland found in works like Denis Florence McCarthy's 'A Dream of the Future' in *The Spirit of the Nation*. Somerville and Ross's nightmare version provides three raucous ballads, 'The Irish Washerwoman', 'One night to the rocks of Yokahn', and 'Lanigan's Ball', as alternative songs which situate this world far indeed from McCarthy's national hopes in 'A Dream of the Future':

> I dreamt a dream, a dazzling dream, of a green isle far away,
> Where the glowing west to the ocean's breast calleth the dying
>   day;
> And the island green was as fair a scene as ever man's eye did
>   see,
> With its chieftains bold, and its temples old, and its homes
>   and its altars free!
> No foreign foe did that green isle know—no stranger band it
>   bore,
> Save the merchant train from sunny Spain, and from Afric's
>   golden shore!
> And the young man's heart would fondly start, and the old
>   man's eye would smile,
> As their thoughts would roam o'er the ocean foam to that
>   lone and 'holy isle'![71]

The ocean foam in Somerville and Ross's 'Holy Island' wreaks havoc. The 'green isle' appears in shadow and darkness. It is where an impoverished peasantry, and its mischievous leaders, would rather do a thing crooked than straight, would rather con their neighbour than earn an honest shilling. Here, as James Canty the leader of misrule notes, drink can be so potent 'it would make a horse out of a cow'.[72]

McCarthy's Catholic nationalist predictions in 'A Dream of the Future' foresee a wonderfully independent Ireland emerging from the bloodshed of war endured by a people 'in abject prayer':

> At length arose o'er that isle of woes a dawn with a steadier
>   smile,
> And in happy hour a voice of power awoke the slumbering
>   Isle!
> And the people all obeyed the call of their chief's unsceptred
>   hand,
> Vowing to raise, as in ancient days, the name of their own
>   dear land!
> My dream grew bright as the sunbeam's light, as I watched
>   that Isle's career
> Through the varied scene and the joys serene of many a future
>   Year—
> And, oh! what thrill did my bosom fill, as I gazed on a pil-

lared pile,
Where a senate once more in power watched o'er the rights
    of that lone green Isle!

McCarthy's dream of the future houses a new Irish government in the ancient Round Tower so that the picturesque artefact becomes heavily weighted with a nationalist significance. Somerville and Ross's nightmare version of McCarthy's dream attacks such picturesque piety. The 'fair hills of holy Ireland' which beckon passing ships to a 'fresh and fragrant strand'[73] become dark and storm-tossed with a beach hardly fresh or fragrant after the Irish have vomited up their booty on Tralalough strand. Unlike the tyrannized Catholics of nationalist balladry who are invigorated by 'the living wells – the cool, the fresh, the pure', Somerville and Ross's cabin folk do not drink holy water to refresh their flagging spirits. Their 'flowing founts' are contraband liquor.[74]

James Canty leads the law and Major Yeates in a merry chase for the missing contraband rum. The Irish Falstaff stashes the goods on Holy Island, a picturesque isle on Corran Lake with its 'jungle' of rhododendrons, a 'ruined fragment of a chapel smothered in ivy and briars', and, naturally enough, a holy well.[75] This ideal picturesque material is shown to be just that – a charming front that conceals all sorts of devious plots and illegal goods. Its renowned holiness (supported by vague fairy stories) provides the greatest protection of all for those hiding things from the law, and James Canty shrewdly dons the religious mask more than once to circumvent the strait-laced rules of British officialdom. At the funeral of the Roman Catholic Bishop of the diocese, Canty secretes the stolen rum on the train which carries the cortège to Cork. His deception works, aided no doubt by the numerous surplices veiling his deeds. Catholicism – the rosary muttered by Mrs Cadogan, the mass attended by the local pillagers, the shrine used as cover for stolen goods – proves to be more of a display or a ruse than a source of spiritual inspiration in 'Holy Island'.

The Northern Newspaper Syndicate, which commissioned Somerville and Ross to write six articles that year, requested that the writers avoid politics except for 'the picturesque Irish species'.[76] Apparently Irish politics could have a picturesque appeal, and perhaps James Canty's evasions, his playfully subversive behaviour, might be of this kind. In the following chapter, the writers' approach to Irish politics will be looked at more closely. For the moment we might note that 'Holy Island', with all its charm and humour, advances serious claims in its attack on Irish Catholicism, and just as the picture-like island is shown to conceal ordinary theft, so too does this picture-like story with its bagpiper and priests, its drunken Irish and clever crooks, reveal the collusion of the Catholic Church and the rising middle class. In the manner of the carnivalesque, Holy Ireland becomes a holy show. Catholic dreams give way to a disorderly, stormy underworld which operates according to its own dictates. 'Holy Island' offers a kind of picturesqueness that disdains idyllic scenery, fairies, and holy wells but still employs the tradition whence the cliché and stereotype derive.

'The Waters of Strife' and 'Holy Island', like most of the Irish RM stories, do not poke fun at merely one kind of myth. Consider once again how 'The Waters of Strife' opens with a panoramic view of Ireland, a distanced perspective of sublime scenery which the English Royal Academy could admire. Or note how 'Holy Island' recalls the terrifying sublime of romantic works like Maturin's *Melmoth the Wanderer* with its opening stormy scenes and madly drunken Irish. These sweeping scenes might be set against Major Yeates's monocular perspective which finds in Bat Callaghan a striking symbol of Irish faction-fighting or which sees James Canty as a benevolent guardian of the people. The short fiction does not necessarily exonerate the ideology shaping either view; rather, it self-consciously reveals how each view remains a picture. In the Irish RM series different kinds of 'pictures' – the landscape, or the portrait, or the monument – conflate history and myth. McCarthy's Round Tower, Carlyle's portrait of Knox, Yeates's miniature of Bat Callaghan: such visions become alternative versions of reality in the Irish RM stories.

CHAPTER 6

Sport/Politics:
The Treasure in the Bog

Reynard, it seems, that lawless Reprobate,
Like Satan, envying our happy state,
Around our Eden often lay in wait.
Stealthily round the walls by night he'd creep,
And through the crannies of the gates would peep.
The trusty Guardians of myself and Wife
Oft made the Ruffian scamper for dear life;
Once they did catch him, and well tanned his hide,
He got away, though sorely scarified;
And for a good while after let us bide.

THOMAS J. ARNOLD AFTER GOETHE, REYNARD THE FOX

Ireland's predominant landscape myth resides in its bogland. Mountains, lakes or streams do not call up the nation as evocatively as does the 'boundless bog', the 'quaking sod', the 'shifting' or 'shaking' soil of this 'spongy gravel'.[1] What Ireland lacks in terms of horizontal scope – wide skies or stretches of forest and grazing field – it makes up for in depth. The limitation of the island's upper reaches, where more often than not the eye is oppressed by lowered clouds or stayed from wandering beyond the immediate by a broken terrain, seems to compel the gaze downwards into the earth where the force of gravity allows it to range unchecked and wondering at the possibilities of the unknown. The legend of St Patrick's hole in medieval depictions of the underworld refers to bogholes in Ireland that lead all the way to purgatory.[2] Various popular late-nineteenth and early twentieth-century treatments of the sublime Irish landscape rely in part on such stories. Bram Stoker's melodramatic adaptation of the legend of St Patrick's banishment of the snake into the land's subterranean depths in *The Snake's Pass* (1890), or George Birmingham's later light-hearted treatment of mysterious bogholes in *Spanish Gold* (1908), recalls this central Irish image. The adventure stories adapt the notion of a hidden Irish underworld to the treasure-hunt motif of popular romance. In both works the hunt in the Irish landscape is rewarded with significant treasure as the land surrenders its mysteries to the improving English entrepreneur or the intrepid Anglo-Irish curate.

Landscape in this chapter, then, comprises not just the physical countryside and the lifestyle of the folk or the big farmers. It also signifies an imagined terrain and the myths and symbols that have been established in the figuration of Ireland throughout the nineteenth century and beyond. Somerville and Ross's fiction deals with both the literary and the physical landscape, and like other Irish writers they are fascinated by the actuality of the bog as well as what it might suggest.

The main attraction of the bogland lies in its hidden treasure. The central conduit to the treasure must be the fox. The activity that incorporates these various elements – land, treasure and fox – is the hunt. Somerville and Ross's later fiction, 'The Whiteboys', published the same year as Birmingham's novel, and their final collaborative work, *In Mr Knox's Country* (1915), parody the quest for hidden treasure in the Irish landscape by employing their favourite pastime, fox-hunting, as a vehicle for satire. Despite the stories' humour, however, the authors' approach to the Anglo-Irish hunt, and their use of 'that lawless Reprobate', Reynard, is far from frivolous. It provides the key to their conception of the Irish landscape and demonstrates the writers' artful use of the short story form.

The frequent depiction of the hunt is relevant for Somerville and Ross's fiction in yet another respect: it introduces a political significance. As indicated by Goethe's comparison of the fox to the devil in *Reynard the Fox*, the fox remains an outsider to human society, forever ready to play tricks and fool unsuspecting victims:

> Reynard, it seems, that lawless Reprobate,
> Like Satan, envying our happy state,
> Around our Eden often lay in wait.[3]

Mr Fox's guile has often been likened to that of politicians. The political nuances of Somerville and Ross's later fiction become apparent when considering their use of the fox and the hunt in relation to their suffragist involvement, Martin Ross's political interests, their growing fascination with beast allegory, and the context of *Blackwood's Magazine* that published many of the later stories.

Somerville and Ross published the politically provocative short story 'The Whiteboys', of *Further Experiences of an Irish RM*, in the illustrated newspaper *The Graphic*. It is their final collection of short stories, *In Mr. Knox's Country*, however, that has been regarded as their most political work. They started writing the stories in 1912, during the Home Rule debate, and published five of the ten stories over the next few years in the conservative Scottish periodical *Blackwood's Magazine*. Allusions to the decline of the Anglo-Irish ascendancy in the stories encourage readers to dismiss the material as 'mordantly nostalgic', a lament for fading Irish feudalism.[4] One story in particular, 'The Finger of Mrs Knox', demonstrates for various critics the authors' autocratic attitude towards land ownership in Ireland, a longing for a time when peasant and patron knew their places and all was right with the world. The historian Patrick Maume argues that this story confirms the writers' unionist politics in the early 1900s.

Maume wrote the entry on Somerville and Ross in the *Oxford Companion to Irish History*. 'Both unionist in politics', says Maume, 'they are sometimes accused of malevolent stage-Irishness'.[5] He connects their politics with that of Martin Ross's elder brother, Robert Martin, who wrote numerous comic Irish songs with a sectarian bias. 'Unionist propaganda' is how Maume describes Robert Martin's material, implying that Somerville and Ross's comic stories come close to being similar in intent.

But as already noted in this study, the women writers did not hesitate to appropriate for their own comic purposes the older brother/cousin's work. Were his politics also up for parody? I have stressed Robert Martin's writing of pantomime for the Dublin theatres in the 1880s and his younger sister's continued interest in that tradition throughout her writing career. This influence might also be taken into account when considering the brother's politics. Robert Martin's interest in popular farce dominated over his political thought. His sister's views were more complex. After her brother's death in 1905 she became increasingly interested in arguing the unionist position in Irish politics and suffragist affairs. By 1912, when Somerville and Ross commenced writing their final collection of stories, Martin Ross had become especially active. Both writers were involved with the Munster Women's Franchise League, and in January the group invited a visiting suffragist,

Miss Gill, to lecture on 'How we won the vote in Norway'. The following month Martin Ross expressed a conservative position in her suffragist tendencies when she wrote to Miss Pankhurst 'declining her militant protest on March 4 because, chiefly, [Martin Ross] belonged to a non-militant suffrage society'.[6]

For Somerville and Ross the 1912 Home Rule Bill (the result of the 'destruction of the veto power of the House of Lords [which] removed the last constitutional obstacle to Home Rule')[7] took on greater political urgency because of their suffragist involvement. As Edith Somerville pointed out when writing to her brother in June, the fortunes of the woman's franchise depended more on the larger game of politics than personal sympathies:

> You may have seen that Lord R. Cecil & Philip Snowden are bringing in a woman's Franchise Amendment to the Home Rule Bill. Redmond is terrified of the 50,000 solid & organised Ulster women, & personally is an Anti. therefore he commands his party, who are mainly Suffies, to vote against it. The Unionist MPs for Ulster are mainly Antis, but they & most of the Unionist party are to vote for it, as it may split the Govt. & the Labour Party.[8]

While Edith Somerville – who would become President of the Munster Women's Franchise League the next year – concentrated on suffragist affairs, her cousin became increasingly involved in mainstream politics.

Martin Ross contributed strenuously to the debate on Home Rule throughout 1912. In January and February she corresponded with the journalist Harold Begbie of the *Daily Chronicle* and the Irish MP Stephen Gwynn, arguing against Home Rule and voicing her suspicions about 'the sudden change in tone of the Irish leaders towards . . . the Landlord Class', the diffidence and occasional warmth which replaced previous attack.[9] In April she attended a unionist meeting in Cork to protest against the Home Rule Bill. The following autumn she described to readers of *The Spectator* a journey from Cork to Belfast to witness the signing of the Covenant against Home Rule. Her description profiles a section of Protestant Ulster made up entirely of workers, ordinary men and women who are willing to 'take their lives and liberties in their hands' to resist an increasingly popular opinion in the southern part of the island.[10] Martin Ross displayed a large understanding of Irish economics and history in these political pieces and, unlike Edith Somerville, never altered or modified her unionist position.

This same year Martin Ross continued to follow developments of the Irish nationalist literary movement. In March she had tea with Edward Martyn and much talk with Lady Gregory in the gardens at Coole. Augusta Gregory had just returned from touring in America with the Irish Players and, no doubt, spoke of the largely successful run of their folk drama notwithstanding mixed reactions to Synge's *Playboy of the Western World*. By the summer Martin Ross was discussing with Carrie Townshend the Gaelic League and the significance of the Irish language. Despite her conviction of the political intent of the League, she recommenced lessons in Irish by the end of the year.

Throughout this period, and although her health was poor, Martin Ross continued to work on the short fiction, and the writing of *Mr Knox's Country* started with the reshuffling of her and Edith Somerville's *Collected Irish Anecdotes*. Sections of the stories rely heavily on this material. John Kane's performance in 'The Aussolas Martin Cat', for instance, comes from these records, while the string of comments on horses and their riders by the 'rustics' in 'The Maroan Pony' might also be found in the collection. As in previous Irish RM stories, the material is framed or staged within the narrative.

In 'The Maroan Pony', for example, the 'Real Primitives' or 'the rustics of Poundlick' act as both a chorus and a backdrop to the races on the banks of the Arrigadheel River. 'Off the stage I have never seen people clear out so fast', remarks one of Major Yeates's party when a race starts.[11] The point is, of course, that no one really is off stage in any of these stories. The commentary of the 'faithful gallery' becomes the true entertainment of the tale as the race merely provides opportunity for testing the audience's wit. 'That horse is no good', says a priest, 'Look at his great flat feet! You'd bake a cake on each of them!' A farmer argues that the same horse has the strength to 'plough the rocks!' while another horse is 'a hardy bit of stuff . . . and nothing in her but a fistful of bran!'[12] The audience/actors are conveniently positioned below Major Yeates and his party of picnickers as they stand on a hillock watching the horses hurl themselves across the turf. The story thus provides a double act or, to be more precise, a play within a play: the race and, framing the race, the rustic revellers. Of course, as in all the Irish RM stories, Major Yeates and Philippa and the rest of their group eventually take to the boards; they become a 'stage mob' when later on in the story they must find the Maroan pony.[13] Appropriately, if incongruously, they discover the missing pony high up in a loft of a pub's outhouse.[14] Now, instead of looking *down* at the horses, the observers find themselves looking *up* at the pony framed in the doorway of as natural a stage set as one could ever hope to find. The Anglo-Irish audience become comical stagehands when they have to get the pony down from its awkward position.

Mr Knox's Country, however, relies on more than Somerville and Ross's transcribed and framed anecdotes. Various elements of the stories directly recall Robert Martin's collection of poetry and stories published in 1899, *Bits of Blarney*, which suggest that the younger sister may have plundered her dead brother's material as well as that of the Irish folk. In 'The Aussolas Martin Cat', for instance, the Englishman who hopes to purchase and improve the decrepit Anglo-Irish estate recalls the Saxon in Robert Martin's 'St. Patrick's Day in the Morning' who discovers that his attempts to improve the debt-ridden castle failed miserably because 'English ideas were only accepted by Hibernians as long as they could get any good out of them'.[15] Then, in 'Comte De Pralines', Somerville and Ross's Englishman disguised as a Frenchman may have originated in Robert Martin's pretend Frenchman in 'Killaloe':

> If disguises you would try, or would prove an alibi,
>   or alter your appearance just for fun,
> You've just one thing to do, go tache [*sic*] French at Killaloe,
>   and your mother will not know you for her son.[16]

In 'Comte De Pralines', Somerville and Ross employ the same French disguise to cause mayhem in Flurry Knox's domain. Finally, Somerville and Ross's last story, 'The Shooting of Shinroe', rewrites Robert Martin's sketch, 'A Connemara Short Cut' from *Bits of Blarney*. Like the Irish material from *Collected Irish Anecdotes*, Robert Martin's Anglo-Irish stuff is reframed or burlesqued in the Somerville and Ross narrative.

Somerville and Ross's later fiction directs attention to a well-trodden countryside. Importantly, the writers rely on different traditions to recreate their comic version of the Irish landscape. Their political intent becomes apparent in the manner in which that landscape is portrayed.

THE TREASURE IN THE BOG

Landscape works as a site of power; it gives 'ruling ideas a natural form'.[17] As already noted in considerations of the picturesque and romantic nationalism, the wild countryside with its crumbling ruins records Ireland's hidden past. The bog, for instance, exists as a political marker of various kinds throughout the eighteenth and nineteenth centuries. Arthur Young's scientific study of the Irish countryside, *Tour in Ireland, 1776, 1777, 1778*, demonstrates the Enlightenment belief in historical progress, that draining the bogs and employing members of agrarian secret societies like the Whiteboys, will improve the land and bring about an economic success which will overcome religious and political differences (a point of view repeated by modern reformers like George Russell and Horace Plunkett at the end of the nineteenth century). Young's overarching theory, his progressiveness, ignored the specifics of Irish cultural life which nineteenth-century novelists set about detailing. Cultural nationalists reclaimed the bog as a threatened source of inspiration. As part of the Irish landscape the bog offered glimpses of an ancient tradition and preserved the artefacts of the national culture.[18]

Somerville and Ross's treatment of the half-hidden treasures of the Irish landscape might be considered in their deployment of the hunt in 'The Whiteboys' of 1908. As mentioned earlier, George Birmingham published his comic novel *Spanish Gold* this same year. Both Birmingham's novel and Somerville and Ross's story exploit the concept of a hidden Ireland and use masks and disguise to question the notion of reality in the Irish countryside. They also recall in different ways Bram Stoker's earlier novel, *The Snake's Pass*. In Stoker's work the treasure in the shifting bog is a chest of French coins and a golden crown. Such treasure indicates wealth accumulated over years of conquest: the gold of strangers (the French of 1798) or the secret resources of vanquished dominions (that of the snake). As Dracula points out to Jonathan Harker in Stoker's later terrifying tale, a conquered and reconquered landscape conceals great reservoirs of unclaimed booty in its depths:

> In old days there were stirring times, when the Austrian and the Hungarian came up in hordes, and the patriots went out to meet them – men and women, the aged and children too – and waited their coming on the rocks above the passes, that they might sweep destruction on them with their artificial avalanches. When the invader was triumphant he found but little, for whatever there was had been sheltered in the friendly soil.[19]

In 1890, with *The Snake's Pass*, Bram Stoker invested the imperial adventure novel with the notion of a hidden Irish underworld enriched by wondrous treasure.[20] An improving English landlord, the novel's hero, reveals the bog's wealth to the world. George Birmingham's later comic novel acknowledges its debt to Stoker in the naming of his hero, the curate John Joseph Meldon, who appears very briefly as Dr Meldon in Stoker's work. Birmingham also includes a real treasure in his novel – two chests of Spanish gold doubloons from 1798 stashed in a boghole on an island off Ireland's western coast. The wily Protestant cleric J.J. Meldon discovers the gold.

George Birmingham's hero in *Spanish Gold*, J.J. Meldon, expert trickster and mischief-maker, works what he describes as a *coup de théâtre* to get his hands on the hidden treasure.[21] His strong sense of play-acting, his artfulness, turns the action of the novel into farce, not unlike the comic situations Flurry Knox masterminds in *Some Experiences of an Irish RM*. Moreover, Meldon's conversation tends to hide his real intentions. Like the topography with its half-hidden recesses and concealed treasures, the adroit talk of the land's occupants reveals only a part of what actually goes on in their heads.

Birmingham's novel offers a commentary on Irish politics demonstrated by its hero's behaviour and which provides insight on Somerville and Ross's approach to politics in their comic writing. J.J. Meldon's manipulation of the truth becomes much more than a beguiling Irish trait in the course of the novel; it becomes a display of political strategy. He adopts different personae and lies outright because the situation demands that he does. He points out that nothing is straightforward in Ireland, and that the Irish mind must adapt accordingly: 'The worst thing about you Englishmen', the curate says to a visiting English politician, 'is that you have such blunt minds. You don't appreciate the lights and shades, the finer nuances, what I may perhaps describe as the chiaroscuro of things'.[22] Meldon thus acts in what must ultimately be described as a political manner: he lies as a pragmatist lies – to discover the truth. 'The test of truth is usefulness', he says to the visiting Chief Secretary, and how can the politician not understand such strategy when his 'own game of politics couldn't be played for a single hour without . . . deceiving innocent people'.[23]

The art of lying as it relates to British colonial policy had already been investigated by Somerville and Ross in their political essay 'An Irish Problem' of 1902 (see Chapter 3). Like J.J. Meldon, the narrator of Somerville and Ross's earlier essay asks if English visitors will ever understand the Irish appreciation for playing with the truth:

> How can [English minds] be expected to realise that a man who is decorous in family and village life, indisputably God-fearing, kind to

the poor, and reasonably honest, will enmesh himself in a tissue of sworn lies before his fellows for the sake of half a sovereign and a family feud, and that his fellows will think none the worse of him for it.[24]

Six years later in 'The Whiteboys' Somerville and Ross examine this kind of Irish politics in their comic fiction. The provocative title of the story promises commentary on agrarian outrage. Initially, however, the title appears to be misleading. The rebellious agents of the story turn out to be a pack of white hounds which seem to have nothing to do with the insurgent practices of the eighteenth- and nineteenth-century secret society. Nonetheless, these wild dogs bought by Flurry, an 'old Irish breed of white hounds, with their truly national qualities of talent, rebelliousness, and love of sport',[25] deliberately recall the nationalist protestors of the past. Their romanticized mystery acts as a camouflage for the real wheeling and dealing of the story.

Flurry buys the dogs from old Mr O'Reilly, who lives hidden in the 'mountain fastness' of Fahoura. He houses his dogs in a grey square tower, probably a towerhouse with its defensive arrow-slits whence the hounds strain their white muzzles. O'Reilly, an Irish-speaking patriarch of the old order, claims the hounds have been in his family since the beginning of the nineteenth century. The O'Reilly family has hunted alongside Anglo-Irish families throughout that time. O'Reilly's brother died gloriously in the chase, unlike the dispirited old patriarch who remains and is 'dying as soft as any owld cow in a boghole'.[26] With sorrow and bitterness O'Reilly sells his nephew's inheritance to Flurry Knox; drink and a modern-day hankering after America have wasted the nephew, Lukey O'Reilly. The dogs – the Whiteboys – unlike contemporary Irishmen, belong to the past. They understand Irish only and follow no law other than their own. They are unmanageable, devour anything that enters their territory, and are the wiliest bunch Flurry has ever come across when he tries them out in the hunt:

> They ignored the horn, eluded Michael, and laughed at Hickey and me; they hunted with blood-thirsty intentness and entirely after their own devices. Their first achievement was to run the earth-stopper's dog, and having killed him, to eat him. . . . The best that could be said for them was that, 'linking one virtue to a thousand crimes', whenever the hounds got fairly out of covert, the Whiteboys were together, and were in front.[27]

These clever beasts, as swift as 'spilt quicksilver' and bold enough, says Mr O'Reilly, to 'take a line over the hob of hell',[28] serve a dual purpose in the text. Dr Hickey (the Mephistophelian figure of the Irish RM stories) knowingly describes them as 'the devil',[29] and as white devils they embody the extreme dimensions of the Irish national character. Like other devilish figures already considered in this book – Melmoth or Harlequin – their anachronistic presence collapses notions of progress or change. But they also unite the Anglo-Irish hunt and Gaelic-Irish tradition. They introduce into the Irish landscape more than one continuous narrative.

The Whiteboys break away from the hunting party and head uphill across a 'green, undefined, entirely treacherous' bog. (In upside-down Ireland, Major Yeates notes, 'water runs uphill, and the subtlest bog holes lie in wait for their prey on the mountain tops'.) Eventually Yeates and Flurry Knox discover the dogs to be heading west towards an old fort (probably a souterrain) which supposedly contains 'holes down in it that'd go from here to the sea'.[30] Like the bog, the hill fort is a conduit to the nethermost regions of Ireland, a hidden hell. A fox 'as big as a donkey' is reported to the Anglo-Irish as having led the Whiteboys right into the bowels of the earth. It seems that they have been swallowed up by a prehistoric fortress and have become, literally, part of the ancient landscape.

The topography of 'The Whiteboys' provides us with a quick survey of the history of the Irish landscape. The unreclaimed bog has escaped eighteenth-century Enlightenment reforms, just as the Whiteboys have remained resolutely wild and untamed. The secret powers of the Irish language (an old farmer tells Yeates that a fox stealing a goose will drop it if shouted at in Irish), the threat of emigration to America, and the markers of the ancient past, those *lieux de mémoire*, the tower and the fort, provide features of an unchanged Irish landscape. This summarizing survey – the bottomless, boundless bog, the hounds who understand only Irish and appear to be entombed in an Irish nationalist monument, the servile farmers who help Flurry by shouting in Irish down the holes and crevices of the fort – proves to be an elaborate hoax, a display that masks what is really going on: the nephew, Lukey O'Reilly, is running a drag to capture his rightful inheritance. The dogs have been crammed into a baker's van which passes the huntsmen in search of their prey. Does *this* action, this canny and witty subterfuge, suggest the hidden Ireland? Whatever the case, the topography ultimately displays its features with self-conscious irony, the Anglo-Irish hunt, the fairy-filled fort in its swampy terrain, the romantic nationalist spirit of the secret societies; these features, whether they belong to an Anglo-Irish tradition, Celtic mythology, or

Gaelic Ireland, congregate as a performance concealing the shady dealings and deep-seated vendettas which lie at the heart of the Irish farmland.

Closer consideration of agrarian outrages of Whiteboyism in the early part of the nineteenth century indicates the appropriateness of Somerville and Ross's conclusion to their story. After 1815 Whiteboyism had as its primary cause of rural disturbance the occupation of the land. The consolidation of land for grazing purposes on the part of improving landlords did not acknowledge the practices and conditions of the small landholders who made up the ranks of the secret society. Thus 'the landlord most obnoxious to the Whiteboys was not the *rentier* who left them alone but the interested improver, anxious to run his estate on sound commercial principles'.[31] The Whiteboys, then, did not resist the landlord system; they resisted a particular kind of landlord, the one who believed in progress (like the English hero/improver revived in Stoker's *The Snake's Pass*). Somerville and Ross's depiction of the Whiteboys' disappearance into the national monument and into the land itself is fitting; equally fitting, however, is their real fate. The capture of the dogs by their 'rightful' owner is appropriate because Lukey O'Reilly has a 'moral right', if not a commercial one, to the animals – and to the land.

'The Whiteboys' reworks notions of antiquarian tourism founded on romantic nationalist ideology. The stylized national landscape, what Katie Trumpener notes to be 'the long-term effect of antiquarian tourism',[32] this half-hidden Irish past, becomes especially suited to Somerville and Ross's romantic irony in their comic short fiction. The linear passage of time, a sense of progress and development, has no bearing in a world that moves freely between past and present. The O'Reilly dogs have been in the family since the beginning of the nineteenth century, and there is a strong sense in this story that these hounds possess supernatural abilities. The features of the story – language, bog, and monuments – suggest a movement downwards into the landscape rather than forwards in time. Place and characters seem to be lost in time, as if the narrative thread itself has slipped through some crevice downwards and outside of historical continuity. Abruptly, then, such a sense is blasted by the reality of the case, the simple fact that turns everything into a show and makes suspect all that has gone before: Lukey O'Reilly in the baker's van stealing back his inheritance. This is the time of the moment. Suddenly attention is drawn from the subject matter to the creative process: the stylization of the subject matter. The writers, in other words, show their hand

and blatantly display the artifice of the material.[33]

The stylized material in 'The Whiteboys' works as a kind of performance masking reality and includes details of both the national landscape and the Anglo-Irish hunt. Both traditions (both classes and the religions they suggest) are staged. Two paintings by Jack B. Yeats might illustrate this point further. *Haute Ecole Act* (1925) and *This Grand Conversation Was Under the Rose* (1943) include a female figure from the hunt and her accompanying clown.[34] Both figures in the first painting are the objects of the circus audience's gaze and all – the audience, the horse and rider, the clown – are surrounded by the sloping canvas of the circus tent. The second painting situates the graceful rider and Pierrot inside the circus tent once again. Their black and white dress recalls Beardsley's illustrations or, more significantly for this study, Charlotte Mullen and Christopher Dysart's black and white clothing in *The Real Charlotte*. More important for the moment, however, is the positioning of the hunt figure alongside the clown inside the circus tent.

As already noted, Jack Yeats shared with Somerville and Ross a conviction that Irish life manifested the spirit of performance usually found on stage. In his novel *The Careless Flower* (1947), Yeats makes his arching circus tent a metaphor for the Irish sky: 'Circus tent above the great round dish of grey-blue sea.'[35] In the painting described above, the colonial rider does not watch or distance herself from the colonized clown because the rider joins the clown on stage. The tent, like the sky in *The Careless Flower*, covers all Ireland. Both clown and rider are members of the Irish circus act. Both the hunt woman and the humble clown perform. All Ireland is a stage. (Plate 10)

In Somerville and Ross's stories, life in Ireland is also an act, and hunting plays an essential role: the characters' antics become a performance. One might argue, of course, that in these stories the 'stage' upon which the characters perform remains an Anglo-Irish construction (a point noted below in the discussion of 'The Comte De Pralines'). Nonetheless the overriding sense of the performative nature of Irish life in short fiction like 'The Whiteboys' remains a vital aspect of Somerville and Ross's work.

The Irish landscape in 'The Whiteboys' serves as a platform for the characters' actions. The topography is ironically stylized rather than realistically realized. Fundamental, however, to the different features of the Irish scene is their shifting or quivering aspect, like the bog itself. Nothing is ever definite or clear in this picture/performance. Everything is half-realized or partially seen. A glimpse of ancient

Ireland lurks in the ruin which houses the Whiteboys, the white devils that recall the furtive adventures of a secret society while participating in the landlord's sport. Their ambiguity is reinforced by the nature of the place in which they disappear. The fortress may have consumed a fox, a calf, even a pack of dogs, but it reveals nothing of its contents. The Irish language, spoken about but never heard, like the fox himself in this story, can bewitch beasts and charm men. We are reminded of the power of a half-hidden history which Maturin describes much earlier in the nineteenth century in *The Milesian Chief*. The Irish hero speaks of Irish music and the source of a melancholy air he hums. A blind bard, he says, composed this air upon his return to the ruined family seat in Ireland. Dying, he wrote the music, as sweet in tone as the song of a dove, but even more beautiful for its unknown words:

> Before he expired on the spot, he poured out his grief to his harp in a strain addressed to the solitary tenant of the ruins – the dove, whose notes the music seemed to imitate. The words are beautiful, but I will not be guilty of doing them in English: their untranslatable beauty is like what we are told of the paintings of Herculaneum, which preserve their rich colours in darkness and concealment, but when exposed to the light and modern eyes, fade and perish.[36]

To see or expose the treasured past, whether that past be conveyed in language or monument, is to lose it. To find the treasure is to know it does not exist.

Perhaps what is most important about the hidden Ireland lies in the fact of its concealment rather than the matter which is supposedly concealed. In the mysterious darkness of the Irish past, a darkness which silences the Gaelic tongue in *The Milesian Chief*, lies the utter attraction of beckoning treasure. In an earlier discussion of *The Real Charlotte*, the 'shifting face' of national character was assessed. Charlotte Mullen never becomes 'real' because she eternally adapts to changing conditions. Her chameleon nature demonstrates in terms of character the concept of the hidden Ireland. This chapter, then, moves from character as representative of the land to the landscape itself as the backdrop to the Anglo-Irish hunt. Like character, Somerville and Ross's landscape cannot be read as one thing or another because it is ever-changing; it is a site of multiple narratives which continue to conceal in their depths some secret source . . . the 'real' Ireland. This propensity to be ever-changing, what Birmingham describes as 'the chiaroscuro of things', the deployment of multiple masks or myths, is in itself political and artful.

With politics in mind, then, let us turn to Somerville and Ross's final collaborative fiction and their boldest work, *In Mr Knox's Country*. To commence this discussion on politics and art, there is none more apt than the messenger himself, Mr Fox.

THE FOX

The Fox never sent a better messenger than himself.[37]

The fox is the supreme trickster in politics and art. Although he bears a central connection to the land, clever Reynard tends to slip his confines. Somerville and Ross's treatment of the fox in their fiction – including occasional children's stories – draws upon his many aliases in history and literature to suggest a complex portrait of the Irish countryside. The fox appears in various guises: the Celtic or fairy fox, Chaucer's Dan Russel, wily Reynard of European beast fable, and the harlequin figure who causes quicksilver changes when he enters the scene, with a flick of the tail rather than the harlequin's wand, carrying within himself the essence of folk laughter. His shifting face provides a key to our understanding of the writers' development of Irish short fiction. As the Irish saying goes, the fox is his own messenger; his shape-changing potential manifests the possibilities of transformation in the modern short story. At the same time he unites the different traditions the comic writers parody in their short fiction, combining within his presence the attributes of the folklore, stage, and Anglo-Irish tradition.

Somerville and Ross's fox, then, may belong to Celtic mythology, a hidden Gaelic Ireland, or European beast fable. His connection to beast fable makes him an integral aspect of the fable form and a natural conduit for satire. Yet he is also a part of the Irish countryside, a feature of the landscape and a central figure of the royal hunt. The fox and his brush rouse the *furor venaticus*, just as harlequin and his wand introduce '*la frontière du merveilleux*'.[38] Thus the fox recalls more than one discourse. Perhaps most obviously he is an aspect of the material world. In pursuit of him, the hunt transgresses physical borders: stone walls, closed gates, turf banks. The hunt ignores boundaries and embraces the Irish landscape as its own.

By its very nature fox-hunting calls upon the united efforts of the countryside to participate in the landlord's sport. Without willing farmers and an affable peasantry, the sport could not succeed. As a result, and as noted in Chapter 1, the hunt emerged as an opportunity to exercise passive resistance on the part of Land League sympathizers. In the early 1880s, for instance, the Land League campaign against fox-hunting employed massed groups of people to tramp through the countryside and disturb any possible prey. The game was ruined but the people had not broken the law.[39]

The repeated summoning of the hunt in Somerville and Ross's later fiction has provoked the sharpest criticism of their work. These 'hunting–stable novelists', as Susan Mitchell dismissed them in 1919, 'whipped-up all life into a froth, piling it lightly over the tragic and dark in Ireland, obscuring reality and, with the most amiable of intentions, inflicting a lasting hurt upon the character of their country.'[40] The pageantry of the hunt smacked of triumphalism. Its ability to cover large tracts of land, the farmer's grazing fields and the tenant's smaller plots, in the pursuit of casual delights belittled the land's allotment to the hard-working folk. The proprietary tone of loud voices atop fine horses ranging across a struggling land seemed to assert ownership and to disdain the new land laws. More generally constant reference to the Irish hunt provoked a feeling that Somerville and Ross remained at odds with the times, clinging to outdated representations of Ireland that belonged more rightly to the illustrated cartoons of *Punch* in the 1800s than the altered political landscape of the twentieth century.

Nationalists like Susan Mitchell understood that the struggle for Irish land in early twentieth-century Ireland took place as much on the page as it did in the fields or courtroom. The Ireland which was to advance into the twentieth century as an independent nation could hardly countenance a landscape which celebrated the quintessentially royal sport of riding to hounds. Daniel Corkery suggests something similar when he asserts in *Synge and Anglo-Irish Literature* that those who did not belong (or whom Corkery could not see as belonging) among the crowds attending an Irish hurling match could not possibly write about those who did.[41]

The additional affront of a *comic* treatment of the hunt, laughing landlords blissfully ignorant of the serious business of Irish political landscaping, gave fuel to smouldering nationalist hearts. The suspicion that the tomfoolery of the Irish RM stories provides a deceptively charming picture concealing aristocratic greed may have contributed to the determination to erase the remnants of an Anglo-Irish tradition from the plundered land, to return to a Celtic Eden, or, at least, to present an Irish landscape emptied of Protestant ascendancy myths.

For some critics, Somerville and Ross's hunting stories continued a tradition they saw as threatening.

By tackling the central symbol of British occupation in Ireland in Somerville and Ross's fiction – fox-hunting – and considering its workings in a wider context, this study notes the more complex treatment of the sport. In fact, if we look closer at Somerville and Ross's writing, we discover that, despite their reputation as writers of fox-hunting, Anglo-Irish aficionados waylaid by an obsession with that 'Sport of Kings' and 'King of Sports',[42] Somerville and Ross did not actually concentrate on the hunt until well into their career. Nonetheless their wholehearted involvement in the royal blood sport, in particular Edith Somerville's position as Master of the West Carbery Foxhounds which she assumed in 1903 (the same year that the Wyndham Act indicated so clearly that the land was changing hands)[43] – such involvement has tended to secure their reputation as members of an élite group tediously preoccupied with outdated posturing and distant from the felt life of a politicized Irish countryside. However, while these writers may have been at odds with the popular attitudes of the time, they were certainly involved with politics. I suggest that the later Irish RM stories might be considered a series of landscapes heavily inscribed by distinctly Anglo-Irish *Weltanschauung* that takes imaginative possession of Ireland's green fields.[44] Declan Kiberd has argued that Somerville and Ross's treatment of the Irish hunt in *The Silver Fox* demonstrates the authors' sympathetic understanding of the Catholic Irish peasantry which admits to the failure of English and Anglo-Irish dealings with Ireland.[45] My treatment of Somerville and Ross's later short fiction shows that while the women writers may have included Catholic participants in the Irish hunt, the country always remained a Protestant ascendancy terrain.

Somerville and Ross started writing the Irish RM stories in 1898, the same year they published their fourth novel, *The Silver Fox*, a work that recalls Bram Stoker's *Dracula*, which also appeared in that year.[46] Both novels elaborate on a concept introduced in earlier works, *Naboth's Vineyard* and Stoker's *The Snake's Pass*: the Irish landscape conceals dark and dangerous depths that contain hints of supernatural forces. In *The Silver Fox* and *Dracula*, the concept becomes a dominating metaphor so that the plots of both works revolve around the literal notion of 'going to earth', to use the hunting term. An animal – fox or wolf – embodies the soul of a human and escapes into the ground like some witch or demon of the underworld, recalling the Celtic myth recorded by Sir James Frazer in his *Golden Bough*. The demon/witch transforms itself into a fox, an animal traditionally burnt in the midsummer festival fires.[47] The 'witch or fairy' fox of Somerville and Ross's novel is appropriated from Irish fairy folklore collected in Galway and West Cork.[48]

The writers' lifelong interest in oral culture may have been sharpened in the late 1890s by the notorious incident of 'witch-burning' in Tipperary in 1895, a case that was well documented and discussed in the English and Irish papers of the time.[49] In *The Silver Fox*, Irish folklore is grafted onto Anglo-Irish traditions and the New Woman novel through the device of the fox. In other words, the animal functions as a fairy for the local people, a familiar of the New Woman, Slaney Morris, and also belongs firmly within the sporting world of the Anglo-Irish ascendancy. At the same time, Somerville and Ross's silver witch works as a device in the novel, a means of enticing the hunters onto the dangerous boggy terrain of Ireland's West. The fox enters the dreams of characters and manifests unknown dimensions of the Irish countryside that an Englishman's reckless improvements (the attempt to lay a railway line across the bog) have stirred up. The silver fox exists on the interface of reality (the land) and the unknown (underground), and its natural environment is a suitably mixed element, the 'spongy gravel' of the bogland.[50]

In the first two collections of Somerville and Ross's Irish RM stories, *Some Experiences* (1898) and *Further Experiences* (1908), various invisible foxes create mayhem and elude capture, flying down crannies and crevices in the Irish countryside like ghosts or fairies. With their sporting novel of 1911, Somerville and Ross introduced a more potent kind of fox into their writing, a 'soldier of fortune': 'that good-looking gentleman of many aliases, Dan Russel the Fox'.[51] Sir Russel Fox of Chaucer's 'Nun's Priest Tale'[52] enters the Irish countryside with his own political suggestiveness, and his introduction indicates the writers' interest in using political allegory in their later short fiction. [53] The fabulist qualities of the fox figure would have especially attracted Edith Somerville, who wrote and illustrated a number of children's stories at this time and evidently enjoyed the satirical potential of the beast material.[54] *The Story of the Discontented Little Elephant*, published in 1912, relied on bold pictures of humanized animal figures for comic effect. Most striking of all her children's books must be her unpublished, handmade book, *Growly-Wowly or the Story of the Three Little Pigs*.[55] Brightly illustrated and with a plot in which the youngest female pig gains the upper hand over the wolf, it turns the familiar tale on its head. A later publication, *Little Red Riding-Hood in Kerry* (1934), shows her

appropriating another fairytale for feminist purposes.[56] Somerville's
children's books gave her an opportunity to include her comic illustrations with her writing, but as evidenced by her rewriting of 'Little Red
Riding-Hood', which has no pictures, she was also strongly attracted to
the allegorical and comic possibilities of fairytale and fable.

Edith Somerville's *Story of the Discontented Little Elephant* is set
'midst Indian trees and plants' and tells of a small elephant who loses
his trunk to a hungry tiger. Somerville's skill and pleasure in employing animals is evident in her accompanying illustrations. (Plate 9) She
had some trouble publishing this work since Mr Longman was more
interested in getting further Somerville and Ross short fiction and did
not see a market in the children's material. Somerville's letters to her
agent detail her frustration with Longmans who wanted to publish a
cheaper and smaller version of the text, while Somerville felt her pictures would not have sufficient impact if reduced. 'My pictures,' she
writes to Pinker in 1911, 'were designed for the "shock tactics",
wh[ich] I believe to be the most modern theory of warfare, especially
with savages (i.e. children)'.[57] Perhaps the profusely bleeding wound
of the poor little elephant is meant for shock tactics as well. Certainly
his brutal punishment and the Indian setting recall the 'Cautionary
Tale[s]' of Mrs Mary Sherwood that both Somerville and Ross knew
well.[58] As noted earlier in this study, *The Real Charlotte* refers to Mrs
Sherwood's ideal Victorian family, the Fairchild Family. Somerville
and Ross's allusion to the Fairchilds, however, is satirical; the English
family represents everything that a family based in Ireland just cannot
be. In a similar way the humiliation of the silly elephant who wasn't
satisfied with the length of his nose might be seen as a comic response
to, rather than a repetition of, Sherwood's Sunday-school tales. The
use of animals rather than humans appears to have given Somerville
the opportunity to explore a world where humiliation and comic
reversals are inevitable and central to the form. The animals and their
escapades belong to a suspended time zone that carnival represents.
Talking animals and discontented little elephants do not appear in
normal life, and Somerville's increasing interest in children's literature and adult comic short fiction in the early 1900s was as much
because of her interest in form as it was with finding a medium to promote her pictures. Somerville and Ross would spend the next few
years writing their final collection of Irish RM stories and in the work
the animals and especially the fox become prominent. Indeed the
humans in this final fiction start mirroring the actions of animals, in
particular the animals that populate the story of Reynard.

The same year that Somerville and Ross published *The Real Charlotte*, Walter Crane's illustrated version of Caxton's *History of Reynard the Fox* appeared. The title page of the children's book depicts Reynard petitioning the lion king at his court and every inch of the illustration has been used to include a range of animals – the picture is filled with animal figures surrounding the slim, entreating figure of the fox. Crane's work might be seen as one of various adaptations of the Reynard story in the late nineteenth century. The beast fable was introduced into children's literature as one of Sir Henry Cole's *Home Treasury Series* of the 1840s and was part of a 'conscious effort . . . to produce well-illustrated and well-designed children's storybooks' that differed from the moralistic and rather sombre children's books of the earlier nineteenth century.[59] Sir Henry Cole was the main force behind the Great Exhibition in 1851. According to Thomas J. Arnold, the translator of Goethe's version of the Reynard fable, the Crystal Palace Exhibition revived interest in Reynard in Britain.[60]

Thomas Arnold published the beautifully illustrated children's book *Reynard the Fox, After the German Version of Goethe* in 1887. Goethe's 1793 version, *Reineke Fuchs,* satirizes the corruption of the *ancien régime* during the period of the French Revolution. Martin Ross, an admirer of Goethe's work and, as already noted, an astute political critic with unionist sympathies, would have appreciated the possibilities of the Reynard fable during a period of Home Rule revival. Moreover, as a keen theatre-goer and lover of pantomime, Martin Ross may have noted the fox's connection to harlequin (who sometimes wore the fox's brush), and probably enjoyed productions of Jonson's *Volpone*, illustrated by Aubrey Beardsley in 1897/98. Both Somerville and Ross admired Beardsley's work.

By the end of the century Reynard had multiple manifestations in both children and adult material: in illustration, in theatre and in texts. When Somerville and Ross started writing their ultimate collaborative work, *In Mr Knox's Country*, they showed a strong interest in the beast epic, 'Reynard the Fox'. The final stories transport the allegory, with its connection to the *commedia dell' arte* demonstrated by *Volpone*, onto Irish terrain, telling the old story in a new way so that the politics of the original fable are recharged with a different tradition.

The first two collections of Irish RM stories, then, appear between two less successful novels, *The Silver Fox* and *Dan Russel The Fox*, which concentrate on the hunt. In the earlier novel the fox is a magical and rather sinister creature reminiscent of the fearsome snakes of Stoker's work. In the later novel, however, Sir Russel Fox comes from folk tradition. Characters manifest the attributes of animals in the opening scenes of the novel, an indicator not only of the writers' love of caricature but also of their growing interest in the use of fable in their fiction. As a result, in the final collection of stories Flurry and Sally Knox have settled into the background, the clown Slipper has disappeared,[61] and Flurry's role as the trickster harlequin subsides. The fox of the novels works as contrivance or part of the picturesque background, but the fox enters the short fiction as if he is coming home. The fox of the Irish RM series, especially the final collection, reflects both the content of the stories and the shape they take. No contrivance occurs because the stories are suspended within an Irish chronotope, carnival time when animals and humans have equal significance, when dogs, horses, and donkeys can nearly talk and the fox is in his element. The fox lives underground and frequently leads his pursuers downwards to the centre of his universe and, in the process, he manifests the main impulse of comic satire with its hell-bent thrusting force.

THE FOX AND MRS KNOX

When Reynard was started he faced Tullamore,
Arklow and Wicklow along the seashore.
We kept his brush in view every yard of the way,
And he took his course thro' the streets of Roscrea.
....
When Reynard was taken, his wishes to fulfil,
He called for ink and paper and pen to write his will;
And what he made mention of they found it no blank,
For he gave them a check *on the National* Bank![62]

In Somerville and Ross's final collection of stories, *In Mr Knox's Country*, a battalion of animals enters the lists – much like the numerous animals populating Walter Crane's illustration of *Reynard the Fox*: varieties of dogs and horses, donkeys, a peacock, turkey-cock, and bull, wood-pigeons, rats, rabbits, cows, goats, plenty of bees and ducks, and an animal frequently masquerading as cat or dog – the fox. From the midst of the beasts, old Mrs Knox of Aussolas Castle emerges as a challenge to the rising middle class and her side-kick, the fox, aids her subterfuge.

The first two stories concentrate upon Mrs Knox's reign as an

Anglo-Irish autocrat of a feudalistic estate who still appears to hold sway in the Irish countryside. The middle stories elaborate upon the increasing significance of a middle-class Dublin family, the McRorys, who have bought into Knox country. One of the family, young and pretty Larkie McRory, wins over Major Yeates and company with her cheeky vitality, her 'street-boy quality of being in the movement'.[63] Thus in the penultimate story of the series, 'The Comte De Pralines', we are not too surprised to discover that the young Dubliner wins the ultimate hunt prize, the fox's brush. However, the parody of the rise of the metropolitan middle-class and Irish women – which Larkie McRory represents – is not the final comment of this collection. The last story, 'The Shooting of Shinroe', continues to satirize the hunting process and the idea of Irish treasure with a final, wonderfully bathetic conclusion to the collection.

In the earlier stories Mrs Knox controls house, servants, and family through personality and guile. In 'The Finger of Mrs Knox' she confronts her ex-tenants in a play for supremacy. Though no longer owning the land and close to her deathbed, she still exercises considerable influence. One of the most pathetic of her ex-tenants, whinging and nearly destitute Stephen Casey, petitions her aid to save him from the mercenary reckoning of Goggins, the gombeen man. Old Mrs Knox drives out with Major Yeates in his new motor car to confront Goggins, a successful merchant who has built his property on the 'blood-money'[64] of the local woods, trees planted by his own grandfather as tenant of the Knox family. Goggins is about to claim Stephen Casey's remaining livelihood, a few starving animals, in return for money owed.

In the midst of old Mrs Knox's high-handed demands that Goggins reduce his claim and Goggins's servile but evasive response, Flurry Knox's hunting party arrives on the scene. A sighting of the fox causes such a hullabaloo that everyone, including Stephen Casey's animals, joins the chase. Major Yeates and Mrs Knox take the car but everyone else sprints off on foot, hoof, or paw after the fox. As always in the Irish RM stories, except for 'The Comte De Pralines' where the beast is slaughtered, the fox escapes. The hounds start chasing Casey's donkey, and Yeates mistakes a dog for a fox. By the end of the tale Yeates finds himself gulled twice, once by Mrs Knox, who leaves the British civil servant to pay Casey's debt, and once by the fox. Luckily for Yeates he has no money. So as a final and clever twist in the story Mrs Knox suggests that Goggins pay Yeates the money owed. Goggins ends up paying himself.

The fox and Mrs Knox are equal in their stratagems and sleight of hand. Each slips away from the various traps set for them. Time ignores them. At age 90-plus, Mrs Knox's existence spans the nineteenth century and she has chased and plotted against many a fox in her time. They collaborate at this stage. Various biographers, following the lead of Lady Gregory, who first noted the resemblance, draw comparison between Mrs Knox and Martin Ross's mother.[65] Mrs Martin's maiden name, Fox, could suggest a connection between the fictional representatives of the old-Irish world: Mrs Knox and the fox.

Even more significant, however, is Somerville and Ross's treatment of the story of Reynard in 'The Finger of Mrs Knox'. A consideration of the popular late nineteenth-century translation of Goethe's version of the Reynard material suggests that Anglo-Irish writers may have appropriated the political allegory in their short fiction.

The stories of the Reynard cycle satirize feudal society through the trickster-hero's ability to outwit established authority. The folk material is the stuff of carnival, when the individual and his anarchic stratagems overcome order and introduce momentary mayhem into the normal state of affairs. The fox is the villain; the lion is the king, the wolf the dupe and the donkey the victim. Reynard is also devilishly clever and takes on the role of unmasker in *Reineke Fuchs*; the fox exposes greed and ambition within the kingdom. His name, as Goethe's translator, Thomas Arnold, points out, comes from the German *Reinhart* and the Flemish *Reinært*, and means 'counsellor' or 'advisor'. His fortress, Malpertuis, means 'an evil hole'.[66]

Various animals whinge to King Noble about Reynard's tricks, pleading for his intercession and help. While some of their stories are true, others are half-fabrications; either they blame the fox for their own misdeeds or mask the fact of their contribution to his unlawful acts. Reynard is the source of envy and resentment in many of his fellow subjects because first, he is the shrewdest among a clever bunch, and second, he has set himself apart from their society. He is an outlaw. When the king sends a series of royal messengers to bring Reynard to justice at court, the fox tricks and humiliates each one of them. Each trick – Reynard fooling Bruin the Bear by appealing to his gluttony for honey; Reynard tricking Tybalt the cat into the trap which has been set for Reynard himself – tells its own story. Finally Reynard's friend the badger brings him to court and the fox arrives believing he can fool them all, even the king himself.

Reynard has few sympathizers and is quickly sentenced to death.

But the wily fox manages once more to trick everyone by hinting at a wondrous hidden treasure, a secret stash concealed deep in the darkness of the earth. Seduced by his own covetousness, the king lets Reynard go, but instead of finding treasure for the king, the fox gobbles up one of the royal messengers and sends his skin back to court. There never was any secret treasure; nonetheless, the lure of diamonds and gold compels the king to heed Reynard's hints. The fox's ultimate trick, then, is to promise wondrous treasure; that promise proves to be the bait which no animal, not even a lion, can resist. However much the king might doubt the existence of the treasure, to ignore the lure is to lose the promise of untold riches.[67]

A number of connections between the fable and *In Mr Knox's Country* might be drawn. Bruin the Bear's gluttony, for instance, is repeated in the Englishman, Chichester, in 'The Friend of Her Youth'. This 'well-fed and *passé* schoolboy'[68] dines on the Derryclare's heather honey like some greedy bear, and he falls into foolishness because of his own stomach. In another story, 'Harrington's', the hidden secrets and 'the thrill of possible treasure-trove'[69] at the auction situated next to a disused gold mine remind us of Reynard's imaginary treasure. The riches of the Irish auction prove to be just as elusive when Yeates ends up bidding for and buying his own ladder. Throughout the Irish RM stories Somerville and Ross capitalize on the notion of the hidden Ireland as a place of treasure, a source of ultimate truth and lost glory, which, however distant or vague, must be respected by the authorities that be. The treasure in the Irish RM stories lurks behind the shifting face of the Irish terrain, safeguarded by an Irish fox.

It is not my intent to list the numerous links between the folk tale and Somerville and Ross's stories, however. Suffice it to say that the fable – and especially the wily fox – resonate throughout their final collection. This politicized material with its connection to the carnivalesque and its use of allegory, which might be considered a kind of masking, contains universal questions about society and power. Goethe's version, as popularized by Thomas Arnold, sets up an argument between the forces of the aristocracy and those of democracy.[70] Reference to the beast fable gives resonance and depth to the Irish material. We might keep in mind, then, that the story of Reynard deals with attempts to control the kingdom, and in Somerville and Ross's short fiction the various visiting English characters to Mrs Knox's/Fox's Castle might be seen as royal envoys attempting to control the wily old trickster. Knox/Fox acts as an outsider in 'The Finger of Mrs Knox', resented for the cleverness and brutality that has given her the upper-hand among the king's subjects, and suspected of holding vast reservoirs of treasure in her decrepit house.

Mrs Knox's position repeats that of the hero of an earlier story by Martin Ross's older brother, Robert, called 'St Patrick's Day in the Morning'. However in Robert Martin's semi-autobiographical tale, the Anglo-Irish landlord, debt-ridden and forced by a changing social system to evacuate his castle, sees himself as victim rather than as master of the situation:

> This hunting season is over, and for the last run of the season the Master is the fox. The Hard Time Hounds will soon run him from scent to view, and there is nothing for him but to look for another country for some seasons to come.[71]

Like his hero in 'St Patrick's Day in the Morning', Robert Martin also left his 'country' (the Martin territory of Galway), pursued by 'the Hard Time Hounds' (Charles Stewart Parnell's pack). Unfortunately he did not discover a pot of gold in Australia with which to recover his estate, as the hero of his fiction does. Somerville and Ross knew both the dream and the reality of his position. Martin Ross would also have recalled the fate of another brother, aptly named Charles Fox Martin, who died in a horse accident while serving in an Indian regiment in Taipeng in 1893.[72]

One might argue that Somerville and Ross, like Robert Martin, reverse Reynard's role in their short story. In the beast fable the fox symbolizes the cleverness of the enlightened individual by demonstrating the stratagems of the royal hunt's prey. By placing autocratic Mrs Knox in Reynard's position, by making the hunter the hunted in a changing Ireland, Somerville and Ross appear to subvert the fabulist material. Such a supposition would fall in with Terry Eagleton's observation on the paradoxical reversal of the Irish ascendancy's perception of itself as victim in Maturin's *Melmoth the Wanderer* or Stoker's *Dracula*. Eagleton reads the alienated and doomed Melmoth as a symbol of the Irish Protestant governing class:

> Their sense of persecution, in part at least, is a dread of the vengeance of those they have persecuted. Estranged from the populace by culture and religion, the elite can easily mistake itself for the marginal, and so misperceive itself as a mirror image of the people themselves. The hunters become the hunted: and this is surely one reason why the figure of the self-lacerating Satanic hero can strike such a powerful resonance.[73]

The exploiter, says Eagleton, 'has put himself beyond the pale of humanity, and so is curiously on terms with those he dispossesses'.[74]

In a similar way Stoker's *Dracula* has been read as an expression of colonial anxiety. The 'old fox', as Van Helsing describes the vampire, is put to the chase by his pursuers when they 'sterilize his lairs, so that he cannot use them of old'.[75] The hunter becomes in the course of the novel the prey of new-world 'knights of the Cross'.[76] In broken English, Van Helsing tells his fellow Christian huntsmen that they will go and 'do what our friend Arthur [Godalming] call, in his phrases of hunt "stop the earths" and so we run down our old fox – so? is it not?'.[77] The reversal of the vampire's role makes him go to ground, like a fox, and assists in Eagleton's perception of the figure as Anglo-Irish ascendancy:

> The ascendancy, too will evaporate once their earth is removed from them, though to wrench it from them will demand rather more than a sprig of garlic and rather less than a stake through the heart.[78]

Somerville and Ross's treatment of the Reynard material does not demonstrate this neat reversal. The writers parody an Anglo-Irish trope as depicted in Robert Martin's story by turning *their* fox into a stage figure. Instead of a misplaced psychological projection that transforms the colonizer into an outlawed figure, the exploiter into the exploited, as Eagleton suggests, I argue that the adoption of marginalized figures like the fox (or harlequin or Mephisto or even Dracula) derives from a burlesque tradition. If we consider the role of the 'hunted' in Ben Jonson's *Volpone*, for instance, popularized at the end of the nineteenth century by Beardsley's illustrations, we discover that the prey has become the hunter in the burlesque form. Such a rehabilitation of the beast fable material does not demonstrate a suppressed anxiety regarding England's role in Europe so much as put into action a fundamental satirical device: everything is turned upside down.

Like Volpone in Jonson's play, Mrs Knox, with her suspected (and coveted) wealth/position, is a manipulator in her own right. If there is any reversal at all in 'The Finger of Mrs Knox', it is that the fox has become the hunter; she has turned the tables on her pursuers. In *Volpone*, we recall that various animal-like characters covet the fox's treasure, his gold: Voltore, the lawyer-vulture, Corvino, the merchant-crow, and Corbaccio, the old man-raven. The treasure as bait and the fox's stratagems, aided by the devilish Mosca (the *Hellequin* of medieval folklore) become artful manipulations whereby the middle-class is exposed in all its gullibility and greed. Somerville and

Ross's treatment of the beast fable works in a similar manner. Mrs Knox and the fox use themselves as bait to expose Goggins's greed. As in Goethe's version of the Reynard story, the fox is the trickster, a comic cousin of harlequin, rather than a victim of the 'Hard Time Hounds' let loose by Irish nationalist politics. Indeed, to discover the possible political purpose of Somerville and Ross's later story, we might consider its context when it first appeared in 1913 rather than rely solely on a comparison to the earlier and rather obvious comic stories of the Irish landowner Robert Martin.

As already noted, 'The Finger of Mrs Knox' pits the craft and authority of a weakened Anglo-Irish autocracy against the opportunistic usury of gombeenism, and thus it is frequently cited as the most political of the Irish RM stories.[79] *Blackwood's* published the story in June 1913; it followed a series of articles debating Asquith's Home Rule Bill introduced in April of the previous year. In 1912 and 1913, *Blackwood's* published four sustained attacks on the Bill. Sir John Pentland Mahaffy of Trinity College Dublin wrote three of these articles. 'What is Nationality?' in February 1912 argued that nationality, a sentiment of brotherhood supported by a supposed commonality of race, home, language and religion, cannot be ascribed to by the Irish in all their differences. The resurgence of the Gaelic language, Mahaffy's pet hate, is a backward step towards isolationism and ultimately stifles progress. 'Will Home Rule Be Rome Rule?' published the following August by Mahaffy, stated the arguments of the minority Irish Protestants and the educated Roman Catholics against the power of the Catholic Church in Ireland as it would expand or be limited with Home Rule. Then, in February 1913, Mahaffy's 'Who Wants Home Rule?' outlined for the *Blackwood's* reader what he saw as dubious support for Home Rule in Ireland and argued against a too precipitate, almost reckless, voting in of the measure. Those who want Home Rule consist of:

> Jackeens, Buckeens, Horse-dealers, Gombeen men, idle sons of strong farmers or of respectable shopkeepers, insubordinate school-teachers, editors of local newspapers, leader writers in the same, patriot poets, bankrupt traders. To all such a new vista of success is opened.[80]

Additional arguments against the Home Rule Bill appear in editorial commentary and in an article published in January 1913 by the imperialist Arthur Page, called 'Ireland and the Empire'. Particular attention in these pieces is given to the Ulster unionists, who would be 'under the heel' of nationalists if Home Rule went through.

Somerville and Ross's story responds directly to the ongoing

Home Rule debate in *Blackwood's Magazine*, but to what extent does the comic fiction support either side of the argument? The direct allusion to the usurpation of the landed gentry through the Irish Land Acts of the early twentieth century in 'The Finger of Mrs Knox' leads analysts to read the story as a critique of the emergence of adept profiteering in the New Ireland.[81] Direct juxtaposition of the old world (Mrs Knox in Aussolas Castle) and the new (Major Yeates's car, reference to cinematography) appears to confirm the sense in this story that a golden, feudal age has passed. For example, Joseph Devlin reads 'The Finger of Mrs Knox' as a romanticization of the 'old feudal order' and Mrs Knox as a manifestation of the writers' 'desired status' to be female autocrats: 'Faced with the evaporation of landlord control and their own double marginality as unattached women, Somerville and Ross created an all-powerful female character able to hold her own, and able to hold the land'.[82] Yet the story's context in *Blackwood's* suggests a gentle dig at Mahaffy's entrenched and biased position, while the deployment of the fox/harlequin material demands that we ask to what extent the feudal backdrop facilitates form. The longing for a Golden Age – as *Volpone* shows with its *commedia dell'arte* figures, whose craving for the fox's treasure satirizes the Renaissance ideal – is echoed in the romantic depiction of past Anglo-Irish glories. In short, though the story is located within an ongoing argument related to land ownership and Home Rule (an argument already shown to be of particular interest to Martin Ross), it presents a complex version that parodies as much as it propagates the unionist position. More important than sentimental musings on the Anglo-Irish past is the modernizing treatment of form.

'The Finger of Mrs Knox' creates an Irish feudal landscape, not to mull over the passage of ascendancy rule, but to incorporate within the short fiction the beast fable material. The antique setting furthers the sense of timelessness we identify with carnival and, more recently, the short story form. The political commentary lies in the authors' reworking of the Reynard fable, rather than their depiction of Ireland as feudal landscape. All those elements perceived to be indicative of the authors' lament for the aristocratic past could also be seen as aesthetic devices used to generate the developing genre of modern short fiction (which *Blackwood's* encouraged) as well as providing an implicit, if uneasy, commentary on the Anglo-Irish role. Aussolas Castle and Mrs Knox, her sycophantic, whining ex-tenant, the hunt and the hounds, 'like creatures in a tapestry hunting scene', the variety of animal and human life, 'from goat to gombeen man',[83] and above all the trickery of both Mrs Knox and the fox directly recall the fable of Reynard. The material is carefully set in the new world so that Yeates and Mrs Knox chase the hunt by car and Mrs Knox's 'rule' possesses no real meaning in modern Ireland. Thus the story recreates the fabulist material and continues its aims by parodying exaggerated perceptions of ascendancy rule (Mrs Knox possesses no real power), British authority in Ireland (Yeates remains bewildered), and nationalist ideals of the rising middle-class (Goggins swindles the poor).

Somerville and Ross's later fiction utilizes multiple discourse to debunk various land myths while, at the same time, erecting upon the Irish literary landscape a structure of Anglo-Irish make. Their intent, to continue establishing within the Irish literary landscape an Anglo-Irish tradition, is complicated by other preoccupying interests: the tension generated by colliding time zones or chronotopes in the Irish countryside, the means by which their subject matter reflects the form their narrative takes, and the political implications of beast allegory when transported onto Irish terrain. These issues reflect upon the authors' political intents during their final years writing together as the popular Irish writers Somerville and Ross.

THE HUNT

What has hunting got to say to politics? Hunting is sport, pure and simple, which everyone has an equal right to enjoy, and if they ride straight like sportsmen, they are admired, no matter what their political ideas may be.

'THE FOX'[84]

The final stories of *In Mr Knox's Country*, 'The Comte De Pralines' and 'The Shooting of Shinroe', offer two different kinds of parodies of fox-hunting and treasure-seeking in the Irish landscape. The first of these stories is a send-up (and celebration) of the Irish hunt as battlefield in the process of empire-building, while the second story uses anticlimax as a final swooping descent into the countryside of the Irish RM series. The first story includes a range of pantomime-like props, elaborate disguise, acrobatics, a country wedding scene, swift alteration of scenery, and heady, nearly frantic, action. The second story is monochromatic, set in shades of grey, and with only a few slow-moving characters. Though the action of both stories takes place in November, 'The Comte De Pralines' presents the rich backdrop of

Castle Knox where the Englishwoman, Lady Knox, presides, and the hunt for the fox takes place in fine, balmy weather, a 'steamy day'.[85] The ever-changing topography includes charming blue lakes, the woods of the demesne, and sleek pastures. This is West Cork. In 'The Shooting of Shinroe' bleak weather and an unchanging landscape of stone, bog, and clumps of furze against a backdrop of 'elephant-grey mountains'[86] suggest that this could be Connemara (though ostensibly the setting is Munster).

Both stories involve the hunt, and though the first includes a fox in its narrative – in fact the plot's climax tells of the killing of the fox – Reynard has disappeared. His mask has changed. Similarly old Mrs Knox no longer figures. Her absence is especially important because killing the fox in 'The Comte De Pralines', like the bloody massacre of the 'old fox' Dracula, has been seen as an act representing the destruction of the Anglo-Irish class.[87] However, though a struggle for position does occur in this story, the Fox/Knox alignment of the earlier part of the collection fades. Instead, an imperial English authority in the shape of Lady Knox presides while Flurry becomes a more remote and intractable presence, with traces of Ulster stubbornness in his lines. In 'The Shooting of Shinroe', then, a desolate and empty Irish landscape has been cleared of the usual RM cast and their prey, the fox. This last story, like one of Jack Yeats's later paintings, 'The Circus Tent Comes Down', where two figures stand alone in a desolate landscape, undercuts the colourful antics of previous work. Somerville and Ross's last story casts its readers downwards into the depths of dark humour. The story ends in the blackness of a wet Irish November night, a suitable place to leave the Irish RM series.

By 1914, when Somerville and Ross were writing 'The Comte De Pralines',[88] Edith Somerville had contributed various essays on the Irish hunt to the sporting magazines. In an article called 'The Irish Citizen' (1913) she claimed that women, like men, could contribute as much to Irish political life as they could to the Irish Horse Show. The women of Ireland, she argued, must 'be given a share in ruling as well as in riding their country'.[89] The victorious rise of the middle-class Dubliner, Larkie McRory, in 'The Comte De Pralines', her capture of the fox's brush, charts a double victory: the success of metropolitan Dublin and Irish women. Yet Larkie's triumph on the early twentieth-century battlefield of Irish cultural politics occurs only with the benign leadership and assistance of a visiting Englishman, Simpson-Hodges, and is manoeuvred through trickery and dogged determination. In this story the Irish hunt turns into a battlefield.

Flurry Knox becomes an Ulster blockade, while Lady Knox represents the English imperial dictate. Both are outdone by middle-class Dublin, a new kind of Englishman who wears masks to achieve his end, and a Catholic priest who leads them to their prize. Both factions, the Protestant bloc and the Catholic confederation, seek as their treasure or prize the capture and execution of Mr Fox.

In 'The Comte De Pralines', the English envoy to Knox's Country, the handsome Simpson-Hodges, deceives his Irish hosts by pretending to be a French Count. Simpson-Hodges is nicknamed 'Mossoo', the same sobriquet as Robert Martin's visiting French 'Mossoo' in his earlier comic song 'Killaloe'. Somerville and Ross's English-Frenchman's skill at caricature is so great that people claim 'he ought to be making a hundred a week on the stage'.[90] Certainly with his bright pink hunting coat and glistening silk hat, his 'mellifluous French', and courteous bows, he seems too French to be true. Ever-alert Flurry suspects mischief and stubbornly resists the bait, throwing Major Yeates 'a look . . . expressive of No Surrender'.[91] Flurry backs off from this play for power in carnival world (by taking up the Protestant Ulster position), and removes himself from the playing field. Larkie, however, has no fear. The Count's ability to disturb the meet at Castle Knox, to cause serious ripples of unease among the usual cast of characters, is comparable to that of the fox himself, who soon arrives to wreak havoc.

The transformation into organized chaos which the fox effects and the ensuing race somewhat disturb Mossoo's subterfuge. Larkie McRory, hot on his handsome heels, learns of his deception when very English expletives slip from his mustachioed mouth. But Larkie, like her forerunner Francie Fitzpatrick in *The Real Charlotte*, is always game for trickery and fun. She admires the Count's ability to swear just as well in French as in English, his oath falling as 'theatrical as a drop-scene, on the close of the first act'.[92] Mossoo proves to be as good as anyone – if not better – at showmanship in Ireland.

Half-way through the chase, the keenest riders, Larkie, Mossoo, Yeates, and Miss Bennett, lose their prey and are waylaid by a priest whose dress, 'an immaculate black coat and top-hat', is as pretty (and as pantomime-like) as that of Mossoo. By the end of the hunt, his significance as a vehicle of change becomes apparent.

The usual suspects have lost the fox and the hounds in their chase across the countryside. Mossoo and the Dubliner, however, are initially stalled by the acrobatic toppling of the former, but they recover well enough to slip away and bring about the grand finale of the chase. When the Irish RM cast eventually arrive at the site of the fox's execution, a field with a small chapel wherein a country wedding group has gathered, they discover that the Englishman, the Dubliner, and the priest have beat them to their quarry:

> We were in the straggling field with furzy patches in it. At the farther end of it was a crowd of country people on horses and on foot, obviously more wedding-guests; back of all, on a road below, was a white-washed chapel, and near it, still on the chestnut horse, was the priest who had headed the morning fox. Close to one of the clumps of furze the Comte de Pralines was standing, knee-deep in baying hounds, holding the body of the fox high above his head, and uttering scream upon scream of the most orthodox quality. He flung the fox to the hounds, the onlookers cheered, Miss McRory, seated on the car-horse, waved the brush above her head, and squealed at the top of her voice something that sounded like 'Yoicks!' Her hair was floating freely down her back; a young countryman, in such sacrificial attire as suggested the bridegroom, was running across the field with her hat in his hand.
>
> Flurry pulled up in silence; so did we. We were all quite outside the picture, and we knew it.[93]

The priest, significantly, spotted the fox and revealed him to the Englishman and the Dubliner. Their imperial contenders of the battlefield, Flurry with his 'iron face' and Lady Knox with a profile 'as inflexible as a profile on a coin – a Roman coin',[94] find themselves outmanoeuvred and no longer part of the tableau (for the moment). The fox is caught and killed in a jubilant and Catholic rite. This victory, of course, is tolerated within Flurry's domain, in Mr Knox's country.

Larkie McRory's triumph in 'The Comte De Pralines' suggests that the story might be read as an allegory of the Anglo-Irish demise. Such a reading, however, misses the nuances of the piece. As in a pantomime, familiar figures, such as Flurry or the fox, adopt different roles in each story. Flurry's original role as trickster has been taken over by the new character, Simpson-Hodges. The fox has also changed his aspect. He may still be Protestant, however, as his swift slaughter by a priest-led middle-class recalls the downfall of another 'Mr Fox' of Irish politics, Charles Stewart Parnell, who adopted the alias when writing to his lover, Katharine O'Shea. Or, the pursuit and slaughter of the fox might recall the persecution of the founding leader of the Society of Friends, George Fox, whom James Joyce described as 'Christfox in leather trews, hiding, a runaway in blighted treeforks, from hue and cry'.[95] The Irish Quakers' marginal position in a society preoccupied by a Protestant/Catholic dynamic is emphasized by the Society of Friends' refusal to swear allegiance to either a royal or a national authority.

Any allegorical reading of the fox's demise in Somerville and Ross's fiction can only be tentative. Thus the fox's end in 'The Comte De Pralines' may not signify as much as the depiction of the Irish hunt as battlefield. The portrayal gives evidence of the colonial heritage of a soldiering family like the Somervilles. It shows the writers' involvement in the war-making enterprise. In fact when writing this story Edith Somerville was particularly interested in the development of the Irish Volunteer Movement that had been set up in response to the Ulster Volunteers,[96] and the summer spent drafting the story also saw outbreak of war in Europe.

The sense that the Irish hunt serves as a mock battle suggests that the particular war being waged in the story is a fair fight, and that both camps are after the same ends. The Irish hunt, like the battlefield, possesses its own laws (however chaotic the sport may appear), just as the 'country' of Mr Knox is its own state, 'a state within a state' as Simon Schama describes the royal hunt:

> For a warrior state, the royal hunt was always more than a pastime, however compulsively pursued. Outside of war itself, it was the most important blood ritual through which the hierarchy of status and honor around the King was ordered.[97]

As Master of the Irish hunt, Flurry Knox rules with despotic intent. His Anglo-Irish world, 'Mr Knox's Country', remains intact whether or not a female Dubliner wins her spurs in this particular chase. The struggle for ascendancy takes place within the Anglo-Irish framework where the rituals and laws are those of the hunt. It does not matter who loses or wins in 'The Comte De Pralines'. All remain in Mr Knox's country and play by the rules of the Anglo-Irish state.

The last story of *In Mr Knox's Country* and the Irish RM stories, 'The Shooting of Shinroe', provides an anti-climactic conclusion to the treasure-hunt in the Irish countryside. The plain tale reduces the fine flourishes of the previous pieces to a single ludicrous event which brings Somerville and Ross's short fiction to a bleakly comic conclusion. The story takes a final swipe at the preoccupying interest of late nineteenth- and early twentieth-century Irish cultural politics, the hidden Ireland or the treasure in the bog. Such an ending to a series of comic turns on Irish affairs seems especially apt as both the content and the form thrust the reader's focus downwards one last time. The use of anticlimax, the subject matter, and the positioning of this story in the collection stress the nature of Somerville and Ross's work as a whole.

'The Shooting of Shinroe' builds on a familiar Irish site, using material already worked by writers like Bram Stoker in *The Snake's Pass* and Robert Martin in 'Connemara Short Cut'. Ostensibly the story is set in the same place as the rest of the collection, but the landscape bears the marks of the West. The eternal presence of water – streams, bogholes, puddles, and the glint of sea in the distance as the sportsmen poach Shinroe mountain – the isolation of the setting and the lowness of the sky, 'like the roof of a marquee,'[98] are reminiscent of land around Recess or Maam Cross as much as Jack Yeats's low circus tent. Major Yeates is not so much a character in this story as a borrowed voice, that of 'Ballyhooly' (Robert Martin's sobriquet), who speaks about a wily Irish solicitor called M'Cabe. The solicitor brings Major Yeates shooting on Shinroe, but they find nothing except a bottle of poitín concealed in a furze bush. Major Yeates believes that they are on a proper shooting expedition and discovers only in the latter half of their search that they are actually poaching on land whose rights have been purchased by an English syndicate – like the Martin stronghold of Ballinahinch Castle.

The topography of Shinroe mountain contains no mysteries. The bogholes and stony terrain yield nothing except for a few cows and sheep. The atmosphere is close, and yet the men's journey seems endless as each turn reveals nothing more than further stone, water, and bogland. M'Cabe's pleasure in the hunt declines steadily and his frustration is furthered by two mundane facts. First, his new set of dentures fits uneasily into his mouth and underscores his normal loquacity with a strange metallic click. Second, the dentist who charged him seven pounds ten for his new teeth, a young upstart with a motorbike, has taken to hunting M'Cabe's territory and catching bagfuls of game.

The pair spends the day chasing the dog that the same dentist lent M'Cabe, getting lost en route, until they are eventually picked up by an outside car bearing two RIC men and their prisoner, a poacher, back to civilization. By now evening has set, and it seems like night in the November countryside. Major Yeates and his companion have trudged the landscape a good eight hours, and M'Cabe gratefully remembers their findings in the bogland, the poitín. He attempts to pull off his glove with his teeth so that he can open the bottle and, ludicrously, out pop his dentures. The teeth fly out the car window into the pitch-black countryside.

A second hunt ensues, and this time M'Cabe's 'gosling-like lisp' and the object of their search – false teeth – shrinks the search to ridiculous proportions. The characters creep along the roadside, 'bent double, like gorillas'[99] and scour the stone and puddles for the missing dentures. The RIC join the hunt, and the parody becomes more pointed when the diligent sergeant thinks he has discovered the missing teeth shining in the darkness:

> 'I see something white beyond you, Mr M'Cabe,' he said respectfully, 'might that be them?'
> M'Cabe swung his lamp as indicated.
> 'No, it might not. It's a pebble,' he replied, with pardonable irascibility.
> Silence followed, and we worked our way up the hill.
> 'What's that, sir?' ventured the sergeant, with some excitement, stopping again and pointing. 'I think I see the gleam of gold!'
> 'Ah, nonthenth, man! They've vulcanite!' snapped M'Cabe, more irascible than ever.[100]

The glimmer of fool's gold in the black boglands of the Irish landscape turns the grand search for Irish treasure, a dominant trope of cultural nationalism and the imperial romance, into a deliberately anticlimactic pursuit. For the second time our heroes do not find anything. Instead the distraction allows the poacher to escape with their only means of transport out of the destitute landscape. The Irish RM series ends with two isolated figures shuffling in the dark – minus teeth, light, and hope – in a blackness as intense and thorough as the deepest boghole of the West, St Patrick's hole, perhaps, and as suitable as possible a position to leave Major Yeates in the conclusion to the parodic farces of Somerville and Ross's stories.

The use of hunting in Somerville and Ross's later fiction clearly raises a political argument. Hunting has everything to do with politics. However, the comic short fiction does not expound a party line or exploit the Irish landscape to detail the workings of opposing political factions so much as undercut and display as false the notion that 'politics' is an abstract reality. Instead the stories demonstrate the craftiness of local politics working within a heavily inscribed Anglo-Irish world, Mr Knox's country. They show how umbrella terms provide a cover for actual deals among the people, and that those transactions inevitably revolve around plots of land, a clutch of livestock, sums of money. The Irish RM stories are a series of burlesques which subvert romantic ideology. At the same time they demonstrate in their make-up a practical and particularly Irish politics at work, what George Birmingham described as the chiaroscuro of thought identifying the flexible Irish mind. *In Mr Knox's Country* might thus be described as stories that demonstrate the manipulation of the system by shifting the point of view as the situation warrants and by exploiting the reader's expectations with regard to such concepts as 'Home Rule' or 'the Irish Problem'.

Although these stories make prominent the Anglo-Irish tradition, the writers' obsession with the landlord's sport does much more than give opportunity to map out an Anglo-Irish literary terrain. Consideration of Somerville and Ross's involvement with pantomime and beast fable suggests a wider interest that reflects both visual and textual influences of the time. The adroit and tricky fox in Somerville and Ross's writing, his multiple masks and comic potential, resists one particular reading of the landlord's sport. The ever-shifting angles of Somerville and Ross's final collaborative work, which Martin Ross believed to be the best of their three collections,[101] display the art of the fox that lies at the heart of the writing. The free-flying fox's passage through these stories, his flight into the earth and multiple aliases, demonstrates the inability of the fiction to capture or to enclose the various masks/traditions of the Irish landscape. His political significance, however, is central, for the fox manifests the strategy and evasion of politics in a tumultuous and difficult terrain. What is more, the short story form finds a fitting proponent in the furtive fox – timeless, evasive, the very essence of political strategy in a tricky world.

Conclusion

In early December 1915, Martin Ross became very ill. Almost immediately the doctors discovered a tumour at the base of her brain. A few weeks later she died, aged 53. Edith Somerville was devastated. Her last sketch of her writing partner, a study in black and white, was carefully worked at Martin Ross's bedside a few days before her death. Martin's profiled face rests on a pillow, as though she were asleep. Her features, exaggerated somewhat by illness, are accentuated further by shadows around her aquiline nose and heavy eyelids. Of her many drawings and caricatures of Martin Ross, this one Edith Somerville prized. Writing to her brother Cameron at the time, she quotes a character from *The Real Charlotte*. The disreputable housekeeper, Norry the Boat, becomes a strange source of comfort during this period of grief:

> It is no use to cry & to weep – As Norry the Boat said, 'You might as well be dancing and singing.' Whether . . . I sit on the safety valve, or whether I cried my grief to the four winds it would make no difference. Half – the best half – of my life & soul is torn away & there are no words & no tears that can cure my trouble.[1]

Somerville's reliance on art and fiction as sources of comfort was rudely interrupted when requests from journalists for information about the collaboration arrived at Drishane House. What everyone wanted to know about this successful writing partnership was who *really* wrote the fiction. Impatient with such questions, Edith wrote to Cameron: 'How abhorrent is to me all the senseless curiosity as to "which held the pen" . . . the books are the thing – not the wretched heart-broken survivor of the once "brilliant literary collaboration" '.[2]

Despite Somerville's claim that 'the books are the thing', critics have always paid particular attention to the biographies of these 'two Victorian maiden ladies'.[3] Perhaps such curiosity resulted from class awareness in Ireland. Indeed, the life concealed behind the demesne wall could beckon as evocatively as any other secret aspect of the Irish landscape. Whatever the case, the collaborators were often perceived as detached from the vital changes of Irish society. Some critics depicted them as rather eccentric types whose partnership recalled the romantic friendship of the Ladies of Llangollen.[4] For many, their works retained an old-fashioned quality, not unlike that ascribed to another female collaboration of the late nineteenth century, the Scottish writers Jane and Mary Findlater. Despite powerful analysis of female poverty and the dualism of character in a novel like *Crossriggs* of 1908, the Findlater sisters came to be associated with outdated productions of the late Victorian popular novel.[5]

The main thrust of Somerville and Ross's work is a modern awareness which develops from the writers' Victorian backgrounds. Somerville and Ross realized in their fiction a complex Irish world which allowed them the possibility of refashioning traditional images in a self-conscious manner. Their collaboration does not so much recall a late eighteenth-century sensibility as it suggests late nineteenth-century possibilities. They decided to write fiction together because they knew it to be worthwhile. After all, their uncles, first cousins Loftus Fox (Martin Ross's uncle) and Joscelyn Coghill (Edith Somerville's uncle), started up the Dublin periodical *Metropolitan Magazine* in the 1830s. Yet another cousin, William G. Wills, published his first fiction in the magazine,[6] and he too worked with various partners to produce popular works. Following such a lead, Robert Martin joined up with others on numerous pantomimes for Dublin's Gaiety Theatre. However Somerville and Ross most successfully managed the art of collaboration by coupling complementary skills, utilizing Edith Somerville's illustrations, and targeting the flourishing magazine business of the 1890s. Their enormous popularity in Britain gives testament to the writers' ability to tap into contemporary concerns while entertaining with a light and sure hand.

Various figures in the fiction represent the dynamic force of modern progress, that quality of 'being in the moment'. In its more positive manifestations, Francie Fitzpatrick and Larkie McRory tease readers with their charming and heedless ability to push ahead. Less attractive but equally compelling is the ugly thrusting forward of grotesque females like Harriet Donovan. The countering of this compulsion with that of a static state (as represented in particular characters like Christopher Dysart or certain manifestations such as the pack of white dogs in 'The Whiteboys') creates a constant friction in the fiction, an uneasy and ever-shifting surface. Charlotte Mullen reflects this ambiguity in her own person. Her progressiveness is complicated by her symbolic meaning in the text. She is a modern woman but she is also a cypher, a kind of harlequin figure. Her 'shifting face' recalls early nineteenth-century Irish characters (Florence Macarthy, Melmoth, Silas Ruthyn) and might be situated within the larger discourse of national character. However, in Somerville and Ross's changing Irish world, this type becomes a new phenomenon. Grotesques like Charlotte Mullen manifest the dynamic realities of late nineteenth-century Ireland as they are informed by a *fin-de-siècle* self-consciousness.

As inheritors of a colonial tradition, Somerville and Ross directly address the dreams and nightmares of the colonial vision. In their satirical novels they concentrate on the shabby underside of Irish life, the half-concealed recesses and muddy crevices of the Irish landscape. The troubling ordinariness of evil and the uneasy effects of casual evasion or half-told truths direct these narratives downwards. The colonial nightmare terrain of *Naboth's Vineyard* has a banality that disturbs more profoundly than the fierce demons of Mephisto's Brocken in *Faust* and is not so unlike the bland colonial dreams of *The Real Charlotte*. Christopher's mission, after all, takes shape only when faced by the troubling, dark forces of the earth.

Because everything in Somerville and Ross's Irish world is turned upside down in the manner of a Gilbert and Sullivan farce, Christopher's Christian dreams become simple delusions. The evangelical mission becomes a conviction that he can teach Francie about poetry. The seemingly harmless belief actually blinds him to ordinary reality and indirectly leads to terrible consequences. We thus witness the destruction of the weak and the vulnerable – the outcast, Julia Duffy, the sickly Mrs Lambert, and the uneducated Francie – because Christopher can only fight shadows rather than confront the emerging power epitomized in the middle-class greed of Charlotte Mullen.

Somerville and Ross's upending of an Anglo-Irish Protestant ethos does not forestall their intent to stake a claim on the Irish literary terrain. Subsuming that intent, however, is the larger demand of the artistic production. This study of Somerville and Ross's recreation of 'Mr Knox's Country' upon the Irish literary landscape cautions against strictly allegorical interpretations of their long and short fiction. Their self-awareness indicates artful manoeuvre of narrative tropes. Thus the historical realities of the period must be considered within an imaginative framework. In other words, to consider Somerville and Ross's work as a mirror of the Protestant ascendancy position, a commentary on its demise, is to ignore the manner in which the writers play with reflection, and to overlook the writers' treatment of form.

Drawing attention to Somerville and Ross's appropriation of popular material in their short stories leads to the conclusion that their fiction operates in a more symbolic manner than has been realized. The same year Somerville and Ross published their first collection of Irish RM stories, Arthur Symons stressed the symbolic potential of the pantomime in 'Pantomime and Poetic Drama'. He argued that 'pantomime, in its limited way, is . . . no mere imitation of nature: it is a transposition, as an etching transposes a picture'. The familiar figures of pantomime re-enact 'universal human experience', and the form within which they appear 'appeals, perhaps a little too democratically, to people of all nations'.[7] The comic figures that wander in and out of Somerville and Ross's fiction possess great demotic charm. But they are cyphers and the writers employ them as agents of transformation in fiction who give a general sense of the Irish countryside rather than representing it realistically.

Somerville and Ross's earlier novels provide glimpses of the Mephisto figure or the outline of a grimacing harlequin in their study of the Irish social terrain. The later concentration on comic short fiction demonstrates a heightened interest in form. The Irish RM stories embrace wholeheartedly the comic sense by introducing an Irish harlequin and his entourage. The hectic antics of Flurry Knox and company take place in the chronotope of festival time and manifest the shape the fiction takes. Then, in Somerville and Ross's final story cycle, *In Mr Knox's Country*, a figure which symbolizes the compelling interests of the writers comes to the fore. Mr Fox not only suggests various layers of the Irish landscape but also symbolizes the nature of the form. 'Unruly Reynard' is his own messenger – not so much a conveyor of a tradition as a manifestation of the form in which he appears.

This study of Somerville and Ross's treatment of the Irish landscape in the comic illustrations and the most significant fiction, that written between 1890 and Martin Ross's death in 1915, profiles an ironic sensibility as it interacts with the realities of Irish cultural life. Despite general notions regarding the Irish cousins – a sense that they were somehow outside of the dynamic changes that were taking place in late nineteenth-century Ireland – Somerville and Ross were far indeed from retiring behind demesne walls to nourish the broken-back pride of a conquered race. They positioned themselves as inheritors of a complex tradition which they restaged on a modern platform and, in so doing, revealed the resulting ambiguities created by conflicts between static and closed conveyors of tradition and the dynamic and open forms of modernism. The writers' developing interest in form to convey the ambiguities of modern life occurred while working within the traditions of their own culture and the political tensions of their time. They possessed an all-consuming interest in land politics, the Irish character, the operation of the law in the countryside, and – above all – money and its lack in the farms and cottages of Ireland. They explored central ambiguities of Irish life through parody and farce, and by using forms such as symbolic realism in *The Real Charlotte*, or grotesque comedy in their short fiction, conveyed certain crises of modern thought.

Somerville and Ross occupy a significant position in late nineteenth-century Irish writing. *The Real Charlotte* reigns as the foremost document of an imaginative reconstruction of the Irish Anglican inheritance in fiction. No other Irish text tackles so directly the ambiguities of an Irish Protestant ethos as manifested in fiction. The Irish RM stories present a symbolic figure of this Protestant inheritance in the shape of Flurry Knox whose darkly comic outlines represent the harlequin of pantomime. Their final collection of stories, *In Mr Knox's Country*, is a remarkable use of traditional material made new, or restaged, to express political allegory in modern form.

Notes

FOREWORD

1. W. B. Yeats, *Explorations* (New York: Macmillan, 1962), p. 27.
2. Somerville and Ross, *The Real Charlotte* (1894; London: Arrow Books, 1990), pp. 122-3.
3. Ibid., pp. 314-15.
4. Ibid., p. 47.
5. Ibid., p. 469.
6. Ibid., pp. 63-4.
7. See below, p. 190.
8. Somerville and Ross, *The Irish RM* (1928; London: Abacus, 1989), pp. 378, 428 and 382.
9. Ibid., pp. 404 and 407.
10. Ibid., p. 405.
11. Ibid., p. 351.

INTRODUCTION

1. Martin Ross, letter to Edith Somerville, 8 August 1901, *The Selected Letters of Somerville and Ross*, ed. Gifford Lewis (London: Faber and Faber, 1989), p. 252.
2. Martin Ross, letter to James Pinker, 24 February 1903, the Pinker Correspondence 3330–1, Manuscripts Department, Trinity College Library, Dublin. The library is hereafter referred to as TCD.
3. Martin Ross, unpublished manuscript, no. 3312–13, Manuscripts Department, TCD.
4. Martin Ross, 'A Subterranean Cave at Cloonabinnia', 1898, *Stray-Aways* (London: Longmans, Green, 1920), pp. 81–82. See also Somerville and Ross, *An Irish Cousin* (1889; London: Longmans, Green, 1903) and *The Silver Fox* (1898; London: Longmans, Green, 1918).
5. Bram Stoker, *The Snake's Pass* (1890; Dingle, Co. Kerry: Brandon, 1990), p. 49. Emily Lawless, 'An Upland Bog', *Belgravia*, XLV (1881), pp. 417–30. Martin Ross's elder brother, Robert Martin, refers to a 'shaking bog and sinking footsteps' in a sketch called 'A Connemara Short Cut' in *Bits of Blarney* (London: Sands, 1899), p. 196.
6. Somerville and Ross, *The Silver Fox*, p. 104.
7. Ibid., p. 100.
8. Lady Morgan (Sidney Owenson), *Florence Macarthy*. I (1818; New York: Garland Publishing, 1979), pp. 114–15. Sheridan Le Fanu, *Uncle Silas: A Tale of Bartram Haugh* (1864; New York: Dover Publications, 1966), p. 170.
9. Daniel Corkery, *Synge and Anglo-Irish Literature* (1931; Cork: Mercier Press, 1966), p. 14.
10. Entitled 'At a Western Hotel', early drafts of the story appear in the *Mr Knox's Country* notebooks; they are first dated May 1912 and are finished in 1915. This story, eventually called 'When I First Met Dr Hickey' of *Some Experiences of an Irish RM*, is one of the final pieces Somerville and Ross would write in collaboration. See nos. 3302 and 3783, TCD.
11. Somerville and Ross, 'When I First Met Dr Hickey', *The Irish RM* (*The Irish RM Complete* 1928, London: Abacus, 1989), p. 31. All references come from this edition of the collected Irish RM stories. Andrew Carpenter echoes this observation in his definition of double vision in 'Double Vision in Anglo-Irish Literature', *Place, Personality and the Irish Writer* (Gerrards Cross: Colin Smythe, 1977). Double vision, however, does not capture the strong sense of theatricality which I ascribe to Somerville and Ross's late nineteenth-century romantic irony. Terry Eagleton interprets such self-consciousness as the late flowering of a nineteenth-century Corkonian renaissance in 'Cork and the Carnivalesque', *Crazy John and the Bishop* (Cork: Cork University Press, 1998), pp. 158–211.

12. *Collection of Irish Anecdotes 1886–1945*, no. 881, Somerville and Ross Collection, Queen's University Library, Belfast. The library is hereafter referred to as QUB.

13. Martin Ross, letters to Somerville, 28 October 1901 and 30 April 1905, *Selected Letters*, ed. Lewis, pp. 253, 274.

14. *Selected Letters*, ed. Lewis, p. 274.

15. Martin Ross, letter to Somerville, 30 April 1905. *Letters*, p. 274. Gifford Lewis names Martin Ross's 'little Fay' as Frank Fay. However, it seems more likely that it was Willie Fay who publicly read Somerville and Ross's 'Poisson d'Avril' and *A Patrick's Day Hunt* in the New Century Club in Dublin. Martin describes the actor as a gas fitter, which seems to be more descriptive of Willie than his brother, who worked as a clerk. Willie played comic and peasant parts which his brother avoided. See Hugh Hunt, *The Abbey: Ireland's National Theatre 1904–1979* (Dublin: Gill and Macmillan, 1979), pp. 33–4.

16. Hilary Robinson, *Somerville and Ross: A Critical Appreciation* (Dublin: Gill and Macmillan, 1980), p. 51.

17. Frank O'Connor, *The Lonely Voice* (London: Macmillan, 1963), p. 36. For further discussion on Somerville and Ross's contribution to the development of the Irish short story, see Heinz Kosok, 'Vorformen der Modernen Kurzgeschichte in der Anglo-Irischen Literatur des 19. Jahrhunderts', *AAA-Arbeiten aus Anglistik und Amerikanistik*, 7 (1982), pp. 131–46.

18. Mario Praz, *The Romantic Agony*, trans. Angus Davidson (London: Oxford University Press, 1970).

19. Charles Baudelaire, 'Les Fenêtres', *Le Spleen de Paris: Petits Poèmes en Prose* (1863; Paris: Les Presses de la Société Parisienne d'imprimerie, 1925), pp. 138–9.

20. Nicholas Daly, *Modernism, Romance and the Fin de Siècle: Popular Fiction and British Culture, 1880–1914* (Cambridge: Cambridge Univeristy Press, 1999), p.8.

21. Ibid., p. 24.

22. Vera Kreilkamp, 'The Big Houses of Somerville and Ross', *The Anglo-Irish Novel and the Big House* (New York: Syracuse University Press, 1998), pp. 112–40; 122. See also Clair Hughes, 'Late Flowering Gothic: The Anglo-Irish Big House Novel', *Australian Victorian Association Journal* (February 1992), pp. 142–50, and Claire Denelle Cowart, 'Ghost Writers?: Somerville and Ross', *That Other World: The Supernatural and the Fantastic in Irish Literature and its Contexts*, I, ed. Bruce Stewart (Gerrards Cross: Colin Smythe, 1998), pp. 231–42.

23. Daly, *Modernism, Romance and the Fin de Siècle*, p. 15.

24. Frank O'Connor, 'Somerville and Ross', *The Irish Times* (15 December 1945), p. 4.

25. Charles Graves, 'Introduction', *Humours of Irish Life* (Dublin: Talbot Press, no date), p. xxv. Geraldine Cummins argued that Somerville and Ross were the 'creators of an Irish "Comédie Humaine"' in *Dr E. Œ. Somerville*, preface by Lennox Robinson (London: Andrew Dakers Ltd., 1952), pp. xii and 44. There is some irony in the comparison of the Irish writers to Balzac by critics like Lennox Robinson and Geraldine Cummins. Balzac described Protestant women as 'schismatics' who lacked an ideal that Catholic women discovered in the Virgin Mary. Honoré de Balzac, 'Introduction', *The Works of Honoré Balzac*, vol. I (1842; Philadelphia: Avil Publishing Co., 1901) pp. lxiii–iv.

26. Morris Collis, *Somerville and Ross* (London: Faber and Faber, 1968); Gifford Lewis, *Somerville and Ross, The World of the Irish RM* (1985; London: Penguin, 1987) and ed., *Selected Letters*.

27. Roz Cowman, 'Lost Time: The Smell and Taste of Castle T' in *Sex, Nation and Dissent in Irish Writing*, editor, Eibhear Walshe (Cork: Cork University Press, 1997), pp. 87–102. Vera Kreilkamp, 'The Big Houses of Somerville and Ross', *The Anglo-Irish Novel and the Big House*, pp. 112–40. Malcolm Kelsall, *Literary Representations of the Irish Country House: Civilisation and Savagery under the Union* (Basingstoke, Hampshire: Palgrave Macmillan, 2003).

28. Recognition of Somerville and Ross's fiction is neglected in *The Field Day Anthology of Irish Writing: Irish Women's Writings and Traditions*, Volumes IV and V (Cork: Cork University Press, 2002) in favour of the works of less well known Irish women writers. An excerpt from Edith Somerville's memoir, *Irish Memories*, and criticism by Roz Cowman, first published in *Sex, Nation and Dissent in Irish Writing*, have been included to offer a biographical or sexual reading of the writers.

29. Otto Rauchbauer, ed., *The Edith Œnone Somerville Archive in Drishane House* (Dublin: Irish Manuscripts Commission, 1995). Declan Kiberd, 'Tragedies of Manners – Somerville

and Ross', *Inventing Ireland* (London: Jonathan Cape, 1995), pp. 69–82, and 'Somerville and Ross: The Silver Fox', *Irish Classics* (London: Granta, 2000), pp. 360–78.

30. Gifford Lewis, *Edith Somerville, A Biography* (Dublin: Four Courts Press, 2005).
31. See Julie Anne Stevens, *Writing and Illustrating Ireland: Somerville and Ross,* exhibition Catalogue, TCD, November to December 2002 (Dublin: Paceprint, 2002).

CHAPTER ONE

1. Carole Fabricant, *Swift's Landscapes* (London: Johns Hopkins Press, 1982), pp. 226; 71. See also Swift's Will in *The Prose Works of Jonathan Swift* xi, ed. T. Scott (London: George Bell, 1907) Note 1, p. 415.
2. W.B. Yeats, 'What is "Popular Poetry"?', *Essays* (London: Macmillan, 1924), p. 12.
3. Martin Ross, draft of 'The Aras of the Sea' (no date), published as 'An Outpost of Ireland' in *Some Irish Yesterdays* (London: T. Nelson & Sons, 1906), no. 3312–13, Manuscript Department, TCD. I believe that Martin Ross is referring to the Aran Islands' landscape as an arras, a densely pictured tapestry.
4. Emily Lawless's fourth novel, *Grania: the Story of an Island,* has attracted most interest, while *Hurrish* is avoided. Gerardine Meaney describes the latter as Lawless's weakest novel in 'Decadence, Degeneration and Revolting Aesthetics: The Fiction of Emily Lawless and Katherine Cecil Thurston' in *Colby Quarterly* 36:2 (June 2000), p. 168. What Lady Gregory described as its 'patronising tone' may explain the tendency to overlook what is often described as a sentimental novel. See Lady Gregory, 26/11/1926, *Journals,* qtd. in Marie O'Neill, 'Emily Lawless', *Dublin Historical Record* vol. XLVIII:2 (autumn 1995), pp. 125–41.
5. Qtd. in relation to *The Real Charlotte* in Lewis, *Edith Somerville, A Biography,* p. 167.
6. Stoker, *The Snake's Pass,* pp. 243–4.
7. Elizabeth Hudson, ed., *A Bibliography of the First Editions of the Works of E. Œ. Somerville and Martin Ross* (New York: The Sporting Gallery, 1942), p. 5. Violet Powell, *The Irish Cousins* (London: Heinemann, 1970), p. 30.
8. Somerville and Ross, *Naboth's Vineyard* (London: Spencer Blackett, 1891), p. 53.
9. John Cronin, *Somerville and Ross* (Lewisburg: Bucknell University Press, 1972), p. 29.
10. B.G. MacCarthy, 'E. Œ. Somerville and Martin Ross', *Studies* xxxiv (1945), pp. 189 and 186. In a letter to Colonel J. Somerville (13 August 1943) Edith agrees with her critics: 'I have long realized that Martin and I made a very great mistake in writing *Naboth's Vineyard*. Not a bad plot but quite unreal characters'. Qtd. in Hilary Robinson, *Somerville and Ross: A Critical Appreciation,* p. 69. The novel never succeeded in Ireland.
11. Cronin, *Somerville and Ross,* p. 29. See also Ann Power, 'The Big House of Somerville and Ross', *The Dubliner* 3.1 (spring 1964), who agrees with the general critical belief that in *Naboth's Vineyard* the authors were unable to enter the minds of their peasant characters because they were 'unable altogether to make the intuitive leap that alone could render their characters convincing' (p. 45).
12. Cronin, *Somerville and Ross,* p. 31.
13. Martin Ross, letter to Edith Somerville, 6 September 1889, *Letters,* p. 154.
14. Margaret Kelleher, 'Late Nineteenth-Century Women's Fiction and the Land Agitation: Gender and Dis/Union', Ireland and the Union: Questions of Identity, SSNCI Conference, Bath Spa University College, 9 April 1999.
15. See Stephen Brown, *Ireland in Fiction* (Dublin: Maunsel, 1916), p. 136.
16. Daly, *Modernism, Romance and the Fin de Siècle,* p. 16.
17. Johann Wolfgang von Goethe, *Faust,* trans. Walter Arndt, ed. Cyrus Hamlin (New York: Norton, 1976) II. V, 11273–89.
18. Somerville and Ross, *Naboth's Vineyard,* p. 10.
19. Daniel Corkery argued that 'our national consciousness may be described, in a native phrase, as a quaking sod. It gives no footing. It is not English, nor Irish, nor Anglo-Irish; as will be understood if one thinks a while on the thwarting it undergoes in each individual child of the race as he grows into manhood.' *Synge and Anglo-Irish Literature,* p. 14. In *Bardic Nationalism* (New Jersey: Princeton University Press, 1997) Chapter 1, Katie Trumpener applies Corkery's term to the Irish bog as it was used in nineteenth-century

travel writing, economic and antiquarian histories, and fiction. I use the term more broadly here and as I understand Corkery's meaning. The 'quaking sod' applies to an ever-shifting terrain made up of competing ideologies and suppressing an elusive reality: the hidden
Ireland.

20. Somerville and Ross, *Naboth's Vineyard*, pp. 1–2.

21. The mudflats seem to suck in the murderer, Dan Hurley. This kind of death occurs frequently in Somerville and Ross's writing. In *An Irish Cousin* Uncle Dominick is swallowed
up in *Poul-na-coppal*; in *The Silver Fox* the bog and its unending holes await the English
visitors; in the story 'Harrington's' of *In Mr Knox's Country* a deep cave nearly becomes
the underground tomb of Major Yeates's son. See Chapter 6 for further discussion.

22. Somerville and Ross, *Naboth's Vineyard*, p. 7.

23. Katie Trumpener points out that the Irish bog, like the swamps of the colonial tropics,
attracts comparisons to hell. Harriet Martineau, for instance, describes the Bog of Allen in
1852 as an image of hell. 'When Connaught became the proverbial alternative of hell, the
great bog was no doubt the uppermost image in men's minds.' (*Letters from Ireland*, p. 76)
Qtd. in *Bardic Nationalism*, Note 35, p. 306.

24. Somerville and Ross, 'Slide Number 42', *The Lady's Pictorial*, 1890, no. 903, QUB. We are
reminded of Leopold Bloom's words when he passes John Howard Parnell outside Trinity
College. Bloom thinks of the dead hero, the brother, lingering like an accusation of murder in the face of John Howard: 'the murderer's image in the eye of the murdered' (James
Joyce, *Ulysses* (New York: Random House, 1986), p. 82. The writers' interest in perspective as it affects cultural politics deepens the ironic intent.

25. Somerville and Ross perceived Parnell's agenda as double-faced, a view given modern context in Conor Cruise O'Brien's work on Parnell. According to O'Brien, this agenda is illustrated by Parnell's incarceration in 1881 and his replacement by 'Captain Moonlight', a
strategy that allowed the politician to maintain his stature in parliament as well as his reputation as a revolutionary. O'Brien describes such tactics as 'a system in which the emotion-
al "residues" of historical tradition and suppressed rebellion could be enlisted in the service of parliamentary "combinations" of a strictly rational and realistic character'. *Parnell
and His Party: 1880–90* (London: Oxford University Press, 1968), p. 351.

26. Somerville and Ross, 'An Irish Landlord of the Future: A Study From Life' (no date), no.
899, QUB.

27. Philip Bull, *Land, Politics and Nationalism: A Study of the Irish Land Question* (Dublin:
Gill and Macmillan, 1996), p. 85. See also Cormac O'Grada, who notes that 'the winners
in the social revolution of 1879–1903 were the farmers, not the farm labourers' because
'unlike the Continental counterparts, Irish agricultural labourers won no concessions in
terms of land in the wake of the Land War' and, 'as predicted by Michael Davitt, the outcome of the Land War traded one form of inequality for another, and gave rise to new
social tensions'. *Ireland: A New Economic History, 1780–1939* (Oxford: Clarendon Press,
1994), p. 264.

28. L. Perry Curtis Jr. 'Stopping the Hunt, 1881–1882: An Aspect of the Irish Land War',
Nationalism and Popular Protest in Ireland, ed. C.H.E. Philpin (Cambridge: Past and
Present Society, 1987), p. 357.

29. Ibid., pp. 373 and 376.

30. Ibid., pp. 381–2.

31. Martin Ross wrote two essays in 1895, 'Quartier Latinities (IV)' in *Stray-Aways* and 'An
Outpost of Ireland' in *Some Irish Yesterdays*, which use Irish economics as literary
metaphor. Her work recalls Dean Swift's satire of the mercantile perspective as presented
by his fictional tradesman, Marcus Brutus Drapier, who assesses worth by arithmetic rather
than blood in 'Letter to the Shopkeepers, Tradesmen, Farmers, and Common-People of
Ireland', in *Swift's Irish Pamphlets*, ed. Joseph McMinn (Gerrards Cross: Colin Smythe,
1991), pp. 59–67. Martin Ross's interest in Irish economics is indicated in a letter to Edith
Somerville in 1905 when she speaks with enthusiasm of her attendance at a financial relations meeting at the Galway Court House where Martin Morris (the son of Lord Killanin)
gives a speech on 'The history of Financial Relations since the Union', *Selected Letters* ed.
Lewis, p. 275.

32. Somerville and Ross, *Naboth's Vineyard*, pp. 160, 229 and 232.

33. Ibid., p. 35.

34. See also David Lloyd's discussion on the lack of an Irish middle class as it impacts upon the

novel form in 'Violence and the Constitution of the Novel', *Anomalous States: Irish Writing and the Post-Colonial Movement* (Dublin: Lilliput Press, 1993), p. 140. Martin Ross, however, had an idea of the middle class as noted in her letter to Stephen Gwynn in 1912: 'I am not quite clear as to what either you or I mean by "middle classes" ', says Ross, 'I think of well-to-do farmers, and small professional people in the towns.' Somerville and Ross, *Irish Memories* (London: Longmans, Green, 1919), p. 321.

35. Somerville and Ross, *Naboth's Vineyard*, p. 95.
36. Ibid., p. 35.
37. Somerville and Ross refer to Olive Schreiner's *The Story of an African Farm* a number of times. See, for instance, a letter from Martin to Edith dated early 1890 in *Letters*, p. 159. A comparison of Schreiner and Somerville and Ross shows similar ambiguities resulting from the authors' feminist sympathies sitting rather incongruously with class or race stereotyping. In the Irish writers' work, the clash of discourse (race, gender, and class) occurs in one character. The resulting ambivalence might be identified as modern ambiguity.
38. Significantly, Vera Kreilkamp in *The Anglo-Irish Novel* and Clair Hughes in 'Late Flowering Gothic' cannot reconcile the later comic stories with their reading of the novels. Perhaps the later comic fiction could be described as 'the comic side of Irish gothic' in that it 'respond[s] to death with frivolous irresponsibility instead of endlessly reiterated excess'. So W.J. McCormack describes W.H. Maxwell's works in his survey of Irish gothic in *The Field Day Anthology of Irish Writing* II (Derry: Field Day Publications, 1991), p. 834.
39. Somerville and Ross, *Naboth's Vineyard*, pp. 41 and 43.
40. Chris Snodgrass, *Aubrey Beardsley, Dandy of the Grotesque* (New York: Oxford University Press, 1995), p. 163.
41. Charles Baudelaire, 'De l'essence du rire', *Œuvres Complètes* II, ed. Claude Pichois (Paris: Éditions Gallimard, 1976), p. 535.
42. Snodgrass, *Aubrey Beardsley*, p. 163.
43. Somerville and Ross, *Naboth's Vineyard*, pp. 47–8.
44. See Michael Beames, *Peasants and Power: The Whiteboy Movement and their Control in Pre-Famine Ireland* (Brighton: Harvester Press, 1983).
45. Lewis, *Edith Somerville, A Biography*, p. 62.
46. Somerville and Ross, *Naboth's Vineyard*, p. 134.
47. Ibid., p. 32.
48. Catherine Marshall points out that 'romantic and idealized genre scenes' of Ireland were 'the order of the day' in the [English] Royal Academy of the 1890s. Human figures were idealized types. *Irish Art Masterpieces* (Southport, Connecticut: Hugh Lauter Levin, 1994), pp. 78–9.
49. Emily Lawless, 'An Upland Bog', *Belgravia* Vol. XLV (1881), pp. 417–30; 417.
50. Thomas Crofton Croker, *Researches in the South of Ireland* (1824) (Shannon: Irish University Press, 1969), p. 13.
51. Lawless, 'An Upland Bog', p. 428.
52. Ibid., pp. 423–4.
53. James Cahalan points out the suitability of Lawless's work to theories advanced in ecofeminism in *Double Visions* (Syracuse: Syracuse University Press, 1999), p. 34. Gerry Smyth notes, however, that much Irish writing relies on an implicit ecological awareness in *Space and the Irish Cultural Imagination* (Basingstoke: Palgrave, 2001). My reading of *Hurrish* draws on such general studies, as well as ecocritical analyses such as William Howarth's study of swampland in 'Imagined Territory: The Writing of Wetlands', *New Literary History: Ecocriticism* 30, 3 (summer 1999), pp. 509–39.
54. Pamela Hinkson, *Seventy Years Young: Memoirs of Elizabeth, Countess of Fingall* (London: Collins, 1937), p. 175.
55. See Eve Patten, 'With Essex in India? Emily Lawless's Colonial Consciousness', *European Journal of English Studies* 3, 3 (December 1999), p. 291.
56. Edith Somerville illustrated her second cousin Ethel Penrose's children's book, *Clear as the Noonday* (London: Jarrold and Sons, 1893), which directly recalls Lawless's description of bogland and has a local woman save the children of the Big House from a dangerous boghole. *The Silver Fox* reuses this scene five years later when a local woman saves a young Englishwoman from a boghole.
57. Somerville and Ross, 'The Anglo-Irish Language', *Stray-Aways*, pp. 184–92; 186.
58. Emily Lawless, *Hurrish* (Belfast: Appletree Press Ltd., 1992), p. 3.

59. Ibid., p. 4.
60. Ibid., pp. 15, 5 and 9.
61. Ibid., pp. 27 and 79.
62. Ibid., p. 63.
63. Ibid., p. 75.
64. Ibid., p. 78.
65. Ibid., p. 79.
66. Howarth uses the phrase 'place-centred' to describe texts that have interested ecocritics since 1990 in 'Imagined Territory', p. 511.
67. Howarth, 'Imagined Territories', p. 511.
68. Somerville and Ross, *Naboth's Vineyard*, pp. 21–2.
69. Ibid., p. 51.
70. Ibid., p. 21.
71. Ibid., pp. 126–7.
72. For further discussion, see Síghle Bhreathnach-Lynch and Julie Anne Stevens, 'The Irish Artist: Crossing the Rubicon', *Local/Global: Women Artists in the Nineteenth Century*, eds. Deborah Cherry and Janice Helland (Aldershot, Hants: Ashgate Publishing, 2006), pp. 137–54.
73. Edith Somerville and Ross, *Irish Memories*, p. 139.
74. Somerville notes reading Darwin's study of facial expressions in man and animals in her diary, 29 February 1888. See Lewis, *Edith Somerville, A Biography*, p. 123.
75. Charles Darwin, *The Expression of the Emotions in Man and Animals* (1872) introduced by Konrad Lorenz (Chicago: University of Chicago Press, 1965), p. xii.
76. Although Punch derives from Pulcinella of the Commedia dell'Arte, the English Punch has characteristics all his own. See George Speaight, *The History of the English Puppet Theatre* (London: Robert Hale, 1990), pp. 218–31. In 'De l'essence du rire', Baudelaire speaks of the marked violence of the English pantomime: '*Il m'a semble que le signe distinctif de ce genre comique était la violence*', p. 538.
77. The influence of the popular pantomime in Irish writing of this period is indicated by Lady Gregory, who writes of a Christmas Punch and Judy show at Coole Park in January 1899. Douglas Hyde and others enact an Irish version for a crowd of local children. The policeman speaks in English, while the other characters speak in Irish. Later on, Lady Gregory would claim this show to be 'the beginning of modern Irish drama'. Qtd. in *Lady Gregory's Diaries, 1892–1902*, ed. James Pethica (Gerrards Cross: Colin Smythe, 1996), Note 9, p. 200.
78. Somerville and Ross, *Naboth's Vineyard*, p. 103.
79. W.C. Glenroy and Dane Clarke, *Harlequin Bryan O'Lynn or The Sleeping Beauty of Erin*, 24 December 1888, National Music Hall, Dublin, theatre programme.
80. L. Perry Curtis Jr. ' "The Land for the People": Post-Famine Images of Eviction', *Éire/Land*, ed. Vera Kreilkamp, catalogue and essays issued in conjunction with Éire/Land exhibition, McMullen Museum of Art, Boston College, 2003 (Chicago: University of Chicago Press, 2003), pp. 85–92.
81. Somerville and Ross, *Irish Memories*, pp. 38–9. Jarlath Waldron, *Maamtrasna: The Murders and the Mystery* (Dublin: Edmund Burke, 1992).
82. Somerville and Ross, *Irish Memories*, p. 34.
83. Ibid., p. 39.
84. *The Freeman's Journal*, 5–10 October 1883.
85. See 'Our Wealthy Dramatists', *Punch* 85 (17 Nov. 1883), p. 240 and 'Review of W.G. Wills and Herman's *Claudian*', *Punch* 85 (22 Dec. 1883), p. 292.
86. John Tenniel, 'O'Caliban', *Punch* 85 (22 Dec. 1883), p. 295.
87. L. Perry Curtis Jr. *Apes and Angels*, rev. ed. (Washington DC; London: Smithsonian Institute, 1997), p. 20. Curtis also notes the use of simianization in Emily Lawless's *Hurrish*. For a response to Curtis's view on caricatures of the Irish, see R. F. Foster's *Paddy and Mr Punch* (London: Penguin, 1993), pp.171–94. For further discussion, see Chapter 3 of this study.
88. Stoker, *The Snake's Pass*, p. 247.
89. Ibid., p. 235.
90. Ibid., p. 116.
91. See Daly, *Modernism, Romance and the Fin de Siècle*, p. 74.
92. Johann Wolfgang von Goethe, 'The Fairy Tale', *Romantic Fairy Tales*, ed. and trans., Carol Tully (London: Penguin, 2000), p. 5.
93. Ibid., pp. 5–6.

94. Stoker, *The Snake's Pass*, p. 246.
95. Somerville and Ross, *Irish Memories*, pp. 29–30.
96. Madeleine Bingham, *Henry Irving and the Victorian Theatre* (London: George Allen & Unwin, 1978), pp. 93–4.
97. See James Clarence Mangan's 'The Man in the Cloak', *Dublin University Magazine* 12 (November 1838), pp. 552–68. I am indebted to Dr David Lloyd for this reference. Mangan not only wore a cloak and a witch's peaked hat but also a 'flax-coloured wig' and 'a huge pair of green spectacles'. Frances Gerard, *Picturesque Dublin, Old and New*, illus. Rose Barton (London: Hutchinson, 1898), pp. 79-80. We can trace these green spectacles (and their self-parodying potential) back through Thomas Moore's *Captain Rock* to Lady Morgan's Molly Magillicuddy in *Florence Macarthy*. Dr Primrose's foolish son, Moses, in *The Vicar of Wakefield* trades the family's horse for a case of apparently useless green spectacles. It seems as though some of them were put to use in both real life and fiction in the next century.
98. Martin Ross, letter to Somerville, 17 April 1887, *Selected Letters*, ed. Lewis, p. 45.
99. Yeats compares Wills to Boucicault in his 1889 article, 'Mr William Wills', *Letters to the New World* (Cambridge, Massachusetts: Harvard University Press, 1934), pp. 69–71. Wilde (whose own name included Wills) was enchanted by Ellen Terry's performance in *Charles I* and reviewed *Olivia* as an imaginatively inspired work. Richard Ellmann, *Oscar Wilde* (New York: Knopf, 1988), pp. 119 and 133.
100. Ellen Terry, *Ellen Terry's Memoirs*, eds. Edith Craig and Christopher St John (1932; Westport, Connecticut: Greenwood Press, 1970), p. 110.
101. Martin Ross, Diaries, QUB.
102. William G. Wills, *Melchior* (London: Macmillan, 1885).
103. The Wills/Martin correspondence (no. 876, QUB) includes few dates, although it evidently spanned the five years 1885–90. His letters include hasty sketches and rather fey, curlicue designs. Frequently arch and even suggestive ('You're very nasty not to have come to Kew. I was cocksure you'd be there'), they nonetheless are dominated by discussion of his work.
104. Rarely does Wills mention Violet Martin's work. He is surprised when he hears of the publication of *An Irish Cousin* in 1889. One gets the impression that the Wills/Martin correspondence devoted itself entirely to Willie Wills's genius.
105. Freeman Wills, *W.G. Wills: Dramatist and Painter* (London: Longmans, Green & Co., 1898), p. 125.
106. Martin Ross wrote in longhand and, according to Collis, she studied German in her teens. Collis, *Somerville and Ross*, p. 22.
107. Freeman Wills, *W.G. Wills: Dramatist and Painter*, p. 201.
108. Bingham, *Henry Irving and the Victorian Theatre*, pp. 214–19. According to Simon Trussler in *The Cambridge Illustrated History of British Theatre* (Cambridge: Cambridge University Press, 1994), the production cost £15,000 and took in nearly £70,000 in its first year and £57,000 in its second (p. 251).
109. As described in an article by Edward R. Russell, editor of the *Daily Post*, in the theatre programme of W.G. Wills's *Faust* at the Royal Lyceum Theatre (16 June 1886), p. 4.
110. References to Willie Wills's version of *Faust* are taken from his brother's summary and quotes. Freeman Wills, *W.G. Wills*, p. 201.
111. Freeman Wills, *W.G. Wills*, p. 201.
112. Edward R. Russell, theatre programme of *Faust*, pp. 5–7.
113. John Tenniel, 'The Open Door!' *Punch* 85 (10 Oct. 1885), pp. 174–5.
114. Somerville and Ross, *The Real Charlotte* (1894; London: Arrow Books, 1990), p. 268.
115. Qtd. in Freeman Wills, *W.G. Wills*, p. 205.
116. Somerville and Ross, *The Real Charlotte*, p. 361.
117. Somerville and Ross, *The Irish RM* (London: Abacus, 1989), pp. 157 and 388.

CHAPTER TWO

1. Otto Rauchbauer notes Somerville's tendency to take different positions in politics in 'An Evaluative Essay', *Drishane Archive*, pp. 202–12. Various critics, like Roz Cowman in one of the few pieces on Somerville and Ross in the *Field Day Anthology* devoted to women's

writing, have suggested a romantic friendship. See 'Lost Time: The Smell and Taste of Castle T.' (1977), *Field Day Anthology*, IV, pp. 1071–3. Most recently Gifford Lewis directs attention to Somerville's nationalist sympathies – especially in her later years – and heterosexual tendencies – especially in her earlier years. See *Edith Somerville, A Biography*. Martin Ross always professed unionist sympathies and this bent influences their joint production with which I am concerned.

2. During the same month in 1886 that Somerville and Ross first met, Somerville was struck by an occurrence noted in her diary. A relation, Emily Herbert, was bequeathed everything in 'Aunt Fanny's will': 'In effect', writes Edith Somerville, 'Emily got everything. Except about 500 to the Somervilles, of wh[ich] Papa & I get 50 each – It is a curious instance of the power of the will – Emily's will, in particular.' Diaries, QUB. Charlotte Mullen is based on Emily Herbert, and the 'power of [a woman's] will' especially interests the writers. For further discussion, see Lewis, *Edith Somerville, A Biography*, pp. 150–1.

3. Somerville and Ross, *The Real Charlotte*, p. 311.

4. Review of Robert Louis Stevenson's *The Master of Ballantrae* and Somerville and Ross's *The Irish Cousin*, *The Old Saloon*, November 1889, pp. 702–5.

5. Somerville and Ross's Diaries, QUB. *The Real Charlotte* was put aside after May 1890 and worked on inconsistently for the next three years. The selection of possible titles for their third novel indicates the divided emphasis on the two main female characters: 'The Welsh Aunt' (their working title), 'Charlotte Mullen's Responsibility', 'A Moral Legacy', 'By an Irish Lake', 'A Dublin Aboriginee', 'Out of the North Side', 'The Revealing of Charlotte', 'A Romance of Two Vulgar Women', and 'Some Romantic Episodes in the Vulgar Life of Charlotte Mullen'. J.H. Berrow (Hilary Robinson), 'Somerville and Ross: Transitional Novelists', PhD Diss., University College Dublin, 1975; Edith Somerville, letter to Cameron Somerville, 13 July 1892, *Drishane Archive*. 'The Welsh Aunt', like the action and characterization of the novel, recalls both Balzac's *Cousin Bette* and Le Fanu's *Uncle Silas*. The working title also suggests Charlotte's betrayal of her promise to her dying aunt: she 'welshes' on her agreement to help Francie.

6. Robert Louis Stevenson, *The Master of Ballantrae* (1889; London: Penguin, 1984), p. 16.

7. Ibid., p. 148.

8. Homi K. Bhabha, *The Location of Culture* (London: Routledge, 1994), pp. 2–3.

9. Martin Ross, 'The Martins of Ross', *Irish Memories*, pp. 6–7.

10. *Somerville and Ross, Irish Memories*, p. 102. See also Edith Somerville's discussion of the arguments in Martin Ross's Dublin household on the Irish Episcopate and the merits of various clergy (pp. 104–5).

11. See, for instance, Martin Ross's letter to Edith Somerville, 11 August 1890, for a description of Robert Martin's theatrical prayer style, 'a mixture of Irving and Beerbohm Tree', *Selected Letters*, ed. Lewis, p. 162.

12. Lewis, *Somerville and Ross*, p. 187; *Drishane Archive*, p. 224.

13. Mark Bence-Jones, *Twilight of the Ascendancy* (London: Constable, 1987), p. 154.

14. Otto Rauchbauer notes that St Barrahane's stained-glass windows (including marvellous work by Harry Clarke) must 'be seen as self-representations of the Castletownshend gentry at a time when their social position was already highly precarious', *Drishane Archive*, p. 177.

15. Qtd. in Moira Somerville's unpublished 'Notes on the Background and Early Life of Edith Oenone Somerville', *Drishane Archive*, B.2.42pp.

16. Jeremiah O'Donovan Rossa, 'O'Donovan Rossa's Prison Life' (1874), *Field Day Anthology*, vol. II, p. 262.

17. According to *The Irish Times*, 13 March 1936, Somerville's 73-year-old brother was shot dead because of 'his interest in young men of the locality who wished to join the Royal Navy'. The attackers left a note saying 'This English agent has sent fifty-two Irishmen to the English forces during the last seven weeks'.

18. Somerville and Ross, *Wheel-Tracks* (London: Longmans, Green, 1923), p. 69.

19. See Bence-Jones, *Twilight of the Ascendancy*, p. 154.

20. Janice Holmes, *Religious Revivals in Britain and Ireland, 1859–1905* (Dublin: Irish Academic Press, 2000), p. 80.

21. Martin Ross, letter to an anonymous 'sir' in Bristol, asking him to accept some leaflets on the Irish question, 7 November 1893, *Drishane Archive*, L.C.11.a. Somerville and Ross worked for the Irish Unionist Alliance in England in 1895. They instructed the East Anglian electorate in Irish politics.

22. Somerville and Ross, *The Real Charlotte*, pp. 31–2.
23. Edith Somerville, letter to Alice Kinkead, 12 March 1899, *Drishane Archive*, L.A.1365.
24. Terence Brown, 'The Church of Ireland and the Climax of the Ages', *Ireland's Literature* (Mullingar: Lilliput, 1988), pp. 51–5.
25. See Foster, 'Protestant Magic', *Paddy and Mr. Punch*, pp. 218–19.
26. Martin Ross, letter to Edith Somerville, no date, 1896, *Selected Letters*, ed. Lewis, pp. 236–8.
27. Jack White states that *The Real Charlotte* presents 'a world untouched by any premonition of change'. *Minority Report: The Protestant Community in the Irish Republic* (Dublin: Gill and Macmillan, 1975), p. 58. I argue that the writers are not so much nostalgically harking back to Protestant-dominated Ireland (as White suggests) as they are presenting the different facets of that tradition to inscribe its reality upon the Irish literary landscape.
28. Father Stephen Brown's extreme view of Somerville and Ross's *Naboth's Vineyard* as a 'loathsome, sordid picture of Ireland', which depicts the Catholic population as 'treacherous' and 'dishonest', suggests a particular attitude towards the Anglo-Irish writers that prevailed in Ireland. Stephen J. Brown, S.J. *Ireland in Fiction* (Dublin: Maunsel and Co., 1919), p. 281.
29. In relation to *The Real Charlotte*'s marginal Catholic characters, we might keep in mind Ruth First and Ann Scott's observation on Olive Schreiner's *The Story of an African Farm* (1883), a novel Martin Ross read twice. First and Scott claim that the neglect of the dominant population of the South African countryside does not diminish the political content of Schreiner's work. Instead, the work shows that 'that was the point of the colonial condition: Africans were kept so far outside white society that that in itself was a statement about it. The European frontier society insulated itself from the indigenous society but internalized the violence it used against it. . . . Olive [Schreiner] was writing, in fact, about what colonialism did to whites.' *Olive Schreiner* (London: Deutsch, 1980), p. 97.
30. Brown, *Ireland's Literature*, pp. 58–9.
31. John Turpin, 'Daniel Maclise and His Place in Victorian Art', *Anglo-Irish Studies* I (1975), pp. 51–2.
32. As Janice Holmes points out, 'although it is easy to characterise the Victorian period as a "crisis of faith" with falling levels of church attendance and the growth of secular activities, it is also possible, paradoxically, to see it as a time of religious revival'. *Religious Revivals in Britain and Ireland*, p. xii.
33. F.S.L. Lyons voices the general critical opinion on *The Real Charlotte* as social record of a dying way of life in 'The Twilight of the Big House', *Ariel* 1, 3 (July 1970), pp. 110–22. More recently, Declan Kiberd in *Inventing Ireland* (London: Jonathan Cape, 1995) argues that the novel is 'a tragic tale of the collapse of big house culture' (p. 72).
34. Somerville and Ross wrote about the loss of the Irish Gentleman in an unpublished essay called 'The Superfluous Gentleman', (no date) no. 899, QUB, where they warn that 'the new rulers of green Erin' must contend with the 'class jealousy & religious intolerance' which has rid the country of its previous governors. In *The Real Charlotte*, however, the portrait of the Gentleman is more complicated.
35. Somerville and Ross, *The Real Charlotte*, p. 266. See Ann Owen Weekes for a feminist reading of Charlotte Mullen's reaction to Eliza Hackett's defection in 'Somerville and Ross: Ignoble Tragedy', *Irish Women Writers* (Kentucky: University Press of Kentucky, 1990), pp. 68–9. Weekes argues that Charlotte Mullen recognizes the male prerogative exercised by the Catholic Church in its Apostolic succession. Charlotte resists this 'male preserve'. Weekes is struck by the deliberate inclusion of theological argument in the text, but does not consider its significance to the Protestant discourse.
36. George Birmingham, 'Catholic', *Spillikins* (London: Methuen, 1926), p. 33.
37. Somerville and Ross, *The Real Charlotte*, p. 67.
38. Ibid., pp. 96, 413 and 415.
39. Ibid., p. 273.
40. Ibid., p. 85. For discussion of the different strands of the Church of Ireland after its disestablishment, see Jack White, *Minority Report*, p. 175. David Hempton points out that the Home Rule crisis of 1886 'brought into sharp focus an Irish Protestant *mentalité*' (p. 226). He quotes the argument of the Protestant Defence Association of the Church of Ireland that 'Romanising tendencies . . . had corrupted the Church of England'. The movement of the Irish High Church Party 'away from an evangelical position, settling upon more sacramentarian thought, was enough to stir a fear of Rome's potential presence in the Church's

fold' (p. 228). '"For God and Ulster": Evangelical Protestantism and the Home Rule Crisis of 1886', *Protestant Evangelicalism: Britain, Ireland, Germany and America c. 1750–1950*, ed. Keith Robbins (Oxford: Basil Blackwell, 1990).

41. Somerville and Ross, *The Real Charlotte*, p. 82.
42. M.N. Cutt, *Mrs Sherwood and Her Books for Children* (London: Oxford University Press, 1974), p. 17. Sherwood's fifty years of writing (1795–1851) produced over four hundred titles. By the end of the 1800s, the principles of Mrs Sherwood's works 'had become part of the very foundation of middle-class family life' (pp. 99–100). An indication of Sherwood's significance might be ascertained in a letter from a Scottish reader to Somerville and Ross. The one detail of *The Real Charlotte* which stirs Mr J.W. Angus's memories of his childhood in Bagnalstown House, Co. Carlow, is not something 'Irish' but something British, Protestant, and colonial: Mrs Sherwood's Fairchild family. Letters to Violet Martin, No. 919, QUB.
43. Cutt, *Mrs Sherwood and Her Books for Children*, p. 7.
44. '"Should you like to see the corpse, my dears?" asked Mr Fairchild. "You never saw a corpse, I think?" "No, Papa," answered Lucy. "We should like to see one."' (qtd. in Cutt, p. 69). Martin Ross echoes the Fairchild's sentiments when she writes to Edith in January 1895 saying, 'I often wish you had seen someone dead – I should like to know how you felt about it, and I think it does one good, though it is excessively painful.' Qtd. in Lewis, *Somerville and Ross*, p. 190. Martin Ross refers to her childhood reading of Mrs Sherwood in 'Quartier Latinities III', *Stray-Aways*, p. 46, and Edith Somerville makes allusions to Mrs Sherwood in *An Incorruptible Irishman* (London: Ivor Nicholson & Watson, 1932), p. 231.
45. Somerville and Ross, *The Real Charlotte*, p. 82.
46. Shorthouse's inspirational sentiments are indicated in *The Spectator*'s review of Shorthouse's writing on 26 December 1891, a month after its review of *Naboth's Vineyard*. Reading Shorthouse after the modern realists is a sensation likened to 'that which Dante must have felt when, issuing from the tortuous cave which led up from the under-world, he came upon the flat, open shore which lay about the foot of the hill of Purgatory; when he stood once more in the upper air, and recognised the far-off quivering of the sea' (p. 931).
47. Mark 4:3. Later on in this chapter, I will discuss the possibility of a typological reading of the text which pays particular attention to religious symbolism, such as Lady Dysart's sowing of seedlings.
48. Somerville and Ross, *The Real Charlotte*, p. 218.
49. Declan Kiberd sees *The Real Charlotte* as 'a novel in the comedy-of-manner mode' in *Inventing Ireland* (p. 77) and argues that the work 'records the collapse of Irish Protestantism into social decorum' (p. 81). I am interested in this record but see the process as transference rather than decline.
50. Somerville and Ross, *The Real Charlotte*, p. 488.
51. Gerald Campbell, *Edward and Pamela Fitzgerald* (London: Edward Arnold, 1904), p. 52.
52. Somerville and Ross, *The Real Charlotte*, pp. 143 and 145.
53. Edith Somerville's great-grandfather, Charles Kendal Bushe, knew Edward Fitzgerald and she quotes from Fitzgerald's letters to his mother recorded in Thomas Moore's *Memoirs of Lord Edward Fitzgerald* in *An Incorruptible Irishman*, p. 78.
54. Somerville and Ross, *The Real Charlotte*, p. 35.
55. Ibid., p. 198. Ensconced as he is within the imperialist and patriarchal traditions and perceiving the Irish landscape and its female occupants as distanced from himself, as Other, Christopher Dysart's mission repeats the imperialist project of 'soul making', the use of Christian evangelicalism in the service of imperial design, which Gayatri Chakravorty Spivak traces in *Jane Eyre*'s St John Rivers in 'Three Women's Texts and a Critique of Imperialism', *Feminisms: An Anthology of Literary Theory and Criticism*, p. 803.
56. Somerville and Ross, *The Real Charlotte*, p. 31.
57. Edith Somerville's uncle Sir Joscelyn Coghill, a prize-winning photographer, photographed his brother-in-law (Edith's father) as a devoutly praying monk clutching rosary beads and a cross. Somerville and Ross, *Wheel-Tracks*, p. 27. Martin Ross also enjoyed photography, and the *Drishane Archive* includes an album of her fine Western landscapes of water and light. In *The Real Charlotte* various characters possess photographs of each other and at one stage Charlotte thrusts Lambert's image into the fire. The photograph, like the Victorian portrait, seems to possess a soul of its own. See Chapter 5 for further discussion.
58. Somerville and Ross, *The Real Charlotte*, pp. 78, 125, 310 and 129.

59. Ibid., pp. 79 and 15.
60. Ibid., pp. 90 and 139.
61. Ibid., pp. 180–1.
62. Pamela's imperial seat recalls Maria Edgeworth's carriage seat in her *Tour of Connemara and the Martins of Ballinahinch*, ed. H.E. Butler (1834; London: Constable, 1950). Indeed, Pamela's bemused kindness towards Francie might be compared to Maria Edgeworth's indulgent affection for the barbaric princess of Connemara, Mary Martin. Edith Somerville refers to Edgeworth's travelogue in *An Incorruptible Irishman*, p. 233, and Somerville and Ross's close familiarity with Mary Martin's history is evident in their travel writing on Connemara, *Through Connemara in a Governess's Cart* (London: W.H. Allen, 1892). Martin Ross, of course, was a Martin of Connemara, one of the wild Irish in Edgeworth's eyes.
63. Somerville and Ross, *The Real Charlotte*, p. 128.
64. Ibid., p. 294.
65. Dante Gabriel Rossetti, 'The Staff and Scrip', *The Works of Dante Gabriel Rossetti* (London: Ellis, New Bond Street, 1911), pp. 59—63. Edith Somerville's younger brother, Boyle, was a keen photographer and traveller who published dictionaries of the languages of the New Hebrides, New Georgia, and the Solomon Islands and took part in the Chilean–Peruvian war in 1880 and the First Egyptian War in 1882. He was very fond of Rossetti's poems and sonnets. See Edith Somerville, letter to Martin Ross, 24 August 1888, *Selected Letters*, ed. Lewis, pp. 112–13.
66. Francie, in constant flight throughout the novel and the object of the male gaze, recalls Daphne pursued by an intoxicated Apollo. Francie is no aborigine for Lambert but a goddess he has set 'upon a ridiculous pedestal' on their honeymoon in Paris. There the couple walks through the gardens of Versailles and reach the Bosquet d'Apollon where Francie sits by the pool, sucking oranges and tossing the peel at a statue of Apollo. Somerville and Ross, *The Real Charlotte*, pp. 399–403.
67. Ibid., p. 49.
68. For a further description of *The Light of the World*, see Robert Hewison ed., *Ruskin, Turner and the Pre-Raphaelites*, (London: Tate Gallery Publishing, 2000) p. 208.
69. For a further discussion of *The Awakening Conscience*, see Hewison ed., *Ruskin, Turner and the Pre-Raphaelites*, p. 209.
70. Somerville and Ross, *The Real Charlotte*, p. 162.
71. While Christopher and Francie study photography, Pamela plays Grieg's *Peer Gynt*. Ironically, the music that stirs Christopher so deeply could be 'In the Hall of the Mountain King', a passage which refers to Ibsen's description of a wild realm. In Ibsen's folk play, Peer Gynt falls for an exotic beauty of the mountains. She leads him to an underground kingdom of trolls. Christopher, too, falls for the natural beauty of an Undine, who may indeed entice the heir of Bruff to some subterranean kingdom of mutant beings. The irony becomes apparent when we consider aristocratic Christopher identifying with the Norwegian peasant farmer. Nonetheless, the 'blood-stirring freshness' of the 'half-civilized northern music' clouds his perspective just as 'the darting flight of the bats' of Bruff weaves a 'phantom net before his eyes' (p. 199).
72. Robert Hewison, 'The Beautiful and the True', *Ruskin, Turner and the Pre-Raphaelites*, p. 13.
73. See George P. Landow, *William Holman Hunt and Typological Symbolism* (London: Yale University Press, 1979).
74. Somerville and Ross, *The Real Charlotte*, p. 312.
75. Martin Ross, letter to Cameron Somerville, 27 May 1894, *Drishane Archive*, L.C.5 a–c.
76. Somerville and Ross, *The Real Charlotte*, p. 165.
77. Ibid., p. 36.
78. Adriaen van der Venne, *Fishing for Souls*, 1614, The Rijksmuseum, Amsterdam, Holland.
79. Somerville and Ross, *The Real Charlotte*, p. 407.
80. *The Athenaeum* 3476 (9 June 1894), p. 738.
81. Somerville and Ross, *The Real Charlotte*, p. 43.
82. Ibid., p. 460.
83. Ibid., p. 96.
84. Charlotte's connection to the supernatural world reminds us of Madame de la Rougierre's peculiar song in Le Fanu's *Uncle Silas*. The governess sings a Bretagne ballad about a queer kind of woman, 'a lady with a pig's head', who has powers that enable her to enter a place where no one goes: the land of the dead. Despite her weird mix of human and animal

attributes, however, she is shunned by both pigs and women. She is a new and strange breed, with her 'mongrel body and demon soul' (p. 32). Madame de la Rougierre's pig-lady is realized in all her full malevolence in Charlotte Mullen, owner of Gurthnamuckla, 'Field of Pigs'.

85. For further discussion on the ambiguity of gender roles in *The Real Charlotte*, see Ann Weekes, *Irish Women Writers*, pp. 71-9.

86. According to Violet Powell, Martin Ross spoke of various readers' comparisons of *The Real Charlotte* to Balzac's *Cousin Bette* during a visit to Scotland and her admission that neither she nor Somerville had read Balzac (*The Irish Cousins*, p. 65). Whether or not the women writers read the great French realist, they appear to have absorbed similar influences to create a figure remarkably similar to Balzac's Lisbeth Fischer.

87. Honoré de Balzac, *Cousin Bette, Part One of Poor Relations* (1846), trans. Marion Ayton Crawford (Harmondsworth, Middlesex: Penguin, 1965), p. 39.

88. Ibid., p. 72.

89. Ibid., p. 82.

90. Ibid., p. 124.

91. For a consideration of the links between the New Woman novel and the decadents of the *fin de siècle*, see Sally Ledger, *The New Woman: Fiction and Feminism at the Fin de Siècle* (Manchester: Manchester University Press, 1997), pp. 94–121.

92. Sarah Grand, *The Heavenly Twins* (1893; Ann Arbor, Michigan: University of Michigan, 1992). Gifford Lewis notes the impact of Grand's controversial novel in Drishane House in *Somerville and Ross*, p. 66

93. Somerville and Ross, *The Real Charlotte*, pp. 252, 294 and 324.

94. *Punch* 99 (6 December 1890), p. 265.

95. Edith Somerville, letter to Cameron Somerville, 13 July 1892, *Drishane Archive* LA 157 a–b.

96. Bhabha, 'Of Mimicry and Man', *The Location of Culture*, pp. 85–92.

97. Ibid., p. 89.

98. Grand, *The Heavenly Twins*, p. 31.

99. Somerville and Ross, *The Real Charlotte*, p. 298. Edith Somerville finished reading 'Oscar Wilde's horrid story' while working on *The Real Charlotte*, 7 September 1890. Diaries, QUB.

100. Five years later Marlow steers his steamboat up the Congo to face a similar opposition of terms generated by colonial occupation. The use of black and white contrast, part of a Manichaean or dualistic argument pervading literature from medieval times, becomes weighted with extra significance throughout the nineteenth century. In the colonial context Christopher Dysart anticipates in his attempts at conversion, and his colonial dreams, the gross transgressions of Kurtz and the 'bewitched pilgrims' in *Heart of Darkness*. In Conrad's novel the visual impact of white on black, a white thread dangling like a necklace around a dying man's throat (which recalls the thin red knife mark around Margaret's throat in *Faust*), the steady stream of ivory wending its way from Kurtz's Inner Station through pitch black forests, starkly declares the immutability of each term. There are strong similarities between these writers' works, but Somerville and Ross's literary agent, James B. Pinker, did not become Conrad's agent until the latter had completed *Heart of Darkness*. The Conrads and the Irish women did have a mutual friend, the artist Alice Kinkead (see *Drishane Archive*, p. 175).

101. Somerville and Ross, *The Real Charlotte*, pp. 22 and 183.

102. Ibid., p. 253.

103. In *A Life of Picasso* II (London: Jonathan Cape, 1996), John Richardson shows how Picasso's 'Harlequin' derives from two watercolours of dancers. In 'Harlequin', the two dancers become one motley figure (pp. 386–7). Such a development is interesting in the light of the kind of figure Charlotte Mullen represents; she is, in effect, two people, male and female, whirling in some mad dance to become a single mad entity, truly 'a soul escaped from hell'.

104. Robinson, *Somerville & Ross*, pp. 100, 105, and 116. Kiberd, *Inventing Ireland*, p. 72.

105. Somerville and Ross, *The Real Charlotte*, p. 204.

106. See Johaan Wolfgang von Goethe, *Faust* I, trans. Walter Arndt, ed. Cyrus Hamlin (New York: W.W. Norton, 1766), ll. 4235-42, 4387–94.

107. Martin Ross, 'Memoir of Robert', no. 10884, TCD. The original manuscript of 'The Martins

of Ross', edited by Edith Somerville for *Irish Memories*, is more about Dublin theatre and Robert Martin's interest in burlesque and pantomime than the final version suggests. See also mention of Robert's involvement in pantomime in *Selected Letters*, ed. Lewis, pp. 17 and 23.

108. 'Memorial to Martin Ross', *The Belfast News-Letter* 24 December 1915. In this article, it is not clear if *Little Doctor Faust* is a pantomime or a song, although it seems to be the former.

109. *The Irish Times* 13, 27, and 28 December 1886.

110. Martin Ross, 'Memoir of Robert', no. 10884, TCD, pp. 19–20.

111. Martin Ross, 'Quartier Latinities III' (1895) *Stray-Aways*, pp. 49–50.

112. The printed programmes of these performances are available in the *Drishane Archive*, M.15.a–b, M.43.a, as well as the scripts of *Sorcerer* and *Poor Pillicoddy*, M.16.a–c and M.17.a–b.

113. Edith Somerville's first work after Martin Ross's death in December 1915, was revising an early pantomime she had written with Ethel Coghill in 1874 called *Chloral or the Sleeping Beauty*, performed in Castletownshend on 7 and 9 September 1916. Somerville and Ross Collection no. 887, QUB. Otto Rauchbauer lists a manuscript of the early version in the *Drishane Archive*, C.8. a–c.

114. Lewis, *Somerville and Ross*, p. 200.

115. Edith Somerville, letters to Martin Ross, 29 April and 3 May 1888, *Letters*, pp. 71–5.

116. W.S. Gilbert and Arthur Sullivan, *HMS Pinafore or The Lass that Loved a Sailor*, D'Oyly Carte Opera Company, 9 April 1888, Gaiety Theatre, Dublin, theatre programme.

117. Somerville and Ross, *The Real Charlotte*, p. 205.

118. Ibid., pp. 205–6.

119. George Gissing, *The Whirlpool* (1897; London: Everyman, 1997), p. 47.

120. *Selected Letters*, ed. Lewis, p. 215.

121. See Martin Ross's fine photographs of churches and architectual detail in the *Drishane Archive* Q.12.a.

122. Kiberd, *Inventing Ireland*, p. 73.

123. Somerville and Ross, *The Real Charlotte*, p. 376.

124. Brown, *Ireland's Literature*, p. 59.

125. Somerville and Ross, *The Real Charlotte*, p. 494.

126. Goethe, *Faust* I, l.111.

127. Stephen Gwynn, 'Lever's Successors', *The Edinburgh Review*, October 1921, p. 351.

128. James M. Cahalan, *The Irish Novel: A Critical History* (Dublin: Gill and Macmillan, 1988), p. 94. Not everyone, of course, adopted this position with regard to *The Real Charlotte*. In 1946, V.S. Pritchett's back-handed compliments on the novel tended to detract from its good reputation. Though he believed the novel to be the first nineteenth-century artistic portrayal of the Anglo-Irish, he argued that its main flaw, killing off Francie, was the result of the writers' 'profound snobbery' (p. 267). Nonetheless, in an article which purported to be about the Irish RM stories, Pritchett spent all his time discussing 'the disquieting people of this one serious novel'. 'The Irish RM', *The Complete Essays* (London: Chatto & Windus, 1991), pp. 263–7.

129. Elizabeth Bowen, rev. of *The Irish Cousins* by Violet Powell, *The Mulberry Tree*, ed. Hermione Lee (London: Vintage, 1999), p. 187.

CHAPTER THREE

1. Review of *Naboth's Vineyard*, *The Daily Express*, 2 November 1891.

2. 'By the Brown Bog: Being some episodes in the life of an Irish DI' by L.P.Y. and H.E.M., *Badminton Magazine*, vols. xxxv–vi (July 1912–June 1913). Somerville and Ross's furious reaction to these eight stories can be found in the Pinker Correspondence, no. 3330–1, TCD.

3. Martin Ross, letter to James Pinker, 21 April 1903, Pinker Correspondence, no. 3330–1, TCD.

4. Anthony Cronin, *Heritage Now: Irish Literature in the English Language* (Dingle, Co. Kerry: Brandon Book Publishers, 1982), p. 82.

5. Martin Ross, 'The Terror in Ireland', *The World*, 5 April 1893, p. 22.

6. Finola O'Kane, *Landscape Design in Eighteenth-century Ireland: Mixing Foreign Trees with the Natives* (Cork: Cork University Press), p. 173.
7. *Selected Letters*, ed. Lewis, p. 39; pp. 137–8.
8. Somerville and Ross, *Wheel-Tracks*, pp. 15–16.
9. Somerville and Ross, *Irish Memories*, p. 107.
10. Robert Louis Stevenson, 'A Penny Plain and Twopence Coloured', *The Magazine of Art* (1884), *Memories and Portraits: Memories of Himself, Selections from His Notebook* (London: Tusitala Edition, 1924), p. 108.
11. Hilary Pyle, 'Jack Yeats: His Miniature Plays', National Gallery Lecture Series, National Gallery of Ireland, Dublin, 23 November 1999.
12. The words of Maria Edgeworth's English visitor, Sir Kit's new wife, in *Castle Rackrent* (1800; Oxford: World's Classic, 1980), p. 27.
13. Maclise's Irish landscape drawings are 'full of references to the picturesque' (p. 24) and he had a special interest in Irish antiquities. See John Turpin and Richard Ormond, *Daniel Maclise (1806–1870)*, exhibition catalogue (London, 1972).
14. James Clarence Mangan, 'The Lovely Land' (1849), *Poems of James Clarence Mangan*, ed. D.J. O'Donoghue (Dublin: M.H. Gill & Son, 1922), pp. 92–4.
15. Fintan Cullen, *Visual Politics: The Representation of Ireland 1750–1930* (Cork: Cork University Press, 1997), p. 6.
16. *The Strand Magazine*, xxiv (1902), p. 138. The front row of the Irish brigade includes Mr Labouchere, Mr Healy, Mr John Morley, Sir William Vernon Harcourt, Mr Gladstone, Mr T.P. O'Connor, Mr Parnell, Mr Biggar, and Mr O'Brien.
17. Edith Somerville, letter to Alice Kinkead, 19 November 1896, Drishane Archive.
18. From *Gedenkausgabe der Werke, Briefe und Gesprache* (Zurich, 1949), p. 719. Qtd. in Allardyce Nicoll, *The World of Harlequin: A Critical Study of the Commedia dell'Arte* (Cambridge: Cambridge University Press, 1963), p. 184.
19. Frank Swinnerton, qtd. in Jeffrey Meyers, *A Biography of Joseph Conrad* (New York: Charles Scribner, 1991), p. 204.
20. See, for instance, Edith Somerville's admiration for Colonel Coghill's physical prowess and vaunted masculinity, as evinced in extracts from his letters recording the bloody conquest of Delhi in 1857 in *Wheel-Tracks*, p. 187 and pp. 192–3.
21. Edith Somerville, 'A Grand Filly', *Badminton Magazine* xxi (April 1897), pp. 379–93; p. 379.
22. Heinz Kosok outlines a familiar pattern employed in nineteenth-century writing that sends an Englishman to Ireland to discover a people and place contradicting previously held notions about Ireland in 'Discovering an Alternative Culture: The Travel-Book Pattern in the Nineteenth-Century Irish Novel', *Das Natur/Kultur-Paradigma in der Englischsprachigen Erzahlliteratur des 19 und 20. Jahrunderts* (Tubingen, 1994), pp. 79–93.
23. Somerville, 'A Grand Filly', p. 381.
24. Somerville's Lisangle house, a 'square yellow box of a house, that had been made a fool of by being promiscuously trimmed with battlements' (p. 380) recalls Edgeworth's description of Ballinahinch, 'a whitewashed dilapidated mansion with nothing of a castle about it excepting four pepperbox-looking towers stuck on at each corner'. Maria Edgeworth, *Tour of Connemara and the Martins of Ballinahinch*, p. 44.
25. Somerville, 'A Grand Filly', p. 390.
26. M.H. Bakhtin, *The Dialogic Imagination* (Austin: University of Texas Press, 1981), p. 163.
27. Edith Somerville, letter to Martin Ross, 25 April 1897, *Selected Letters*, ed. Lewis, pp. 243–4.
28. *Badminton Magazine* vii (July–December 1898). In October 1898 'Great Uncle McCarthy' appeared, in November 'Trinket's Colt', and in December 'In the Curranhilty Country'. The remaining stories of *Experiences of an Irish RM* appeared in *Badminton* from January to December 1899.
29. *Irish Memories*, p. 258. See also Somerville, '*Happy Days!*' (London: Longmans, Green, 1946), p. 65.
30. In 1885 George Moore published a pamphlet called *Literature at Nurse or Circulating Morals* (London: Harvester Press, 1976) attacking the censorship of the Mudie circulating library and the requirement of an expensive three-volume novel form (which would die out with printing developments in the 1890s). Moore's 1883 novel, *A Modern Lover*, had been refused circulation by Mr Mudie because 'two ladies in the country had written to him to

say that they disapproved of the book' (*Literature at Nurse*, pp. 3–4).

31. Somerville is referring to the use of the feminine stereotype in the visual arts. 'Paris Notes', *International Art Notes* (March 1900), p. 10. Reference to the 'eternal feminine' as idealized womanhood recalls the final lines of Goethe's *Faust* Part II, Act V: 'Human discernment/Here is passed by;/Woman Eternal/Draw us on high'.

32. See, for instance, Somerville, 'Period Aunts', *'Happy Days!'* (London: Longmans, Green, 1946), pp. 36–49; p. 40.

33. James Thorpe, *English Illustration: The Nineties* (London: Faber and Faber, 1985), pp. 73–4.

34. In *A Magazine of Her Own? Domesticity and Desire in the Women's Magazine, 1800–1914* (London: Routledge 1996), Margaret Beetham points out that the English women's magazine provides a site for frequently conflicting discourse, where the appeal to a woman's class (her ladylike behaviour, her moral and physical perfection, her social position) might clash with the magazine's commercial demands or where the popularity of women's fashions might conflict with the need for more serious material for the woman of the 1890s.

35. Somerville and Ross, *Irish Memories*, p. 261.

36. Rauchbauer, ed., *The Edith Œ. Somerville Archive in Drishane*, I.71.a.

37. Edith Somerville, 'High Tea at McKeown's', *Black and White*, Christmas Number (1900), pp. 16–19.

38. Somerville and Ross, 'High Tea at McKeown's', *All on the Irish Shore* (London: Longmans, Green, 1903), p. 164.

39. Maurice Sendak, interviewed in the introduction to *Victorian Color Picture Books*, ed. Jonathan Cott (New York: Allen Lane, 1984), points out that most of the illustrator's work of the Victorian period used a conventional female face, 'a typical look of the time', rather than personalized portraiture: 'It's hard to see *through* the Victorian veneer', says Sendak; 'these are faces that are just *put on*'. He calls them 'glib faces' (p. xii).

40. Edith Somerville, letter to Pinker, 19 July 1904, the Pinker Correspondence 3330–1, TCD. Somerville repeats frequently in her letters to Pinker her belief that an illustration must do more than repeat a story's contents.

41. Anne Crookshank and the Knight of Glin, *Watercolours of Ireland 1600–1914* (London: Barrie & Jenkins 1994). The authors admire Somerville's work more for her illustrations than her oils (p. 231).

42. Stuart Sillars, *Visualization in Popular Fiction 1860–1960* (London: Routledge, 1995), p. 73.

43. *The Strand Magazine*, xx (December 1900), p. 604.

44. John Ruskin, 'Of the Turnerian Picturesque', (1856) *Modern Painters*, IV, ed. David Barrie (London: André Deutsch, 1987), p. 430.

45. Somerville and Ross, 'The Boat's Share', *The Strand Magazine*, xxix (January–June 1905), p. 79.

46. Ibid., p. 73.

47. Ibid., p. 73.

48. The opposition of appearance and reality that the Irish peasant manifests in the face of English law (and which occurs over and over again in the Irish RM stories) dominates one of Somerville and Ross's possible sources for the Irish RM stories, *Recollections of an Irish Police Magistrate and Other Reminiscences of the South of Ireland* by Henry Robert Addison (London: Ward, Lock, and Tyler, 1862). In the first story, 'The Bird's Nest', for instance, an apparently respectable Irish peasant family conceals in its cottage the bloodied instruments the family used to batter some drunken men to death. These stories are supposedly based on the real-life exploits of the chief magistrate of police in Limerick in the 1820s, Thomas Philip Vokes. I consider this source in greater detail in my next chapter.

49. Edith Somerville, address, 'The Educational Aspect of Women's Suffrage', Munster Women's Franchise League, 15 December 1911, in 'Essays on Irish and Suffragette Affairs' by E. Œ. Somerville, 1910–25, no. 898, QUB.

50. Martin Ross, 'For Better, For Worse', *Cornhill Magazine* (September 1906), pp. 356-65; p. 363.

51. Ibid., pp. 364–5.

52. Lewis, *Edith Somerville, A Biography*, p. 447.

53. 'In Sickness or in Health' provoked a strong response in Martin Ross's Catholic friend Maud Wynne, who argued, 'I acknowledge the Irish are rather *sexless*, but I will not allow

unromantic!' For the Catholic, romantic love arose from a greater love for God, said Wynne. 'Don't you think . . . materialism . . . has led to the world being over sexed. In our hardy forefather's time it was not the same. There it was a case of first come first taken, no picking & choosing'. 26 December 1906, Letters to Violet Martin, no. 919, QUB.

54. Edith Somerville, 'West Carbery as Sketching Ground', *International Art Notes* (May 1900), pp. 83–4.
55. Ibid., p. 84.
56. Malcolm Andrews, ed., introduction, *The Picturesque: Literary Sources and Documents*, I (Robertsbridge: Helm Information, 1994), pp. 10–11.
57. 'Children of the Captivity', *Some Irish Yesterdays* (London: T. Nelon & Sons, 1906), pp. 269–81. Violet Powell claims that the writing of the collection can be attributed solely to Martin in *The Irish Cousins*, p. 84. See also Edith Somerville's later discussion of Carleton's 'humiliatingly exaggerated buffooneries' in 'Stage Irishmen and Others', *Stray-Aways*, p. 242.
58. *Some Irish Yesterdays*, p. 275. Martin Ross's essay may owe its argument to Evan Evans's eighteenth-century poem 'A Paraphrase of the 137th Psalm, Alluding to the Captivity and Treatment of the Welsh Bards by King Edward I' ('What!—shall the Saxons hear us sing,/ Or their dull vales with Cambrian music ring?'). Qtd. in Trumpener's *Bardic Nationalism*, p. 2.
59. Pinker Correspondence, no. 3330–1, TCD.
60. George Eliot, *Daniel Deronda* (1876; London: Penguin, 1986), p. 193.
61. O'Kane, *Landscape Design in Eighteenth-century Ireland: Mixing Foreign Trees with the Natives*, pp. 156–7.
62. Peter Womack, *Improvement and Romance: Constructing the Myth of the Highlands* (London: Macmillan, 1989), p. 62. See also Simon Schama, *Landscape and Memory* (London: Fontana Press, 1995), pp. 466–9.
63. Ibid., p.3.
64. Ibid., p. 62.
65. Ibid., pp. 62-5.
66. John Ruskin, 'Of the Turnerian Picturesque' (1856) *Modern Painters*, IV, ed. David Barrie (London: André Deutsch, 1987), p. 427.
67. Ibid., pp. 427–33.
68. In 'The Metropolitan Picturesque', *The Politics of the Picturesque*, eds. Copley and Garside (Cambridge: Cambridge University Press, 1994), pp. 282–98, Malcolm Andrews notes that nineteenth-century civic awareness and an increasing presence of the poor within the metropolis demanded such a response. He also argues that Ruskin 'refashioned' the picturesque to 'equip it for a new role on the stage of cultural politics' (p. 297).
69. Ruskin, 'Of the Turnerian Picturesque', *Modern Painters*, p. 428.
70. Trumpener, 'The Bog Itself: Enlightenment Prospects and National Elegies', *Bardic Nationalism*, pp. 37–66.
71. Lady Morgan, *Florence Macarthy*, I (1818; New York: Garland Publishing, 1979), p. 44. The term 'aesthetiquarian' is used to describe such perusals of the Irish countryside by Trumpener in *Bardic Nationalism*, p. 144.
72. David Wilkie, letter to Sir William Knighton, 30 August 1835. Qtd. in Fintan Cullen's *Visual Politics: The Representation of Ireland 1750–1930* (Cork: Cork University Press, 1997), p. 124.
73. Thomas Hardy laments the changes wrought in the English countryside in 'The Dorsetshire Labourer' of 1883. *Thomas Hardy's Personal Writings*, ed. Harold Orel (London: Macmillan, 1967), pp. 168–91; 181.
74. On 15 August 1901, Martin Ross writes in her diary that 'there was only one case, of the drowning of a sheep, but J.O'Loghlen & W. McDermot worked it for an hour and a half for all it was worth'. In September, the cousins began to write their article about the Carna Petty Sessions; on 9 October, Martin sent the article to Maxse, editor of *The National Review*, who accepted it for £20. Diaries, QUB.
75. Somerville and Ross, 'An Irish Problem', *The National Review* 38 (September 1901–February 1902), p. 407. In 1903 Somerville published in the same magazine a political commentary, 'The Desired of the People', with the byline 'A Looker-On', which deplored the Catholic priest's influence in politics as well as the rising power of the 'strong farmer' who is motivated by personal interest to garner as much power as possible in a

changing country. This piece lacks the vibrant humour of 'An Irish Problem' but is more consistent with the commentary on Ireland in *The National Review*. Discussion articles from the unionist and nationalist viewpoints, such as 'A Final Land Measure' by 'A Landlord', 'Ireland and the Tariff', and 'Ireland – Retrospect and Forecast', appeared the same year.

76. Martin Ross, letter to Pinker, 22 February 1903, Pinker Correspondence, no. 3330–1, TCD.

77. Somerville and Ross, 'An Irish Problem', p. 407. For further discussion on Somerville and Ross's positioning of themselves as outsiders in Ireland and their consequent challenge to traditional notions of Irish identity, see Anne Oakman, 'Sitting on "The Outer Skin": Somerville and Ross's *Through Connemara in a Governess Cart* as a Coded Stratum of Linguistic/Feminist "Union" Ideals', *Eire-Ireland* 39: 1&2 (Spring/Summer 2004), pp. 110–35.

78. George Birmingham, 'Law and Order, and the Camera', *The Adventures of Dr Whitty* (London: Methuen, 1913), p. 174. In this series of comic stories detailing the art of manipulating the system and having plenty of fun while at it, 'The Interpreters' also satirizes the use of the Irish language in the West of Ireland.

79. Edgeworth, *Castle Rackrent*, p. 109.

80. Somerville and Ross, 'An Irish Problem', pp. 418 and 408.

81. Ibid., p. 409.

82. William Makepeace Thackeray, *The Irish Sketchbook*, *The Works of William Makepeace Thackeray*, XXIII (London: 1911), p. 21. See also Heinz Kosok's discussion of Thackeray's description in 'The Travel-Book Pattern in the Nineteenth-Century Irish Novel'.

83. Sympathy for the Boers thrived in the West of Ireland, to the extent that Lady Gregory included in her collection of folk songs and stories, *Poets and Dreamers* (1903; New York: Kennikat Press, 1967), a chapter on 'Boer Ballads in Ireland'. According to Gregory, and as Somerville and Ross indicate in 'An Irish Problem', it was the small farmers of Ireland who looked 'with special sympathy on their fellows in the Transvaal' (p. 42).

84. Sydney Brooks, 'Our Next Blunder in South Africa', *The National Review* 37 (June 1901), pp. 524–32.

85. Martin Ross, *A Patrick's Day Hunt*, illustrated by Edith Somerville (London: Constable, 1902). The following chapter considers this work more closely.

86. John Wilson Foster, 'The Irish Renaissance, 1890–1940: prose in English', *The Cambridge History of Irish Literature*, volume II, eds. Margaret Kelleher and Philip O'Leary (Cambridge: Cambridge University Press, 2006), p. 116.

87. Somerville and Ross's argument that English might be renewed and work with other languages to create a vibrant means of expression continues to be offered as an alternative response in twentieth-century post-colonial discourse. African writers such as Chinua Achebe and Ngugi wa Thiong'o, for instance, reconsider the dominance of English within a mixed African culture. In 'The African Writer and the English Language' (1975), Achebe states that African writers might adopt the language of colonialism to suit their own ends, while Ngugi in 'The Language of African Literature' (1986) argues that the use of the native tongue is part of the 'anti-imperialist struggle' (p. 451). See *Colonial Discourse and Post-Colonial Theory*, eds. Williams and Chrisman (Hertfordshire: Prentice Hall, 1994), pp. 428–34; 435–55. Martin J. Croghan introduces Anglo-Irish writers such as Edgeworth and Somerville and Ross into this post-colonial debate in 'Maria Edgeworth and the Tradition of Irish Semiotics' in *International Aspects of Irish Literature*, ed. Toshi Furomoto et al. (Gerrards Cross: Colin Smythe, 1996), pp. 340–8, and in *Demythologizing Hiberno-English*, Working Papers in Irish Studies (1990).

88. For further discussion of Yeats's painting, see Adele M. Dalsimer, ' "The Irish Peasant Had All His Heart": J.M. Synge in *The Country Shop*', *Visualizing Ireland: National Identity and the Pictorial Tradition*, ed. Adele Dalsimer (Boston: Faber and Faber, 1993), pp. 201–30.

89. Stanley Weintraub, *Whistler: A Biography* (Glasgow: William Collins Sons & Co., 1974), pp. 198, 207.

90. Martin Ross, 'The Martins of Ross', *Irish Memories*, pp. 29–30.

CHAPTER FOUR

1. Somerville's artistic education was mainly shaped by her extended visits to France. She spent various stints in Paris throughout the 1880s (84, 85, 86, 87). In 1894 Martin joined Somerville as she worked in Délécluse's studio, and, in 1898, they went to an artists' colony in Étaples near Boulogne. In 1899 Somerville returned to Paris for four months and worked in Délécluse's studio in the morning and with the illustrator Cyrus Cuneo in the afternoon. *Irish Memories*, pp. 263–5; Francis Gillespie, introduction, *Dr Edith Œnone Somerville 1858–1949*, exhibition catalogue, Drishane House, 5–9 September 1984.
2. Martin Ross, diary of 1899, QUB. See also Edith Somerville, 'Paris Notes', *International Art Notes*, no.1 (March 1900), pp. 10–13.
3. James McNeill Whistler, letter to *The World*, 22 May 1878, qtd. in Stanley Weintraub, *Whistler* (New York: Weybright and Talley, 1974), p. 441.
4. Somerville and Ross, *Irish Memories*, p. 265.
5. Paul Henry, *An Irish Portrait* (London: B.T. Batsford, 1951), p. 11.
6. As editor of *The Woman's World*, Wilde rejected Somerville's pictures. See Somerville, letter to Martin, no date, *Selected Letters*, ed. Lewis, p. 155. In later years Somerville neglected to mention this meeting and denied knowing Wilde. Edith Somerville, letter to Mr Symons, 14 December 1935, William Andrews Clark Memorial Library, UCLA.
7. Oscar Wilde, review of *Ismay's Children* by May Laffan, *The Woman's World* (November 1887–October 1899), p. 84.
8. Oscar Wilde, *The Picture of Dorian Gray*, *The Works of Oscar Wilde 1856–1900* (London: Collins, 1948), p. 112–13.
9. Qtd. in Thomas Crofton Croker, *Researches in the South of Ireland* (1824; First ed. rpt., Shannon: Irish University Press, 1969), p. 13.
10. Somerville and Ross, 'Great-Uncle McCarthy', *The Irish RM*, p.11.
11. Mikhail Bakhtin, *The Dialogic Imagination*, p. 163.
12. Maureen Waters, *The Comic Irishman* (Albany: State University of New York Press, 1984), pp. 15–16. Joep Leerssen, *Remembrance and Imagination* (Cork: Cork University Press, 1996), p. 171.
13. Frank O'Connor's claim that Somerville and Ross remained firmly within the English realist tradition does not recognize the French influence on Somerville's artwork or what other critics saw as a French influence in their writing, as mentioned in Chapter 2. Possibly following the lead of Charles Graves who thought the women writers' unsympathetic portrait of Charlotte Mullen had been drawn 'in the spirit of Balzac', various critics have compared Somerville and Ross to Balzac. See Frank O'Connor, 'Somerville and Ross,' *Irish Times* (15 Dec. 1945), p. 4, and Charles Graves, 'Introduction', *Humours of Irish Life* (Dublin: The Talbot Press, no date), p. xxv. More recent exploration of the French influence on Somerville and Ross's writings is found in Guy Fehlmann, *Somerville and Ross: Témoins de l'Irlande d'hier* (Caen: Association des publications de la Faculté des Lettres et Sciences Humaines de l'Université de Caen, 1970), pp. 309–11.
14. Henry Robert Addison, *Recollections of an Irish Police Magistrate and Other Reminiscences of the South of Ireland* (London: Ward, Lock, and Tyler, 1862). Virginia Crossman points out various similarities between the Irish RM stories and Addison's text in 'The Resident Magistrate as Colonial Officer: Addison, Somerville and Ross', *Irish Studies Review* 8,1 (2000), pp. 28–33.
15. Síghle Bhreathnach-Lynch and Julie Anne Stevens, 'The Irish Artist Crossing the Rubicon', *Local/Global*, eds. Cherry and Helland, p. 139.
16. Enid Welsford, *The Fool: His Social and Literary History* (London: Faber and Faber, 1935), pp. 307–8.
17. Jane Abdy, *The French Poster* (London: Studio Vista, 1969). Théophile-Alexandre Steinlen, *Steinlen's Drawings* (New York: Dover Publications, 1980). I am grateful to Peter Murray of the Crawford Gallery in Cork for suggesting Steinlen's possible influence on Somerville's illustrations.
18. Edith Somerville in a letter to Alice Kinkead in Paris, 26 January 1898, thanks her for sending *Gil Blas*. Drishane Archive.
19. Martin Ross, diary, 28 October 1901, QUB.
20. Qtd. in Michele Hannoosh, *Baudelaire and Caricature* (Pennsylvania: Pennsylvania State University Press, 1992), p. 115. Hannoosh argues that 'caricature, like the realist novel, is

nothing less than the art of the nineteenth century' (pp. 115–17).

21. *Le Charivari*, founded by Charles Philipon, took over from *La Silhouette* (1829) and *La Caricature* (1830) in 1832. *La Caricature* had collapsed because of libel suits. Though initially a left-wing paper, *Le Charivari* lost its political edge under the Second Empire (1852–70). However throughout the nineteenth-century French illustrated papers voiced anarchist and royalist views and 'the flood was unleashed with the law on the liberty of expression (29 July 1881) . . . by the end of the century there were six thousand papers in Paris alone'. Michel Melot, *The Art of Illustration* (New York: Rizzoli International Publications, 1984), pp. 155–6.

22. Henry James, 'Honoré Daumier' (1890), *Picture and Text* (New York: Harper and Brothers, 1893), p. 116.

23. Charles Baudelaire, 'De l'essence du rire', 'Quelques caricaturistes français', and 'Quelques caricaturistes étrangers' *Œuvres Complètes*, p. 529.

24. Ibid., p. 532.

25. Somerville and Ross, *Irish Memories*, p. 270.

26. John Leech, illus., 'The Claddagh – Galway', *A Little Tour in Ireland*, by 'An Oxonian' (London: Bradbury & Evans, 1859).

27. Somerville and Ross, *A Patrick's Day Hunt* (1902), *Some Irish Yesterdays*, pp. 119–20.

28. Edith Somerville, letter to James Pinker, 25 October 1902 Pinker Correspondence, no. 3330–1, TCD.

29. Somerville, illus., *A Patrick's Day Hunt* by Martin Ross.

30. Croker, *Researches in the South of Ireland*, p. 21.

31. Ibid., p 13.

32. John Brewer, 'Culture, Nature and Nation', *Pleasures of the Imagination: English Culture in the Eighteenth Century* (London: HarperCollins Publishers, 1997), pp. 615–61.

33. Ibid., p. 622.

34. O'Kane, *Landscape Design in Eighteenth-Century Ireland*, p. 156.

35. Ibid., pp. 4 and 157.

36. Ibid., p. 658.

37. See Neil Buttimer's analysis of Croker's treatment of the Irish national character as dependent upon his response to accounts of the 1798 rebellion (especially Sir Richard Musgrave's anti-Catholic account) in 'Remembering 1798', *Journal of the Cork Historical and Archaeological Society* 103 (1998), pp. 1–26.

38. Leerssen, *Remembrance and Imagination*, p. 160. See also Seamus Deane. 'Irish National Character 1790–1900', *The Writer as Witness: Literature as Historical Evidence*, ed. Tom Dunne (Cork: Cork University Press, 1987), pp. 90–113. In his discussion of the traditional or Celtic virtues ascribed to the Irish national character by the works of Sylvester O'Halloran, Charles Vallancey, Charles O'Conor, and so on, Deane notes the use of the sublime which brings about a new primitivism to counter the revolutionary culture of novelty, simplicity, and respect for mechanical regularity. Amateur antiquarianism, he notes, provided exotic origins while Irish poetry and music furthered the notions of Ireland's unique character. Deane stresses the Anglo-Irish writer's reaction to British caricature of the Irish and the consequent redemption of the peasant as a preoccupation during the first half of the century.

39. Leerssen, *Remembrance and Imagination*, p. 160.

40. Thomas Philips Vokes, letters, State of the Country Papers, National Records Office, Dublin, 29 January, 26 February, 23 June, and 10 August 1824, SOC/2618/19, SOC/2618/36, SOC/2618/85, and SOC/2619/13.

41. Virginia Crossman, 'The Resident Magistrate as Colonial Officer', *Irish Studies Review*, 8, 1 (2000), endnote 10, p. 31.

42. See Penny Bonsall, *The Irish RMs* (Dublin: Four Courts Press, 1998), pp. 17–19. Bonsall provides a summary of the resident magistrate's position during the 1860s but does not mention Addison's influential text.

43. Henry Robert Addison, 'The Bird's Nest', *Recollections of an Irish Police Magistrate*, p. 11.

44. Ibid., p. 14.

45. Ibid., p. 102.

46. 'Our Portrait Gallery – no. xxiii: Henry R. Addison, Esquire', *Dublin University Magazine* xviii (July–December 1841), pp. 505–6.

47. See Virginia Crossman, 'The Resident Magistrate as Colonial Officer', p. 24, and *Local*

Government in Nineteenth-Century Ireland (Queen's University of Belfast: Institute of Irish Studies, 1994), pp. 96–7.

48. Robert J. Martin and E.A.P. Hobday, *The Forty Thieves; or Ali Baba and the Black Sheep of Baghdad* (Dublin: W.J. Alley, 1886), p. 10.

49. Lewis, *Edith Somerville, A Biography*, p. 225.

50. For further discussion on genre transformation as it affects national character, see Katie Trumpener, 'National Character, Nationalist Plots: National Tale and Historical Novel in the Age of *Waverly*, 1806–1830', *English Literary History* 60 (1993).

51 Qtd. in Ainslee Armstrong McLees, *Baudelaire's 'Argot Plastique': Poetic Caricature and Modernism* (Athens, Georgia: University of Georgia Press, 1989), endnote 5, p. 158. I have relied on McLees's translation of *démêler* as unmasking.

52. As noted in Ainslie Armstrong McLees, *Baudelaire's 'Argot Plastique'*, p. 7.

53. Honoré de Balzac, *Théorie de la démarche*, qtd. in Judith Wechsler, *A Human Comedy: Physiognomy and Caricature in 19th Century Paris* (London: Thames and Hudson, 1982), p. 22.

54. Balzac, *Cousin Bette*, p. 9.

55. Baudelaire, 'Le Miroir', *Le Spleen de Paris*, pp. 150–1.

56. Sigmund Freud, *Wit and Its Relation to the Unconscious*, trans. A.A. Brill (1905; New York: Dover Publications, 1993), p. 325.

57. Ibid., pp. 322 and 326.

58. Charles Robert Maturin, *The Milesian Chief* (1812; New York: Garland Publishing, 1979), pp. iv–v.

59. Florence Macarthy, a national hero in a national tale, is reduced and altered by the extreme conditions of life in Ireland. She possesses a chameleon-like character, ever-changing and ever-shifting, which survives in the Irish world by slipping on one mask after another. Lady Morgan, *Florence Macarthy* III (New York: Garland Publishing, 1979), pp. 273–4.

60. James Clarence Mangan, 'The Wandering Jew', *The Collected Works of James Clarence Mangan*, ed. Jacques Chuto (1837; Dublin: Academic Press, 1996), pp. 377–80.

61. At the end of the eighteenth century, Immanuel Kant addressed 'National Characteristics, so far as They Depend upon the Distinct Feeling of the Beautiful and Sublime' to categorize nationality according to different kinds of taste (the French taste in poetry, for instance, runs to the Beautiful while the English aesthetic preference leans towards the Sublime). *Observations on the Feeling of the Beautiful and Sublime*, 1764, trans. John T. Goldthwait (Berkeley; London: University of California Press, 1960), p. 97.

62. For further discussion on the relationship of Burkean notions of the sublime and the Irish national character, see Richard Haslam, 'Representation and the Sublime in Six Irish Writers: A Study of Edmund Burke, Lady Morgan, Charles Maturin, James Clarence Mangan, Joseph Sheridan Le Fanu, and William Carleton', Ph.D. 1991, Trinity College Dublin.

63. Baudelaire, 'De l'essence du rire', p. 526.

64. Ibid., p. 531.

65. Charles Maturin, *Melmoth the Wanderer* (1820; London: Oxford University Press, 1968), p. 352.

66. Baudelaire, 'De l'essence du rire', p. 531.

67. Charles Baudelaire, 'Of the Essence of Laughter', *Baudelaire: Selected Writings on Art and Literature*, trans. P.E. Charvet (London: Penguin, 1972), p. 147.

68. Homi Bhabha, *The Location of Culture*, p. 67.

69. Ibid., pp. 74–5. Bhabha applies Freud's use of fetishism ('the disavowal of difference') to his study of stereotyping (p. 74).

70. Martin J. Croghan, *Demythologizing Hiberno-English*, p. 1. See also Croghan's later work on Edgeworth and her use of stereotyping, or 'symbolic violence', in stage-Irish portrayals. 'Maria Edgeworth and the Tradition of Irish Semiotics', *International Aspects of Irish Literature*, pp. 340–8.

71. L. Prerry Curtis Jr. *Apes and Angels*, p. 147. Curtis refers to Somerville's use of a 'simian simile' as used by the Prendevilles in *Big House of Inver* to describe insurgent Irish: 'The Gorillas'. The implication is that Somerville (as 'gentry of Ireland') may have shared the Prendevilles' view (p. xxxiii).

72. Roy Foster emphasizes in his survey of representations of the Irish in *Punch* from the 1840s up until the end of the century the ambiguity of their depiction. He concludes that they are

'a threatening underclass rather than a colonized subrace'. *Paddy and Mr Punch*, p. 192. More recently, in a review of Curtis's revised edition, Catherine Eagan points out that the revisionists' primary reason for stressing ambivalence instead of racism [in English carica- ture of the Irish] is their conviction that Curtis's exclusion of the factors of class and reli- gion in his binary model of civilized and savage comes dangerously close to simplistically equating anti-Irish racism with racism directed against non-Europeans' (p. 27). English cari- cature of Africans, argues Eagan, may not have needed the visual signals ascribed to the Irish (simianized characteristics) because blackness already denotes the status of the African. Eagan thus suggests the significance of the 'fact of blackness' in English caricature. The white skin of the Irishman, like the ambiguous politics of his state, complicates the binary model which black and white, ape and angel, suggests. 'Simianization Meets Postcolonial Theory', *The Irish Literary Supplement* (Fall 1997), pp. 27–8.

73. See, for instance, Richard Lebow, *White Britain and Black Ireland: The Influence of Stereotypes on Colonial Policy* (Philadelphia: Institute for the Study of Human Issues, 1976). Further discussion on the use of binary extremes of black and white, such as Leslie Fiedler's work in the United States, demonstrates the utilization of chiaroscuro for multiple purposes. Fiedler analyses the moral significance of black and white in the nineteenth-century novel in 'The Power of Blackness: Faustian Man and the Cult of Violence', *Love and Death in the American Novel* (1960; New York: Stein and Day, 1975).

74. Edward Said also aligns Irish and black races. For Said, Ireland is not part of his construc- tion of the West. Instead, he uses Ireland to point out the connection between 'black' and 'white' colonies (such as Ireland and Jamaica) by referring to the French caricaturist Honoré Daumier, whose drawing of a black Jamaican and a white Irishman 'explicitly con- nects Irish whites and Jamaican Blacks'. *Culture and Imperialism* (London: Vintage, 1994), p. 162.

75. Frantz Fanon, *Black Skin, White Masks* (London: Pluto Press, 1986), p. 110.

76. George Moore, Lecture on Impressionism, Dublin 1904, Appendix A, *Hail and Farewell* (1911) ed. Richard Cave (Gerrards Cross: Colin Smythe, 1985), pp. 662–3.

77. Fintan Cullen identifies the influence of notions of Irishness in formal portraiture by Reynolds and Wilkie. He points out that while portraits of the 'Third Earl of Bellamont, 1773–4' and 'Daniel O'Connell, 1836–8' are influenced by stage-Irish types and *Punch* cari- catures, they indicate a more general belief in the Irishman's ability to be utterly charming or utterly diabolical, which results in ambiguous portrayal. *Visual Politics*, p. 104.

78. Henry James, 'Honoré Daumier' (1890), *Picture and Text*, 1893, p. 118.

79. James Clarence Mangan, 'The Man in the Cloak: A Very German Story', *Dublin University Magazine*, vol. 12 (Nov. 1838), pp. 552–68. Terry Eagleton notes Mangan's self-con- sciousness when Mangan describes the act of pretending that one's own plagiarised text is the original as 'anti-plagiarism'. As Eagleton argues: 'whereas plagiarism proper claims the parasitic text as original, this mischievous reversal reduces the source text to secondary sta- tus'. *Heathcliff and the Great Hunger* (London: Verso, 1995), p. 266.

80. I have taken the liberty of applying Clarence Mangan's observations on Dr Anster's trans- lation of Goethe's *Faust* to Mangan's plagiarism of Balzac. See James Clarence Mangan, *Irishman*, 21 April 1849 in James *Clarence Mangan: Selected Writings*, ed. Seán Ryder (Dublin: University College Press 2004), p. 409.

81. Martin Ross, letter to Edith Somerville, 1896, *Selected Letters*, ed. Lewis, p. 240.

82. *The Savoy*, ed. Arthur Symons, 1–8 (January–December 1896). From No.2 (April 1896). Yeats's poetry dominated the magazine.

83. Roy Foster, *W.B. Yeats* I (Oxford: Oxford University Press, 1997), pp. 157–9. Max Beerbohm sends up the notion of diabolism in his satire of a fictional decadent 1890s' poet, 'Enoch Soames'. Soames, a Catholic Diabolist, who writes a book called *Negations* and a collection of poems called *Fungoids*, sells his soul to a Devil who looks like Salvador Dali. *The Bodley Head Max Beerbohm*, ed. David Cecil (London: The Bodley Head, 1970), pp. 55–86.

84. Welsford, p. 288.

85. Ibid., pp. 290–1.

86. Mikhail Bakhtin, *Rabelais and His World*, trans. Helene Iswolsky (1965; Bloomington: Indiana Press, 1984), pp. 396–7.

87. David Mayer, *Harlequin in His Element: The English Pantomime, 1806–1836* (Cambridge: Harvard University Press, 1969), pp. 4–5.

88. The English pantomime used the stage Irishman, and with Catholic emancipation in 1829, he began to show greater possibilities. His improved profile is reflected in a number of pantomimes of this period. Initially, in Charles Farley's 'Harlequin and Friar Bacon' in 1820, the drunken Irish characters of Donnybrook Fair appear solely in the harlequinade. In 'Harlequin and the Eagle' of 1826, the Irish characters, the peasant lovers, Cormac and Mary, feature throughout the pantomime, changing into Harlequin and Columbine later on. In 'Harlequin Pat and Harlequin Bat' of 1830, 'the Ireland of musical comedy and tourist brochures is complete'. Brian Boru and his bride, Norma, are changed to Harlequin and Columbine by St Patrick and the harlequin bat becomes the inevitable shillelagh. Mayer, *Harlequin in his Element*, pp. 254–6.

89. Mayer, *Harlequin in his Element*, p. 5.

90. Welsford, *The Fool*, p. 217.

91. Ibid., p. 299.

92. Baudelaire, 'De l'essence du rire', p. 541.

93. Somerville and Ross, 'The Policy of the Closed Door', *The Irish RM*, p. 174.

94. Somerville and Ross, 'Sharper than a Ferret's Tooth', *The Irish RM*, p. 383.

95. Roz Cowman reads *Experiences of an Irish RM* as 'a manifesto of erotic joy', a 'Greek pastoral idyll' with Flurry Knox, 'the Lord of the Animals' as the incarnation of Dionysus. The name Florence is androgynous and Great-uncle Denis of the first Irish RM stories refers directly to the Latinate Dionysius (pp. 100–1). 'Lost Time: The Smell and Taste of Castle T', *Sex, Nation and Dissent in Irish Writing*, pp. 87–102. The 'erotic joy' that Roz Cowman notes is well-concealed for this reader.

96. Bakhtin, 'Forms of Time and of the Chronotope in the Novel', *The Dialogic Imagination*, pp. 84–5; 159.

97. Baudelaire, 'De l'essence du rire', p. 540.

CHAPTER FIVE

1. Martin Ross, Draft of 'Cheops in Connemara' (13 June 1889) no. 884, QUB.

2. Edgar Allan Poe, 'The Philosophy of Composition', *The American Tradition in Literature* I, eds. Sculley Bradley et al. (New York: Grosset and Dunlap, 1977), p. 881.

3. Frank O'Connor, *The Lonely Voice* (London: Macmillan, 1963). For further discussion on Frank O'Connor's neglect of the anecdotal kind of story in his discussion of the development of the modern short story, see Valerie Shaw, *The Short Story: A Critical Introduction* (London: Longman, 1983), p. 88.

4. Somerville and Ross's Diaries, 1898. QUB.

5. Stephen Crane was hailed by Edward Garnett as 'the chief impressionist of the age' and by Conrad as 'the impressionist *par excellence*'. Qtd. in Sergio Perosa, 'Naturalism and Impressionism in Stephen Crane's Fiction', *Stephen Crane: A Collection of Critical Essays*, ed. Maurice Bassan (Englewood Cliffs, New Jersey: Prentice Hall, 1967), p. 91. Joseph Conrad, 'Preface', *The Nigger of Narcissus* (1897; London: Gresham Publishing, 1925), p. ix.

6. James Joyce, *Ulysses* (New York: Random House, 1986), p. 115.

7. Rachbauer, *Drishane Archive*, p. 184.

8. Diaries, QUB.

9. Augusta Gregory had tried to learn Irish before 1897 but only persevered after being inspired by the general enthusiasm generated by the visits of Standish O'Grady, Horace Plunkett, and Douglas Hyde during the summer of that year. See James Pethica, ed., *Lady Gregory's Diaries, 1892–1902*, pp. 151–2.

10. Edith Somerville, letter to Martin Ross, 25 April 1897, *Letters*, pp. 242–3.

11. Pethica, ed., *Lady Gregory's Diaries*, pp. 152–3.

12. Crossman, *Local Government in Nineteenth-Century Ireland*, pp. 96–7.

13. Hilary Robinson notes how closely Somerville and Ross's fiction follows the material in 'Stock Pot Memories' (*Collection of Irish Anecdotes*). She thus sets about proving the authenticity of the Hiberno-English used in Somerville and Ross's work. *Somerville and Ross*, pp. 51–5.

14. Somerville and Ross, 'The Anglo-Irish Language' (1910), *Stray-Aways*, p. 184.

15. P.J. Mathews, *Revival: The Abbey Theatre, Sinn Féin, the Gaelic League and the Co-operative Movement* (Cork: Cork University Press, 2003), p. 11.

16. Augusta Gregory, 'Ireland, Real and Ideal', *The Nineteenth Century* (November 1898), pp. 769–82; 779.

17. Bakhtin, *The Dialogic Imagination*, p. 163.

18. Lewis, *Somerville and Ross*, p. 226.

19. Somerville and Ross, ''Lisheen Races, Second-Hand', *The Irish RM*, p. 93.

20. Nevill Coghill's description of mss XII, which was used for 'The Boat's Share' is in his Catalogue, no. 3783, TCD. Early drafts of the two stories are found in no. 3290, TCD.

21. Somerville and Ross, 'Lisheen Races, Second-Hand', *The Irish RM*, p. 96.

22. Ibid., p. 94.

23. Ibid., pp. 103 and 107.

24. Somerville and Ross, 'The Last Day of Shraft', *The Irish RM*, p. 337.

25. Ibid., pp. 347–8.

26. *The Spirit of the Nation* becomes an important source of Irish nationalist sentiment in Edith Somerville's later novel, *Mount Music* (London: Thomas Nelson & Sons, 1919). The hero, Larry Coppinger, finds his 'young soul burning with hatred for England, borrowed from the Bards of "The Nation" office' (p. 34).

27. Joep Leerssen speaks of the foregrounding of martial topics in the national iconography of *The Spirit of the Nation*: 'such a martial tendency marks a change from the mellower tones of Moore and foreshadows the machismo of Standish O'Grady'. Leerssen notes the appearance of two Irish military histories by Matthew O'Conor (1845) and John O'Callaghan (1854) during this period. *Remembrance and Imagination*, pp. 148–9. The mock battles of the Irish R.M. stories parody this discourse.

28. Somerville and Ross, 'Great-Uncle McCarthy', *The Irish RM*, p. 11.

29. In December 1897, Somerville and Ross sent six chapters of a 'hunting story' to James Pinker. As mentioned in Chapter 3, much of this unfinished work, 'A Man of the People', they used in the Irish R.M. stories. Most of 'A Closed Door' and 'A Misdeal' comes from the earlier work. See 'A Man of the People', no. 880, QUB. The 'man of the people' in the earlier unpublished work, Michael Kavanagh, anticipates Flurry Knox, although the former character's folk wisdom and closeness to the land becomes less obvious in Flurry, the landowner. Nonetheless Flurry's idyllic background as a 'man of the people' (corrupted through past family marriages into the Knox family) indicates the influence of the pastoral idyll in the Irish RM stories. For discussion of the role of 'a man of the people' in the idyll, see Bakhtin, *The Dialogic Imagination*, p. 235.

30. Lady Morgan, *Florence Macarthy*, III, p. 110.

31. Somerville and Ross, 'Great-Uncle McCarthy', *The Irish RM*, pp. 8, 10 and 18.

32. McCarthy has nine poems in the 1864 edition of *The Spirit of the Nation*. His popularity is indicated by the presence of his collected poems in Leopold Bloom's bookshelf in *Ulysses*. The marker in Bloom's text rests on page five, which according to the 1881 edition is the table of contents. Perhaps Bloom never got round to reading the actual poems.

33. Leerssen, *Remembrance and Imagination*, p. 14.

34. According to Hardiman, Timothy Sullivan (Thaddeus Hibernicus) composed this lament for 'the last of Munster's genuine stock, MacCarthy's royal line' in the eighteenth century. As titular king of Munster, Denis MacCarthy 'retained much of the dignity appertaining to the ancient Irish chief'. His clan dominated in the south but was eventually 'broken down by [its] own divisions rather than the power of [its] enemies'. The remains of this Irish family, says Hardiman, were 'sons bred to low trades, uneducated paupers, some of whom are still living – *Sic transit gloria Mundi*'. *Irish Minstrelsy or Bardic Remains of Ireland*, II (London: Joseph Robins, 1831), pp. 272–9; 418–20.

35. Denis Florence McCarthy, 'The Clan of MacCaura', *The Ballad Poetry of Ireland*, ed. Charles Gavan Duffy (1845), fortieth edition (Dublin: James Duffy, 1869). The extensive notes to this ballad set about establishing the connections of the McCarthy family to ancient nobility. In *Florence Macarthy*, Lady Morgan had already suggested a similar line of descent for the Munster family. The name Florence 'comes from the Spanish name Florianus, which the Macarthies brought with them on their way from Scythia' (I: p. 261).

36. Denis Florence McCarthy, ed., 'Introduction on the Early Religion and Literature of the Irish People', *The Poets and Dramatists of Ireland* and *The Book of Irish Ballads*. One volume (Dublin: James Duffy, 1846), pp. 15–18.

37. Joep Leerssen, *Remembrance and Imagination*, pp. 109–12.

38. Somerville and Ross, 'Oh Love! Oh Fire!', *The Irish RM*, pp. 226 and 235.

39. Ibid., p. 232.
40. Somerville and Ross, 'The Policy of the Closed Door', *The Irish RM*, p. 169.
41. Somerville and Ross, 'A Horse! A Horse!', *The Irish RM*, p. 355.
42. A possible source for Somerville and Ross's parody of complacent religiosity might be found in Lady Carbery's description of visiting Protestant missionary friends to Castle Freke in the late nineteenth century. These pompous and comfort-loving evangelicals request their hostess to produce suitable sinners for their missionary work; unfortunately, Mary Carbery knows none but asks a few friends to help out. Included is Somerville's cousin, Hewitt Poole. Lady Carbery reports in her journal that the missionaries are disgusted with their audience 'who ask them inconvenient questions about miracles, etc.' Most likely a follow-up report on missionaries who are not 'too good to have a first-rate cook and comforts' made its way back to the Somerville home in Castletownshend. Jeremy Sandford, ed., *Mary Carbery's West Cork Journal, 1898–1901* or 'From the Back of Beyond' (Dublin: Lilliput, 1998), pp. 96–100.
43. In 'Great-Uncle McCarthy', the Knoxes are described as 'Black Protestants' descending from 'a godly soldier of Cromwell' (p. 11). Gifford Lewis tells us that neither the Somervilles nor the Martins 'were Cromwellian in origin' and 'their families' connections with England had been brief; England was used only as a staging post for the Somervilles on their journey to Lowland Scotland, and for the Martins on their journey to the West of Ireland'. Lewis, *Edith Somerville, A Biography*, p. 29. The satire of the Knox family, then, is not self-satire but directed at another strain of Anglo-Irish.
44. John Turpin and Richard Ormond, *Daniel Maclise (1860–1870)*. John Turpin, 'Daniel Maclise and his Place in Victorian Art', pp. 51–69.
45. John Townshend married Lady Catherine Barry who descended from MacCarthy Reagh, according to genealogist and lawyer, Eoin O'Mahony. See Lewis, *Edith Somerville, A Biography*, p. 17. Presumably this is the same John Townshend.
46. In a letter to David Laing published in *Proceedings of the Society of Antiquaries of Scotland* (Edinburgh: Society of Antiquaries of Scotland, 1855), Thomas Carlyle argues that the portrait, like a 'lighted candle' by which one might read the biography of a historical figure, becomes an essential part of historical record (p. 174).
47. Nina Auerbach, *Woman and the Demon: The Life of a Victorian Myth* (Cambridge, Mass.: Harvard University Press, 1982), p. 192.
48. Thomas Carlyle, 'The Portrait of John Knox', *Fraser's Magazine*, XI, LXIV (April 1875), pp. 407–39.
49. Fred Kaplan, *Thomas Carlyle: A Biography* (Cambridge: Cambridge University Press, 1983), p. 515.
50. Thomas Carlyle, *On Heroes, Hero-Worship and the Heroic in History* (London: Routledge, 1841), pp. 192–5.
51. See, for instance, Carlyle's letter to Duffy written a year after his visit to Ireland, 15 September 1850. *Conversations with Carlyle* (London: Sampson Low, Marston & Co., 1892), pp. 158–62. Duffy also records that their one serious argument was a disagreement about Ireland and what Carlyle saw to be Ireland's resistance to the Reformation (pp. 223–8).
52. James Anthony Froude, *Thomas Carlyle: A History of His Life in London, 1834–1881*, II (London: Longmans, Green, 1884), pp. 336–8.
53. Ibid., p. 340.
54. For instance, Gifford Lewis notes that Martin Ross's family referred to her in early years as 'Our Little Carlyle' in *Selected Letters*, p. 25. See also Edith Somerville, 'Two of a Trade', *Irish Writing*, eds. D. Marcus and T. Smith, no. 1 (1946), p. 83.
55. Somerville and Ross, 'The Waters of Strife', *The Irish RM*, pp. 76–7.
56. Penny Bonsall, *The Irish RMs: The Resident Magistrates in the British Administration in Ireland*, p. 46.
57. F.S.L. Lyons, *Ireland Since the Famine* (London: Fontana, 1971), pp. 216–18.
58. Somerville and Ross, 'The Waters of Strife', *The Irish RM*, p. 80.
59. See, for instance, ' "Up for the Green!" A Song of the United Irishmen' (1796): 'Tis the green—oh! the green is the colour of the true/ And we'll back it 'gainst the orange, and we'll raise it o'er the blue!/ For the colour of our fatherland alone should here be seen—/ The colour of the martyred dead—our own immortal green'. *The Spirit of the Nation* (rev. ed. 1845; Dublin: James Duffy, 1866), p. 118.

60. Somerville and Ross, 'The Waters of Strife', *The Irish RM*, p. 86.
61. Ibid., p. 91.
62. *Penny Readings for the Irish People*, II (Dublin, 1879), pp. 120–3.
63. J.C. Beckett, *The Making of Modern Ireland 1603–1923* (London: Faber and Faber, 1981), p. 264.
64. *The Spirit of the Nation* (1843; Dublin: James Duffy, 1864), p. 40.
65. David Lloyd, 'The Spirit of the Nation', *Nationalism and Minor Literature* (Berkeley: University of California Press, 1987), pp. 63; 71.
66. Edith Somerville, *An Enthusiast* (London: Longmans, Green, 1921), p. 147.
67. *Henry IV, Part One*, I.ii, *William Shakespeare, The Complete Works*, ed. Alfred Harbage (New York: Viking, 1975), p. 673.
68. Somerville and Ross, 'Holy Island', *The Irish RM*, p. 151.
69. Ibid., pp. 152–3.
70. Ibid., p. 153.
71. *The Spirit of the Nation* (1864), pp. 112–14.
72. Somerville and Ross, 'Holy Island', *The Irish RM*, p. 157.
73. Samuel Ferguson, 'The Fair Hills of Ireland', *Irish Verse*, ed. Brendan Kennelly (London: Penguin, 1981), p. 196. According to Seán Ryder, Ferguson's 1834 poem idealizes the Irish landscape to argue a Protestant, liberal viewpoint. 'The Politics of Landscape and Region in Nineteenth-Century Poetry', *Ireland in the Nineteenth Century: Regional Identity*, eds. Leon Litvak and Glenn Hooper (Dublin: Four Courts Press, 2000), pp. 171–4.
74. J.D. Fraser, 'The Holy Wells', *Ballad Poetry of Ireland*, ed. Charles Gavan Duffy (1845), reproduction of the fortieth edition (1869: New York: Scholars' Fascimiles & Reprints, 1973), pp. 216–17. 'Holy Island' responds to a tradition of Irish ballads which sacralize Ireland, poems like Fraser's anti-imperialist ballad or Ferguson's romantic translation of an old Irish song.
75. Somerville and Ross, 'Holy Island', *The Irish RM*, p. 162.
76. Letter to James Pinker, 14 December 1899, Pinker Correspondence, no. 3330–1, TCD.

CHAPTER SIX

1. Daniel Corkery, *Synge and Anglo-Irish Literature*, p. 14; Robert Martin, 'A Connemara Short-Cut', *Bits of Blarney*, p. 196; Somerville and Ross, *The Silver Fox*, p.117. Seamus Heaney celebrates the layered Irish landscape in poems like 'Bogland' in *Door into the Dark* (1969), *New Selected Poems 1966–1987* (London: Faber and Faber, 1990), pp. 17–18, or his essay '*from* Feeling into Words' (1974), *Finders Keepers: Selected Prose, 1971–2001* (London: Faber and Faber, 2002), pp. 21–3. Echoing Daniel Corkery, Heaney likens the bog to the Irish national consciousness (p. 22). I am interested in the bog as a landscape myth and also the vertical motion that it suggests for nineteenth-century writers. The bog, like the abyss, serves as a symbol of the sublime.
2. See, for instance, Bakhtin, *Rabelais and His World*, p. 388.
3. Thomas James Arnold, *Reynard the Fox, After the German Version of Goethe*, illustrated by Wilhelm von Kaulbach and Joseph Wolf (London: John C. Nimmo, 1887), p. 47.
4. Cronin, *Somerville and Ross*, p. 73.
5. S.J. Connolly, ed., *Oxford Companion to Irish History* (Oxford: Oxford University Press, 1998), p. 520.
6. Martin Ross's Diary, 1912, QUB.
7. Lyons, *Ireland Since the Famine*, p. 287.
8. Edith Somerville, Letter to Cameron Somerville, 4 June 1912, *Drishane Archive*, L.A. 771.
9. Somerville and Ross, *Wheel-Tracks*, p. 220. For Martin Ross's letters to Stephen Gwynn, see *Irish Memories*, pp. 315–23.
10. Martin Ross, 'The Reaping of Ulster', *The Spectator*, 5 October 1912, pp. 504–5.
11. Somerville and Ross, 'The Maroan Pony', *The Irish RM*, pp. 486–8.
12. Ibid., pp. 490 and 493.
13. Ibid., p. 500.
14. The pony's position on high in 'The Maroan Pony' mirrors the pony's position down below in 'Trinket's Colt' in Somerville and Ross's first collection of stories. Perhaps it is the repetition of this device which leads John Cronin to conclude that in *In Mr Knox's*

Country, 'the writers fall back on situations often exploited before'. Reading these final stories, he says, one suffers from 'a strong sense of *déjà-vu*' (p. 74). My analysis, however, demonstrates the authors' reworking of similar material to create different effects. Moreover, viewed side by side the two stories create a topsy-turvy effect which emphasizes the pantomime-like world of the Irish RM stories.

15. Robert J. Martin ('Ballyhooly'), *Bits of Blarney* (London: Sands, 1899), p. 28.
16. Ibid., p. 36.
17. Schama, *Landscape and Memory*, p. 17.
18. Trumpener, *Bardic Nationalism*, pp. 37–66. Malcolm Kelsall considers another landscape myth, the Irish country house ideal, in relation to the 'dialectically opposed' positions of Young's Enlightenment view and that of post-Union nationalism. Kelsall argues that both viewpoints translate the landscape and its markers according to their different political agenda. *Literary Representations of the Irish Country House*, pp. 5–10.
19. Stoker, *Dracula* (1898; New York: W.W. Norton & Co., 1997), p. 27.
20. Daly, 'The imperial treasure hunt: *The Snake's Pass* and the limits of romance', *Modernism, Romance and the Fin de Siècle*, pp. 53–83.
21. George Birmingham, *Spanish Gold* (1908; London: The Bodley Head, 1973), p. 127.
22. Ibid., p. 183.
23. Ibid., pp. 185 and 187.
24. Somerville and Ross, 'An Irish Problem', *The National Review*, p. 419.
25. Somerville and Ross, 'The Whiteboys', *The Irish RM*, p. 404.
26. Ibid., p. 408.
27. Ibid., p. 413.
28. Ibid., p. 409.
29. Ibid., p. 415.
30. Ibid., pp. 411–16.
31. Beames, *Peasants and Power: The Whiteboy Movements and their Control in Pre-Famine Ireland*, p. 131.
32. Trumpener, *Bardic Nationalism*, pp. 52–3.
33. 'The Romantic ironist . . . assumes a prominence in his narrative that is the antithesis of the half-hidden reticent position associated with the more traditional ironist. . . . The narrator holds center of the stage, disposing his characters and arranging his material before our very eyes so that we see not the finished product but the creative process.' Lilian R. Furst, 'Romantic Irony and Narrative Stance', *Romantic Irony*, p. 300. See also the Russian formalists' discussion of this technique of 'laying bare' the contrivance of fiction in *Russian Formalist Criticism*, eds. Lemon and Reis (Lincoln: University of Nebraska, 1965) and in Boris Eichenbaum, *O. Henry and the Theory of the Short Story*, trans. I.R. Titunik (1925; Michigan: University of Michigan, 1968).
34. *The Haute Ecole Act* first appeared as a drawing for the *Broadside* in January 1913. The rider in the drawing is unaccompanied but appears as a circus act. *This Grand Conversation Was Under the Rose* first appeared as Yeats's illustration of the Irish political ballad, 'The Grand Conversation Under the Rose' in *A Broadsheet* of August 1903. The illustration, a drawing of Napoleon Bonaparte, differs entirely from the later oil painting. Nonetheless, Hilary Pyle's tracing of the refashioning of these images in *Jack B. Yeats: A Catalogue Raisonné of the Oil Paintings*, volumes I and II (London: André Deutsch, 1992) demonstrates the artist's early treatment of these themes – when Somerville and Ross were publishing the Irish RM stories.
35. Qtd. in Pyle, *Catalogue Raisonné* II, pp. 787–8.
36. Charles Maturin, *The Milesian Chief* (1812; New York: Garland Publishing, 1979), I, pp. 184–5. Katie Trumpener argues that these words re-enact the 'paradox of memory and obliteration' (*Bardic Nationalism*, p. 9) and does not draw a connection between the comparisons of Ireland's language and land to the paintings preserved by Herculaneum's darkness. I stress such a comparison and choose to dwell somewhat on Maturin's description. The darkness here does not refer to the chiaroscuro technique which the novelist applies in *Melmoth*; nonetheless, darkness preserves colour. Light (modernism) paradoxically douses colour, depth, and meaning. Light is progress, what Baudelaire would later describe with different intents as a 'smoky beacon light', which in terms of Art cannot denote advancement: 'This modern lantern . . . sends out beams of darkness over the whole domain of knowledge.' 'The Universal Exhibition of 1855', *Baudelaire: Selected Writings*, pp. 120–1.
37. Somerville and Ross, *Collection of Irish Anecdotes, 1886–1945*, no. 881, QUB.

38. Baudelaire, 'De l'essence du rire', p. 541.
39. Philip Bull, *Land, Politics and Nationalism: A Study of the Irish Land Question*, pp. 123–5. Perry Curtis, 'Stopping the Hunt, 1881–1882'. Somerville and Ross, *The Silver Fox*, pp. 72–4; *Dan Russel The Fox*, pp. 238–42. See also my discussion in Chapter 1.
40. From *The Shamrock and the Irish Emerald*, a weekly paper which included articles by Corkery and Boyd. Qtd. in Hilary Pyle, *Red-Headed Rebel: Susan L, Mitchell, Poet and Mystic of the Irish Cultural Renaissance* (Dublin: Woodfield Press, 1998), p. 191.
41. Corkery, *Synge and Anglo-Irish Literature*, p. 13.
42. E. Œ. Somerville, 'Hunting in Ireland', *Irish Travel*, III, 2 October 1927, p. 295.
43. Lyons, *Ireland Since the Famine*, p. 219. Bull, *Land, Politics and Nationalism*, pp. 152 –3.
44. As Simon Schama points out in *Landscape and Memory*, 'landscapes can be self-consciously designed to express the virtues of a particular political or social commentary' (p. 15).
45. Kiberd, *Irish Classics*, p. 375.
46. E. Œ. Somerville and Martin Ross, *The Silver Fox* (1898; London: Longmans, Green, 1918). Bram Stoker, *Dracula* (1898; New York: W.W. Norton, 1997).
47. James Frazer, *The Golden Bough* (New York: Macmillan, 1947), pp. 656–7.
48. Somerville and Ross record a story told by Thady Hennessy of Castletownshend about a beast, half dog and half cat, with a bark like the 'squeal of a seagull' living in the woods. QUB Ms 17/1–4/B. Transcribed by June Hilary Berrow, in appendix c: Folk material, 'Somerville and Ross: Transitional Novelists', PhD thesis, UCD (January 1975).
49. Angela Bourke, *The Burning of Bridget Cleary: A True Story* (London: Pimlico, 1999). As Angela Bourke points out, the reporting of Bridget Cleary's murder brought into sharp focus the confrontation of two radically different ways of perceiving the world in late nineteenth-century Ireland; modern systems of order faced the deep-seated traditions and ways of apprehending reality of the Irish country people. Somerville and Ross consider the same theme in *The Silver Fox* and give precedence to Irish folk traditions. More to the point, the writers adapted these traditions as their own. Edith Somerville believed in fairies and owned a fairy shoe. See Somerville and Ross, *Collection of Irish Anecdotes*, book one, QUB.
50. Somerville and Ross, *The Silver Fox*, p. 117.
51. Somerville and Ross, *Dan Russel the Fox* (London: Methuen & Co., 1911), pp. 233–4.
52. Geoffrey Chaucer, 'The Nun's Priest Tale', *The Canterbury Tales*, trans. Nevill Coghill (Baltimore, Maryland: Penguin, 1952), p. 244. Nevill Coghill was Somerville's nephew and according to Gifford Lewis possessed the best knowledge of the Somerville and Ross manuscript material. *Edith Somerville, A Biography*, pp. 437–8.
53. The political potential of Dan Russel is indicated in Chaucer's naming of his fox as 'daun Russel' (Sir Russel), which suggests to J. Leslie Hotson a possible dig at the sly evasions of Sir John Russel (a pretence of madness to avoid execution) upon the return of Henry IV to England. 'Colfax vs. Chauntecleer', *Chaucer: Modern Essays in Criticism*, ed. E. Wagenknecht (London: Oxford University Press, 1978), p. 112.
54. Edith Somerville wrote *The Story of the Discontented Little Elephant* (1912) in 1911 and in the same year hoped to interest publishers in an adaptation of Southey's 'Crocodile King' as an illustrated children's book. See her letter to James Pinker, 18 November 1911, no. 3330–1, TCD. Edith Somerville was alert to the political significance of the fox figure. In a later essay called 'Dan Russel the Fox', she points out that English hunters of the past called their prey 'Charlie' after Charles James Fox. Somerville and Ross, *The Sweet Cry of Hounds* (London: Methuen, 1936), p. 5.
55. Edith Somerville, *Growly-Wowly or the Story of the Three Little Pigs*, private collection. See Julie Anne Stevens, *Writing and Illustrating Ireland* (Dublin: Paceprint, 2002), p. 31.
56. Edith Somerville, *Little Red Riding-Hood in Kerry* (London: Peter Davies Ltd., 1934).
57. Edith Somerville, letter to James Pinker, 25 November 1911, Pinker Correspondence, no. 3330–1, TCD.
58. Edith Somerville quotes Mrs Sherwood in 'Picnics', Somerville and Ross, *Some Irish Yesterdays*, p. 57.
59. Rodney K. Engen, *Walter Crane as a Book Illustrator* (New York: St. Martin's Press, 1975), pp. 7–8.
60. Thomas J. Arnold, 'Introductory Letter,' in *Reynard the Fox*, p. xxiii.
61. Somerville and Ross echoed Maria Edgeworth's claim that Thady in *Castle Rackrent* was her only character drawn from real life (see Emily Lawless, *Maria Edgeworth* (London:

Macmillan, 1904), pp. 89–90) when they asserted that Slipper alone had his basis in fact (*Irish Memories*, p. 258). Nonetheless, when they started drafting the stories which would make up their final collection, Slipper was sacrificed. Their most successful character, the one who came closest to stage-Irishness, was dropped from the programme.

62. 'Reynard the Fox', Qtd. in Somerville and Ross, *The Sweet Cry of Hounds*, pp. ix–x.
63. Somerville and Ross, 'The Comte De Pralines', *The Irish RM*, p. 567.
64. Somerville and Ross, 'The Finger of Mrs Knox' *The Irish RM*, p. 442.
65. Collis, *Somerville and Ross*, p. 148; Powell, *The Irish Cousins*, p. 166. Lady Gregory was Mrs Martin's cousin.
66. Arnold, *Reynard the Fox*, p. xxv.
67. Ibid. I have concentrated on the first half of Arnold's treatment of Goethe's version.
68. Somerville and Ross, 'The Friend of Her Youth', *The Irish RM*, p. 453.
69. Somerville and Ross, 'Harrington's', *The Irish RM*, p. 472.
70. Roger H. Stephenson argues that Goethe's treatment of the beast fable is not a straight-forward attack on the French Revolution – as is often argued – but a wider discussion that includes a satire of the corruption of the *ancien regime*. 'The Political Import of Goethe's Reineke Fuchs', *Reynard the Fox: Social Engagement and Cultural Metamorphoses in the Beast Epic from the Middle Ages to the Present*, ed. Kenneth Vartry (New York: Berghahn Books, 2000), pp. 191–207.
71. Robert Martin, *Bits of Blarney*, p. 18.
72. Lewis, *Edith Somerville, A Biography*, pp. 163–4.
73. Terry Eagleton, *Heathcliff and the Great Hunger* (London: Verso, 1995), p. 191.
74. Ibid., p. 192.
75. Stoker, *Dracula*, p. 255.
76. Ibid., p. 278.
77. Ibid., p. 255.
78. Eagleton, *Heathcliff and the Great Hunger*, p. 215. Bruce Stewart cautions against reading *Dracula* as 'allegory of the landlord–tenant relations', which sees the vampire as a 'portrait of the Anglo-Irish landlord', in 'Bram Stoker's *Dracula*: Possessed by the Spirit of the Nation?' *Irish University Review* 29, 2 (autumn/winter 1999), pp. 238–55. My findings with regard to Somerville and Ross lead me to agree with Stewart's conclusions.
79. Patrick Maume has mentioned this story a number of times to me as an example of Somerville and Ross's politics, which might be better understood by considering Robert Martin's stories. I am grateful to him for emphasizing the significance of Robert Martin's work, although I argue that Somerville and Ross exploit rather than merely repeat the older brother's point of view.
80. *Blackwood's Magazine* CXCIII. MCLXVIII (Feb. 1913), pp. 245–53.
81. Julian Moynahan, *Anglo-Irish* (Princeton: Princeton University Press, 1995), p. 196.
82. Joseph Devlin, 'Comedy and the Land: Somerville and Ross's Irish RM' *Studies in Anglo-Irish Fiction and Balladry*, by Devlin, Kehler, and Curran, Working Papers in Irish Studies, 94–1 (Fort Lauderdale, Florida: Nova University, 1994), p. 21.
83. Somerville and Ross, 'The Finger of Mrs Knox', *The Irish RM*, pp. 442 and 447.
84. Harry Sargent, hunting enthusiast, writing as 'The Fox' in *The Irish Times*, 4 October 1881. Qtd. in L. Perry Curtis Jr. 'Stopping the Hunt, 1881–1882: An Aspect of the Irish Land War', *Nationalism and Popular Protest in Ireland*, p. 377.
85. Somerville and Ross, 'The Comte De Pralines', *The Irish RM*, p. 560.
86. Somerville and Ross, 'The Shooting of Shinroe', *The Irish RM*, p. 580.
87. Devlin, 'Comedy and the Land', pp. 25–6.
88. Draft of 'The Comte De Pralines', 25 June 1914, no. 7674, TCD.
89. Draft of 'Irish Citizen' published in *Horse Show Number* (August 1913). See also draft of 'To Open the Season', no. 7676, and draft of a review of John Lane's publications on hunting (probably 1914), no.7674. Finally, in a draft of a review of 'Sport in Art' by W. Baillie Grohmann, dated 12 July 1913, no.7675, TCD, Somerville states that sport and art stand somewhat at a distance, although she admires the treatment of the hunt in 'The Lady of the Lake'.
90. Somerville and Ross, 'The Comte De Pralines', *The Irish RM*, p. 556.
91. Ibid., pp. 558–9.
92. Ibid., p. 563.
93. Ibid., p. 572.

94. Ibid., p. 573.
95. Joyce, *Ulysses*, p. 159. It is just as likely that Somerville and Ross may have had Charles James Fox and the young William Pitt in mind when writing 'The Comte De Pralines'. Somerville points out later in her career that the fox's name in England was at one time 'Charlie' after Charles James Fox. See note 54 in this chapter.
96. Lewis, *Edith Somerville, A Biography*, p. 273.
97. Schama, *Landscape and Memory*, pp. 144–5.
98. Somerville and Ross, 'The Shooting of Shinroe', *The Irish RM*, p. 581.
99. Ibid., p. 588.
100. Ibid., p. 589.
101. Cummins, *Dr E. Œ. Somerville*, p. 30.

CONCLUSION

1. Edith Somerville, letter to Cameron Somerville, 10 December 1915, *Drishane Archive*, L.A. 935 a–c.
2. Edith Somerville, letter to Cameron Somerville, 6 January 1916, *Drishane Archive*, L.A. 938 a–c.
3. Norman Jeffares, *Anglo-Irish Literature* (London: Macmillan Press, 1982), p. 211.
4. Though Somerville and Ross visited Lady Eleanor Butler and Miss Sarah Ponsonby's home during their Welsh tour, they did not identify with the couple. It seems likely that their pilgrimage retraced the steps of their Great-grandfather Charles Kendal Bushe, who wrote to his wife of his visit in 1805 to the Ladies of Llangollen. See *Beggars on Horseback* (Edinburgh: William Blackwood & Sons, 1895) and *An Incorruptible Irishman*, pp. 169–71.
5. Jane and Mary Findlater, *Crossriggs* (1908; London: Virago, 1986).
6. Freeman Wills, *W.G. Wills*, p. 30.
7. Arthur Symons, 'Pantomime and the Poetic Drama', *Studies in Seven Arts* (London: Constable, 1906), pp. 381–4.

Select Bibliography

PART ONE: SOMERVILLE AND ROSS'S WORKS

I. UNPUBLISHED MATERIAL BY MARTIN ROSS

'Memoir of Robert' (no date), no. 10884, Manuscripts Department, Trinity College Library, Dublin.

'An Irish Goldmine' (no date), no. 3312–3313, Manuscripts Department, TCD.

Draft of 'Cheops in Connemara', 13 June 1889, no. 884, Somerville and Ross Collection, Queen's University Library, Belfast.

Correspondence with William G. Wills, 1885–90, no. 876, Somerville and Ross Collection, QUB.

II. UNPUBLISHED MATERIAL BY EDITH SOMERVILLE

Correspondence with Cameron Somerville, 30 April 1879–12 May 1910, *Edith Œnone Somerville Archive in Drishane House*, ed. Otto Rauchbauer (Dublin: Irish Manuscripts Commission, 1995), L.A.1–L.A.938.

Correspondence with Alice Kinkead. 8 March 1895–12 March 1899. *Drishane Archive*, L.A.1365–L.A.1378

'Essays on Irish and Suffragette Affairs, 1910–1925', no. 898, Somerville and Ross Collection, QUB.

Drafts of 'Irish Citizen' (published in *Horse Show Number*, August 1913), 'To Open the Season', reviews of John Lane's publication on hunting and *Sport in Art* by W. Baillie Grohmann (12 July 1913), nos. 7676, 7674 and 7675, Manuscripts Department, TCD.

Letter to Mr Symons, 14 December 1935, William Andrews Clark Memorial Library, UCLA.

III. Unpublished material by Somerville and Ross

Diaries, 1873–1915 (incomplete), Somerville and Ross Collection, QUB.
'An Irish Landlord of the Future: A Study from Life' (no date), no. 899, QUB.
'The Superfluous Gentleman' (no date), no. 899, QUB.
Collection of Irish Anecdotes, 1886–1945 (4 books), no. 881, QUB.
Correspondence with James B. Pinker, 1898–1934, 3330–1; 4276–7, Manuscripts Department, TCD.
'At a Western Hotel' (published as 'When I First Met Dr Hickey') 1912–1915, nos. 3302 and 3783, Manuscripts Department, TCD.
A Man of the People, unfinished novel written between 1879–99, no. 880, Somerville and Ross Collection, QUB.
Ballyhooly's Troupe of Wax-Works, 1891, theatre programme, *Drishane Archive*, M.43.a
Draft of 'The Comte De Pralines', 25 June 1914, no. 7674, Manuscripts Department, TCD.

IV. Published Material

a.) Magazine publications (chronological order)
Somerville, Edith Œ. *A Mule Ride in Trinidad*, The Graphic (summer 1888).
Somerville, Edith Œ. and Martin Ross. 'Slide Number 42' (*The Lady's Pictorial* 1890), no. 903, Somerville and Ross Collection, QUB.
Ross, Martin. 'The Terror in Ireland', *The World* (5 April 1893), pp. 22–3.
Somerville, Edith Œ. 'A Grand Filly', *Badminton Magazine*, 21, 4 (April 1897), pp. 379–93.
Somerville and Ross. *Some Experiences of an Irish RM*, Badminton Magazine, July 1898–December 1899.
Somerville, Edith Œ. 'High Tea at McKeowns', illus. by Max Cowper, *Black and White*, Christmas Number (1900), pp. 16–19.
Somerville, Edith Œ. 'Paris Notes', *International Art Notes*, 1 (March 1900), pp. 10–13.
Somerville, Edith Œ. 'West Carbery as Sketching Ground', *International Art Notes* (May 1900), pp. 83–4.
Somerville and Ross. 'An Irish Problem', *The National Review*, 38 (September 1901–February 1902), pp. 407–19.
(Somerville, Edith Œ.) 'A Looker-On', 'The Desired of the People', *The National Review*, 42, 247 (September 1903), pp. 120–9.

Somerville and Ross. 'The Boat's Share', *The Strand Magazine*, xxix (Jan.–June, 1905), pp. 72–80.

Ross, Martin. 'For Better, For Worse', *Cornhill Magazine* (September 1906), pp. 356–65.

Ross, Martin. 'The Reaping of Ulster', *The Spectator*, 5 October 1912, pp. 504–5.

Somerville and Ross. 'The Finger of Mrs Knox', *Blackwood's Magazine*, CXCIII, MCLXXII (June 1913), pp. 735–46.

Somerville, Edith Œ. 'Hunting in Ireland', *Irish Travel*, III, 2 (October 1927), pp. 295–8.

b.) Book publications (chronological order)

Somerville (as Geilles Herring) and Ross. *An Irish Cousin* (1889; London: Longmans, Green, 1903).

Somerville and Ross. *Naboth's Vineyard* (London: Spencer Blackett, 1891).

Somerville and Ross. *Through Connemara in a Governess's Cart* (London: W.H. Allen, 1892).

Somerville and Ross. *The Real Charlotte* (1894; London: Arrow Books, 1990).

Somerville and Ross. *Beggars on Horseback* (Edinburgh: William Blackwood, 1895).

Somerville and Ross. *The Silver Fox* (1898. London: Longmans, Green, 1918).

Ross, Martin. *A Patrick's Day Hunt*, illus. by Edith Œ. Somerville (London: Constable, 1902).

Somerville and Ross. *All on the Irish Shore* (London: Longmans, Green, 1903).

Somerville and Ross. *Some Irish Yesterdays* (London: T. Nelson & Sons, 1906).

Somerville and Ross. *Dan Russel the Fox* (London: Methuen, 1911).

Somerville and Ross. *Irish Memories* (London: Longmans, Green, 1918).

Somerville and Ross. *Mount Music* (London: Longmans, Green, 1919).

Somerville and Ross. *Stray-Aways* (London: Longmans, Green, 1920).

Somerville and Ross. *An Enthusiast* (London: Longmans, Green, 1921).

Somerville and Ross. *Wheel-Tracks* (London: Longmans, Green, 1923).

Somerville and Ross. *The Big House of Inver* (London: William Heinemann, 1925).

Somerville and Ross. *The Irish RM Complete* (1928), rpt. as *The Irish RM* (London: Abacus, 1989).

Somerville and Ross. *An Incorruptible Irishman* (London: Ivor Nicholson & Watson, 1932).

Somerville and Ross. *The Sweet Cry of Hounds* (London: Methuen, 1936).

Somerville and Ross. *'Happy Days!'* (London: Longmans, Green, 1946).

Somerville and Ross. *The Selected Letters of Somerville and Ross*, ed. Gifford Lewis (London: Faber and Faber, 1989).

c.) Edith Œnone Somerville's works for children (and some adults)

Chloral or the Sleeping Beauty, A Fairy Extravaganza by Two Flappers, by E. Œ. Somerville and Ethel Coghill (unpublished) (1874; revised by E. Œ. Somerville in 1916), no. 887, QUB.

The Kerry Recruit, An Old Irish Song, illustrated by E. Œ. Somerville (London: Perry, 1889).

Clear as the Noonday, by Ethel Coghill Penrose and illustrated by E Œ. Somerville (London: Jarrold and Sons, 1893).

Growly-Wowly or the Story of the Three Little Pigs, written and illustrated by E. Œ. Somerville (handmade book; unpublished and undated), private collection.

Slipper's ABC of Foxhunting, written and illustrated by E. Œ. Somerville (London: Longmans, Green, 1903).

The Story of the Discontented Little Elephant, written and illustrated by E. Œ. Somerville (London: Longmans, Green, 1912).

Little Red Riding-Hood in Kerry, by E. Œ.Somerville (London: Peter Davies Ltd., 1934).

PART TWO: BIOGRAPHICAL AND CRITICAL WRITING
ON SOMERVILLE AND ROSS

Bence-Jones, Mark. *Twilight of the Ascendancy* (London: Constable, 1987).

Berrow, J.H. (Hilary Robinson). 'Somerville and Ross: Transitional Novelists', Ph.D. University College Dublin, 1975.

Bhreathnach-Lynch, Síghle and Julie Anne Stevens. 'The Irish Artist: Crossing the Rubicon'. *Local/Global: Women Artists in the Nineteenth Century*. Eds. Deborah Cherry and Janice Helland (Aldershot: Ashgate Publishing, 2006), pp. 137–54.

Bonsall, Penny. *The Irish RMs: The Resident Magistrates in the British Administration of Ireland* (Dublin: Four Courts Press, 1998).

Bowen, Elizabeth. Rev. of *The Irish Cousins*, by Violet Powell, *The Spectator* (31 January 1970), rpt. in *The Mulberry Tree: Writings of Elizabeth Bowen*, ed. Hermione Lee (London: Vintage, 1999), pp. 185–8.

Cahalan, James. *The Irish Novel: A Critical History* (Dublin: Gill and Macmillan, 1988).

—— ' "Humor With Gender': Somerville and Ross and the Irish RM', *The Comic Tradition in Irish Women Writers*, ed. Theresa O'Connor (Florida: University Press of Florida, 1996), pp. 58–72.

Coghill, Nevill. 'E. Œ. Somerville and Martin Ross: Detailed Catalogue of Mss. made by Nevill Coghill before sale at Sothebys, 30 July 1946', presented to TCD March 1964 by Nevill Coghill, no. 3783, Manuscripts Department, TCD.

Collis, Maurice. *Somerville and Ross* (London: Faber and Faber, 1968).

Cowart, Claire Denelle. 'Ghost Writers?: Somerville and Ross', *That Other World: The Supernatural and the Fantastic in Irish Literature and its Contexts*, ed. Bruce Stewart (Gerrards Cross: Colin Smythe, 1998), pp. 231–42.

Cowman, Roz. 'Lost Time: The Smell and Taste of Castle T', *Sex, Nation and Dissent in Irish Writing*, ed. Eibhear Walshe (Cork: Cork University Press, 1997), pp. 87–102, rpt. *The Field Day Anthology of Irish Writing*, IV (Cork: Cork University Press, 2002), pp. 1071–3.

Croghan, Martin J. *Demythologizing Hiberno-English* (Boston: Working Papers in Irish Studies, 1990).

Cronin, Anthony. *Heritage Now: Irish Literature in the English Language* (Dingle, Co. Kerry: Brandon Book Publishers, 1982).

Cronin, John. *Somerville and Ross* (Lewisburg: Bucknell University Press, 1972).

Crossman, Virginia. 'The Resident Magistrate as Colonial Officer: Addison, Somerville and Ross', *Irish Studies Review*, 8, 1 (2000), pp. 23–33.

Cummins, Geraldine. *Dr E. Œ. Somerville* (London: Andrew Dakers Limited, 1952).

Devlin, Joseph. 'Comedy and the Land: Somerville and Ross's Irish RM', *Studies in Anglo-Irish Fiction and Balladry*, Working Papers in Irish Studies, 94–1 (Florida: Nova University, 1994), pp. 1–30.

Fehlmann, Guy. *Somerville and Ross: Témoins de l'Irlande d'hier*

(France: Association des Publications de la Faculté des Lettres et Sciences Humaines de l'Université de Caen, 1970).

Gillespie, Francis (comp.). 'Introduction', *Dr Edith Œnone Somerville 1858–1949*, exhibition catalogue, Drishane, Castletownshend (5–9 September 1984).

Graves, Charles. 'Introduction', *Humours of Irish Life* (Dublin: The Talbot Press, no date), pp. xiii–xlviii.

—— 'Martin Ross', *The National Review*, LXXI (May 1918), pp. 349–59.

Gregory, Lady Augusta. Letter to Mrs Martin, 21 October 1889, no. 920, Somerville and Ross Collection. QUB.

—— Letter to Violet Martin, 1914, no. 920, Somerville and Ross Collection, QUB.

Gwynn, Stephen. 'The Secret of Ireland', *Macmillan's Magazine*, LXXXIII (November 1900–April 1901), pp. 410–19.

—— 'Lever's Successors', *The Edinburgh Review*, October 1921, pp. 346–57.

—— *Irish Literature and Drama* (London: Nelson & Sons, 1936).

Hudson, Elizabeth, ed. *A Bibliography of the First Editions of the Works of E. Œ. Somerville and Martin Ross* (New York: The Sporting Gallery, 1942).

Hughes, Clair. 'Late Flowering Gothic: The Anglo-Irish Big House Novel', *Australian Victorian Association Journal* (February 1992), pp. 142–50.

Jeffares, Norman. *Anglo-Irish Literature* (London: Macmillan Press, 1982).

Kelsall, Malcolm. *Literary Representations of the Irish Country House: Civilisation and Savagery under the Union* (Basingstoke, Hampshire: Palgrave Macmillan, 2003).

Kiberd, Declan. 'Tragedies of Manners – Somerville and Ross', *Inventing Ireland* (London: Jonathan Cape, 1995), pp. 69–82.

—— 'Somerville and Ross: The Silver Fox', *Irish Classics* (London: Granta Books, 2000), pp. 360-78.

Kosok, Heinz. 'Vorformen der Modernen Kurzgeschichte in der Anglo-Irischen Literatur des 19. Jahrhunderts', *AAA-Arbeiten aus Anglistik und Amerikanistik*, 7 (1982), pp. 131–46.

Kreilkamp, Vera. 'The Big Houses of Somerville and Ross', *The Anglo-Irish Novel and the Big House* (New York: Syracuse University Press, 1998).

Lewis, Gifford. *Somerville and Ross: The World of the Irish RM* (1985; London: Penguin, 1987).

—— 'Introduction', *The Real Charlotte* (Dublin: A&A Farmar, 1999), pp. vii-xv.

—— *Edith Somerville, A Biography* (Dublin: Four Courts Press, 2005).

L.P.Y. and H.E.M. (Mr. Yates and Miss Mahon). 'By the Brown Bog: Being some episodes in the life of an Irish D.I.', *Badminton Magazine*, xxxv–xxxvi (July 1912–June 1913).

Lyons, F.S.L. 'The Twilight of the Big House', *Ariel*, 1, 3 (July 1970), pp. 110–22.

MacCarthy, B.G. 'E. Œ. Somerville and Martin Ross', *Studies*, xxxiv (1945), pp. 183–94.

Maume, Patrick. 'Somerville and Ross', *Oxford Companion to Irish History*, ed. S.J. Connolly (Oxford: Oxford University Press, 1998), p. 520.

'Memorial to Martin Ross', *The Belfast News-Letter* (24 December 1915).

Mitchell, Hilary. 'Somerville and Ross: Amateur to Professional', *Somerville and Ross: A Symposium* (Queen's University of Belfast: Institute of Irish Studies, 1968).

Moynahan, Julian. *Anglo-Irish* (New Jersey: Princeton University Press, 1995).

Murphy, Rev. J.J. 'The Country Houses of Ireland', 'The "Town Houses" of the Colonial Ascendancy in Dublin', 'Social Life of the Ascendancy as Described by Themselves', 'The Ascendancy and the Gael', *The Catholic Bulletin*, XIII, 6–10 (June–October 1923), pp. 369–73, 440–4, 625–9, 708-11.

Oakman, Anne. 'Sitting on "The Outer Skin": Somerville and Ross's *Through Connemara in a Governess Cart* as a Coded Stratum of Linguistic/Feminist "Union" Ideals', *Eire-Ireland*, 39, 1 & 2 (spring/summer 2004), pp. 110–35.

O'Connor, Frank. 'Somerville and Ross', *The Irish Times*, 15 December 1945, p. 4.

—— *The Lonely Voice* (London: Macmillan, 1963).

Powell, Violet. *The Irish Cousins* (London: Heinemann, 1970).

Power, Ann. 'The Big House of Somerville and Ross', *The Dubliner*, 3, 1 (spring 1964) pp. 43-53.

Pritchett, V.S. 'The Irish R.M.' *The Living Novel* (1946), rpt. in *The Complete Essays* (London: Chatto & Windus, 1991), pp. 263–7.

Rev. of *The Master of Ballantrae* by Robert Louis Stevenson and *The Irish Cousin* by Edith Somerville and Martin Ross, *The Old Saloon* (November 1889), pp. 702–5.

Rev. of *Naboth's Vineyard* by Somerville and Ross, *The Daily Express* (2 November 1891).

Rev. of *The Real Charlotte* by Somerville and Ross. Athenaeum, no. 3476 (9 June 1894), p. 738.

Rev. of *Some Experiences of an Irish RM* by Somerville and Ross. *Freeman's Journal* (10 November 1899).

Rev. of *Some Experiences of an Irish RM* by Somerville and Ross. *Punch* (14 August 1901), p. 116.

Robinson, Hilary. *Somerville & Ross: A Critical Appreciation* (Dublin: Gill and Macmillan, 1980).

Rossa, Donovan. 'Major Thomas Somerville', qtd. in Moira Somerville, 'Notes on the Early Background and Early Life of Edith Œnone Somerville', unpublished essay, *Drishane Archive*, B.2.42pp.

Shaw, G.B. Letter to Edith Somerville, 18 January 1922, *Drishane Archive*, L.B.315. a-e.

Stevens, Julie Anne. *Writing and Illustrating Ireland: Somerville and Ross*, exhibition catalogue, TCD (Dublin: Paceprint, 2002).

Waters, Maureen. *The Comic Irishman* (Albany: State University of New York Press, 1984).

Weekes, Ann Owen. *Irish Women Writers* (Kentucky: University Press of Kentucky, 1990).

PART THREE: FURTHER CRITICAL READING

Abdy, Jane. *The French Poster* (London: Studio Vista, 1969).

Achebe, Chinua. 'The African Writer and the English Language', 1975, *Colonial Discourse and Post-Colonial Theory*, eds. Williams and Chrisman (Hertfordshire: Prentice Hall, 1994), pp. 428–34.

Addison, Henry Robert. *Recollections of an Irish Police Magistrate and Other Reminiscences of the South of Ireland* (London: Ward, Lock and Tyler, 1862).

Andrews, Malcolm. 'The Metropolitan Picturesque', *The Politics of the Picturesque*, eds. Copley and Garside (Cambridge: Cambridge University Press, 1994), pp. 282-98.

—— ed. *The Picturesque: Literary Sources and Documents*, I (Robertsbridge: Helm Information, 1994) 2 volumes.

Arnold, Thomas James. *Reynard the Fox, After the German Version of Goethe*, illus. by Wilhelm von Kaulbach and Joseph Wolf (London: John C. Nimmo, 1887).

Auerbach, Nina. *Woman and the Demon: The Life of a Victorian Myth* (Cambridge: Harvard University Press, 1982).

Austen, Jane. *Mansfield Park* (1814; London: Penguin, 1996).

—— *Northanger Abbey* (1818; New York: Norton, 2004).

Bakhtin, Mikhail. *Rabelais and His World*, trans. Helene Iswolsky (1965; Bloomington: Indiana University Press, 1984).

—— *The Dialogic Imagination* (Austin: University of Texas Press, 1981).

Balzac. Honoré de. 'Introduction', *The Works of Honoré Balzac*, vol. I (1842; Philadelphia: Avil Publishing Co., 1901), pp. lxiii–iv.

—— *Cousin Bette, Part One of Poor Relations* (1846), trans. Marion Ayton Crawford (Harmondsworth: Penguin, 1965).

Baudelaire, Charles. *Le Spleen de Paris: Petits Poèmes en Prose* (1863; Paris: Les Presses de la Société Parisienne d'imprimerie, 1925).

—— *Baudelaire: Selected Writings on Art and Literature*, trans. P.E. Charvet (London: Penguin, 1972).

——'De l'essence du rire', *Œuvres Complètes*, II, ed. Claude Pichois (Paris: Éditions Gallimard, 1976), pp. 525–43.

Beames, Michael. *Peasants and Power: The Whiteboy Movement and their Control in Pre-Famine Ireland* (Brighton: Harvester Press, 1983).

Beckett, J. C. *The Making of Modern Ireland 1603–1923* (London: Faber and Faber, 1981).

Beerbohm, Max. 'Enoch Soames', *The Bodley Head Max Beerbohm*, ed. David Cecil (London: The Bodley Head, 1970).

Beetham, Margaret. *A Magazine of Her Own? Domesticity and Desire in the Women's Magazine, 1800–1914* (London: Routledge, 1996).

Bhabha, Homi K. *The Location of Culture* (London: Routledge, 1994).

Bingham, Madeleine. *Henry Irving and the Victorian Theatre* (London: George Allen & Unwin, 1978).

Birmingham, George. *Spanish Gold* (1908; London: The Bodley Head, 1973).

—— *The Adventures of Dr Whitty* (London: Methuen, 1913).

—— 'Catholic', *Spillikins* (London: Methuen, 1926), pp. 24–35.

Bourke, Angela. *The Burning of Bridget Cleary: A True Story* (London: Pimlico, 1999).

Brewer, John. 'Culture, Nature and Nation', *Pleasures of the Imagination: English Culture in the Eighteenth Century* (London: HarperCollins Publishers, 1997), pp. 615–61.

Brooks, Sidney. 'Our Next Blunder in South Africa', *The National Review*, 37 (June 1901), pp. 524–32.

Brown, Stephen. *Ireland in Fiction* (Dublin: Maunsel, 1916).

Brown, Terence. 'The Church of Ireland and the Climax of the Ages', *Ireland's Literature* (Mullingar: Lilliput Press, 1988) pp. 49-64.

—— *The Life of W.B. Yeats* (Dublin: Gill and Macmillan, 1999).

Bull, Philip. *Land, Politics and Nationalism: A Study of the Irish Land Question* (Dublin: Gill and Macmillan, 1996).

Buttimer, Neil. 'Remembering 1798', *Journal of the Cork Historical and Archaeological Society*, 103 (1998), pp. 1–26.

Cahalan, James. *Double Visions* (Syracuse: Syracuse University Press, 1990).

Campbell, Gerald. *Edward and Pamela Fitzgerald, Being some Account of their Lives Compiled from the Letters of those who knew them* (London: Edward Arnold, 1904).

Campion, J.T. 'Ninety-Eight', *Penny Readings For the Irish People*, II (Dublin, 1879), pp. 120–3.

Carbery, Lady Mary. *Mary Carbery's West Cork Journal, 1898–1900* (Dublin: Lilliput Press, 1998).

Carlyle, Thomas. *On Heroes, Hero-Worship and the Heroic in History* (London: Routledge, 1841).

—— Letter to David Laing, *Proceedings of the Society of Antiquaries of Scotland* (Edinburgh: Society of Antiquaries of Scotland, 1855), p. 174.

—— 'The Portrait of John Knox', *Fraser's Magazine*, XI, LXIV (April 1875), pp. 407–39.

Carpenter, Andrew. 'Double Vision in Anglo-Irish Literature', *Place, Personality and the Irish Writer*, ed. Andrew Carpenter (Gerrards Cross: Colin Smythe, 1977), pp. 173-89.

Chaucer, Geoffrey. *The Canterbury Tales*, trans. Nevill Coghill (Baltimore, Maryland: Penguin, 1952).

Conrad, Joseph. *The Nigger of Narcissus* (1897; London: Gresham Publishing, 1925).

'Convent Education of Irish Girls', editorial, *Freeman's Journal*, 5–10 Oct. 1883.

Corkery, Daniel. *Synge and Anglo-Irish Literature* (1931; Cork: Mercier Press, 1966).

Croker, Thomas Crofton. *Researches in the South of Ireland Illustrative of the Scenery, Architectural Remains and the Manners and Superstitions of the Peasantry with an Appendix containing a*

Private Narrative of the Rebellion of 1798 (1824; Shannon, Ireland: Irish University Press, 1969).

Crookshank, Anne and the Knight of Glin. *Watercolours of Ireland 1600–1914* (London: Barrie & Jenkins, 1994).

Crossman, Virginia. *Local Government in Nineteenth-Century Ireland* (Queen's Univeristy of Belfast: Institute of Irish Studies, 1994).

Cullen, Fintan. *Visual Politics: The Representation of Ireland 1750–1930* (Cork: Cork University Press, 1997).

Curtis Jr., L. Perry. 'Stopping the Hunt, 1881–1882: An Aspect of the Irish Land War', *Nationalism and Popular Protest in Ireland*, ed. C.H.E. Philpin (Cambridge: Past and Present Society, 1987), pp. 349–402.

—— *Apes and Angels: The Irishman in Victorian Caricature*, revised edition (Washington D.C.: London: Smithsonian Institution, 1997).

—— ' "The Land For the People": Post-Famine Images of Eviction', *Éire/Land*, ed. Vera Kreilkamp, catalogue and essays issued in conjunction with Éire/Land exhibition, McMullen Museum of Art, Boston College, 2003 (Chicago: University of Chicago Press, 2003), pp. 85–92.

Cutt, M.N. *Mrs Sherwood and her Books for Children* (London: Oxford University Press, 1974).

Dalsimer, Adele M. ' "The Irish Peasant Had All His Heart': J.M. Synge in *The Country Shop*.' *Visualizing Ireland: National Identity and the Pictorial Tradition*, ed. Adele Dalsimer (Boston: Faber and Faber, 1993), pp. 201–30.

Daly, Nicholas. *Modernism, Romance and the Fin de Siècle: Popular Fiction and British Culture, 1880–1914* (Cambridge: Cambridge University Press, 1999).

Darwin, Charles. *The Expressions of the Emotions in Man and Animals* (1872), introduced by Konrad Lorenz (Chicago: University of Chicago Press, 1965).

Deane, Seamus. 'Irish National Character 1790–1900', *The Writer as Witness: Literature as Historical Evidence*, ed. Tom Dunne (Cork: Cork University Press, 1987), pp. 90–113.

Duffy, Charles Gavan, ed. *The Spirit of the Nation* (1843; Dublin: James Duffy, 1864).

Duffy, Charles Gavan. *Conversations with Carlyle* (London: Sampson Low, Marston & Co., 1892).

Eagan, Catherine. 'Simianization Meets Postcolonial Theory', rev. of

Apes and Angels (revised edition) by Perry Curtis, *Irish Literary Supplement* (Fall 1997), pp. 27–8.

Eagleton, Terry. *Heathcliff and the Great Hunger* (London: Verso, 1995).

—— 'Cork and the Carnivalesque', *Crazy John and the Bishop* (Cork: Cork University Press, 1998), pp. 158–211.

Edgeworth, Maria. *Castle Rackrent* (1800; Oxford: World's Classics, 1980).

—— *Tour of Connemara and the Martins of Ballinahinch* (1834), ed. H.E. Butler (London: Constable, 1950).

Eichenbaum, Boris M. *O. Henry and the Theory of the Short Story*, trans. I.R. Titunik (Michigan: University of Michigan, 1968).

Eliot, George. *Daniel Deronda* (1876; London: Penguin, 1986).

Ellmann, Richard. *Oscar Wilde* (New York: Knopf, 1988).

Engen, Rodney K. *Walter Crane as Book Illustrator* (New York: St Martin's Press, 1975).

Fabricant, Carole. *Swift's Landscapes* (London: Johns Hopkins Press, 1982).

Fanon, Frantz. *Black Skin, White Masks* (London: Pluto Press, 1986).

Ferguson, Samuel. 'The Fair Hills of Ireland', *Irish Verse*, ed. Brendan Kennelly (London: Penguin, 1981), p. 196.

Fiedler, Leslie. *Love and Death in the American Novel* (1960; New York: Stein and Day, 1975).

Findlater, Jane and Mary. *Crossriggs* (1908; London: Virago, 1986).

First, Ruth and Ann Scott. *Olive Schreiner* (London: André Deutsch, 1980).

Foster, R.F. *Paddy and Mr. Punch* (London: Penguin, 1993).

—— *W.B. Yeats*, I (Oxford: Oxford University Press, 1997).

Fouqué, Friedrich de la Motte. 'Undine' (1811), *Romantic Fairy Tales*, ed. and trans. Carol Tully (London: Penguin, 2000), pp. 54–125.

Fraser, J. D. 'The Holy Wells', *Ballad Poetry of Ireland*, ed. Charles Gavan Duffy, rpt. of fortieth edition (New York: Scholars Fascimiles & Reprints, 1973), pp. 216–17.

Frazer, James. *The Golden Bough* (New York: Macmillan, 1947).

Freud, Sigmund. *Wit and Its Relation to the Unconscious*, 1905, trans. A.A. Brill, 1916 (New York: Dover Publications, 1993).

Froude, James Anthony. *Thomas Carlyle: A History of His Life in London, 1834–1881*, II (London: Longmans, Green, 1884) 2 vols.

Garber, Frederick, ed. *Romantic Irony* (Budapest: Coordinating Committee of a Comparative History of Literatures in European Languages, 1988).

Gerard, Frances. *Picturesque Dublin, Old and New*, illus. Rose Barton (London: Hutchinson, 1898).

Gilbert, W.S. and Arthur Sullivan. *HMS Pinafore or The Lass that Loved a Sailor*, D'Oyly Carte Opera Company, Gaiety Theatre, 9 April 1888, Dublin, theatre programme.

Glenroy, W.C. and Dane Clarke. *Harlequin Bryan O'Lynn or The Sleeping Beauty of Erin*, National Music Hall, 24 December 1888, theatre programme.

Goethe, Johann Wolfgang von. 'The Fairytale', *Romantic Fairy Tales*, ed. and trans. Carol Tully (London: Pengun, 2000), pp. 2–32.

—— *Faust*, trans. Walter Arndt, ed. Cyrus Hamlin (New York: W.W. Norton, 1976).

Goldsmith, Oliver. *The Vicar of Wakefield* (1766; New York: New American Library, 1961).

Grand, Sarah. *The Heavenly Twins* (1893; Ann Arbor, Michigan: University of Michigan, 1992).

Gregory, Lady Augusta. 'Ireland, Real and Ideal', *The Nineteenth Century* (November 1898), pp. 769–82.

—— *Poets and Dreamers: Studies and Translations from the Irish* (1903; New York: Kennikat Press, 1967).

—— *Autobiography* (Gerrards Cross: Colin Smythe, 1974).

—— *Lady Gregory: Selected Writings*, eds. Lucy McDiarmid and Maureen Waters (London: Penguin, 1995).

—— *Lady Gregory's Diaries, 1892–1902*, ed. James Pethica (Gerrards Cross: Colin Smythe, 1996).

Hannoosh, Michele. *Baudelaire and Caricature* (Pennsylvania: Pennsylvania State University Press, 1992).

Hardiman, James. *Irish Minstrelsy or Bardic Remains of Ireland*, II (London: Joseph Robins, 1831), 3 volumes.

Hardy, Thomas. 'The Dorsetshire Labourer' (1883), *Thomas Hardy's Personal Writings*, ed. Harold Orel (London: Macmillan, 1967), pp. 168–91.

Haslam, Richard. 'Representation and the Sublime in Six Irish Writers: A Study of Edmund Burke, Lady Morgan, Charles Maturin, James Clarence Mangan, Joseph Sheridan Le Fanu, and William Carleton', Ph.D, 1991, Trinity College Dublin.

Heaney, Seamus. 'Bogland' (1969), *New Selected Poems 1966–1987* (London: Faber and Faber, 1990), pp. 17–18.

——'from Feeling into Words' (1974), *Finders Keepers: Selected Prose, 1971–2001* (London: Faber and Faber, 2002), pp. 14–25.

Hempton, David. ' "For God and Ulster": Evangelical Protestantism and the Home Rule Crisis of 1886', *Protestant Evangelicalism: Britain, Ireland, Germany and America c.1750–1950*, ed. Keith Robbins (Oxford: Basil Blackwell, 1990).

Henry, Paul. *An Irish Portrait* (London: B.T. Batsford, 1951).

Hewison, Robert, ed. *Ruskin, Turner and the Pre-Raphaelites* (London: Tate Gallery Publishing, 2000).

Hinkson, Pamela. *Seventy Years Young: Memoirs of Elizabeth, Countess of Fingall* (London: Collins, 1937).

Holmes, Janice. *Religious Revivals in Britain and Ireland, 1859–1905* (Dublin: Irish Academic Press, 2000).

Hotson, J. Leslie. 'Colfax vs. Chauntecleer', *Chaucer: Modern Essays in Criticism*, ed. E. Wagenknecht (London: Oxford University Press, 1978), pp. 98–116.

Howarth, William. 'Imagined Territory: The Writing of the Wetlands', *New Literary History: Ecocriticism*, 30, 3 (summer 1999), pp. 509–39.

Hunt, Hugh. *The Abbey: Ireland's National Theatre 1904-1979* (Dublin: Gill and Macmillan, 1979).

James, Henry. *Picture and Text* (New York: Harper and Brothers, 1893).

Joyce, James. *Ulysses* (New York: Random House, 1986).

Kant, Immanuel. *Observations on the Feeling of the Beautiful and Sublime*, 1764, trans. John T. Goldthwait (Berkeley; London: University of California Press, 1960).

Kaplan, Fred. *Thomas Carlyle: A Biography* (Cambridge: Cambridge University Press, 1983).

Kelleher, Margaret. 'Late Nineteenth-Century Women's Fiction and the Land Agitation: Gender and Dis/Union' SSNCI (Society For the Study of Nineteenth-Century Ireland) Conference, Bath Spa University College, Bath (9–11 April 1999).

Kelleher, Margaret and Philip O'Leary. *The Cambridge History of Irish Literature*, II (Cambridge: Cambridge University Press, 2006).

Kosok, Heinz. 'The Travel-Book Pattern in the Nineteenth-Century Irish Novel', *Das Natur/Kultur-Paradigma in der Englischsprachigen Erzahlliteratur des 19 und 20. Jahrhunderts*, Festschrift zum 60, Geburtstag von Paul Goetsch (Tübingen, 1994), pp. 79–93.

Landow, George P. *William Holman Hunt and Typological Symbolism* (London: Yale University Press, 1979).

Lawless, Emily. 'An Upland Bog', *Belgravia*, XLV (1881), pp. 417–30.

—— *Hurrish* (1886; Belfast: Appletree Press, 1992).

—— *Maria Edgeworth* (London: Macmillan, 1904).

Lebow, Richard Ned. *White Britain and Black Ireland: The Influence of Stereotypes on Colonial Policy* (Philadelphia: Institute for the Study of Human Issues, 1976).

Ledger, Sally. *The New Woman: Fiction and Feminism at the Fin de Siècle* (Manchester: Manchester University Press, 1997).

Leech, John. 'The Claddagh – Galway', frontispiece illus. *A Little Tour of Ireland* by 'An Oxonian' (London: Bradbury & Evans, 1859).

Leerssen, Joep. *Remembrance and Imagination* (Cork: Cork University Press, 1996).

Le Fanu, Sheridan. *Uncle Silas: A Tale of Bartram Haugh* (1864; New York: Dover Publications, 1966).

Lemon, Lee and Marion J. Reis. *Russian Formalist Criticism: Four Essays*, ed. Paul A. Olson (Lincoln: University of Nebraska Press, 1965).

Lloyd, David. *Nationalism and Minor Literature* (Berkeley: University of California Press, 1987).

—— 'Violence and the Constitution of the Novel', *Anomalous States: Irish Writing and the Post-Colonial Movement* (Dublin: Lilliput Press, 1993), pp. 125–62.

Lyons, F.S.L. *Ireland Since the Famine* (London: Fontana Press, 1971).

McCarthy, Denis Florence. 'A Dream of the Future', *The Spirit of the Nation* (1843), pp.112–14.

—— 'The Clan of MacCaura', *The Ballad Poetry of Ireland*, ed. Charles Gavan Duffy (1845; Dublin: James Duffy, 1869).

—— *The Poets and Dramatists of Ireland* and *The Book of Irish Ballads*, 1 volume (Dublin: James Duffy, 1846).

Mc Cormack, William. 'Irish Gothic and After' *The Field Day Anthology of Irish Writing*, II (Derry: Field Day Publications, 1991), pp. 831–54.

McLees, Ainslie Armstrong. *Baudelaire's 'Argot Plastique': Poetic Caricature and Modernism* (Georgia: University of Georgia Press, 1989).

Mahaffy, Sir John Pentland. 'What is Nationality?', 'Will Home Rule Be Rome Rule?' and 'Who Wants Home Rule?', *Blackwood's Magazine* (1912–13), pp. 245–53.

Mangan, James Clarence. 'The Wandering Jew' (1837), *The Collected Works of James Clarence Mangan*, ed. Jacques Chuto (Dublin: Irish Academic Press, 1996), pp. 377–80.

—— 'The Man in the Cloak', *Dublin University Magazine*, 12 (November 1838), pp. 552–68.

—— 'Dr. Anster's translation of Goethe's *Faust*', *Irishman* (21 April 1849), *James Clarence Mangan: Selected Writings*, ed. Seán Ryder (Dublin: University College Press, 2004), p. 409.

—— 'The Lovely Land' (1849), *Poems of James Clarence Mangan*, ed. D.J. O'Donoghue (Dublin: M.H. Gill, 1922), pp. 92–4.

'The Manly Maiden: Modern Types, no. xxii', *Punch*, 99 (6 December 1890), p. 265.

Marshall, Catherine. *Irish Art Masterpieces* (Southport, Conn.: Hugh Lauter Levin, 1994).

Martin, Robert. *Bits of Blarney* (London: Sands, 1899).

Martin, Robert and E.A.P. Hobday. *The Forty Thieves; or Ali Baba and the Black Sheep of Baghdad* (Dublin: W.J. Alley, 1886).

Mathews, P.J. *Revival: The Abbey Theatre, Sinn Féin, the Gaelic League and the Co-operative Movement* (Cork: Cork University Press, 2003).

Maturin, Charles. *The Milesian Chief* (1812; New York: Garland Publishing, 1979).

—— *Melmoth the Wanderer* (1820; London: Oxford University Press, 1968).

Mayer, David. *Harlequin in his Element: The English Pantomime, 1806–1836* (Cambridge: Harvard University Press, 1969).

Meaney, Gerarding. 'Decadence, Degeneration and Revolting Aesthetics: The Fiction of Emily Lawless and Katherine Cecil Thurston', *Colby Quarterly*, 36, 2 (June 2000), pp. 157–75.

Melot, Michel. *The Art of Illustration* (New York: Rizzoli International Publications, 1984).

Merry, Tom. *Ireland For Ever*, caricature of Lady Butler's *Scotland For Ever!*, oil painting, *The Strand Magazine*, XXIV (1902), p. 138.

Meyers, Jeffrey. *A Biography of Joseph Conrad* (New York: Charles Scribner, 1991).

Moore, George. *Literature at Nurse or Circulating Morals: A Polemic on Victorian Censorship* (1885), ed. Pierre Coustillas (England: Harvester Press, 1976).

—— Lecture on Impressionism (1904), *Hail and Farewell*, ed. Richard Cave (Gerrards Cross: Colin Smythe, 1985), pp. 647–63.

Moore, Thomas. *The Memoirs of Captain Rock, the Celebrated Irish Chieftain, with Some Account of his Ancestors* (London, 1824).

Morgan, Lady (Sidney Owenson). *The Wild Irish Girl* (1806; New York: Garland Publishing, 1979), 3 volumes.

—— *Florence Macarthy* (1818; New York: Garland Publishing, 1979), 3 volumes.

'Murder of Co. Cork Admiral', *The Irish Times*, 26 March 1936.

Neale, John Mason. 'Hymn 527', *Church of Ireland Hymnal* (1862; Dublin, 1941), p. 708.

Newnes, George. 'Editorial', *The Strand Magazine*, XX, 120 (December 1900), p. 604.

Ngugi wa Thiong'o. 'The Language of African Literature' (1986) *Colonial Discourse and Post-Colonial Theory*, eds. Williams and Chrisman (Hertfordshire: Prentice Hall, 1994), pp. 43–55.

Nicoll, Allardyce. *The World of Harlequin: A Critical Study of the Commedia dell'Arte* (Cambridge: Cambridge University Press, 1963).

O'Brien, Conor Cruise. *Parnell and His Party: 1880–90* (London: Oxford University Press, 1968.

O'Donovan Rossa, Jeremiah. 'O'Donovan Rossa's Prison Life' (1874), *The Field Day Anthology of Irish Writing*, II (Derry: Field Day, 1991), pp. 260–3.

O'Grada, Cormac. *Ireland: A New Economic History, 1780–1939* (Oxford: Clarendon Press, 1994).

O'Kane, Finola. *Landscape Design in Eighteenth-Century Ireland: Mixing Foreign Trees with the Natives* (Cork: Cork University Press, 2004).

O'Neill, Marie. 'Emily Lawless', *Dublin Historical Record*, XLVIII, 2 (autumn 1995), pp. 125–41.

'Our Portrait Gallery – no. xxiii: Henry R. Addison, Esquire', *Dublin University Magazine*, no. xviii (July-December 1841), pp. 505–6.

'Our Wealthy Dramatists', rev. of W.G. Wills's *Charles the First*, *Punch*, 85 (17 November 1883), p. 240.

Patten, Eve. 'With Essex in India? Emily Lawless's Colonial Consciousness', *European Journal of English Studies*, 3, 3 (December 1999), pp. 285–97.

Perosa, Sergio. 'Naturalism and Impressionism in Stephen Crane's Fiction', *Stephen Crane: A Collection of Critical Essays*, ed. Maurice Bassan (Englewood Cliffs, New Jersey: Prentice Hall, 1967), pp. 80–94.

Poe, Edgar Allan. 'The Philosophy of Composition', *The American Tradition in Literature*, I, eds. Sculley Bradley *et al.* (New York: Grosset and Dunlap), pp. 887–96.

Praz, Mario. *The Romantic Agony*, trans. Angus Davidson (London: Oxford University Press, 1970).

Purser, John W. *The Literary Works of Jack B. Yeats* (Gerards Cross: Colin Smythe, 1991).

Pyle, Hilary. *Jack B. Yeats: A Catalogue Raisonné of the Oil Paintings*, 2 volumes (London: André Deutsch, 1992).

—— *Red-Headed Rebel: Susan L. Mitchell, Poet and Mystic of the Irish Cultural Renaissance* (Dublin: Woodfield Press, 1998).

—— 'Jack Yeats: His Miniature Plays', National Gallery Lecture Series, National Gallery of Ireland, Dublin, 23 November 1999.

Rafroidi, Patrick. *Irish Literature in English: The Romantic Period (1789-1850)*, I (Gerrards Cross; Colin Smythe, 1980).

Rev. of *Ariel* in the Gaiety, *Punch*, 85 (20 October 1883), pp. 184–5.

Rev. of *Blanche, Lady Faloise* by John Shorthouse, *Spectator* (26 December 1891), p. 931.

Revs. of *Bluebeard* by Robert Martin, *The Irish Times*, 13, 27, and 28 December 1886.

Rev. of W.G. Wills and Herman's *Claudian*, *Punch*, 85 (22 December 1883), p. 292.

Richardson, John. *A Life of Picasso, II: 1907–17* (London: Jonathan Cape, 1996), 2 volumes.

Rossetti, Dante Gabriel. 'The Staff and Scrip', *The Works of Dante Gabriel Rossetti* (London: Ellis, New Bond St., 1911), pp. 59–63.

Ruskin, John. 'Of the Turnerian Picturesque', *Modern Painters*, IV, 1856, ed. David Barrie (London: André Deutsch, 1987).

Russell, Edward G. 'Review of "Faust" by William G. Wills', Lyceum Theatre, 16 June 1886, theatre programme.

Ryder, Seán. 'The Politics of Landscape and Region in Nineteenth-Century Poetry', *Ireland in the Nineteenth Century: Regional Identity*, eds. Leon Litvak and Glenn Hooper (Dublin: Four Courts Press, 2000), pp. 169–84.

Said, Edward. *Culture and Imperialism* (London: Vintage, 1994).

The Savoy, an illustrated quarterly, ed. Arthur Symons, nos. 1–8 (January–December 1896).

Schama, Simon. *Landscape and Memory* (London: Fontana Press, 1995).

Schreiner, Olive. *The Story of an African Farm* (1883; London: Penguin, 1993).

Script of *Poor Pillicoddy*, Drishane Archive, M.16.a–c, M.17.a–b.

Script of *Sorcerer* by Gilbert and Sullivan, Drishane Archive, M.15.a–b, M.43.a

Sendak, Maurice. 'Interview', *Victorian Color Picture Books*, ed. Jonathan Cott (New York: Allen Lane, 1984).

Shakespeare, William. *Henry IV, Part One, William Shakespeare. The*

Complete Works (New York: Viking, 1975).

Shaw, Valerie. *The Short Story: A Critical Introduction* (London: Longman, 1908).

Sillars, Stuart. *Visualization in Popular Fiction 1860–1960* (London: Routledge, 1995).

Smyth, Gerry. *Space and the Irish Cultural Imagination* (Basingstoke: Palgrave, 2001).

Snodgrass, Chris. *Aubrey Beardsley, Dandy of the Grotesque* (New York: Oxford University Pres, 1995).

Speaight, George. *The History of the English Puppet Theatre* (London: Robert Hale, 1990).

Spence, Joseph. ' "The Great Angelic Sin": The Faust Legend in Irish Literature, 1820–1900' *Bullán*, 1, 2 (autumn 1994), pp. 47–57.

Spivak, Gayatri Chakravorty. 'Three Women's Texts and a Critique of Imperialism', *Feminisms: An Anthology of Literary Theory and Criticism*, eds. Warhol and Herndl (New Jersey: Rutgers University Press, 1991), pp. 798–814.

Steinlen, Théophile-Alexandre. *Steinlen's Drawings* (New York: Dover Publications, 1980).

Stephenson, Roger H. 'The Political Import of Goethe's Reineke Fuchs', *Reynard the Fox: Social Engagement and Cultural Metamorphoses in the Beast Epic from the Middle Ages to the Present*, ed. Kenneth Vartry (New York: Berghahn Books, 2000), pp. 191–207.

Stevenson, Robert Louis. 'A Penny Plain and Twopence Coloured', *The Magazine of Art* (1884), *Memories and Portraits & Other Fragments* (London: Tusitala Edition, 1924), pp. 103–9.

—— *The Master of Ballantrae* (1889; London: Penguin, 1984).

Stewart, Bruce. 'Bram Stoker's *Dracula*: Possessed by the Spirit of the Nation?', *Irish University Review*, 29, 2 (autumn/winter 1999), pp. 238–55.

Stoker, Bram. *The Snake's Pass* (1890; Dingle, Co. Kerry: Brandon, 1990).

—— *Dracula* (1898; New York: W.W. Norton & Co., 1997).

Swift, Jonathan. 'Letter to the Shopkeepers, Tradesmen, Farmers, and Common-People of Ireland', *Swift's Irish Pamphlets*, ed. Joseph McMinn (Gerrards Cross: Colin Smythe, 1991), pp. 59–67.

—— 'Will of Jonathan Swift', *The Prose Works of Jonathan Swift*, xi, ed. T. Scott (London: George Bell, 1907).

Symons, Arthur. 'Pantomime and the Poetic Drama', *Studies in Seven Arts* (London: Constable, 1906), pp. 381–4.

Tenniel, John. 'Crowning the O'Caliban', *Punch*, 85 (22 December 1883), p. 295.

—— 'The Open Door!', *Punch*, 85 (10 October 1885), pp. 175–6.

Terry, Ellen. *Ellen Terry's Memoirs*, eds. Edith Craig and Christopher St John (1932; Westport, Conn.: Greenwood Press, 1970).

Thackeray, William Makepeace. *The Irish Sketchbook, The Works of William Makepeace Thackeray*, XXIII (London: 1911).

Thorpe, James. *English Illustration: The Nineties* (London: Faber and Faber, 1985).

Trumpener, Katie. *Bardic Nationalism: The Romantic Novel and the British Empire* (New Jersey: Princeton University Press, 1997).

—— 'National Character, Nationalist Plots: National Tale and Historical Novel in the Age of Waverley, 1806–1830', *English Literary History*, 60 (1993).

Trussler, Simon. *The Cambridge Illustrated History of British Theatre* (Cambridge: Cambridge University Press, 1994).

Turpin, John and Richard Ormond (compilers). *Daniel Maclise, 1806–1870*, The Arts Council of Great Britain Catalogue of the Maclise Exhibition at the National Portrait Gallery, London, 3 March–16 April 1972 and National Gallery of Ireland, Dublin, 5 May–18 June, 1972.

Turpin, John. 'Daniel Maclise and his Place in Victorian Art', *Anglo-Irish Studies*, I (1975), pp. 51–69.

' "Up For The Green!" A Song of the United Irishmen', 1796, *The Spirit of the Nation*, rev. ed. 1845 (Dublin: James Duffy, 1866), pp. 118–19.

Valle-Inclan, Romon del. *The Grotesque Farce of Mr Punch the Cuckold* (Warminster: Aris and Phillips, 1991).

Venne, Adriaen van der. *Fishing for Souls*, oil painting, 1614, The Rijksmuseum, Amsterdam, Holland.

Vokes, Thomas Philips. Letters to William Gregory, 29 January 1824, 26 February 1824, 23 June 1824, nos. 2618/19, 36, 85, State of the Country Papers, National Records Office, Dublin.

—— Letter to Gaulburne, 10 August 1824, no. 2619/13. State of the Country Papers, Dublin.

Waldron, Jarlath. *Maamtrasna: The Murders and the Mystery* (Dublin: Edmund Burke, 1992).

Wechsler, Judith. *A Human Comedy: Physiognomy and Caricature in 19th Century Paris* (London: Thames and Hudson, 1982).

Weintraub, Stanley. *Whistler: A Biography* (Glasgow: William Collins, 1974; New York: Weybright and Tally, 1974).

Welsford, Enid. *The Fool: His Social and Literary History* (London: Faber and Faber, 1935).

White, Jack. *Minority Report: The Protestant Community in the Irish Republic* (Dublin: Gill and Macmillan, 1975).

Wilde, Oscar. Rev. of *Ismay's Children* (by May Laffan), *The Woman's World* (November 1887–1899), p. 84.

—— *The Picture of Dorian Gray* (1890), *The Works of Oscar Wilde, 1856–1900* (London: Collins, 1948), pp. 17–167.

Wills, Freeman. *W.G. Wills: Dramatist and Painter* (London: Longmans, Green, 1898).

Wills, William G. *Melchior* (London: Macmillan, 1885).

—— *Faust*, theatre programme, Royal Lyceum Theatre, 16 June 1886.

Womack, Peter. *Improvement and Romance: Constructing the Myth of the Highlands* (London: Macmillan, 1989).

Yeats, William Butler. 'What is Popular Poetry?', *Essays* (London: Macmillan, 1924), pp. 3–14.

—— 'Mr. William Wills', *Letters to the New World* (Cambridge, Mass: Harvard University Press, 1934), pp. 69–71.

Index